W9-DJB-008

Full-Court Quest

Also by Linda Peavy and Ursula Smith

Women Who Changed Things

Dreams into Deeds

The Gold Rush Widows of Little Falls:
A Story Drawn from the Letters of Pamelia and James Fergus

Women in Waiting in the Westward Movement:
Life on the Home Frontier

Pioneer Women:
The Lives of Women on the Frontier

Frontier Children

Frontier House
(with Simon Shaw)

Pamelia
(libretto for opera by Eric Funk)

Full-Court Quest

The Girls from Fort Shaw Indian School
Basketball Champions of the World

Linda Peavy & Ursula Smith

UNIVERSITY OF OKLAHOMA PRESS : NORMAN

Library of Congress Cataloging-in-Publication Data
Peavy, Linda S.
Full-court quest : the girls from Fort Shaw Indian School, basketball
champions of the world / Linda Peavy and Ursula Smith.
p. cm.
Includes bibliographical references and index.
ISBN 978-0-8061-3973-9 (hardcover : alk. paper)
1. Fort Shaw Indian School (Great Falls, Mont.)—Basketball—History.
2. Basketball for girls—Montana—Great Falls—History.
3. Basketball for women—Montana—Great Falls—History.
4. Indian athletes—Montana—Great Falls—History.
5. Basketball—United States—History.
6. Basketball for girls—United States—History.
I. Smith, Ursula. II. Title.
GV886.P43 2008
796.323—dc22
2008015313

Credits for illustrations can be found on page 480.

The paper in this book meets the guidelines for permanence and
durability of the Committee on Production Guidelines for Book
Longevity of the Council on Library Resources, Inc. ∞

Copyright © 2008 by Linda Peavy and Ursula Smith. Published
by the University of Oklahoma Press, Norman, Publishing
Division of the University. Manufactured in the U.S.A.

All rights reserved. No part of this publication may be reproduced, stored in
a retrieval system, or transmitted, in any form or by any means, electronic,
mechanical, photocopying, recording, or otherwise—except as permitted
under Section 107 or 108 of the United States Copyright Act—without
the prior written permission of the University of Oklahoma Press.

1 2 3 4 5 6 7 8 9 10

To the memory
of the girls who lived
the story we tell
and to
their descendants and tribal kin

Contents

Preface

AT A TIME WHEN WOMEN'S BASKETBALL IS DRAWING THE ATTENTION of sports fans around the globe, few of these fans realize that more than a century ago girls' teams playing full-court "basket ball" were already challenging long-held assumptions about women and athletics. And, at a time when indigenous peoples around the world are reclaiming their heritage and celebrating their history, few Indians—or non-Indians for that matter—have any idea that the best of the best, a team one Missouri reporter described as ten "aboriginal maidens" from Montana, overcame racial and gender barriers to emerge as basketball champions of the 1904 St. Louis World's Fair.[1]

The story of the Fort Shaw team's journey to St. Louis had its beginnings a dozen years earlier, in 1892, with the establishment of an off-reservation government school for American Indian children at an abandoned military fort in central Montana, and, at almost the same time—but on the other side of the country—with the invention of the game of basketball.

From this serendipitous convergence of events, ten young women came together to form a virtually unbeatable team. The oldest of the girls was nineteen, the youngest fifteen. Some of them were veterans of boarding school life, Fort Shaw style, while others had been enrolled at the school for barely a year. Hailing from American Indian communities and reservations across Montana and Idaho, the players represented seven different tribes, some of them with long-standing animosities toward one another: Minnie Burton, Lemhi Shoshone; Genie Butch, Sarah Mitchell, Katie Snell, and Nettie Wirth, Assiniboine; Genevieve Healy,

Gros Ventre; Belle Johnson, Piegan; Rose LaRose, Shoshone-Bannock; Flora Lucero, Chippewa; and Emma Sansaver, Chippewa-Cree.

Despite their tribal diversity, by the spring of 1904 these ten young women had melded into a team whose energy and skills amazed and delighted the crowds that packed community halls and gymnasiums across Montana to watch them play this game of "basket ball" as no one else could play it. The Fort Shaw style was marked by speed and teamwork, by hustle and endurance. But basketball was not their only claim to fame, for their "entertainments" were an integral part of their public appearances—from their mandolin concerts to their gymnastic routines to their highly choreographed pantomimes and recitations.

These multitalented girls were not just "ten little Indians." They were ten distinct personalities whose cultural and family backgrounds influenced their achievements on the court and off as surely as did their boarding school experiences. They came to Fort Shaw with different motivations and expectations, different languages and legacies, different attitudes and aptitudes. There at Fort Shaw, as a group and as individuals, they made the most of what they were offered, acquiring new knowledge, forming new friendships, and gaining new confidence and skills.

Ultimately, their athletic and artistic talents took them from the narrow confines of an Indian boarding school in rural Montana to the wonders of a world's fair, where they were both objects on display and full participants in a grand adventure. Center stage, center court, over the course of a summer and into the fall they performed before some 3 million spectators from across the nation and around the globe and returned to Fort Shaw with a gleaming silver trophy declaring them "champions." Their hard-won skills and determination gave them entrée to a world traditionally closed to women of color. In turn, they shattered stereotypes and reshaped expectations, thereby broadening opportunities for their gender and their race.

Like many athletes who achieve stardom during their high school years, the girls from Fort Shaw Government Indian Boarding School would never again enjoy the fame that had been theirs during those heady days in St. Louis. Though they played together as a team through one more year, they gradually began to leave school, marry, and raise families. Inevitably, their lives took them in separate directions, and the closing of Fort Shaw in 1910 left them with no gathering point for reunion and reverie. For the most part, they lost contact with one another and became all but invisible to the fans who had once followed their every game. And while their descendants and tribal kin continued to treasure their stories, as the decades rolled by and Native Americans became more and more aware of the cultural losses incurred under the federal policy of "assimilation and acculturation" that lay at the heart of the Indian education program, celebrating anything connected with government boarding schools became anathema.

Yet, as is so often the case, especially within American Indian communities, heroic achievements have a way of becoming a part of oral tradition, finding their way into stories of sometimes mythic proportions. To those elders who are only a generation or so away from the girls themselves, the Fort Shaw players were not only basketball champions of the St. Louis World's Fair, they were Champions of the World, a team whose exploits were not only the stuff of history but the stuff of legend as well.

It was with the goal of documenting the history and exploring the legend that we began researching the story of the girls from Fort Shaw Indian School. The narrative that follows conforms to the facts as best we could ascertain them from tribal, state, and federal records; vintage newspapers and journals; and the personal papers and family records shared with us by descendants of the players, their classmates, and Fort Shaw faculty and staff. Those facts were often difficult to establish. Newspaper accounts and government records were sometimes at odds; family records, obituaries, and scrapbooks contained information that contradicted as often as it confirmed data gleaned from public records.[2]

These difficulties notwithstanding, we have sifted and weighed these sometimes disparate elements and woven them into a story solidly rooted in fact. In shaping this narrative we have also drawn upon our own informed sense of prevailing conditions and attitudes to conjure the day-to-day realities of those who lived the story we tell. That said, we share the sentiments expressed by a high school junior in his poem about old Fort Shaw—the military post established to subdue the Indians, then transformed into a school designed to assimilate them. Opening with a description of the origins of that fort, the poem closes with lines that remind us of the limitations of history, biography, and art:

> We'll never know.
> We were never there.[3]

What we *do* know, and have known almost from the first, is that our examination of the incredible journey of the girls from Fort Shaw Indian School has taken us on an incredible journey of our own—one that began with the chance discovery of a single photograph in the archives of the Montana Historical Society in January 1997 and evolved into a ten-year cross-cultural collaboration that in itself became an integral part of the story. The memories and memorabilia of our collaborators—especially the descendants and tribal kin of the Fort Shaw players—have not only given us invaluable insights into the personalities of these ten young women but have also enabled us to ground their stories in the particulars of tribal traditions and family dynamics. In addition, their patience and encouragement have sustained us in our efforts to place the experiences of the Fort Shaw team within the larger context of western American history, women's history, American Indian history, and the early history of basketball.

But we are not the first to tell the story that has been entrusted to us.

"Back in the time of your great-grandmother," the elder begins, "there was once this team of Indian girls who played basketball better than anyone else in the world."

And it could well be that whatever biographical fragments, whatever facts and figures we have found to document the lives and accomplishments of the girls from Fort Shaw, might, in the end, be less crucial to our understanding of the significance of those lives and accomplishments than the elder's quiet assurance: "There was once this team of Indian girls . . ."

Full-Court Quest

St. Louis World's Fair
Saturday, October 8, 1904

THE DAY HAD DAWNED UNUSUALLY CRISP. A FRONT HAD MOVED through the night before, bringing rain that had scoured the air of its heaviness and left a freshness that seemed to bode well for the afternoon's game, an event that was already beginning to draw spectators a full hour or more before the referee's whistle. On the plaza in front of the Model Indian School the boys in the band were assembling for a pregame concert.

Some of the inhabitants of the Indian village that spread out at the base of the hill had moved up the slope to take their place on the fringe of the plaza where, for once, they would be the observers rather than the observed. They stood back from the roped-off playing field, keeping their distance from the men in fedoras and three-piece suits who were accompanied by corseted, tiny-waisted women in bustled, ankle-length skirts and mutton-sleeve blouses. Little girls in pinafores and high-top button shoes clung to their mothers' skirts while little boys kept breaking away, worrying their parents by appearing and disappearing in the increasingly large crowd.

Inside the Model Indian School itself the girls from Fort Shaw were donning navy middies and bloomers and then helping one another add the final touch—a bright little ribbon of silk at the end of each girl's long braid. Their shoes were tightly laced, their stockings pulled up and bound so that not a wrinkle showed between shoe tops and bloomer hems.

In the wide hallway the girls waited for Miss Crawford's signal to go out onto the porch of the school and make their presence known to the fans below. The officials were already down on the field. The boys in the

Indian School Band had started through their series of numbers again while still more people were making their way from the platform at the "Indian Station" on the fair's Intramural Railway, across the sweep of lawn, and toward the school plaza. Suddenly someone—maybe Belle Johnson, the captain, but more likely Genevieve Healy, well known for her high jinks—picked up the ball and bounced it on the hardwood floor of the hallway. Once, twice. The echo rang through the emptiness, for all who would normally be indoors busy with schoolwork or domestic chores were outdoors awaiting the game. Then a pass, a dribble, and a second pass that set up the semblance of a well-rehearsed play, with Minnie Burton feigning a shot at an imaginary goal. Miss Crawford's raised hand brought instant order, but that brief interlude had relieved the rising tension and readied the team to push open the double doors and move out onto the porch.

With their appearance, a roar went up from a crowd stretching out to the very edges of the fence separating the hogans, grass huts, and tepees of the village from the school atop Indian Hill. After the quiet darkness of the hallway, the noise and glare were momentarily unnerving, but the girls quickly regained their composure and nodded their thanks to the crowd. The cheers continued and someone—again, most likely that impish Gen Healy—bounced the ball on the concrete floor of the porch. A quick pass around, a few dribbles, and then the entire team fell into place, all ten of them, two lines of five, standing as if in military formation, for the intramural train had pulled into Indian Station, and the Missouri All-Stars were stepping off the train and onto the platform, suited up and ready for the game that would determine the champions of the 1904 St. Louis World's Fair.

As the All-Stars moved single file toward the plaza, the crowd opened up to let them pass through. On the porch of the school, the girls from Fort Shaw formed a circle, heads together, arms around one another's shoulders. Then the players broke out of their circle and moved down the steps, ready to meet their opponents in a contest that was as much about a confluence of cultures as it was about how well young women at the turn of the twentieth century could play this game called "basket ball."

A Confluence of Cultures

HOLDING THE STRAIGHT END OF HER PEELED WILLOW BRANCH at the ready, forked tip raised high overhead, Pea-boa stood in a tightly knotted circle with a dozen of her Bannock teammates, shoulder to shoulder with an equal number of Shoshone. All eyes were on the buckskin double ball the girl in the center of the field held by the slender leather strip that connected its two sand-filled pouches. Having already jostled for position, the players seemed frozen in place as the "double ball" was swung back and forth, back and forth in an ever lengthening arc, then sent hurtling upward, end over end, a brown bird climbing into blue sky and hanging there for an almost imperceptible second before plummeting toward the thicket of waving saplings below.[1]

Pea-boa jumped high, stabbing the air and feeling the weight of the ball against her stick. Then came the clatter of wood against wood, the jabs and shouts and flying elbows as the ball seemed caught in the circle until the connecting strip of buckskin was snagged by one of the willows and whipped over the heads of the players and down to a second group of girls waiting to snare the flying length of leather and pass it from player to player toward the opponent's goal.

This was a game of stamina, for the cottonwood poles at opposite ends of the playing field were some two hundred yards apart. It was a game of courage, for the crashing of bodies and slashing of sticks grew more frenzied with every exchange of the ball. It was a game of strategy, for keeping the ball in play required deft footwork and well-placed passes. And it was a game of teamwork, for cooperation and unselfish moves were essential to success.

Pea-boa now raced down the field, staying just far enough ahead of those who pursued her to be the one to catch the final pass and, in one smooth whip of her willow stick, send the twinned leather balls sailing toward one of the shorn branches of the "goalpost" to land in the crotch between limb and pole, caught like a bird in a snare.

An interested observer of this double-ball match, played on a summer's day in what would come to be known as the Lemhi Valley of Idaho, was a Shoshone youth named Pea-wa-um. This young man was looking to choose his bride from among those who excelled in this time-honored competition—the only team sport among Plains Indians reserved exclusively for women—for he would need to marry a strong and healthy mate who could bear his children and handle with ease the physically challenging tasks that would fall to her. Pea-boa was such a woman, and the speed and strength and stamina she showed on the playing field were her legacy to the descendants of this Shoshone-Bannock union—including her granddaughter, Minnie Burton, who would one day mirror her prowess on another field of play.[2]

Pea-boa's people were hunters and gatherers who spent the summer months ranging as far west as the Camas Prairie of Idaho, where the women dug roots and harvested berries, and as far east as the three forks of the Missouri River, where the men hunted the buffalo whose flesh and hides, bones and sinews, were the source of food, shelter, and clothing not only for the Shoshone-Bannocks but for other Native peoples of the region as well. Encounters with rival bands of Crows and Sioux had lent an element of danger to these hunting expeditions for decades, but since the signing of the Fort Laramie Treaty of 1851, tribal warfare had diminished somewhat. There at Laramie, envoys from Washington had met with the heads of nine nations and as many as ten thousand of their peoples to forge an agreement whereby emigrants bound for the goldfields of California or the green fields of Oregon would be allowed safe passage through Indian homelands and hunting grounds. In return, the government would guarantee certain annuities and set aside a vast reserve in which the indigenous peoples of the plains could live and fish and hunt and wander at will—as long as the members of each tribe remained within the boundaries assigned to them and respected the lands of their neighbors.[3]

Under the vague terms of this agreement, which would be altered several times in the next two decades, Pea-boa's Shoshone-Bannocks were "assigned" the lands they had occupied and traversed for generations in present-day southeastern Idaho and southwestern Montana. The Crows were given a swath of land across the Yellowstone Valley. The Nakota Sioux, or Assiniboines, the Piegan Blackfeet, the Gros Ventres, and the River Crows were all consigned to what was called the Blackfeet Reserve, an area encompassing some 23 million acres, bound by the Rockies on the west and the Dakotas on the east, and stretching from the Canadian border on the north to the Musselshell River on the south.[4]

~

In the north-central reaches of that vast reserve, nearly four hundred miles as the raven flies from the Lemhi Valley where Pea-boa was born, another Indian girl was coming of age in the mid-nineteenth century. Born in a camp near the confluence of the Teton and Missouri Rivers, Can-kte-win-yan was only six years old when her father, Got Wolf Tail, a chief of the Red Bottom band of the Assiniboines, agreed to the terms of the Laramie Treaty. The treaty made little difference to the child, since her people were already living within their assigned area. Her father continued to lead hunts for buffalo and antelope, and her mother, Walking Blue Mane, and the other women of the tribe continued to carry out the tasks that had been theirs for centuries.[5]

Like her mother and grandmother before her, as Can-kte-win-yan grew older she engaged in the northern plains version of double ball. And, like Pea-boa, she was no doubt adept at the game, for her name translated as Woman That Kills Wood, indicating strength and agility. She learned how to cut and carry wood for the fire and how to skin out a buffalo, scrape and stretch the hide, and cut the meat into thin strips to be hung on racks to dry. She learned how to take down a tepee, prepare it for travel, then set it up again at the new camp, lifting the heavy buffalo hides into place and securing them on lodge poles cut for that purpose.[6]

But Woman That Kills Wood was, like so many of her people, caught up in a progression of changes that were all but inevitable, given the steady influx of whites onto the plains. When she was in her mid-teens, her father's band set up their camp near the point where the Poplar River flows into the Missouri. The head of the trading post at that site was Henry Archdale, a young Englishman who watched the chief's pretty daughter with interest. Sometime in 1860 he struck a bargain with Got Wolf Tail that allowed sixteen-year-old Woman That Kills Wood, whom he called Susan, to live with him, thereby becoming his wife *a la façon du pays*—"according to the custom of the country."[7]

By the 1860s the influence of white culture had become increasingly apparent to the Assiniboines and their neighbors, not only through the intermarriage of white men and Native women but also through the influx of goods from the East that provided enticing alternatives to traditional ways of working and dressing. Guns, metal knives, and awls were being used by many tribes, including the Red Bottom band of the Assiniboines. At the post, Susan Archdale, Woman That Kills Wood, had access to kettles, pots, and other cooking utensils. The men in her tribe were wearing woolen shirts and trousers as often as they wore traditional dress. Susan and the women of her band dressed in calico blouses and woolen skirts as often as in buckskin dresses.[8]

Having become a woman of two cultures, Susan Archdale suddenly found herself in limbo some eight years later when Henry Archdale disappeared—or died—during a trip down the Missouri. Left with the care of a toddler and a newborn, she returned to her people, setting up her tepee near that of her mother and her younger brother, Red Dog, who had assumed leadership of the band upon the death of their father. There at the camp near the Dakota border, she met a German immigrant, now a soldier with the U.S. infantry, sent west to help build the forts intended to subdue the still-warring Indian tribes. Sometime in 1869 she married this Jacob Wirth, and their union, also *a la façon du pays,* produced a number of children, including Nettie Susan Wirth, who would one day travel to St. Louis—the site of her father's army training—to engage in skirmishes of a different sort in a world far removed from the one in which her mother had grown up.[9]

~

Other bands of Assiniboines chose to settle farther west along the Missouri, in the vicinity of present-day Poplar, Wolf Point, and Frazer, Montana. Among those who crisscrossed the northern tier of the Blackfeet Reserve were the grandmothers and great-grandmothers of Katie Snell, Genie Butch, and Sarah Mitchell, girls whose Assiniboine mothers had married men with white blood and strong feelings about the importance of having their children seize the opportunities offered by government schools. Although these fathers could not have known it at the time, one such opportunity would be their daughters' participation in the world's fair that celebrated the centennial of the 1803 Louisiana Purchase.[10]

The Louisiana Purchase had signaled the beginning of the end of life as the Indians living within that vast expanse had known it. During the first half century following that historic event, there was relatively little encroachment by whites. This was especially true in the northern Rockies. Things began to change, however, in 1846, with the establishment of a trading post at Fort Benton, the farthest navigable port on the Missouri. Fur traders, adventurers, and settlers from points east began to travel upriver, infiltrating the western reaches of the Blackfeet Reserve. Because Fort Benton served as an Indian agency as well as a trading post, government rations were meted out there at set times during the year. As a result, the Gros Ventres, Piegans, and Assiniboines found it advantageous to establish camps near the fort.[11]

By the early 1860s, with the discovery of gold in Montana Territory, prospectors, peddlers, and entrepreneurs by the thousands were traveling up the Missouri to Fort Benton by steamboat, then heading south and west in wagons or on horseback, bound for the goldfields of Bannack and Virginia City. Some of these immigrants stayed on in Fort Benton to ply their trades as carpenters, barkeeps, and merchants. In due time, many of those who had failed to make their fortunes in the mines wandered back to the port where they had landed and sought work there. Thus the white population of Fort Benton continued to grow, and while many, indeed most, of the Piegan and Gros Ventre women who had grown up in camps on the outskirts of that settlement married men within their tribes, others married white men and raised children whose lives would straddle both worlds. Two of those mixed-blood children, Belle Johnson and Genevieve Healy, would one day excel in a sport invented in New England and exported worldwide, even to a remote Indian school in Montana.[12]

Considered legitimate occupants of the Blackfeet Reserve, the Assiniboines, Gros Ventres, and Piegans were entitled to the rations promised to members of those tribes who accepted the terms of the Laramie Treaty. Another group of Natives, who lacked legal claim to the land, but for whom it had long been a summer hunting area, continued to migrate freely across the Medicine Line separating the United States and the British possessions to the north, to the consternation of government agents for whom the 49th parallel was sacrosanct. These people were the Métis, a proud, mixed-blood nation descended from generations of intermarriages between French Canadian trappers and Chippewa and Cree tribeswomen.[13]

Métis customs and culture were largely an expedient blend of two disparate lifestyles. Métis settlements along Canadian streams featured small houses and garden plots, but when out on the plains for the buffalo hunts of June and September, they lived in skin tepees or in canvas tents. They conversed in a language as mixed as their blood line, a potpourri of Chippewa, Cree, and French, with a sprinkling of English words and phrases. Their dances were sprightly jigs accompanied not by the sonorous beat of the drums but by the lively strains of French folk tunes played on fiddles, some of which—like the tunes themselves—had been transported across an ocean and a continent to be passed down through successive generations. And in place of rituals overseen by medicine men, Métis hunters relied on blessings bestowed by priests, since for the most part their religious beliefs were those of the French Blackrobes.[14]

Considered wards of the British Commonwealth, those Métis who wandered south of the line and onto the Blackfeet Reserve were tolerated but not welcomed. They received no rations from the American government, but as long as game was plentiful they asked for nothing more than to be left alone to follow their way of life. Considered illegal immigrants, they were ineligible for the educational opportunities eventually offered by mission and agency schools supported or established by the Bureau of Indian Affairs (BIA), a branch of the U.S. Department of the Interior.[15] Still, in time, many of these "British Indians" found their way into the educational system. One of those students was Emma Rose Sansaver, a young woman destined to represent her school, her people, and the government's Indian education system at the Louisiana Purchase Exposition of 1904.[16]

But that honor would be a long time coming, for Emma Sansaver had yet to be born, the school she would eventually attend had yet to be established, and the sport that would be her vehicle to momentary fame had yet to be invented. The Blackfeet Reserve that had been a seasonal home for her people had not yet been carved into reservations, and the upheavals caused by that action were another two decades away. Nevertheless, by 1867 the forces that would sweep Emma and her teammates toward the ultimate confluence of cultures—the St. Louis World's Fair—had already been set in motion by the U.S. government's decision to establish yet another military outpost, a fort named for Civil War hero Robert Shaw and located in the Sun River Valley of newly established Montana Territory.[17]

End of an Era

❧⁂❧

DECEMBER 1891. A PARADE OF SORTS WAS MOVING THROUGH THE town of Sun River. The faces of the few white officers among row after row of black enlisted men stood out like the scanty patches of last week's snow still visible here and there against the frozen ground. The march of the buffalo soldiers of the 25th Regiment, their lumbering wagons laden with whatever the government deemed worth saving, marked the end of an era for the people of Montana's Sun River Valley.[1]

As the last of the troops disappeared, merchants and bankers, farriers and freighters returned to their work, still mulling the impact of the closing of the military post that had been a source of income as well as security. Established in 1867 just east of the intersection of the Sun River and the Mullan Road that provided a vital link between the bustling river port of Fort Benton and the goldfields of Helena and beyond, Fort Shaw had once been considered an essential part of the government's strategically situated military installations in the region.[2]

The fort was also an essential element in the lives of the settlers of the Sun River Valley. Seeing the last of the detachment passing by set off yet another round of discussions. On one thing they were all in agreement. There was no denying the old military post had outlived its usefulness. Those marauding Indians whose tribal squabbles and occasional raids on whites had called for a fort in the first place would not likely come riding into the valley to stir up trouble again. Those new reservations had solved the Indian problem once and for all.

"What problem?" an old-timer interjected. In his view the valley's Indian troubles had vanished on that below-zero night back in 1870 when Colonel Baker's regiment had wiped out a Piegan camp on the Marias, breaking the spirit of the Blackfeet once and for all. You might say the soldiers at Fort Shaw had done themselves out of a job a long time ago and that everything since had just been for show.[3]

There had, indeed, been plenty of show, plenty of spit and polish and posturing over the past two decades. And why not, argued those who had benefited most from the brisk trade with the fort that had bolstered the local economy. Who would expect any less of the region's largest and most elaborate fort, the regimental headquarters for the Military District of Montana Territory? Unlike most of the outposts thrown up in the first frenzied years of the Indian wars, Fort Shaw was laid out with an eye to aesthetics. The main buildings—officers' quarters, barracks, administrative offices, hospital, storehouse, and guardhouse—faced inward on a 400-by-400-square-foot parade ground. A bakery, laundry, workshops, stables, and other outbuildings complemented the handsome structures at the center of the complex.[4]

Lawns and shrubs graced the barracks and officers' quarters. Cottonwoods lined the edges of the boardwalks surrounding the parade ground. Water from the river ran through a system of ditches, irrigating hayfields but also nourishing lawns, trees, and shrubs as well as the gardens that provided fresh produce for mess hall and dining room. By the mid-1870s Fort Shaw had become a veritable oasis, largely due to the efforts of Frances Gibbon, wife of the fort's commanding officer, Brigadier General John Gibbon. The post was a cultural oasis as well, boasting a school, a library, and a 120-foot-long building for dances, recitals, and theatrical productions. These events had been welcome diversions for those valley residents who were invited to join the officers and their wives for an evening's entertainment at the post that came to be known as "the Queen of Montana's Indian Forts."[5]

Those were the glory days, said the ladies of the valley who had donned their finest gowns and enjoyed many an evening of dancing or theatre at the post. The men might talk all they liked about the bravery of Fort Shaw's soldiers during the Sioux wars—and their role in the later engagement against Chief Joseph's band of Nez Perce in the Big Hole Basin. The womenfolk held fast to memories of music and dancing and theatre the likes of which had never before been seen in the valley—and would likely never be seen again. Furthermore—and in this they were unified—exposure to such social and cultural events had had a positive influence on their children.[6]

They could only hope that influence had been strong enough to prevail over the negative example set by the unkempt and unruly urchins in the Indian camp on the other side of the river. Something should have been done about that camp years ago. There was nothing that *could* be done, their husbands had told them from the first. There were no rules against setting up tepees around a military post. Some of those Blackfeet men worked at the fort. Others were trusted scouts. Still others, some of them white, were trappers who bartered with the soldiers, trading pelts and meat for knives and guns and blankets. Those men served a useful purpose. But what of their wives—and the other Indian women in the camp? That was the problem, the ladies had long been saying. They knew without being told that a sizeable number of those "other" women, some no older than fourteen or fifteen, could also be said to serve "a useful purpose." The number of half-breeds in the camp left no doubt of that.[7]

At least with the final closure of the fort there would be no further excuse to have Indians hanging around in the valley. And no further excuse for colored soldiers to come into town on weekends, strutting about as if they belonged there.[8]

But neither would there be any further demand for the goods and services supplied by Sun River's merchants and ranchers. That fact had been apparent from the first mention of the fort's closure. Yet, in the three years since, no one had managed to come up with a solution to what had, on this very afternoon, become a pressing problem indeed. At one point there had been talk of making Fort Shaw the fledgling state's new capital, though no one had put much store by that rumor. Then there was the push to transform the old fort into an agricultural college. Now, that was a plan the locals had supported. Might-have-beens and should-have-beens aside, something had to be done to bring new life to the valley. One thing was certain, said the wisest among them, if the people of the valley did not solve this problem on their own, the government would solve it for them.[9]

Birth of a Game

DECEMBER 1891. JAMES NAISMITH WAS STUMPED. DR. GULICK, dean of physical education at the Springfield YMCA Training School, had asked his thirty-year-old instructor to come up with an indoor game that would keep the students active through the long, cold Massachusetts winter, something challenging and competitive enough to engage the young men between the football and baseball seasons. No gymnastics or barbells or anything of the sort. Something requiring teamwork as well as agility. The assignment that had seemed simple enough at first had turned into a series of dead-ends. During the previous few weeks, Naismith had introduced his gym class to adaptations of football, rugby, soccer, lacrosse. With no success. Players were bruised and bloodied. Windows were shattered.[1]

Now, with increasing pressure from his superior, Naismith had come to the conclusion that there was nothing to do but invent an entirely new game. Given the constraints of the school's gymnasium, he decided against any use of a bat or a racket, although he did not rule out the use of a ball, a sizeable one that could be thrown from man to man. There would be no running with the ball, no tackling. Instead, players would pass the ball to their teammates, with the object of moving the ball down the floor to the opponents' end of the gym and into the hands of a player close enough to toss it into some sort of goal.

Considering the roughness that had been a part of his earlier adaptations of goal-centered sports, Naismith had come to see the players' all-out assault on an opponent's goal for what it was. These men were accustomed to winning, and in their minds roughness was the means to that end. But what if winning required a different style of play? What if the goal was out of reach of the players? And there he had it. Elevating the goal would make the accuracy and arc of the throw more important than the brute strength of the players. As the idea took shape, James Naismith began to scratch out some basic rules. First, the basics, then "no shouldering, holding, pushing, tripping or striking. . . ."

The next morning he handed his scribbled notes to Miss Lyons, the department secretary, and asked her to type them up at her earliest convenience. Then he went in search of the necessary equipment—a ball and some goals. A soccer ball was the first thing that came to his hand, and in no time the building superintendent had located the goals—a pair of peach baskets. Not exactly the goals Naismith had envisioned but good enough for now. Calling for a ladder, he nailed the baskets to the lower edge of the balcony, one at each end of the gym, both ten feet above the floor.

Back at the office he found the neatly typed sheet containing the thirteen rules of his new game lying on his desk. With hasty thanks to Miss Lyons, he hurried back to the gym where he posted the sheet on the bulletin board, confident that he had finally come up with a good game, one so different from outdoor sports that novelty alone should appeal to his students.

But, as always, the proof was in the playing.

Would his eighteen ruffians even give his game a chance? There was hope, for once the class was assembled, he saw the curiosity roused by those two peach baskets. They were goals, he explained. And here is the way this game is played. One by one, he read off the rules, pausing to answer questions. And when their impatience was at its peak, he led them to the center of the gym where he divided them into two teams of nine each. Designating two opposing players as the "centers," he tossed the ball up between them. The first-ever game of "basket ball" was under way.[2]

It was not long before James Naismith knew he had a success on his hands. The new sport became popular almost overnight. But Naismith's reward was not in the game's popularity. It was in the way that "basket ball" fit into the overall goals of the YMCA. As a firm believer in the cause of "muscular Christianity," he embraced the concept that good health and physical fitness enhanced one's spiritual life—and vice versa. His new game not only fostered physical fitness, it called for sportsmanship and teamwork, the basic ingredients of muscular Christianity.[3]

Teamwork. To Luther Gulick, Naismith's superior at the Springfield Y, the new sport's critical quality was teamwork. Gulick was not only looking for something that would bring young men into YMCA gymnasiums during the winter months, he was also concerned about a larger social problem. In the late nineteenth century, with immigrants pouring into the country, American society was becoming increasingly diverse and, at the same time, increasingly fragmented. Simple as it sounded, a game demanding teamwork could be a vehicle for reaching isolated, dispossessed individuals. It could be a means of building a sense of community within ethnic groups and, ultimately, of assimilating them into American society. In other words, basketball could be the "fix" for a very modern problem.[4]

With Gulick's hearty endorsement, Naismith published the rules of the new game in the January 1892 edition of *The Triangle*, the YMCA's monthly journal. The article, modestly titled "Basket Ball," carried a sketch of seven players, all intent on a ball hovering over a basket hung above a gymnasium floor. "We present to our readers a new game . . . which seems to have those elements in it which ought to make it popular among the Associations," Naismith wrote. "Any number of men" could play at once, with the size of the teams depending on "the size of the floor space." Two goals and a ball were the only equipment required. By calling for "physical judgment and co-ordination of every muscle," the new game would contribute to the "all-around development" of the athlete, including improvements in agility and teamwork. This was a game requiring "science and skill," rather than sheer strength, and it was to "be played by gentlemen in a manly way."[5]

Even as he urged that his rules be respected, Naismith encouraged competitive play between different YMCAs and asked instructors to "report any points that might be amended." Refinements would come in due time—and in great numbers. But with the January 1892 publication of the rules of his new game, Naismith had put the ball in play. The only truly American game was about to take on a life of its own.[6]

Phoenix Rising
1892

❧❧❧

WILLIAM WINSLOW, M.D., ARRIVED IN GREAT FALLS, MONTANA, on a chilly afternoon in late April 1892. It had been a long, wearisome trip from Indian Territory (Oklahoma), and he had passed the interminable hours on the train reading and rereading the BIA agent's reports on conditions at Fort Shaw. On that basis alone, he was buoyed by the thought that he had quite possibly been handed the best position the Indian School Service had to offer. Admittedly, starting a new school at an abandoned military post in an area only a few years removed from fierce conflicts between whites and Indians was a daunting assignment. But it was a worthy challenge for an experienced educator coming off a commendable performance as principal teacher and physician at Chilocco, one of the country's most prestigious Indian boarding schools.[1]

By the time the train pulled into the station at Great Falls, the dog-eared pages of the agent's reports were showing the effects of the long journey—and so was Dr. Winslow. Eager as he was to reach his final destination, he was in no shape to continue his journey without a good night's rest, and he sought out the Park Hotel. Come morning, he would be ready for the trip to the Sun River Valley to see for himself this erstwhile military fort that was about to become the nation's fourteenth off-reservation Indian boarding school.[2]

Knowing a comfortable bed awaited him, Dr. Winslow was content to linger over supper, then treat himself to an aperitif in front of the fireplace. Unaccustomed as he was to moments of total leisure, his thoughts remained centered on what lay ahead. Under his charge this fledgling school in the wilds of Montana would soon be on a par with

Chilocco and, in due time, would rise to the level of Haskell—or even Carlisle. No. Not Carlisle. Carlisle was unassailable. But everything else was possible. Everything.

Rising early the next morning, fully refreshed, Dr. Winslow telegraphed his wife to let her know of his safe arrival, then sent a messenger to arrange for a driver and buckboard to carry him out to Fort Shaw. Having learned that the twenty-five-mile trip could take four to five hours, depending on road conditions, he enjoyed a hot breakfast but decided to forgo a second cup of coffee in favor of getting under way.[3]

Soon he was traveling west on the streets of Great Falls, crossing the bridge that spanned the Missouri, and heading out onto the plains. As the miles rolled by, Dr. Winslow, a curious man both by nature and training, peppered his driver with questions—about prominent landmarks, about local personalities, about the general attitude of the valley's settlers toward Indians and Indian schools. But as morning stretched into afternoon, the two men fell silent, each lost in his own thoughts.

Conversation was sparked again, however, as the buckboard rolled into the bustling town of Sun River. As the horses trotted down Main Street, past stores, saloons, and hotels, townspeople turned their heads as if they knew exactly who was passing through and exactly where he was going. On impulse Dr. Winslow tipped his hat in the direction of two ladies who seemed glued to the boardwalk in front of the mercantile.

⌒

Now there's a gentleman for you. The remark drew a laugh from the others standing outside the barbershop. But what we need for the school is another general. Who else will be able to ride herd on a bunch of little savages? I say we give him a chance, the druggist offered. Brains could be better than brawn when it comes to getting a school up and running. And I guess he has brains. I've heard he's a doctor, not just another teacher. So let's see if he can't turn that old fort into a successful school.

For Indians.

The wait-and-see attitude of those who still lingered outside their shops long after the buckboard had gone on its way was understandable. This was not the solution they would have chosen to the problem of how to recoup the losses suffered since the closing of Fort Shaw. Indeed, at the *Rising Sun*'s first mention of turning the old complex into an Indian school, there had been much wringing of hands, mostly among the women who thought they had seen the last of the Indians once the fort had closed down. Hadn't the government spent enough money moving those people to their own reservations? Weren't there schools on those reservations? Wouldn't those children be better off among their own? What possible sense could it make to go out and gather them up from the four corners of the earth and plop them down right here in the Sun River Valley?[4]

Yet as no brighter prospect materialized and possibility moved toward reality, there had been increasing support for the project, mostly among the men for whom opening an Indian boarding school seemed a better alternative than closing down a business or selling off cattle and losing a ranch.[5]

In the end, of course, the decision had not been theirs to make. Though it would surely be theirs to live with.

~

Not long after leaving Sun River, Dr. Winslow's driver pointed toward a dot on the distant horizon. Fort Shaw. In time the outlines of buildings and cottonwood trees came into view. But as the buckboard swung onto the road leading to the post, the complex that had looked so promising from a distance began to appear bleak, almost foreboding. When the driver pulled the horses to a halt at the edge of an overgrown square, the new superintendent could only stare in disbelief. Surely this shabby, disheveled place was not the "campus" so glowingly described in the special agent's reports. Nor did it resemble in any way the photographs the War Department had passed on to the BIA when the old fort was decommissioned. In one glimpse William Winslow's lofty aspirations concerning his school in the wilderness vanished.[6]

In the nearly two years during which the reserve had stood empty, deterioration and vandalism had wrought extensive damage. "Every-thing loose had evaporated," the disappointed doctor noted in his first report to Washington. Fences were "scattered over the grounds in con-fusion." A family had taken up residence in one set of the officers' quar-ters "and kept the adjoining set for a milk house." They had turned an-other building into a shelter for chickens, for whom "the yards, walks, porches, and parade ground made a splendid roaming ground." Cattle and horses had ambled at will over boardwalks and onto porches, even entering some of the buildings through doors that had been left ajar— or were missing altogether, having been removed, along with windows, by settlers who apparently considered anything left on an abandoned military post good for the taking. The sheds behind the main buildings were "in every degree of confusion." Of particular concern to physician Winslow was the condition of the outhouses, which he described as "toppling over . . . so as to make a hot-bed for contagion."[7]

Having been led to believe that Fort Shaw was in every way suit-able for the instruction of 250 or more Indian students, Dr. Winslow now made haste to advise his superiors of the darker reality. Toward that end, he undertook his own survey of the land and the buildings. Of the compound's twenty-five structures, he judged fifteen to be, at best, in "fair" condition, the others in "poor" or "very poor" condition. Next, he explored the entire reserve, choosing the 10,000 acres of arable land and desirable pasture that lay in closest proximity to the buildings. Also included in the allotted acreage was the land running the length of the nine-mile ditch from the Sun River that had supplied the old fort with the water necessary for irrigation and domestic use. Satisfied with his choices, he ordered the remaining 19,000 acres released for settle-ment.[8]

Over the next few months Dr. Winslow worked against the calendar, doing his best to prepare the school for occupancy in the fall. He called for bids from merchants and suppliers in Great Falls as well as in the valley, then authorized the purchase of lumber for new siding for the old adobe walls. Fences and roofs had to be repaired, doors and win-dows replaced, and the barracks remodeled into boys' and girls' dor-mitories. The kitchen, hospital, chapel, laundry, and faculty housing, including the quarters he would eventually share with his wife, had to be refurbished and made ready for use.[9]

As the weeks and months rushed by and the construction work lagged far behind schedule, the exhausted superintendent conceded his inability to meet this challenge on his own. Without a capable contractor to help him oversee the completion of the school's physical plant, that monumental task would never be completed by the start of fall semester. And without a clerk to help him make sense of all the invoices, receipts, and other paperwork that had begun to overwhelm him, he would soon be taken to task by his superiors in Washington. It was time to call for reinforcements.

The Pleases, two of the seven Chilocco educators he had persuaded to follow him to Fort Shaw that fall, came immediately to mind. J. H., who would be heading up the school's industrial arts department, and his wife, Mary Jane, who would be school clerk as well as assistant matron, could not have been a better match for his needs. Trusted veterans of the Indian School Service, the two were mature enough to deal with the chaos and confusion they would encounter. But would they be willing to forgo their summer plans and come at once to his rescue? Within a week the Pleases were settled into their makeshift quarters. J. H. took charge of construction and renovation, and Mary Jane was well on her way to restoring Dr. Winslow's desk to its customary state of order.[10]

Freed from the need to be everywhere at once, Winslow turned his attention to other vital, though heretofore neglected tasks. Restored buildings, fine as they might be, were useless until properly furnished and equipped. To outfit the classrooms he ordered desks, readers on the first- through fifth-grade levels, grammar and math books, history and geography texts, twenty gross of foolscap paper, four gross of steel pens, five pints of black ink, two hundred slates, and two hundred slate pencils.[11]

For the dormitories being readied for the arrival of the first cadre of students, Winslow ordered 140 iron beds and a like number of pillows and mattresses, as well as wash bowls, pitchers, and chamber pots. For the kitchen and dining hall, he ordered plates, cups, bowls, flatware, pitchers, pots and pans. From Chicago merchants approved by the Indian School Service, he authorized the delivery of boys' overalls, suspenders, "hickory" shirts, and caps. For the incoming girls, he requisitioned dresses, nightgowns, and dozens of woolen and cotton hose. For the sewing room from which all other clothing would soon be coming, he ordered quantities of calico, denim, gingham, flannel, and wool.[12]

~

While Superintendent Winslow went feverishly about the work of preparing the campus for the arrival of faculty, staff, and students, the commissioner of Indian affairs back in D.C. was sending letters to agents at reservations across Montana, Idaho, northern Wyoming, and eastern Washington, announcing the establishment of the new industrial training school at Fort Shaw, an educational institution he predicted would be "one of the most important in the Indian Service." The commissioner directed all agents to "cooperate with Superintendent Winslow in his efforts to secure a large enrollment for the new school," being certain that the children selected already had "a fair knowledge of English."[13]

Stripping American Indian youth of their native languages was a major tenet in the government's goal of assimilation and acculturation through education. Immersion in the ways of their conquerors; abandonment of their native dress; rejection of their sacred and secular customs and traditions; and acceptance of the white man's religion, values, and vocations were all a part of a policy one historian has termed "education for extinction." As Col. Richard Henry Pratt, superintendent of Carlisle, the nation's first and foremost off-reservation boarding school, put it, the aim of the educator was "[to] kill the Indian . . . [to] save the man."[14]

In the late nineteenth century, off-reservation schools such as Carlisle and Fort Shaw were but one aspect of the government's overall program for Indian education. Fort Shaw School would, at its peak, be able to accommodate no more than 350 students. Thousands of other Indian youngsters in the Rocky Mountain West were enrolled in reservation agency schools. Hundreds more were attending Catholic and Protestant mission schools that were receiving per-pupil allowances for

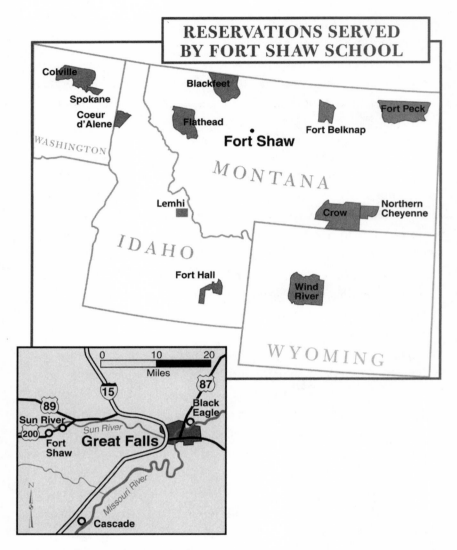

RESERVATIONS SERVED BY FORT SHAW SCHOOL

Colville

Spokane

Coeur d'Alene

WASHINGTON

Blackfeet

Flathead

Fort Shaw

Fort Belknap

Fort Peck

MONTANA

Lemhi

IDAHO

Crow

Northern Cheyenne

Fort Hall

Wind River

WYOMING

0   10   20
Miles

15

87

89

Black Eagle

Sun River

200

Sun River

Fort Shaw

Great Falls

N

Missouri River

Cascade

Great Falls/Fort Shaw area today.

offering academic and vocational programs in line with federal policies.[15]

Among those students whose studies would begin at reservation and mission schools across Montana and Idaho in 1892 were ten little girls who would, over the next decade, become classmates at Fort Shaw Indian Boarding School and, in due time, teammates on a legendary basketball team. By the time the commissioner of Indian affairs was sending out bulletins concerning the opening of the new school in the Sun River Valley, most of these girls, coming as they did from mixed parentage, already had "a fair knowledge of English," and each of them would arrive at Fort Shaw already grounded in the ways of the white world.[16]

In due time any wariness arising from their diverse family, tribal, and educational backgrounds would give way to a sense of sisterhood. But that summer and fall of 1892, as William Winslow went about the business of readying the Fort Shaw campus for occupancy, neither he nor they had any idea of the adventures that lay ahead.

Routine and Ritual
1892

By late August 1892, Dr. Winslow's wife, Josephine, had joined him at Fort Shaw. There she was made welcome by Mr. and Mrs. Pleas, who were, by now, quite at home in their new surroundings, and by the five other Chilocco educators, all of whom had arrived on campus earlier that month. The Roberts sisters, Belle and Ida, would form the heart of the teaching staff, and Belle, the older sister, would also serve as matron. Upon the arrival of the students, Mrs. Pleas would add the role of assistant matron to her work as school clerk and Mr. Pleas would take up his post as head of the industrial arts program. Byron White was already preparing his carpentry shop, while his wife, Olive, had the sewing room in order and was beginning work on uniforms that could serve as models for the ones the girls would soon be making. Until she had the help of incoming students, Clara Blanchard would be handling all the faculty and staff laundry on her own.[1]

Pleased as he was to have such a solid core of experienced employees, all of whom had worked well together at Chilocco and were familiar with the routines and regulations of off-reservation schools, Dr. Winslow knew that core would need far more support in handling a full complement of students. But, as it turned out, Winslow did not need to enlarge his staff as quickly as he had anticipated. Construction and remodeling were taking far longer than expected, and in early September the new superintendent resigned himself to postponing the school's opening until January.[2]

In late fall that date was altered once again, this time by news that a disastrous fire had swept through the Fort Peck agency school at Poplar, leaving the school's student body without classrooms. Agent C. R.

A. Scobey wired the news to Winslow, with a plea to take these Assiniboine children in before they drifted back into their old ways. Scobey asserted—and Winslow concurred—that the youngsters should adjust well to life at Fort Shaw, being already accustomed to school routine. Winslow now committed himself and his skeleton crew to having Fort Shaw's dormitories, bathhouses, kitchen, and dining room facilities ready for the arrival of forty or fifty boys and girls from Fort Peck in late December. They would be traveling by rail, and he would send wagons to meet them at the station and transport them to Fort Shaw. With the students—to Winslow's relief—would come J. L. Baker, superintendent of the ill-fated agency school, and his wife, Henrietta, who had been the matron at Fort Peck and would become the cook at Fort Shaw.[3]

With the addition of the Bakers to the staff, Winslow could make this work. In a sense, this little emergency had enabled him to reach his original goal. Fort Shaw would welcome its first students in 1892. In December, rather than September, admittedly, but in terms of his permanent record—and that of the school—it was the year, not the month, that mattered.

∼

As word of the imminent arrival of the Fort Peck students made its way up and down the Sun River Valley, tensions heightened. Whereas local residents had been led to believe the first enrollees at Fort Shaw would be Blackfeet children, now they were told that Assiniboines were on their way to the valley. What other surprises awaited them? Old worries surfaced. How would the presence of so many Indian children affect the well-being of the area's white settlers? How could so few teachers control so many students, especially the older ones who were likely accustomed to roaming when and where they pleased? What if these dark-skinned little savages were not really as well disciplined as Superintendent Winslow had promised?[4]

These children were likely to be more homesick than hostile, someone ventured, more in need of support than discipline. Most of them had likely never been so far away from their families.

Then the rejoinder: What kind of parents would allow their sons and daughters to go to a school so far from home?

While holiday preparations and celebrations served as momentary distractions from such discussions, the post-Christmas lull was disrupted by news that the children and their escort from the Fort Peck Reservation had made the transfer at Great Falls and were bound for Sunnyside station, where wagons were waiting to bring them to Fort Shaw. Sure enough, early on the evening of December 27 the little caravan rolled into the town of Sun River. As the wagons bounced their way along the rutted, snow-packed road that led to Fort Shaw—still some eight miles distant—curious citizens pulled aside their parlor curtains. Families silhouetted by lamplight stared into the darkness, doing their best to determine the number of students in each wagon, a difficult task since the youngsters sat huddled under blankets, four and five abreast, and some of the smaller ones were cuddled in the arms of older brothers or sisters. There must be forty of them. Maybe fifty.[5]

And this was only the beginning.

~

In truth there were only thirty-five boys and girls crowded into the wagons that passed through Sun River that December evening, and among those thirty-five was six-year-old Nettie Susan Wirth. It was her first time away from her mother and father, and had she been old enough to grasp just how much time would pass before she saw her parents and home again, perhaps she would have been less easily comforted by the presence of her two older sisters, twelve-year-old Lizzie and nine-year-old Louise.[6]

Like many other students in that wagon caravan and like many more who would enroll at Fort Shaw over the months and years ahead, the Wirth sisters were children of an Indian mother and a white father. For Nettie and her siblings, "assimilation and acculturation" was not only government policy but a way of life. Indeed, their family was a blend of starkly different cultures. Their maternal grandfather, Got Wolf Tail, had been chief of the Red Bottom band of Assiniboines, while their paternal grandfather, Johann Wirth, had owned a bakery in a village near Stuttgart, Germany. Nettie was the youngest of eight born to her widowed mother, Susan Archdale—Woman That Kills Wood—and her German-immigrant father, Jacob Wirth.[7]

On that frosty December morning when the agency school superintendent, J. L. Baker, took little Nettie from her father's arms and hoisted her into the railway car that would carry her almost 350 miles farther west, her mother could not be comforted. Up until then, Susan Wirth had shared her husband's belief that white man's schooling was the best preparation for their children's survival and success in a rapidly changing world. Indeed, that fall Susan had even accompanied her girls to the agency school, sharing a desk with Nettie, to see for herself exactly what they were being taught. And, just two months before this December day, she had given in to the pleas of their oldest daughter, Christine, and had watched her leave for Carlisle. But sending her three youngest girls away was another matter altogether. Yes, she had heard Agent Scobey say that the loss of the reservation school meant parents at Fort Peck had no choice but to send their children to Fort Shaw. But she vowed to defy Agent Scobey's edict, even if doing so meant never receiving government rations again. She and Jacob had fought for days over the matter, right up to the time of the girls' departure. Yet her husband's will—and that of the agent—prevailed, and as the locomotive sounded its whistle and lurched into motion, the wails of Woman That Kills Wood mingled with the sobs of the other mothers clustered around the railroad platform.[8]

This overwhelming sense of loss was not limited to the adults who stood staring after the westbound train until only a trail of black smoke was left to see. The emotions of the boys and girls aboard that train mirrored those of their elders. Yet their faces did not give them away. Even in the midst of bewilderment and distress, no one cried, not even the youngest among them.

In time, the excitement of the journey began to work its magic, especially after Superintendent and Mrs. Baker passed around peppermint candies and oranges, the Christmas treats they had ordered some weeks before the fire. Mrs. Baker led them in a carol or two, then told them they were free to move around as long as they didn't leave their own railroad car. They should take advantage of this opportunity, the superintendent told them. It was not every day an Indian child had a chance to ride on a train, let alone to see a city as big as the one they were headed toward.

At midday, the travelers were allowed to open the little bundles of food their mothers and grandmothers had packed for them. That meal was bittersweet for the older children, aware as they were that this would be their last taste of home for a long, long time. Too hungry and inno-cent to be bothered by such thoughts, the younger travelers devoured their food with gusto, then returned to their games or to gazing out the smoke-hazed windows. The novelty of the ride had worn off by the time the train pulled into the Sunnyside station outside Great Falls, and anxieties rose as they stepped off the platform and were herded into the wagons that would take them on the last leg of their journey.[9]

At Fort Shaw, the campus and staff were well prepared for the chil-dren's arrival on that evening of December 27. The children were led into the dining room for a light supper and a brief welcome by Superin-tendent Winslow. Then came the mandatory separation of siblings and friends, with the boys disappearing off into their own world. Lizzie and Louise Wirth were sent to the older girls' dormitory, while Miss Roberts led Nettie and her friend Mattie Hayes to the "little girls' dorm," where kerosene lamps burned brightly and rows of beds stretched out to greet them. Identical nightgowns were laid out on top of wool blankets.

Yet before Nettie could slip into one of those warm gowns, she had to step out of the clothes she had worn from home and undergo a thor-ough inspection. Naked and shivering, she closed her eyes and held her breath as Miss Roberts dusted her head for lice. Directed toward one of the washstands arrayed along the far wall of the dormitory, Nettie hurried across the bare floorboards. At the washstand, she squared her little shoulders and said not a word as Mrs. Pleas poured water from the tall white pitcher into the smooth white bowl, then scrubbed her down with lye soap, head to toe. After a quick rinsing with water splashed from the pitcher, she was left to dry herself with one of the towels hung on hooks beside each stand. By the time her ordeal was over, Nettie was more than ready to pull on her flannel gown and snuggle under the covers.[10]

Yet whatever pleasure she might have had taken in the thought of having her very own bed faded the moment she slipped between the sheets. Accustomed as she was to the shared warmth of her sisters, the new bed felt cold and strange and empty. Was she sufficiently weary from the long day of travel to drift off to sleep at once? Or was she still too frozen from her washdown and too haunted by her mother's cries to sleep at all that night? Were her dreams, if she dreamed at all, filled with images of home or visions of what might lie ahead?

Wherever her dreams might have taken her on that cold December night, with the coming of dawn and the sound of the bugle, she awoke to the realities of her new life at Fort Shaw Indian School.

~

The staff at Fort Shaw had little time to congratulate themselves on the opening of the newest campus in the Indian School Service, for Dr. Winslow was determined that the thirty-five children newly arrived from the Fort Peck Reservation would be familiar enough with the routine and ritual of campus life to help indoctrinate the Blackfeet students who were due to arrive within days. The move to an off-reservation school could be a bit overwhelming, even for those with prior exposure to boarding school life. The sooner these students realized how much more would be expected of them at Fort Shaw, the sooner they could begin to meet those expectations. At the heart of it all lay that sine qua non—regimentation. There would definitely be tighter regimentation.

Nettie Wirth learned that lesson her very first morning at Fort Shaw. Before the last notes of reveille had faded, Miss Roberts appeared in the doorway to hurry the girls into their new uniforms—full-length worsted dresses and wool stockings—and herd them down to the dining hall for breakfast. Boys' tables were on one side, girls' on the other, and Nettie immediately saw Lizzie and Louise seated at a long table covered with a gleaming white cloth. Slipping into place between her two sisters, Nettie snuggled as close to Lizzie's side as she could, but she said not a word, since Miss Roberts had warned them that there would be no chatter during meals.[11]

As the senior boy or girl at each table filled and passed the bowls of oatmeal, Dr. Winslow rose to introduce the teachers and staff members who would ensure that lessons were learned and rules were followed. Discipline would be the key to success here at Fort Shaw, and in the world beyond. No foolishness would be tolerated. English, and only English, would be spoken on the campus. From this day forward students were to apply themselves to their academic studies and master the vocational skills upon which their livelihood would someday depend. Over the course of this first full day on campus, they would learn more about the specific duties they would be assigned. Immediately after breakfast they were to rise and move out to the parade ground—not in the lackadaisical manner in which they had entered the dining hall, but with purpose and pride. On the parade ground they would be divided into squadrons, boys in one squadron, girls in the other, and taught the rudiments of marching.[12]

For the next hour on that cold and blustery late December morning the thirty-five uniformed students marched in ragged lines up and down the square, their feet pounding the frozen ground, their breath condensing in white puffs as they did their best to keep in step. Back and forth they marched, glancing down the lines to check their position, squaring up, and staring straight ahead once more. Finally came the command that allowed them to catch their breath. But there was no breaking formation as the girls and boys moved in their separate columns to begin the next activity of the morning—tours of the grounds and buildings that would give them some idea of the weekday routine at Fort Shaw.

As the boys marched off toward the shops on the fringe of the campus, the seventeen girls from Fort Peck Agency School filed into the administration building and into the larger of two classrooms on the second floor. There Nettie slid into one of the double desks that stood row on row in the center of the room. Glancing around, she marveled at the surrounding shelves full of textbooks, stacks of writing paper, boxes of quill pens and lead pencils, and piles of slates. She had not seen anything like this back at Fort Peck. A map of the states and territories adorned one wall. A globe sat on the teacher's desk.[13]

Behind that desk stood Dr. Winslow himself. Taking up where he had left off at breakfast, the superintendent launched into a lengthy description of the academic challenges awaiting them at Fort Shaw. Eloquent though he was, much of his rhetoric was lost on many of the girls sitting in front of him, some of whom were still struggling with their English and others who, like Nettie, were too young to comprehend his vocabulary.

While the superintendent held forth in the classroom, Mr. Pleas led the boys around the campus, pointing out the sites where they would hereafter be spending their morning hours learning carpentry, blacksmithing, and the fundamentals of plowing, planting, tilling, and harvesting. The fine points of tending livestock–cattle, horses, pigs, and chickens—would also be part of the lessons. Every boy, Mr. Pleas told them, would learn how to milk, just as every girl would learn how to skim off cream, churn butter, and make cheese, some to be sold and some to be used in the school's kitchen.[14]

As the bell sounded for the noon meal, the boys marched back toward the campus square and the girls moved in step out of the classroom, through the main hall of the administration building and out onto the boardwalk, to join the faculty and staff in the dining hall for the midday meal. Immediately thereafter, the boys took their turn in the classroom presided over by Superintendent Winslow, while the girls were introduced to the various domestic arts that would fill their afternoons.

Big and little girls alike followed Mrs. White into the sewing room. In the center stood an impressive array of sewing machines, their treadles waiting to be pumped by feet already feeling the unaccustomed pinch of button-up leather shoes. Shelves on one wall were stocked with bolts of gingham and denim, spools of thread, papers of needles and pins. Nettie was wide-eyed. Even Lizzie and Louise had never seen a room like this. Then on to the handiwork area where embroidery and lacework would be mastered. And finally into the ironing nook where the little girls would learn to smooth out pillowcases and tablecloths and the older students would turn out the starched shirts and collars worn by Dr. Winslow and the other men on the faculty, the fine blouses of the female teachers, and the aprons and caps of the kitchen staff.[15]

In the kitchen, Mrs. Baker, who had been their matron at Fort Peck and who would be teaching them cooking here at Fort Shaw, was up to her elbows in flour, turning out loaves of bread for the evening meal. A dozen or more loaves were already shaped and rising. The wood in the fireboxes crackled as the ovens heated to baking temperature, and pots of stew simmered atop the stove. Pies baked before dawn that morning were stored in warming compartments above the stoves. It was clear the kitchen would be a busy place from the earliest hours of the day until the last dish was washed and put away at night—and it was equally clear that once the rest of the students arrived, the cook would need many hands in order to put three meals a day on the table.

From the warm kitchen the girls stepped out into the cold once more. Feeling the growing chill of the afternoon, they marched down to the laundry house, with its water buckets, washtubs, and scrub boards. The outhouses next door needed no introduction, nor did the dormitory rooms to which the girls returned for further instruction on how to make their beds—which, according to Miss Roberts, had been left in an abysmal mess that morning—and how to fold and store their night-clothes, uniforms, and undergarments in the trunk at the foot of each bed. Brooms were fetched and floors were swept. Kerosene lamps were trimmed. Wash basins neglected that morning in the haste to move to breakfast were rinsed out and wiped dry, and empty pitchers were lined up along the dormitory steps.

To Nettie's great relief, the supper bell finally rang. And by the time the evening meal was over, by the time she and the younger girls had cleared the tables and the older girls had scoured clean the dishes, pots, and pans, Nettie was glad enough to head back toward the dormitory. Exhausted by all she had done and learned, she was more than ready to pull off her dress, pull on her nightgown, and drop into bed. The bugle would sound again at 6:00 A.M., and the marching and the lessons would begin all over again.[16]

With his teachers and staff as worn out as his students, Dr. Winslow did not keep them long at that evening's gathering. Their first full day had proven to his satisfaction that this crew could hold up its end of things until he could fill out its ranks. He was also satisfied with the way the Fort Peck students had already begun adjusting to the daily routine. They would set a fine example for the newcomers. He was proud of them, and he meant to tell them that at breakfast in the morning. Routine and ritual: the basis of a Fort Shaw education.

Recruitment, Runaways,
and Reinforcements
1893
❦

THERE WAS NO BREAK IN ROUTINE ON NEW YEAR'S DAY, 1893, as Dr. Winslow pressed to have everything ready for the expected arrival of the youngsters from the Blackfeet Reservation. Not that he was especially worried about melding the Piegan children into the routine. All of them were his recruits, more or less, although his trip to the reservation last fall had been far less fruitful than he had anticipated. Based on the agent's assurances that the Blackfeet were progressive people who knew the value of a good education, he had set out under the assumption that a good number of the reservation's school-aged children would soon be attending Fort Shaw. Yet a few days of interviews with parents and grandparents had given him cause to question that assumption.

It seemed the agent had failed to share a crucial bit of information. The Blackfeet were still recovering from the shock of seeing forty-five of their boys taken off to Carlisle three years back. With that day seared in their minds, they had ever since been leery of government schools of any stripe, although the mission schools had fared somewhat better. Seventy boys and girls were attending Holy Family on Two Medicine River, and fifty or so had been sent to St. Peter's in the Sun River Valley.[1]

Deciding to lower his expectations and bide his time, Winslow focused on the more positive aspects of his trip north. Consider the case of Jenny Johnson. This comely and intelligent widow—Nearly Died, as she was known to her people—had seemed not only open, but eager, to have her children receive the best education available, as long as they did not have to travel too far from home. Or from her. In fact, when she had enrolled her five oldest in the new agency school at Willow Creek west of Browning, a half-day's journey from their home at Heart Butte, she had followed them there, leaving her youngest in her mother's care. At the time of Winslow's recruiting visit that fall she was working as a laundress at Willow Creek School and keeping a close eye on her children.[2]

Adept as he had become at making quick assessments of the attitudes and aptitudes of Indian children, Superintendent Winslow had noted at once that both of Jenny Johnson's oldest girls, Mary and Belle, were capable students and potential leaders. The two clearly belonged at Fort Shaw *if* their mother could be persuaded to send them there. On the basis of her rapt attention to his recital of the advantages his school could offer, Winslow had left the reservation all but certain that, come January, widow Johnson would be entrusting her children to his care.

But to his great disappointment, there were no Johnsons among the eighteen Blackfeet boys and girls who arrived at Fort Shaw on Tuesday, January 3, 1893.[3] Still, there was much to be thankful for. Diversity counted almost as much as numbers in this business of getting an off-reservation school up and running, and for the moment Winslow was satisfied with the number and the vigor of the Piegan youngsters whose names Mrs. Pleas inscribed in the records that evening. And he was more than satisfied with the way the students from Fort Peck had stepped forward to share their freshly acquired knowledge and skills with the newcomers.

With some degree of pride of place, the Assiniboines had introduced their incoming classmates to the routine in the dorms and answered their questions about what lay ahead. All of this was in English, of course, and according to Miss Roberts, the communication achieved during those brief exchanges had laid the basis for further halting attempts at conversation later that evening. Even in the little girls' dorm, her giggling Piegan and Assiniboine charges had made a game of lobbing random and often incomprehensible English words and phrases back and forth until "lights out." For Superintendent Winslow, the fact that whispered conversations in their own languages would have begun the minute lamps were extinguished and doors were closed did not lessen the import of Miss Roberts's observations.

His students had just realized an unexpected benefit of learning the white man's tongue. Yet it would be years before Dr. Winslow—and the Indian School Service as a whole—would come to see an unexpected consequence of mandatory use of the English language. By stripping students of their native tongues and forcing them toward a hard-won knowledge of the English language, off-reservation boarding schools like Fort Shaw were not only fulfilling the government's goal of diminishing tribal identities but were also fostering the beginnings of the pan-tribalism that would one day prove invaluable to American Indians in their united push toward changes in federal policy, which no one tribe could have brought about on its own.

It would also be years before the import of Superintendent Winslow's persistence in recruiting Jenny Johnson's children would become fully evident when her second daughter, Belle, became captain of the basketball team that showed the state, the nation, and the world the benefits of teamwork across tribal lines.

That January of 1893 William Winslow's aspirations went no further than turning children from diverse tribal cultures into a unified student body. Accordingly, the formal indoctrination of his first contingent of students from the Blackfeet Reservation started the morning after the group's arrival on campus. That introduction to life at an off-reservation boarding school began on the parade ground as the Piegan youngsters were melded by size and gender into the squadrons of boys and girls from Fort Peck. Rank beginners themselves only seven days earlier—and admittedly still less than perfect in the drills—the Assiniboine "veterans" felt a sense of pride as they demonstrated the quick little skip essential to recovering from a misstep. Morning drill over, designated Assiniboine students escorted their new classmates on the tours through which they themselves had so recently been introduced to campus life.

∼

While Dr. Winslow reflected with pleasure on the way his school and his student body were shaping up, three of the oldest Piegan boys had already begun plotting their escape. Faced with the dismal prospect of confinement, regimentation, and harsh discipline, they made their bid for freedom within days of arriving at Fort Shaw. Setting out before the rest of the campus was stirring, they followed the river west, then turned north, planning to keep on moving until they reached the border of the Blackfeet Reservation. Dr. Winslow fumed at the news of their disappearance, even as he realized that he had no reason to expect Fort Shaw to be any different in this respect from any other school in which he had served, or, indeed, from any other school in the system.[4]

He lost no time in sending out search parties in every direction. As news of the incident spread, valley residents counted their horses and kept a sharp lookout for dark-skinned strangers. When the boys had not been found by nightfall, Superintendent Winslow's displeasure gave way to concern. It was likely they were caught out in the open, somewhere between school and home, on a night when temperatures would be well below freezing. Perhaps lost. Possibly injured or ill.

While such thoughts meant a sleepless night for their superintendent, his teen-aged truants were safe, though miserably cold and hungry. When seventy-five miles proved to be much farther than their legs could carry them in a single day, they set up a makeshift camp. Afraid a fire would give them away, they shivered their way through a seemingly endless night. With the coming of dawn, they turned back toward Fort Shaw, no longer confident that they could find their way home without a road to guide them but knowing they could retrace their steps and get back to the school.[5]

Angry, but greatly relieved, when the runaways made it back to campus in time for supper the next evening, Superintendent Winslow announced to the wayward boys—and their fellow students—that such actions would not be tolerated. Suitable punishment would be meted out, and precautionary measures would be taken to prevent such occurrences in the future. Shamed, but unrepentant, the three runaways stared at their plates.[6]

Retreating to his office, Winslow considered his dilemma: Why should he mar the Fort Shaw record by reporting this incident? Was there any need to record an instance in which homesick boys had left the campus, seen the error of their ways, and returned of their own volition? Of course, the tiny article in the *Rising Sun* had, in a sense, already made the incident a matter of record. Still, he convinced himself that just this once he was justified in not reporting the boys' absence to his superiors, and there was certainly good reason to keep the word from spreading to other reservations. Appearances. So much depended on appearances. Community support. Federal funding. Recruitment success.[7]

The best way of protecting his image and that of the school was to prevent students from running away in the first place. With another group from the Blackfeet Reservation due to arrive before month's end, he would put his entire staff on the alert for any signs of discontent. Not that the Piegan students would be any more likely to strike out for home than students from any other tribe, were it not for the fact that their reservation was so much closer to school than the others. Any Assiniboine setting out for Fort Peck would be hard put to make those three hundred and fifty miles without hopping a freight.

He would like to have more Assiniboine boys and girls, lots more. And recruiting them should be relatively easy. After all, no one knew exactly when the burnt-out agency school would reopen and everyone knew that Indian children *had* to attend school *somewhere*. But not necessarily at Fort Shaw. Not if Woman That Kills Wood had her way. Still upset with both her husband and the agent for sending her girls so far from home, Susan Wirth was doing her best to help other mothers avoid that same fate. But there were others with more positive views of Fort Shaw. One of the most influential men on the reservation, David Mitchell, son of the legendary fur trader and Indian agent, David Dawson Mitchell, had allowed two of his daughters, fifteen-year-old Josephine and six-year-old Nancy, to go to Fort Shaw aboard the very same train that had taken the Wirth sisters west.[8]

On the basis of Mitchell's decision, other parents were weighing the pros and cons of allowing their children to go to Fort Shaw. Joe Butch, a well-known rancher whose Assiniboine wife had drowned that November, had been reluctant to send his three girls away so soon after their mother's death. Now the timing seemed right, and two of the girls, eleven-year-old Josepha and seven-year-old Rosa, would soon be on their way to the school His youngest, six-year-old Genie, would not be with them, however, having persuaded her father to let her stay at home on the ranch—at least until the Poplar school was rebuilt.[9]

The news spread quickly and set still more families talking. If that school in the Sun River Valley was good enough for David Mitchell's and Joe Butch's girls, it should be good enough for their sons and daughters too. Little by little, resistance was giving away to acquiescence, and the agent at Fort Peck let Dr. Winslow know that more Assiniboine children would be coming sometime in early February. Just how many he could not say, given the fluctuating moods of the parents on his reservation.

Suddenly Winslow realized that Fort Shaw's student population would likely double within the next three weeks. Such an increase in enrollment would require an increase in staff. Finding teachers this far into the school year would be all but impossible, although he would write to officials in D.C. and hope for a miracle. He would normally have despaired of doing much better in filling staff positions, considering the poor timing, except for a recent BIA directive that not only authorized, but encouraged, offering such jobs to qualified Indian youth who had completed their schooling.[10]

Accordingly, Winslow invited three recent Carlisle graduates from the Blackfeet Reservation to serve as "Indian assistants." They should be particularly effective role models for some of his more reluctant Piegan scholars. Needing female assistants as well as male, he chose one of his most mature and responsible students, fifteen-year-old Josephine Mitchell, assuring her that she could continue her studies even while gaining invaluable work experience. And from a recommendation forwarded to him by one of the Ursulines at St. Peter's, he chose another female assistant, a seventeen-year-old who had been born in the shadow of old Fort Shaw.[11]

~

February 10, 1893. Josephine Langley's long buggy ride down from the Blackfeet Reservation was a journey through time as well as space. Seeing the Bird Tail rise up in the distance had taken her back to her years at St. Peter's Mission. And moving ever closer to the lamp-lit windows of Fort Shaw stirred childhood memories of watching those flickering lights through the mist that rose up from the river separating the world of the Blackfeet encampment from that of the soldiers on the other side.[12]

Her father, a trapper turned military scout, had been free to bridge those worlds, and he had availed himself of that freedom, crossing the river more than once in search of female companionship. Josie's mother, Many Kills, had just turned sixteen at the time thirty-two-year-old Louis Langley visited the tepee she shared with her mother, Always Singing, and her baby sister, Annie. Not long thereafter, the two were married, *a la façon du pays,* and by the time Josie was born the following summer, they were living with eighteen-month-old Annie in a tepee of their own.[13]

Those early childhood years were happy times for Josephine Langley. She spent long summer days playing with Annie and the other children at the camp, running freely along the riverbanks, weaving garlands from the flowers growing among the prairie grasses and following the older girls all the way out to the base of the buffalo jump at Square Butte, where they gathered bones to be carried home and fashioned into all sorts of playthings—from little log houses to poles for toy tepees fashioned from scraps of deerskin or buffalo hide. Their make-believe world was a classroom as big as all outdoors.

For Josie, life provided so few glimpses of her father that in time she stopped asking where he was and when he would be home again. By the early 1880s, Louis Langley, always a drifter, had disappeared from her life all together. By the middle of that decade, Many Kills had a new husband: young Charles Choquette, the Piegan son of one of the Sun River Valley's most prosperous ranchers. Education was important to the Choquette family, and in spring of 1885, nine-year-old Josie Langley and three of the Choquette girls were among the first enrollees in St. Peter's newly established school for Indian girls. She was to spend the next seven years of her life at the mission school, staying on with the Ursulines even after her mother and stepfather had left the valley and moved onto the Blackfeet Reservation.[14]

She could not have been in a better place for having her abilities and talents appreciated and nurtured. Impressed by her eagerness to learn, her excellence in her studies, and her leadership abilities, the sisters at St. Peter's encouraged Josie's interest in becoming a teacher. Knowing that Carlisle offered teacher training, they recommended her for admission there. Sixteen-year-old Josephine Langley was an ideal candidate for the school in the East, yet her application was summarily rejected. Colonel Pratt held to his long-standing rule against accepting students who might bring contagion to his school, and Josie suffered from trachoma, a chronic, potentially blinding eye infection that had plagued her since her earliest days at St. Peter's.[15]

Serendipitously, Dr. Winslow's offer of a staff position at Fort Shaw now rekindled dreams Josie had all but abandoned. Yes, she would have to start at the bottom of the ladder as an Indian assistant, but with hard work she could move up in the ranks of the Indian School Service. And by continuing her studies while working at Fort Shaw, she could eventually qualify for the civil service exam required of teachers in the system. Those bright prospects aside, by accepting this post, she would, in a very real sense, be going home.[16]

~

As Superintendent Winslow had hoped, Josephine Langley's first-hand knowledge of boarding-school life served her well as she assumed her duties at Fort Shaw. Having spent so many years away from her own mother, she understood the loneliness that could overwhelm a child newly removed from home and family. She took special notice of the youngest students, including six-year-old Nettie Wirth. She also reached out to the oldest Wirth sister, Lizzie, an enthusiastic eleven-year-old who seemed destined to rise to the top of her class in everything from mathematics to gymnastics. Yet even someone like Lizzie could run out of energy, lose her confidence, and find herself in need of encouragement and support. In such moments, Josie would be there for Lizzie, just as the sisters at St. Peter's had been there for her.[17]

Being there for all of her students while keeping up with her own studies became increasingly difficult as the steady influx of boys and girls continued over the course of Josie's first semester on campus. Beginning with a student body of 35 the previous December, Fort Shaw enrollment had grown to 139 by April 1893. With numbers came diversity. Having begun her tenure at Fort Shaw with only Piegans and Assiniboines in her care, within two months of her arrival on campus, Josie was working with Cheyenne, Crow, and Yankton Sioux youngsters.[18]

~

Diversity would be a major theme in the opening remarks Dr. Winslow was drafting as he oversaw preparations for his school's first closing exercises. Mandated events intended to showcase student achievements and demonstrate the effectiveness of the government's Indian education program, these year-end programs varied in quality from the barebones offerings at struggling agency schools to the elaborate productions of the nation's finest off-reservation institutions. While he had no illusions of equaling the events staged at Carlisle or Haskell, Winslow intended to mount a show that would entertain as well as enlighten visitors who would spread the good news concerning the remarkable progress being made at Fort Shaw Indian School.

He had plenty of help in achieving those goals as his faculty and staff pushed their students to the limit. Long hours were given to perfecting gymnastics exercises and precision drills. Demanding rehearsals of recitations and songs were the order of the day. Yet Dr. Winslow's primary focus was on the quality of the academic and industrial displays that would attest to the progress his students were making in all areas of study. Excellence across the board was a must, given his need to impress not only officials in D.C. and local politicians but also valley residents, many of whom remained openly skeptical as to whether Indian boys and girls could ever become truly "educated."

On Friday, June 30, 1893, satisfied that his students were ready to answer that question, Superintendent William Winslow threw open the campus, welcoming one and all to Fort Shaw's well-publicized year-end exercises. His opening address was followed by a tour of the premises, including classrooms and workrooms, barns, shops, and sheds. Then the crowd reconvened for a "literary entertainment" that began with a march onto the parade ground, a rousing rendition of "America," and a salute to the flag. Club-swinging and barbell exhibitions, precision drills, and a series of recitations and choral numbers followed, and the voices of visitors blended with those of the students in the afternoon's closing number, "God Be with You 'til We Meet Again." The women of the valley who were in attendance that day could not help but think back on the musical entertainments they had so enjoyed during the glory days of the old fort.[19]

An article in the *Great Falls Tribune* attested to the success of Fort Shaw's first closing exercises. According to the reporter, the quality of the academic work on display was "a great surprise to those . . . who have been more used to thinking [of] the Indian and the scalping knife than of the Indian and the slate and pencil." Achievements in the industrial arts were equally impressive. The boys had made good use of their newly acquired carpentry skills, "putting in floors, wainscoting, and doing general repairs on buildings." The older boys had "taken care of horses and cows . . . built eight miles of fence [and] put in twenty-five acres of garden." The girls were becoming proficient housekeepers and cooks and had turned out "2,700 different articles" in the sewing room. In sum, the achievements of these Indian boys and girls, many of whom "had come from the camp six months ago, . . . would have been a credit to any white school."[20]

For Superintendent Winslow, the 1892–93 school year could not have ended on a better note.

Foreshadowings
1893

JUNE 1893. WILLIAM BURTON HAD DECIDED TO ATTEND THE closing exercises at the agency school on Idaho's Lemhi Reservation only because his daughters needed his support now more than ever. They had lost their mother barely two months ago, and he was struggling to fill that hole in their lives. Disillusioned as he was by the deplorable conditions at the school, he simply could not let Rosie and Minnie down. This poor excuse for a school was the only form of education available to his children right now, and he wanted them to know that he supported the work they were doing, the progress they were making in their lessons.[1]

Shifting uncomfortably on the hard bench, Burton endured Agent Monk's desultory remarks—the only item on the "program." For Lemhi agents, it was an oft-told tale: the woes of administering an undersized, underfunded reservation, the challenge of persuading the Indians to adhere to the government's policies, the difficulties of gaining the attention of the bureaucrats in Washington . . . it all seemed insurmountable. As tribal interpreter, Burton had gotten to know George Monk well enough to have little patience with the man, although he realized that Monk had a hard go of it, given Chief Tendoy's adamant stance against anything the white man might propose—whether it was giving up their language; forsaking their native dress in favor of the drab garments provided by the government; complying with federal mandates against seasonal migrations to distant hunting, fishing, and gathering grounds; or especially, giving up their children to the white man's school.[2]

While many Lemhi parents shared Chief Tendoy's opinions and followed his example—even going so far as to hide their children when the agent came to call— Burton took exception to Tendoy's beliefs. His status on the reservation was second probably only to that of the chief himself, and Burton attributed this to his having gotten the white man's education and mastered the white man's language. He wanted no less for his children. He was convinced that only by learning English and mastering the lessons taught at government schools would Lemhi boys and girls be able to make their way in this rapidly changing world. There had never been any question that his children would go to school, and soon enough, he hoped, to a better school than this one.[3]

For now, though, his girls were numbered among the mere handful of children—no more than thirty-four this year—who attended the Lemhi Agency School. While Monk seemed focused on eliminating the influence of the "blanket Indians" who wandered the school grounds at will, Burton wished the man would show more concern about what went on *inside* the building, including hiring competent teachers and providing adequate textbooks.[4]

As the agent droned on, Burton focused on the days that lay ahead. With school ending, he would be bringing his girls back into the house where their mother had so recently died in childbirth and where their five-year-old brother was still asking when she and the baby would be coming home. He could count on fourteen-year-old Rosie to assume many of the household duties, including the care of little Willard. And he knew that Minnie would want to do her part. Yet, as had been the case almost all of her young life, she was far more likely to seek out the company of her grandmother Pea-boa. She was, after all, a "grandmother's grandchild," an honored position for any little girl, but one with special meaning for a child who treasured the stories of her grandmother's feats on the double ball field and was determined that she too would be the best there was at the game.[5]

He was right about that. On the very first day of summer vacation, Pea-boa took Minnie down to the banks of the Lemhi River, and together the two of them chose a forked willow stick just the right size for an eight-year-old.

~

Superintendent Winslow would not be going to Chicago this summer after all. The folder of clippings and railroad schedules that had sat on the edge of his desk for months might as well be filed away for good. The 1893 World's Columbian Exposition would have to go on without him. Not that his presence would be missed, except, perhaps, by some of his teaching colleagues of years gone by. Several had written, urging him to arrange his trip to the fair to coincide with theirs, and he had even penciled in possible departure dates on his calendar. He had accumulated more than enough vacation days to allow for a leisurely exploration of the fair's White City, and he had already drafted a letter to officials in D.C. requesting travel funds.[6]

There was ample justification for government support of a sojourn that would be as educational as it was enjoyable. Indeed, failing to take advantage of such an opportunity could even be viewed as a dereliction of duty, especially given this exposition's ethnological displays, including an exhibit of items from Carlisle Indian School. Indeed, Colonel Pratt himself would be there with a delegation of his students, including Carlisle's famed marching band.[7]

While Pratt's years of dedicated service to the school he had established had earned him the right to travel the world if he so wished, Winslow's need to nurture his own little school left him no such choice. There would be other world's fairs. There might even be a time when Fort Shaw students would be part of an international exposition. Such things were not beyond the realm of possibility, but getting his school to that level would require diligence, hard work—and sacrifice. He would not be going to Chicago because he was duty-bound to stay where he was for the summer.

Duty-bound, but not homebound. There would still be travel. Just not beyond the borders of Montana.

Future Prospects
1893–1894

THE END OF FORT SHAW'S FIRST FULL SEMESTER DID NOT MEAN students would be going home for summer break. In keeping with BIA guidelines, Dr. Winslow believed that children who were allowed to spend that much time with their families would likely lose their command of the English language—along with their fragile grasp of the manners and mores of civilized society. And there was always the distinct possibility that children who were allowed to go home on vacation might not return in the fall.[1]

Unlike many of their classmates who longed to be at home with their families, the Wirth sisters were somewhat relieved not to be returning to Fort Peck that summer of 1893. The few letters they had received from their father had made it clear that there was more tension in the household than ever. Under ordinary circumstances, his decision to send them to Fort Shaw would no longer be their mother's primary focus, he said. But circumstances at home were far from ordinary. In the months since their departure for school, Tina Archdale, the half sister they had never heard of, much less seen, had returned to the reservation angry, resentful, and full of stories of the cruelty and humiliation she had endured at the hands of the white couple who, years before, had taken her to California, promising to raise her as a daughter. Whites were not to be trusted, Tina ranted, including the two her mother had married. Henry Archdale had abandoned her, and Jacob Wirth had let their daughters be sent three hundred miles from home.[2]

Little Nettie could hardly believe that their home had changed that much in her absence. If only she had refused to get on that train. Lizzie tried to explain to her that their parents' relationship was not something they could "fix" by going home for the summer. Their return might even make things worse. As if they even had any choice in the matter. That decision was out of their hands, as was the situation back home on the reservation. It was time to start thinking instead about what a summer at Fort Shaw might be like. Lizzie was sure that the vacation schedule would be different enough from the school schedule to keep their thoughts from wandering toward home too often.

And she was right.

The summer sun rose early and set late in Montana's Sun River Valley. Those long daylight hours kept the boys outside tending the livestock and working the garden. And although the girls were confined to kitchen, laundry, and sewing room for much of the day, at least their drills with dumbbells and Indian clubs were moved outdoors. With academic work suspended, the daily regimen was a lot more relaxed. Midday picnics often broke up the work routine. Hikes led by teachers and staffers were a favorite activity, especially the climb up Square Butte, whose steep walls Josie Langley had scaled as a child and from whose flat summit she had looked down on the soldiers drilling on the parade ground. There were campouts along the upper reaches of the Sun River, and even a wagon journey up north into the Sweetgrass Hills. While such outings did not completely erase the tug of home and family, activities during the summer months at Fort Shaw were sufficiently different from those of the school year to constitute a much-needed break for students as well as faculty and staff.[3]

But not for Superintendent Winslow. Recruitment, that Sisyphean task, would be his focus through the summer months.

∽

William Winslow reached for his spectacles, straining to read the small print on the map spread out on his desk. Here was Fort Shaw. The tip of his forefinger anchored him there for a moment, then carried him north along the by-now familiar road to the southern edge of the Blackfeet Reservation. He needed to pay another visit to the widow Johnson. But that could wait until summer's end. He traced his way back down to Fort Shaw, then lifted his finger and set down a penny to hold his place as he leaned back to take in the whole of Montana. The six reservations, though faintly marked, were evident enough, as was the fact that the government had achieved its goal of locating them sufficiently far apart to make it difficult, if not impossible, for any of the tribes to join forces again as the Sioux and Cheyennes had at the Little Bighorn. And they were sufficiently far apart to make it difficult, if not impossible, for any one man to visit all of those reservations in the course of a single summer.[4]

The penny atop Fort Shaw seemed so small and insignificant compared with the miles and miles of sparsely inhabited land that must be traversed over the course of the next two months. Winslow lifted the map abruptly, letting the penny slide to the floor. For a man who had wanted to ride the rails all the way to Chicago, he was uncharacteristically reluctant to hitch up his buggy and head for the depot in Great Falls. He was also reluctant to travel the back roads of the Fort Belknap Reservation—alone—on the unlikely chance that somewhere within one of those isolated Gros Ventre camps he would find parents willing to send their children to Fort Shaw.

The recently established agency school at Fort Belknap had not yet met its own enrollment quota and could therefore hardly afford to send any of its students to Fort Shaw. From his correspondence with the Ursuline sisters at St. Paul's Mission on the southwestern edge of the reservation, he judged them to be equally reluctant to give up any of their pupils. His strategy would be to seek out influential white fathers who believed in the importance of a good education for their mixed-blood children and persuade them of the benefits offered at Fort Shaw. They, in turn, might then persuade others to send their youngsters to the school in the Sun River Valley. That may not happen overnight, but Winslow had been in this business long enough to know that persistence and patience were a recruiter's greatest assets.[5]

The agent met Dr. Winslow's midmorning train at the station at Harlem and transported him directly to the Fort Belknap Agency School on the reservation's northern edge. There Winslow made the most of his limited time, conversing with the matron and two of the teachers, then wandering off by himself to chat with some little boys who were weeding the garden and with a group of older girls at work in the laundry room. Just before noon he addressed a small gathering of parents who were clearly there at the agent's behest. All to no apparent avail.

Over dinner the agent proffered the names of two former military scouts who were raising Indian families on the southern end of the reservation. Although both men had several children, neither had, as yet, sent any of them to school, a puzzling situation, since both men seemed progressive enough in other matters. James Snell, who had given up scouting and freighting for farming, had four school-aged youngsters, but he seemed unlikely to let go of them, given his Assiniboine wife's firm belief that children belonged at home with their parents. In the agent's opinion, Fannie Black Digger was not an unreasonable woman, but she could be stubborn, especially where family matters were concerned.[6]

Colonel William Healy, a rancher who ran a trading post down on Lodge Pole Creek, had a half-dozen Gros Ventre children who were, or soon would be, ready for school. In this case, the agent predicted, their mother's opinion was not likely to count for much. Although he had been to the trading post on more than one occasion, he had never laid eyes on the woman. She kept to her bed, he was told, too weak and sickly and worn out to do much of anything else. Except have more babies, so the joke went. Too many children in too short a time, some said. Every one of them a blessing, according to Father Eberschweiler. Most likely those little blessings would all be sent to the sisters at St. Paul's, the agent said, considering that Healy, German and Catholic to the core, had donated the land on which the mission was built.[7]

Seeing James Snell as the more promising prospect, Winslow inquired as to the best way to get to the Snell family farm. The *only* way, the agent responded, was to take the train over to Dodson, then go down from there by way of a fairly well-traveled road that paralleled the reservation's eastern border. That meant catching the last eastbound train that evening, reserving a horse and buggy at the livery stable, then getting as much sleep as he could. Tomorrow would be a long day.

The next morning, just as the sun was streaking the sky, William Winslow climbed into the buggy, glanced behind him to be sure his valise, his packet of food, a flask of water, and a bag of oats for his horse were well secured, then started out on the long, dusty ride south. Although his directions were good and his progress steady, it was mid-afternoon before he came upon fields of beans and potatoes, carrots and cabbage, corn and cucumbers—vegetables similar in kind, if larger in size, to the ones being grown by the boys back at Fort Shaw.

The tall, sturdy man who stepped out from the farmhouse beyond the fields was ready enough to hear compliments on his crops, which, he told the superintendent, were finding a ready market among the miners down at Zortman, a boomtown just beyond the reservation's southern border. Not that this was all his doing, he said. Much of the credit for his success went to his wife, for it was her land that he tilled and her work in the fields, as well as in the house, that had enabled him to expand their operation. Having come so far, Dr. Winslow must surely come in for supper and stay the night with them. What better way could there be for sampling the bounty of those productive rows?[8]

Inside the house, Winslow found everyone busily engaged in chores. Nine-year-old Jennie was cutting up venison for stew. Six-year-old Catherine—Katie—appeared at the top of the stairs to the root cellar, cradling onions in her apron. While those two girls worked alongside their mother in the kitchen, five-year-old Mabel kept little Daisy out of mischief, and without waiting to be asked, eight-year-old Richard brought in more wood and stoked up the fire in the cookstove before joining the menfolk at the kitchen table.[9]

By Winslow's standards, the Snell family was enjoying a good life, one forged from two cultures and showing steady progress away from the primitive habits of the one and toward the more civilized ways of the other. The children moved from conversing with their mother in Nakoda to answering their father's questions and his own in fairly fluent English. These youngsters were obviously ideal candidates for enrollment at Fort Shaw. Their work ethic was exemplary, and here again, much of the credit must surely go to their mother, Fannie Black Digger Snell. She had spoken nothing in English beyond her initial greeting and had sat through the meal in silence, but Winslow had the feeling she had missed very little of what had been said.

When the table was cleared and mother and daughters were washing up the dishes, Superintendent Winslow eased into the topic he'd come so far to discuss. Snell's response was cordial, but firm. He was well aware that his children must have a good education. In fact, if there were a day school nearby, they would likely be students there. But sending them off to boarding school, even the agency boarding school, could well do more harm than good. For now his son and daughters were learning all they needed to learn. English, of course. And a bit of arithmetic. Plus raising crops, milking cows, tending chickens, and keeping house. Schooling had its place, of course, but children belonged at home with their families. It was almost as if the silent woman at the dishpan were speaking her piece through his voice.

The next morning, after thanking Mrs. Snell for her hospitality and the fine meals he had enjoyed at her table and the lunch she had packed for him, Winslow said his goodbyes all around. His buggy was wait-ing, the reins held by young Richard, who had obviously groomed, fed, and watered the horse that would carry the superintendent on the next leg of his journey. Embarrassed a bit by Dr. Winslow's profuse thanks for his efforts, the boy nodded and disappeared into the house, leaving his father the opportunity for a final word with the superintendent. As much as he hated the idea of sending his children away from home, Snell said, he couldn't help being impressed by what Winslow had had to say about Fort Shaw. Yet he remained cautious. Perhaps he would enroll the four oldest at the agency school this coming fall. But sending them as far away as Fort Shaw was out of the question. Maybe someday. But not now.[10]

Not now. Still, the seed had been planted, and as Winslow climbed into his buggy, he knew it was only a matter of time before James Snell would be enrolling his children at Fort Shaw—and influencing other families to do the same.

Colonel Healy provided a challenge of a different sort. Dr. Winslow's timing was less than ideal. As he had learned from his host of the pre-vious evening, the children he had hoped to enroll had just lost their mother. Honkow, or White Eagle, had died shortly after the birth of a baby girl. In a sense, according to James Snell, these Healy children had been motherless for quite some time. With the steady decline of Honkow's health, the childcare, cooking, and housekeeping duties had fallen to an easygoing young Frenchman called Ponley.[11]

Neither their caretaker nor the children were in sight when Colonel Healy met Dr. Winslow at the gate to the ranch and ushered him into the house. Anticipating the superintendent's reasons for such a long journey, the colonel got in the first word. "As to the education of my children, . . . " he began. As if on cue, John, Harry, Nettie, Genevieve, and William, ages nine to two, burst through the door and raced around and around the table, a virtual whirlwind of flying arms and legs. Their shouts and screams woke baby Maude, who added her howls and shrieks to those of her siblings. Unaccustomed as he was to such pandemonium, Winslow looked toward their father, anticipating a sharp command that would end the deafening uproar. None was forthcoming, either from the colonel or from Ponley, who had followed the children into the house and was now leaning against the door jamb, paring his nails.[12]

Raising his voice so as to be heard above his boisterous brood, Colonel Healy returned to the subject at hand. He had supported the school at St. Paul's Mission from its beginnings. From all reports the Ursuline sisters had things in good order. Maybe he would send some of his children there in the fall. Maybe not. There was no rush to send them anywhere. Observing the children's roughhousing and their incessant chatter in a mixture of Ponley's French and their mother's Gros Ventre, Dr. Winslow thought otherwise, but held his peace.[13]

The noise ended almost as abruptly as it had begun as Ponley lifted the crying baby from her cradle and herded his little mustangs back into the yard. Winslow could have spoken, now that the room was quiet again, yet the colonel was reaching for his cane. The conversation, such as it was, was obviously coming to a close. As Healy ushered him out the door and back to the gate, he assured his guest that the good sisters at St. Paul's would be waiting for him. Though their fare was simple, their hearts were kind, and his bed would be clean and comfortable. He could tell them all about his new school. Perhaps they could even spare a pupil or two.

Then, lest there be any doubt as to his own position, William Healy declared he had no intention of sending any of his children all the way to the Sun River Valley for their schooling. Although he could understand Dr. Winslow's need to fill his quota, his children were not pawns to be moved around at the whim of nuns and agents. Or superintendents. Still, he would think the matter over. Talk to a few other parents. Maybe in time there would be Gros Ventre students at Fort Shaw.

Maybe. Maybe not. Such were the ups and downs of recruiting. Patience would pay off in the end. Even such a crusty old fellow as Healy would see, in time, the need for some sort of education for his lively offspring. And given his obvious sense of himself, he would also see the prestige to be gained by sending his children to one of the nation's best off-reservation schools.[14]

~

By the time Fort Shaw classes resumed in September, Dr. Winslow had reason to think his school was moving ever closer to his vision for it. He now had in place a music department, a necessity at any top-notch institution in the Indian Service. Eugene Parker, an accomplished musician from South Dakota, was putting together an orchestra and a brass band for the school that, before long, would be known as one of the best in the state of Montana. And another new faculty member, Sarah Patterson, was introducing the girls to the violin, cello, guitar, and mandolin. Music lessons had become a central part of life at Fort Shaw, and the school's first Christmas pageant, held on December 23, 1893, featured numbers by the new Fort Shaw orchestra.[15]

No one enjoyed that program more than two of the valley's most prominent women. Both had belonged to the little orchestra General Gibbon's wife had put together, the one playing the cello, the other the flute. In Christmas programs of years past, their sons had always been Joseph, the wise men, or the shepherds, and their daughters Mary or the angels. Now the tinsel halos and gossamer wings on the little Indian cherubs were all but identical to the ones the cellist had once designed for the valley's youngest performers. Angels are angels, she whispered to her companion. And Christmas is always Christmas.

Their report of that evening's performance led other Sun River townspeople to join them for Fort Shaw's patriotic pageant on Washington's Birthday. Each event seemed more impressive than the last, and the valley's citizens began bringing their children to these programs, hoping they would be inspired to take their own music lessons more seriously. At the closing exercises of June 1894, Indian assistants, including Josie Langley, escorted visitors on tours of the campus facilities. Students were posted in workrooms and shops to explain their projects—and, not coincidentally, their command of English. After sharing a meal in the dining hall with the visitors—who were noticeably impressed by the impeccable table manners of the young Indians—the students launched into an evening program that opened and closed with performances by Mr. Parker's band.[16]

Those closing exercises were prelude to an even more impressive program given in early August when the school hosted a regional gathering of Indian educators, a week-long institute the local *Rising Sun* billed as "the most interesting event that has ever transpired in the Sun River Valley." Indeed, the meeting drew some prominent national figures, most notably William Hailmann, the newly installed superintendent of Indian schools, and Carlisle's own Richard Henry Pratt. Hailmann came in order to acquaint himself with this school in the West that was drawing so much attention. Pratt came on a recruiting mission. He hoped to find prospects for Carlisle among the older Fort Shaw students, and he was looking forward to meeting with George Monk, agent for the Lemhi Reservation.[17]

After years of fruitless attempts to lure Lemhi children to Carlisle, Pratt had received word that the Lemhi interpreter, William Burton, who had recently lost his wife, was thinking of sending his two daughters, fifteen-year-old Rosie and nine-year-old Minnie, to Carlisle. Agent Monk had spoken so highly of Rosie and Minnie Burton that Pratt was eager to bring the girls east, and he intended to "settle all the details" at this summer conference. On that count Pratt was destined to be disappointed, although at the time his train pulled into the depot at Great Falls and was met by the buggy that would deliver him to Fort Shaw, he had no way of knowing that Agent Monk had decided not to attend the institute after all.[18]

Even so, Pratt's trip to Montana would ultimately prove fruitful.

When the buggy pulled up to the entrance to Fort Shaw School that August morning, Josephine Langley was excited to be among the Indian assistants detailed to welcome the legendary figure. She knew the colonel would never remember her earlier application or the circumstances under which it had been rejected. But now she had the chance, in person, to impress him with her restored health. Before the week was out, Colonel Pratt had invited Josephine Langley to return with him to Carlisle. Ready as she was to accept that invitation on the spot, Josie asked to have her entry deferred until January in order keep her commitment to Dr. Winslow for the fall semester.[19]

Among the other students who caught Pratt's eye was Lizzie Wirth, but before Lizzie even had time to write home about Colonel Pratt's invitation, she received news that trivialized her own. In a scene evidently witnessed by many on the reservation, her mother, Woman That Kills Wood, had humiliated her father, raging at him in Assiniboine, chasing him with a knife, and going off with a man named Grasshopper. The news, with all its embellishments, soon enough reached the ears of the other Assiniboine students at Fort Shaw and swirled around the Wirth sisters. With the home situation so unsettled, Lizzie was loath to leave her younger sisters. She was barely fourteen. She would get to Carlisle one of these days. All in good time.[20]

For now there was plenty to look forward to right there at Fort Shaw, and she could hardly wait for September and the start of the new school year.

"Basket Ball for Women"
1894

SEPTEMBER 1894. SMITH COLLEGE, NORTHHAMPTON, MASSACHUSETTS. Senda Berenson dismissed her sophomores, closed the gymnasium doors, and headed for the administration building, hoping against hope that this month's issue of *Physical Education* would be waiting for her. But once again she returned to her office disappointed and empty-handed. Dropping into her chair, she stared at the manuscript on the corner of her desk, resisting the temptation to read it one last time. After all, it was too late to make any further changes. And too late for any misgivings about sharing her beliefs concerning the future of women's basketball with other physical education instructors across the country.[1]

Her rationale for adapting the game in ways that eliminated all roughness and rudeness, while emphasizing teamwork and athleticism, seemed solid enough. Yet there were sure to be fierce rebuttals from those who rejected out of hand any attempt to alter the one sport that allowed, even encouraged, women and girls to break free of Victorian restraints—at least those imposed on women of all but the working class. To Berenson's way of thinking, this was no time to be unreasonable. To refuse to adapt the game would be to risk having it banned altogether. As for being afraid to set forth one's ideas before they were perfectly formed, what if James Naismith had felt he wasn't ready to take a chance with his rudimentary rules for the game?

She had read and reread that brief article Naismith had published in the *Triangle*, and with each reading she had become more and more convinced that this new sport was exactly what she needed to engage the young women who passed through her physical education classes at Smith College, the very women most restrained by Victorian "ideals." She was constantly working against their abysmal ignorance of the value—and the fun—of exercise. One could hardly blame the girls themselves, given societal views on the delicate nature of the female sex—and given the lack of any team sports for women. Her students had simply never had a chance to know the exhilaration that comes from an athletic contest pitting team against team, nor had she, for that matter.[2]

Then, early in that fall semester of 1892, Berenson had made her move. Two peach baskets were hung at a height of ten feet at each end of the college gymnasium, just as Naismith had instructed. A soccer ball was secured. The women of Smith were about to learn the game of basketball, and the game itself was about to change the world of women's athletics. Although there was as yet no way Senda Berenson could have realized the full impact of her actions, she soon had plenty of proof that basketball would alter forever her girls' perceptions of appropriate physical exercise for women as well as their perceptions of themselves.[3]

She had begun by introducing the game to her freshmen, expecting only a few of them to take to the sport. To her surprise, their enthusiasm was so great her sophomores demanded a chance to play. In spring of 1893, when one class challenged the other to a match and asked that their friends be allowed to come to the game, she had agreed, assuming only a few students would drop by to watch the action. And action there was aplenty. She remembered that first game in great detail, and she would ultimately commit her memories to print.[4]

Contrary to her expectations, "the whole college with class colors and banners turned out." The balcony filled up first, with the earliest arrivals "sitting on the edge dangling their legs." Latecomers ended up standing against the walls. Excitement had reached fever pitch by the time she tossed up the ball to begin the game. Thereafter the gym reverberated with the deafening screams and cheers of the onlookers—all of them female, for on that day, and for some years to come, no men were allowed into the gym to witness women in bloomers and stockings go tumbling head over heels after a loose ball.[5]

Excluded or not, the men of Northampton did not have to wait long to find out what had gone on behind closed doors. The next day's paper reported the news: "Gladiators," it called the players in its description of the wild and wooly action. As Berenson read the article, she feared that "the staid citizens of the Valley [would] wonder whether Sophia Smith had been wise to found a college in which young women might receive an education equal to that accorded to young men!"[6]

Over the course of the next two years, that bothersome question had been raised so often, in one guise or another, that it could no longer be ignored. Yes, women should be allowed to play basketball, for—as Berenson's forthcoming article for *Physical Education* made amply clear— this "splendid game" had done more than any other to "develop the athletic spirit in women." Yet encouraging women and girls to play a game that fostered "physical courage, self-reliance, quickness, alertness . . . and enthusiasm" did not mean requiring them to play by rules written for men and boys. Equality did not mandate imitation. If the only way to keep women's basketball from being banned altogether was to "change a few rules and make a few others," she, for one, stood ready to make those changes.[7]

As Berenson was to learn, being willing to make changes and being successful in implementing them were hardly one and the same thing. The young women at Smith and most of the other elite colleges in the Northeast adapted well to the changes Berenson set forth—six to a team, with the players assigned to specific sectors of the court. But her "girls' rules," and similar, even more restrictive adaptations soon to be introduced by others, would so drastically slow the game and alter the dynamics of the sport that many high school and college teams— especially those west of the Mississippi—would ignore them and opt to play by "boys' rules."[8]

Including the girls' team from Fort Shaw Indian Boarding School.

Elusive Dreams
1895–1896

❦

JANUARY 1895. THE TWO-HOUR WAIT AT THE GREAT FALLS DEPOT gave Josie Langley time to reflect on what was, and on what would be. Behind her were her family and friends on the reservation and at school. Ahead of her was the great adventure of Carlisle. The Indian assistants back at Fort Shaw who had been to Carlisle had inspired her with their memories of the school and with their assurances that by getting her training there she would be qualified to teach at any Indian school in the country. Over her Christmas vacation at home on Birch Creek, her mother and sister had supported her aspirations, confident that she would return to Montana better prepared to help her people.

Knowing that it might be years before she would see her mother and Annie again, Josie had given every minute of that vacation to them, except for the afternoon she'd spent with Jenny Johnson. The two had first met the summer Josie returned from her studies at St. Peter's and heard the tragic story of the young Blackfoot woman whose husband, a rancher in Kibby Canyon, had been killed in a logging accident. Waiting only long enough to take care of matters at the ranch—and to give birth to her sixth child—the twenty-eight-year-old widow moved herself, her newborn daughter, and her five other children into her mother's lodge on the reservation.[1]

Intrigued by the story, Josie had ridden over to Blacktail Creek that summer to meet this intrepid woman, Nearly Died. Within an hour or so she had come to understand the widow's rumored lack of interest in finding another man to look after her. Charles Johnson was clearly still at the center of her life. He had been a tall and handsome man, Nearly Died told her, fair-haired and blue-eyed like his German ancestors. As if words weren't enough, she pointed to a photograph taken before Charlie had left his parents' home in upstate New York, and then she began to tell their story.[2]

She had been sixteen in 1878, and Charles Johnson nearing thirty, when he showed up in Fort Benton and dropped by the Piegan encampment. By the time her family broke camp and moved back to their winter quarters on the reservation, Nearly Died had become Jenny Johnson. Soon the couple was living on a ranch in Kibby Canyon, some twenty miles south of Fort Benton, and the children came in quick succession—Mary in 1880, Charles in 1881, William in 1884, Belle in 1886, and James in 1887. With so many children to care for, Nearly Died longed for the company of her family, and her husband had honored her wishes. Leaving her pregnant with their sixth child, he set out for the settlement of Heart Butte on the southern edge of the Blackfeet Reservation, where he began cutting logs and building a home on Blacktail Creek, near his wife's family. The house was only a few courses up when Charles Johnson was crushed to death by rolling logs.[3]

Now, on a cold day in late December 1894, Josie and Jenny were once again enjoying each other's company. It had been almost two years to the day since their first meeting, for Josie had not been home since she began her work at Fort Shaw. This late December visit had been prompted by more than her desire to spend an afternoon with a woman she admired. Dr. Winslow had asked her to drop in on Widow Johnson and encourage her to allow her older children to transfer to Fort Shaw. Josie's visit was timely. Fifteen-year-old Mary was begging to follow in Josie's footsteps, and even fourteen-year-old Charlie, who had always said he would never go that far from his mother, was beginning to long for something better than what the agency school had offered so far.[4]

Realizing she would not be able to put them off much longer, Jenny Johnson was glad to be able to ask Josie Langley questions she would never dare ask Dr. Winslow: Were the teachers kind and understanding? Or were the horror stories told by the runaways true?[5] Were the dormitories warm? Was the food good—and plentiful? Won over by Josie's reassurances and enthusiasm, Nearly Died made up her mind. Her children would finish out the school year at Willow Creek, but in the fall she would allow Mary and Charlie to go to Fort Shaw. Over William's objections, she would send him too. And by the time Josie had completed her studies at Carlisle and returned to work at Fort Shaw, perhaps the three youngest Johnsons—Belle, James, and Ida—would be there to welcome her.

The decision had not been an easy one, for Nearly Died's children had been the focus of her life in the years since her husband's death. But she had vowed to raise them in a way that honored his memory, and that meant providing them with the education he had always said they would need in order to move with ease between his world and hers. If, as Josie assured her, Fort Shaw would provide that kind of education, then Nearly Died was prepared to let them go.

~

The shrill whistle announcing the arrival of the train brought Josie back to this raw January afternoon. Once she boarded that train, she knew there was no looking back. Yet come what may, this was the dream that had tantalized her for years.

As the long miles rolled past, Josie watched the ever-varying scenes out the window, dozed in her seat, snacked on box lunches bought at whistle stops, and constantly checked the transfer instructions sent along with the tickets by Colonel Pratt. Once the train crossed into Pennsylvania, she never closed her eyes, afraid she might miss her station. Finally, the conductor called out the words she'd been waiting for: "Carlisle Junction."[6]

~

The campus was beautiful. More beautiful even than Fort Shaw. Past the iron gates lay the perfectly landscaped quadrangle, new dormitories, a new gymnasium. The scene caught Josie by surprise. It was what she had imagined—but somehow even more. For one thing, as she soon discovered, there were four hundred students at Carlisle, twice as many as at Fort Shaw. And the new dormitory featured amenities beyond anything she had envisioned—electric lights rather than kerosene lamps lit the apartment she was to share with three other young women, and central steam heat, not a woodstove, warmed the building against the winter chill.[7]

In some ways, though, day-to-day life at Carlisle turned out to be hardly different from what she had known back home, first at St. Peter's and then at Fort Shaw. The daily regimen was almost identical to campus routine in the Sun River Valley, although the academics were more challenging. And there were many more activities and programs, including physical culture classes in a well-equipped gymnasium. Fort Shaw had offered only calisthenics, club swinging, wand drills, and barbells for girls and track and field events for boys. Here at Carlisle there was a major emphasis on team sports, competitive team sports. Especially, but not limited to, football.[8]

It was not football that interested Josephine Langley, however. She was drawn to a new game being played by her female classmates, one that reminded her of her grandmother's descriptions of the game of double ball. Like double ball, this new game, "basket ball," required teams of girls to protect their own goal while trying to get the ball to the opponents' goal. But instead of many girls using forked sticks to fling the double ball to teammates down the field, this game was limited to ten girls, five on each side, and the players passed a round leather ball from one teammate to another in hopes of getting close enough to the opponent's basket to score a "field throw."[9]

It took some time to get used to the pace of this game, which seemed to Josie to be played at breakneck speed. There were two twenty-minute "halves," and those halves flew by, for the clock never stopped. Not while the referee was releasing the ball from the net after every successful field throw and bringing it back to center court for a jump ball, not when the referee called a foul and awarded a "free throw," not when an errant ball went out of bounds and had to be retrieved, not when an injured player was being helped from the floor. The running clock kept the scores low, but the action was fast-paced and spirits were high.[10]

Josie was enthralled by this new game, and she was good at it. At nineteen, she was a few years older than many of the girls with whom she played, and the leadership skills she had developed over the years served her well. She saw the need for strategy and teamwork as well as speed and stamina, and her team usually won its games. Although the competition at Carlisle was limited to games against teams made up of her classmates, she knew that other schools in the East—and even a few out on the West Coast—were playing basketball against one another. These games were reportedly played behind closed doors, with no men or boys allowed. If there were those who felt the game was too rough and unladylike for young women—and Josie knew there were people who thought that—she was not among them. For her, running up and down the floor of the gym, stretching and twisting and turning, bouncing and passing and shooting a ball, were more invigorating than any other physical culture activities in which she had ever engaged. She was determined to take this game home to Fort Shaw.[11]

~

While Josie was honing her skills back east, life at the school in the Sun River Valley went on much as it had before her departure—with one exception: A sports program was developing at Fort Shaw. It came in the person of Louis Goings, a Shoshone raised in Wyoming and educated at the Indian school in Pierre, South Dakota. Only eighteen at the time of his arrival on campus shortly after Josie's departure for Carlisle, Goings had come to Fort Shaw as a faculty member, charged with teaching the cobbler's trade. But he brought more than shoemaking to the campus that spring of 1895. Back in South Dakota, baseball had become his passion, and his interest in organizing a Fort Shaw team prompted Winslow to think of building an athletic program modeled after the one at Carlisle.[12]

Gloves, balls, bats, and bases were ordered. The girls in sewing class provided blue serge uniforms for the team's first game. On June 22, for a game against the men's team from nearby Choteau, students and staff lined the newly laid-out diamond. Lizzie Wirth and the other girls who had created the handsome uniforms worn by the equally handsome boys led their classmates in cheering for the Indians. Although the school lost by a score of 14 to 10, it seemed that testing the talents of Fort Shaw players against those of other teams was an idea whose time had come.[13]

~

Dr. Winslow was looking forward to fall semester, convinced that the 1895–96 school year would be the one in which he finally achieved his enrollment goal of 250 students. Among the incoming pupils would be a sizeable contingent from the Willow Creek school on the Blackfeet Reservation, and Jenny Johnson's three oldest children—Mary, Charles, and William—were a part of that group. From the Fort Belknap Reservation he was expecting three of James Snell's children—Jennie, Richard, and Katie—all of whom had been eager to go to Fort Shaw ever since his recruiting visit two summers before. According to their father, a couple of intervening and unhappy terms at the agency school had made them all the more excited about the transfer.[14]

Yet nine-year-old Katie, initially the most enthusiastic of all the Snell children, had, at the very last minute, begged to stay on at the Fort Belknap Agency School rather than leave her younger sister Mabel there alone. Just over a year apart in age, the two had shared a bed in the cold and drafty girls' dorm, and Katie had always looked out for her little sister, a "frail" child by all reports. At first Katie had tried to persuade her parents to let Mabel go with her to Fort Shaw, insisting she could take care of her there just as well as she had at the agency school. But Fannie Black Digger had stood firm. Mabel needed to stay closer to home, so they could bring her back to the farmhouse if she got sick again this year. Still not convinced she was doing the right thing, Katie reluctantly joined Jennie and Richard on the journey to Fort Shaw.[15]

All through that journey, Katie made mental notes of everything she thought would be of interest to Mabel—meeting Mr. Parker at the siding at Harlem, just north of Belknap Agency, the train ride to Great Falls, the wagon ride to Fort Shaw. Mostly Katie wanted to tell Mabel how *long* it seemed to take to get from home to school. And then, once at school, how she had been taken to the little girls' dorm to be scrubbed down and fitted into a new uniform before being escorted into the dining hall and assigned her place at table. The next morning brought the introduction to classroom work, and in the afternoon, the sewing room. Katie's eyes went at once to Nettie Wirth, who had been so kind to her at supper and in the dorm. Her new friend was sitting at a sewing machine, hemming a tablecloth. As her feet worked away at the treadle, she looked up and gave Katie a welcoming smile.

That very evening Katie wrote Mabel of the long train ride and of all the things she could look forward to at Fort Shaw. She wrote her parents too, eager to share her new world with them. All students were required to write home, in English, at regular intervals, but Katie would have written anyway. She knew her father would read every single word aloud to her mother. She couldn't help but wonder about other students who might have to depend on the agent to translate their letters to their parents. How would they know whether what they had written was what their parents actually heard?[16]

Katie posted her letters in the very next mail, counting up the days it would take for Mabel's to get to the agency school at Fort Belknap and then how long it might take for Mabel's answer to reach Fort Shaw. But one week and then another passed without a reply. Then at long last, Jennie's, Richard's, and Katie's names were called as the mail was being handed out in the dining hall. Katie hurried forward, certain she must have a letter from Mabel. But it was her father's handwriting on the envelope, and the letter was addressed to all of them.

The message inside was short and to the point: At ten to ten in the morning on Friday, November 8, Mabel Snell had died in her dormitory bed. A sudden "sinking chill" had carried her off. The news had been telegraphed to Colonel Healy's trading post that very day, then carried across the valley by one of the colonel's ranch hands. James Snell had hitched up the horses at once and headed north. Neither he nor his wife had been informed that Mabel was sick, although the agent insisted he would have sent word had he realized how ill she was. Those apologies were little comfort to the grieving parents who laid the little girl's body on a bed of hay in the wagon, covered it with a blanket, then turned south toward Lodge Pole Creek. Home at last, eight-year-old Mabel Snell was laid to rest the following afternoon.[17]

With Josie Langley away at Carlisle, the task of comforting Katie fell to Miss Roberts. She should not blame herself for what happened, the matron told her. Mabel had died so suddenly there was nothing she or anyone else could have done to save her. Katie found little solace in the words. At least Mabel would have died in her arms instead of alone in a cold bed with no one she loved beside her.

⌒

Another letter from another father reached Fort Shaw not long after the one carrying news of Mabel Snell's death. Correspondence from Jacob Wirth had been scarce since late January when he had written to tell his girls of his marriage to Lydia Kennedy, a Santee Sioux. His daughters had been more relieved than surprised by the news, for they had fretted over their father's welfare ever since their mother had deserted him for another man.[18]

The news in this current letter was good. Jacob Wirth was now the baker at the reopened agency school on Poplar Creek, and he and his new wife were living in a large house in the circle of government and Indian homes there in Poplar. Prospects were looking up at the school; the new superintendent who had arrived that very month—a tall, red-headed Scotsman named Fred Campbell—seemed just the man to put the place in order. But no matter how this Campbell might improve the agency school, Jacob Wirth remained convinced that Fort Shaw was the place for his girls. There was no point in their coming back to the reservation to stay until they finished their schooling, although he couldn't help wishing they would soon make it home for a visit, so they could meet his new wife and see his fine house.[19]

⌒

Josephine Langley was on the train home from Carlisle that December of 1895, some nine months earlier than she had planned. Her old nemesis, trachoma, had flared up, diminishing her vision and making her a likely carrier of the disease. In accordance with Colonel Pratt's strict health policies, she had been sent back to her reservation. Once she was under her mother's care and free of the relative stress of life at Carlisle, the infection subsided and her vision began to improve—as it always had after these episodes in the past. By early January Josie was sufficiently recovered to resume her post as Indian assistant at Fort Shaw.[20]

Dr. Winslow greeted her with warmth. And with a challenge. While the boys' physical culture program was flourishing under the direction of Louis Goings—as evidenced by the new baseball team—the girls' program was all but nonexistent. Her excitement about the athletic training at Carlisle had been evident in her letters. Might she be interested in taking over the girls' physical culture program here at Fort Shaw? Her enthusiasm and leadership, coupled with her newly acquired knowledge of gymnastics and of this new game of basketball, made her the perfect candidate for the post of instructor of physical culture classes for girls.[21]

Josie could not have been more pleased. She had joined the staff at Fort Shaw as an Indian assistant, with the dream of working her way up to a teaching position, and this new assignment was a big step toward fulfilling that dream. She must, of course, prove herself by tending to the basics of physical culture first. But once she got that program up and running, she would add basketball to the curriculum. She would have to explain the game as she had learned to play it. She might be hampered by lack of nets and a proper ball, but she had her court—the gymnasium that had served as theatre and dance hall for the old military post. Its dirt floor, hard-packed by legions of heavy-booted soldiers, was an ideal surface for bouncing a ball. And there was plenty of room for full-court play up and down its 125-foot length. True, the space was not without drawbacks. The ceiling was definitely too low to allow for much of an arc on the shot that would send the ball through the iron-ringed net. But the sky would be their only limit once she had moved the girls onto the outside court she intended to mark off just beyond the parade ground as soon as snow gave way to grass.[22]

By late spring, Josie had begun teaching the basics of basketball to those who showed the most interest and enthusiasm, among them the Wirth sisters and Nettie's new friend and dormmate, Katie Snell. She first drilled them in making crisp passes to one another. Then she divided them into teams and set them to deflecting or intercepting the passes of their opponents. She taught them the advantages of bouncing—or "dribbling"—the ball anytime they were too closely guarded to get off a shot or pass to a teammate. She made do with a soccer ball borrowed from Louis Goings for those first few months, confident that soon enough she could persuade Superintendent Winslow to invest in a regulation ball—and a pair of baskets.[23]

Dr. Winslow at first seemed open to the idea of making these purchases, but ultimately he turned down the request. For now. He would have no time to work on next year's budget until the end of the term, and there were no funds left for such amenities in this year's budget.

Once more Josie Langley knew the disappointment of a dream deferred.

A Wise Investment
1896–1897

❧

BASKETBALL EQUIPMENT? NOT LIKELY.

With limited funds available, Dr. Winslow's budget plans necessarily began with the bare essentials—salaries for faculty and staff; food and clothes for students; supplies for classrooms, workrooms, shops, and farming and livestock operations; and funds for maintaining the facilities of his aging campus. Little wonder any additional requests, especially anything that might seem the least bit frivolous, had to be justified.

On the other hand, filling Josephine Langley's request could be a wise investment in the future of the school. If improving his athletic program for girls would move his institution in the direction of Carlisle, then Josie must surely have her basketball and nets. He put those items near the top of his budget for the coming year, although he balked at ordering the rubber-soled shoes she had described, sure that Louis Goings could find a catalog model and have the boys in the cobbler shop create a suitable match, likely with soles of leather. Uniforms were also out of the question. Even though Josie had convinced him of the advantages of bloomers for all gymnastics exercises, the budget would not stretch that far. For the time being, the girls would play in their long skirts, cumbersome though they were.[1]

His budget drafted, Superintendent Winslow turned his attention to recruiting more students for the coming term. Although his school was actually becoming crowded, he had to continue to recruit in order to increase his chances of having the BIA approve the eventual expansion of the physical plant.

He took stock of his prospects. He was corresponding on a regular basis with the new superintendent at the revitalized Fort Peck Agency School. Knowing the young man realized the worth of off-reservation schools, he was convinced that in due time F. C. Campbell would be sending the brightest and best of his students to Fort Shaw. He could also count on a goodly number of Piegan transfers, since the reputation of the agency school at Willow Creek had grown worse even as that of Fort Shaw had grown better. Pleased with the positive reports of her oldest daughter, Jenny Johnson had decided to send her three youngest children to Fort Shaw that coming September. And thanks to Colonel Healy's influence, the Gros Ventres from Fort Belknap were beginning to be well represented on campus.[2]

~

At least one of those Gros Ventre children—one of the colonel's own—would have preferred to be going just about anywhere except to Fort Shaw. Or to any other school. Genevieve Healy had begun her formal education at St. Paul's Mission School as a five-year-old in the fall of 1893, barely nine months after her mother's death and on the heels of Dr. Winslow's visit that summer. A wild child by all accounts, she much preferred riding across the open range to sounding out letters in a classroom where she was obliged to hold her tongue, speak only English, and obey every order issued by the sisters. She did her best to convince her father to come and get her, complaining that she had never been so hungry, or so cold, or so miserable.

The whole school felt like a prison to Gen Healy after years of running free and taking her lessons from the land, from Ponley, and from her father and his wranglers. And sometimes from her grandmother, aunts, and uncles on the reservation, although visits with her mother's people had become less and less frequent and then had stopped altogether once her father had made up his mind to provide his children with the education they needed to become productive citizens in the white world. With her father set on this new path, Gen's complaints went unheeded, and she resigned herself to life at St. Paul's.[3]

By fall 1894 St. Paul's enrollment was inching upward, and with growth came diversity. Most of the students were still Gros Ventre, but each year brought a few more Assiniboines from other areas on the reservation. And there were even a few Chippewa-Cree, or Métis, children from what Colonel Healy termed "the breed camp" along the edge of Fort Assinniboine, some fifty miles west of Fort Belknap Agency. Perhaps precisely because her father had warned her against having anything to do with "those dirty Cree," or perhaps because nine-year-old Emma Rose Sansaver, one of those forbidden companions, offered kindness and help with adjusting to life at St. Paul's, Gen was soon seeking out her company. Despite their difference in age, the two girls had much in common. They were both semi-orphans: Emma was fatherless and essentially motherless; Gen was motherless and essentially fatherless.[4]

But there the similarities ended. Young as she was, Gen resented and resisted every order issued by the sisters, while Emma seemed to take pleasure in doing their bidding. While both girls were obviously bright, Gen spent most of her time playing tricks on the nuns and her dormmates, while Emma devoted most of her time to her studies. While both girls worked well with their hands, Gen would deliberately misplace her embroidery hoop and thread during sewing class, while Emma did her cross-stitching with patience and care. But this alliance of opposites was sundered at the end of Gen's first year at St. Paul's when Colonel Healy suddenly decided to transfer his children to the agency school—perhaps because he had finally paid attention to their litany of complaints about conditions at St. Paul's. But for his daughter Gen, life at the agency school with its cold and drafty dorms, greasy food, and harsh discipline was, if anything, worse than life at St. Paul's. Still, at least there was no catechism to learn and no mass to attend, and she found she enjoyed singing the hymns that were part of the school's sporadic chapel services.[5]

The agency school had a number of Gros Ventre children who, like Gen, lived in or around Lodgepole, although most of its students were Fort Belknap Assiniboines. There were no Chippewa-Crees, and if Gen's boldness had led her to ask why, she would have been told in short order that the U.S. government was not obliged to educate "British Indians." Once again showing a preference for girls beyond her own circle, six-year-old Gen sought out the company of the Snell sisters, Jennie, Katie, and Mabel, whose family lived on a farm, a ride of just an hour or so across the foothills from the Healy ranch. She was particularly drawn to eight-year-old Katie, and the two became friends. Once again opposites seemed to attract, for Katie Snell was a peaceful, purposeful child while Gen Healy was feisty and unpredictable. But this friendship, too, was destined to be short-lived. In the fall of 1895 Katie and her older siblings transferred to Fort Shaw School, traveling in the same group as Gen's eleven-year-old brother, John.[6]

Far from being envious of her brother's opportunity to attend a bigger school, Gen had been glad she would not be going so far away that it would be impossible to ever get back to her father's ranch. For that was her plan—to go back home if she had to walk every step of the way. And she was, indeed, home by late November, having managed to convince her father to withdraw her from the agency school before it was too late. Everybody seemed to be getting sick, and after seeing her classmate Mabel Snell come down with fever and chills and die right there in the dorm, not two beds away from her own, she was afraid to stay at school for fear the same thing might happen to her.

Had Colonel Healy not still been shaken by the telegram the school had sent to his trading post for immediate delivery to James Snell, he would likely have been more skeptical of the motives of this wily child of his. But given these special circumstances, he had sent Ponley up to the agency school to bring her back to the ranch, supposedly just until spring term. Yet January came and went with Gen helping Ponley pitch hay to the cattle and horses, feed the chickens, and gather the eggs. And then came calving time. Busy as he was with his own work at the trading post and natural as it seemed to have his daughter at home with her younger brother and sister, the colonel never gave another thought to her schooling until it was time to send Ponley back up to the agency school to bring Harry and Nettie home for the summer. His oldest, John, was already on his way home from Fort Shaw, thanks to his father's letter insisting he was needed on the ranch.[7]

It was John's favorable opinion of his new school that had influenced Colonel Healy to announce that all of his children—except four-year-old Maude—would be transferred to Fort Shaw for the 1896–97 school year. Even Willie seemed pleased at the prospect of following his big brothers and sisters off to this far-distant school. But not Gen. Her expectations of life at Fort Shaw were colored by her attitude toward the two schools that had already darkened her days.[8]

~

Ten-year-old Belle Johnson's expectations of life at Fort Shaw were based on the reports of her older sister, Mary, who had done so well during her first year there that she had earned an appointment as Indian assistant for the upcoming year. Mary had nothing but praise for the school, as had Belle's oldest brother, Charlie. On the other hand, Willie, her next-oldest brother, had spent that summer filling the ears of his younger siblings with descriptions of the harsh discipline, the senseless routine, and the bad food that awaited them at Fort Shaw. If their mother made him go back to that school, he vowed he was going to run away—and take James with him. Indeed, on their journey to Fort Shaw that September of 1896, Willie and James sat in the back of the wagon, plotting an escape just as soon as they got there. Mary would not let her younger sisters sit anywhere near those two, furious as she was at Willie's attitude. Fortunately, six-year-old Ida fell promptly to sleep. Belle remained wide awake, eager as she was to catch her first glimpse of the school she had waited so long to attend.[9]

~

Just as she had promised, Josephine Langley was on hand to welcome Jenny Johnson's three youngest children when their wagon rolled onto the campus. To Josie's surprise—and pleasure—Belle asked at once to see the gymnasium. The physical culture program at Willow Creek had been nonexistent, and Belle was eager to learn how to drill with barbells, toss Indian clubs—and learn to play the new game Mary had come home talking about. For her part, Josie was eager enough to take all the girls into the gymnasium that autumn semester, so she could show off the equipment she had requested and Dr. Winslow had finally purchased.

As the girls filed in for the first physical culture lesson of the new year, Josie stood just inside the open door, bouncing a real basketball, just like the one she had used on the court at Carlisle. They could still come into the gym to practice their dribbling, but for the most part, she said—at least until winter set in—they would be doing their running and passing and dribbling on the grassy field beyond the parade ground. Pointing out the brand-new baskets positioned at each end of her outdoor "court," Josie announced the time had come to learn how to send the ball soaring upward and through the hoop. There would be hours of practice, both from the field and the free-throw line, before they were ready to try to shoot against the interference of a player from the other team. And there would be hours and hours of more practice before they would be ready to play a real game, even among themselves.

Over the course of the fall 1896 semester, everyone in physical culture class had a turn at learning to pass and shoot, even the younger girls. Eight-year-old Gen Healy begged to be allowed to play with the group just older than she, the group that included ten-year-old Katie Snell, her friend from the agency school at Fort Belknap, and another ten-year-old, Belle Johnson, who had taken an instant liking to the sport. In fact, Belle seemed to like almost everything about Fort Shaw, with academic courses and domestic arts being almost as exciting to her as basketball.[10]

Work in the classroom would never be exciting for Gen Healy, but lessons in the music room were. She was drawn to the mandolin, her "tater bug," and she had begun to master that instrument before the end of her first semester at Fort Shaw. She was good, and she knew it, although she also knew it would take a while to catch up with Nettie Wirth, who had grown up listening to the classical music her German-born father played on his violin and who had been playing the mandolin since the year she had come to Fort Shaw. Clearly one of the school's most accomplished instrumentalists, Nettie knew musical talent when she heard it, and she appreciated Gen's enthusiasm as much as her skills. The two of them were soon playing and singing together, sometimes contenting themselves with old standards, sometimes composing words and music of their own. A fast friendship was forming, despite the two-year difference in their ages.[11]

But then Gen had always gotten along well with girls older than she was—including Katie Snell, whose company she had enjoyed back at the agency school at Fort Belknap. It seemed natural the two would bond again once they were reunited at Fort Shaw, but Gen had been uncharacteristically reticent around her one-time friend. Gen had, after all, been at the agency school all last year, including the cold November day when Katie's little sister Mabel had died. Yet there seemed to be no easy way for either of them to bring up the subject of Mabel's death.

The court was the one place where their awkwardness fell away. As the two girls ran up and down the worn grass of the playing field, passing the basketball off to one another, the give-and-take of that action seemed to bridge the gap between them. With Josie Langley putting them through their paces, the two found a way of communicating feelings neither of them could voice.

～

With the coming of winter, Josie had the outdoor baskets taken down and mounted at either end of the gymnasium. Indoor games would now be the order of the day. And there would be extra practices for her most talented players. She had no illusions about building a team that could compete against other schools. For one thing, she knew of no other schools in Montana playing basketball. For another, she doubted there would ever be sufficient funds to develop a full-fledged program in team sports for girls. But she was determined to develop several Fort Shaw squads that would be well enough matched for her players to experience what she had in intramural games back at Carlisle.

The girls were still getting used to playing indoors again when, one late November afternoon, Dr. Winslow came into the gym with a tall, broad-shouldered, redheaded man he introduced to Josie as the superintendent of the Fort Peck School. He explained that Mr. Campbell had accompanied a group of new students from Poplar and had asked to look in on the Wirth sisters, as he had promised their father he would do. As Josie moved to stop the action on the court, Campbell raised his hand. She need not do that. He had a few minutes and, truth be told, he'd like to watch the game. He could visit with Lizzie and Nettie when their practice was over.[12]

Everything about the Fort Shaw campus had impressed Fred Campbell that afternoon, and nothing so much as the sports program that his counterpart was developing. An all-star catcher during his undergraduate days at the University of Kansas, Campbell knew how much being part of an athletic team could enrich a student's life. He had heard about the baseball club that Louis Goings had developed last spring here at Fort Shaw, and he had sought out the young man earlier that afternoon. Now here Winslow had something going for girls as well. Basketball. He had heard about the game. Anyone associated with the Y, anyone with an interest in sports, had heard about basketball. But he had never seen it played. If he could trust what he was seeing, this was a game that offered nothing but excitement and fun for those involved.[13]

When Winslow excused himself to get back to the office, Campbell leaned back against a pillar and watched the girls racing up and down the court, full of energy, full of the joy of competition. Although he'd never met them, he was pretty sure he could pick out the Wirth sisters from the other girls. He would be able to tell their father that from everything he had seen, they were thriving at Fort Shaw.

~

By the start of spring semester Josie had the foundation for two squads. She formed one around fifteen-year-old Lizzie Wirth, whose leadership skills she had noticed during her first year at Fort Shaw. Though only ten, Lizzie's little sister, Nettie, was already handling and shooting the ball as well as anyone else in the gym. Another Assiniboine, Mattie Hayes, who had come to the Sun River Valley in that first contingent of Fort Peck students, was also a solid player. And there were several younger players, like Belle Johnson, whose talents were beginning to match their enthusiasm.

If Josephine Langley's girls were still a long way from knowing their way around a basketball court, they were learning that this game took discipline, dedication, and teamwork. She would continue to stress those essentials even as she pushed her players to the limit, for she had a plan in mind. She intended to ask Dr. Winslow to schedule an exhibition game during closing exercises for the 1896–97 school year. She knew his approval of her request would depend on the girls' readiness to show their skills to advantage. Yet it was with considerable confidence—and not a little boldness—that she requested one bolt of white cotton twill and one bolt of red from the seamstress, Mrs. Cushman, enlisted the woman's help in turning a rough sketch into a pattern, then set her players to work in the sewing room, creating their own uniforms, the bloomers and middies they would wear for the exhibition game they would play at closing exercises.[14]

~

Excellence in all areas would be expected of the students in that year-end program, and by the beginning of April everyone on campus was focused on the entertainment planned for that event. When Lizzie Wirth was not practicing basketball, she was practicing four-part harmony with Rosa Lucero, a fifteen-year-old transfer from St. Peter's. Though Josie Langley had been much older than Rosa during her own years at the mission school, she remembered Rosa as the little girl with the big voice. The child had been a curiosity of sorts at St. Peter's. Her father was rumored to be a red-headed Spaniard who had brought her there as a young child soon after the death of her Piegan mother, then gotten on with his life, marrying a Chippewa-Cree woman, begetting more children, and forming a partnership with a local cattleman. But those were only rumors, while Rosa Lucero's voice was the real thing.[15]

It was the thought of hearing that voice that had moved Philip Lucero to announce to his wife that he would attend the closing exercises at Fort Shaw on the last day of June and that he intended to take two of their little girls along with him so they could hear their half sister sing. Nine-year-old Flora could hardly believe her ears. It was unusual enough for her father to leave off his gambling and drinking up at Dupuyer long enough to come home at all. It was more unusual still for him to take her and Emma on any trip, especially such a long one as he was now proposing. And it was strangest of all to think that at long last they would be meeting their mysterious half sister, something their mother had vowed would never happen.

A red-headed Spaniard indeed, Philip Lucero got more than his share of stares as he spent that afternoon of June 30 at Fort Shaw with a crowd of three hundred other parents and visitors, listening to the marching band; touring classrooms, workrooms, and shops; then watching the day's athletic events. First the boys, who engaged in foot races, hurdles, pole vault, and broad jump. Next came the girls, who had this year set aside barbells and Indian clubs in favor of a leather sphere the Indian assistant in charge identified as a "basket ball."[16]

Suddenly a whistle blew and the action began, with two teams of girls, five to a side, running, passing, and arcing the ball high overhead in an attempt to put it through one of the two baskets at either end of the field. The two squads Josie Langley put on the playing field next to the parade ground that day were made up of the older girls who had been practicing together ever since Josie's return from Carlisle—plus Josie herself and ten-year-old Nettie Wirth. The other younger girls, including Gen Healy, Katie Snell, and Belle Johnson, were seated cross-legged along the sidelines, watching with the rest of the spectators as the action surged back and forth. The teams were evenly matched, and the final score stood 7 to 6. The entire demonstration lasted no longer than the customary calisthenics drills, but the crowd was captivated. Maybe it was the novelty of seeing girls engage in such strenuous, rough-and-tumble play. Maybe it was appreciation for the skill involved in throwing a ball through an iron hoop high overhead. For whatever reason or reasons, never before had staff or students or visitors shown such enthusiasm for an athletic event at Fort Shaw.[17]

As engaged in the game as the other parents and guests seemed to be, Philip Lucero's patience was wearing thin. He had not come to tour the campus or to watch ten Indian girls run up and down a field in pursuit of a ball. He had come to see his daughter sing. At last the outdoor events came to an end and everyone was invited into the chapel for the musical and literary program. And still the waiting went on. The band played several numbers. Then there were recitations, followed by a piano duet and still more recitations. And finally came the performance

Lucero had come so far and waited so long to see—Rosa, his oldest daughter, lifting her lovely voice in song.[18]

Other attendees, and even the students and faculty, had their favorites among the many elements of the program that day. In the eyes of Josie and her players, the basketball exhibition was the highlight of the afternoon. Among those who likely shared Josie's opinion were a number of girls in the audience, including the daughters of several Sun River Valley residents. Their mothers would undoubtedly have voted for the needlework they saw in the sewing room that day, while their fathers would have been most impressed by the gardens and the condition of the livestock. But their daughters had been inspired by the unpredictable—the sight of girls their own ages running and jumping as if their very lives depended on getting a round ball into a net goal.

Ironically, the Great Falls papers, both of which within a few years would be covering every game played by the girls from Fort Shaw Indian School, offered not a single comment on the afternoon's crowd-pleasing demonstration of this new sport. It was their loss, as history would prove, for they were scooped by the little *Choteau Montanian* that described the game and gave the score—but failed to note that the girls from Fort Shaw Indian School had given Montanans their first glimpse of basketball.[19]

Widening the Circle
1897

"BASKET BALL FOR GIRLS."

That one-line mention of a field event in the program for the closing exercises at Fort Shaw School in June 1897 needed no commentary
to pique the interest of Fred Campbell, superintendent of the agency
school over at Fort Peck. He was glad to see that the young Indian assistant he'd met on his visit to Fort Shaw last November had persisted
in developing the sport over there. As far as he knew, the school was
the only educational institution in Montana—white or Indian, college
or high school—to incorporate basketball into its physical culture curriculum.[1]

He would have enjoyed seeing the exhibition game, but he had hesitated to leave Ella alone with their two lively little boys. She seemed to
be in the family way again and needed as much help as he could give
her. Still, he regretted having missed not only the game but the whole of
the closing exercises. By all reports, Superintendent Winslow's year-end
programs were entertaining as well as educational. By rights, he should
have been on hand to applaud the performances of students from his
own reservation and bring back to their parents descriptions of their
excellence in precision marching, recitations, musical performances,
and athletic events.[2]

Including basketball for girls.

Nine-year-old Flora Lucero had plenty to think about during the
long wagon ride home to the cabin in Choteau. At Fort Shaw she had
seen a different side of her volatile father. He had been visibly moved by

Rosa's singing, obviously proud of her performance and pleased by the crowd's applause. Now that she knew it was possible to please this man she so often feared, Flora was determined to earn the kind of praise he had given her half sister. But how? Even if her father allowed her to transfer to Fort Shaw, she would never be able to equal Rosa's academic or musical accomplishments. Perhaps she would find her place in the domestic arts. Her mother had already begun to teach her to hem and mend and put on buttons. With further instruction she might be able to sew fine dresses herself. Or create beautiful lacework. Perhaps. But there was something else—an ace up her sleeve, as her father would say. She knew she could learn to play this new game called basketball as well as any of the girls at Fort Shaw. She was strong. She was quick. She was focused. And she loved the challenge of chasing down the very chicken her mother had picked out for dinner, zigzagging this way and that in her dogged pursuit of the chosen bird—while her mother looked on and laughed.[3]

Rose Jocko Lucero, Rosa's mother, hardly ever laughed. Given away by her father shortly after her birth and the death of her mother, she had, in turn, been bartered as a teenager to a forty-year-old man she barely knew. He had moved her into his spacious, well-furnished ranch house, where two Piegan girls did all the cooking, washing, and cleaning. But from the first, Rose had hated being the virtual slave of this red-bearded Spaniard who was as disparaging of her lineage as he was proud of his own. The tensions that had always been a part of their marriage increased dramatically during the winter of 1886–87 when howling blizzards and temperatures well below zero decimated Lucero's livestock operation. Selling what cattle he had left to his ranching partner, he moved his wife into a cabin in nearby Choteau.[4]

Flora was born the following winter. Emma, Lawrence, and Lena followed in quick succession, with each pregnancy more difficult for Rose than the last.[5] Philip drifted from one odd job to another, always aware that a man approaching fifty could never earn enough to regain the status he had worked a lifetime to achieve. Drinking eased his despair and gambling fueled his hopes. Poker became his obsession, and he soon developed a reputation for playing a high-stakes game.

When he won, his wife was given a share of his bounty to meet house-hold expenses. When he lost, she stretched what she had squirreled away. Somehow she managed to keep her children fed and clothed, and most of the time she was able to keep them out of their father's way when he came home drunk and angry and broke. She also managed to fend off his talk of sending all four of them away to St. Peter's, where his oldest daughter, Rosa—child of his long-dead Piegan wife—was reportedly doing so well. On this point, Rose stood her ground. If a white man's education was what her children needed to escape the life she had led, what good would it do to send them off to some *Indian* school? Why not start making that move toward a new identity by sending them to school with their white neighbors there in Choteau?[6]

For once, Rose Lucero had her way. Flora, Lawrence, and Emma were enrolled in the public school, while their half sister, Phillip's oldest daughter, continued on at St. Peter's—and then Fort Shaw.[7]

It was Rosa's success at Fort Shaw that caused Philip to pressure his wife to allow Flora and Emma to transfer there in the fall. Having seen the school at its best that summer's day, the two girls took their father's part in the matter. Their mother finally conceded. Indeed, she would have had no qualms whatsoever about having her girls go off to Fort Shaw Indian Boarding School had it not been for that one damning word—*Indian.*

~

Superintendent Winslow brightened when Mrs. Pleas handed him the letter that had just come in from St. Paul's Mission School over on the Fort Belknap Reservation. Ever since attaining their enrollment quotas and qualifying for government support for their school, the sisters at St. Paul's had been increasingly open to sending their more advanced students his way. Their transfers were primarily Gros Ventres, but they sometimes sent him Assiniboine children as well. Winslow welcomed students from these tribes, but he found himself vaguely troubled by the contents of this particular letter. The Ursuline sisters had nothing but praise for the achievements and talents of the two young girls they were now recommending for transfer. He had no doubts about the accomplishments of the two, for he recognized the family name from a recruiting visit to St. Paul's the previous summer. And he recalled how impressed he had been by a rendition of "Te Deum" performed by a young pianist introduced to him as Emma Rose Sansaver. He had also met Emma's younger sister, Flora. Both girls seemed bright and, thanks to their years at St. Paul's, both were fluent in English. Excellent prospects for transfer—or so it would seem.[8]

Winslow's unease had to do with the scanty information the letter provided as to the girls' tribal background. Although they were identified as "Sioux," their surname—"Sansaver"—suggested a Métis heritage. Normally this seeming discrepancy would have posed no problem for him, since the BIA's edict barring enrollment of Métis children in government schools did not apply to those who had at least one parent classed as a "reservation Indian." In this particular case, however, no reservation affiliation was given. Therein lay his dilemma. Over the years of his superintendency, he had conscientiously resisted the temptation to visit any of the Métis settlements scattered across Montana, even though they represented a vast, untapped reserve of prospective students, many of whom, like the Sansaver girls, would no doubt have been ideally suited to life at Fort Shaw. Despite continual pressure from Washington to enlarge the school's population, he had never wavered from his position.[9]

Until now.

He could still see young Emma Sansaver's face as she bent over the keys, mesmerized by the music she played. Sioux? Not to his eye. But who was he to doubt the integrity of the Catholic sisters? Dipping pen into inkwell, he scrawled out his reply. The Sansaver sisters were welcome to transfer to Fort Shaw, along with any other candidates the Ursulines saw fit to send his way. He would expect the girls later that month.

~

There was no denying the Métis heritage of Emma Rose Sansaver. The Sansaver, or Sansauver, family came from a long line of mixed-blood peoples whose skin was the color of *bois brule*—scorched wood.

Emma's parents, Marie Rose LaFromboise and Edward Sansaver, were both natives of Canada, although in the tradition of their people they had joined their tribal kin in migrations back and forth across the Medicine Line as the seasons dictated. Only after the first of Louis Riel's failed attempts to create a Métis sanctuary in their native country put an end to their seasonal migrations, did Marie and Edward Sansaver choose to establish full-time residence on the vast Blackfeet Reserve. As "British Indians," however, they were ineligible for the various types of government assistance available to the nations for whom the reserve had originally been set aside.[10]

Obliged to support his family on his own, Edward Sansaver had moved from one Métis camp to another, finding what work he could as a day laborer, then joining a group of wranglers hired to herd cattle between the upper reaches of the Missouri and the Canadian border. Steady income was a good thing for a man with a growing family, but long absences from his wife and children were not. Thus, when the construction of Fort Assinniboine, some five miles south of Havre, offered opportunities for skilled and unskilled laborers, Edward moved his family to a newly established Métis settlement at the northern edge of the fort and signed on with the brick-making crew. Over the next few years the ongoing expansion of the post provided sporadic but welcome work and wages for the area's Métis population.[11]

The ragged little settlement in which Edward and Marie Sansaver and other Chippewa and Cree refugees had been given permission to live consisted of numerous tepees and a few log structures. It was there in what the neighboring whites called the "breed camp" that Emma Rose Sansaver, the couple's third child, was born in August 1886. She joined an older sister, Mary, and a brother, Isadore. Two years later the family was complete with the birth of another girl, Flora.[12]

While Emma and her siblings played with other children in the camp, their mother cooked meals over an open fire, washed their clothes in water from the creek, and fought the dust and grime of high-plains living. There were evenings of storytelling and dancing to sprightly tunes played on the fiddle. If the camp was crude, the family was secure, for Edward's wages from wrangling and construction work at the fort provided sufficient income to meet the basic needs of his wife and four children.

That security was abruptly shattered in June 1890 when Edward, who had suffered from consumption most of his life, contracted pneumonia while moving cattle across the open range in a driving rainstorm. He died at the age of thirty-two, leaving his wife and children in less-than-ideal circumstances. It soon became obvious that Marie Rose Sansaver, who had begun to seek solace in drink, would not be able to provide adequately for her children. Mary, only thirteen, took over most of her mother's responsibilities, including the care of eight-year-old Isadore, three-year-old Emma, and one-year-old Flora. But there were limits to Mary's ability to care for—and protect—her younger siblings. When their mother subsequently entered into a stormy relationship with Joseph Rondo, conditions at home rapidly deteriorated. Seeing the necessity of moving the Sansaver children to a better environment, relatives enrolled all four at St. Paul's Mission School in late spring of 1891.[13]

Emma found the regimentation and order of mission school life a welcome change from the confusion and chaos at home. Having effectively lost her mother from the moment Marie Sansaver took up with Joseph Rondo, the six-year-old formed a close attachment to the sisters who were charged with her care and education and who buffered her from the abusive situation she had left behind. Within months of her arrival at St. Paul's she had settled into a comfortable routine, and over the next few years the predictability and peace of the mission school— and the presence of her siblings—restored the sense of security she had lost with her father's death. Not even Mary's marriage and departure from the school the year she turned eighteen disturbed the relative tranquility of Emma's world.[14]

But life took yet another turn in 1897 when the Ursuline sisters, recognizing the promise of eleven-year-old Emma and nine-year-old Flora, recommended them for transfer to Fort Shaw. Emma had mixed emotions about the plan. She did not like the idea of leaving behind her brother Isadore, who had already announced his intentions to leave St. Paul's and move back home to do what he could to protect their mother from Rondo's abuse. Nor did she like the idea of being uprooted yet again and sent more than 150 miles from St. Paul's and the women who had mothered as well as taught her. Even as she and Flora boarded the train at Havre that September of 1897, she was still trying to imagine what it would be like to attend classes that were not presided over by sisters clad in black from head to toe. Yet, having taken to heart the lessons those sisters had taught by precept and example, she was determined to accept whatever lay ahead.[15]

On the Lemhi Reservation in southeastern Idaho, thirteen-year-old Minnie Burton, was also caught up in change beyond her control. Agent Edward Yearian had just announced that the game of double ball would no longer be played on the reservation. The news came as a shock, though perhaps Minnie should have realized that this edict was coming, considering Yearian's ongoing campaign against gambling. While there was no denying that gambling had always been an integral part of double ball, there was also no denying that double ball had always been an integral part of Shoshone tradition.[16]

Having only recently been allowed to play the game with the older girls and women, Minnie was just beginning to develop the speed, stamina, and agility that had characterized the legendary play of her grandmother, Pea-boa. Now the agent's decree had put an end to the clatter and clash of forked willow sticks, the flight of the buckskin balls through the air, the headlong race toward the goal, and the cheers of those who lined the field. For Pea-boa, the decree marked the end of an era. For Minnie Burton, it marked the end of her dreams of carrying on her grandmother's legacy.

The waning of one game for girls and women coincided with the waxing of another. In a retrofitted armory still farther west in April 1896—a year prior to the agent's banning of double ball on the Lemhi Reservation—the University of California at Berkeley hosted Stanford University in the country's first women's intercollegiate basketball game. Men and boys were excluded from Armory Hall, but the teams otherwise chose to ignore the "girls'rules" so carefully set forth by Senda Berenson—including her insistence that competitive attitudes be discouraged in players and spectators alike. To the reporter who covered the game for the *San Francisco Chronicle*, the seven hundred onlookers "roared until the glass doors in the gun cases shivered at the noise." The crowd's involvement was all the encouragement the athletes needed. "Sometimes with a slump and a slide three girls would dive for the ball and end in an inextricable heap of red, white and blue." Yet, the reporter continued, "In less time than it takes to read [this sentence] they were all planted firmly on their own two feet, flushed, perspiring, intensely in earnest and oblivious of everything except the ball." When Stanford won by a score of 2 to 1, their fans raised a cheer suggesting that competition was a vital component of this new game of women's basketball:

> Who made the basket?
> Why do you ask it?
> Sure, it was Stanford,
> Without half a try.
> Berkeley cannot win,
> Without our permission.
> She'll make a goal
> In the sweet by-and-by.[17]

Transitions
1897–1899

Superintendent Winslow himself met Emma and Flora Sansaver at the Sunnyside station in late September. One look reinforced his earlier instincts concerning the Métis heritage of the "Sioux" sisters he assisted into his buggy—and confirmed his memory of Emma Sansaver as the girl at the piano at St. Paul's. On the ride out to the school, Emma and Flora answered his questions politely if timidly, but from that limited exchange, Winslow was convinced the girls would have no trouble catching up with those students who had started the fall semester a month earlier.[1]

Emma Sansaver was well settled into Fort Shaw routine by the time the Lucero sisters, nine-year-old Flora and seven-year-old Emma, arrived at the school the second week of October 1897.[2] She felt an immediate rapport with the two girls, for the flamboyant, obviously inebriated father who accompanied them reawakened painful memories of Joseph Rondo. As she had at St. Paul's, Emma Sansaver kept such thoughts at bay by immersing herself in her studies. She was determined to meet the high expectations of her teachers, the two Misses Roberts, and she gave long hours to practicing the piano.

Flora Lucero was also soon absorbed in school activities, though, unlike Emma Sansaver, she barely tolerated her mornings in the classroom. It was the afternoons she looked forward to—first in the sewing room, where she was learning to use the sewing machine and embroidery hoop, and then in Josie Langley's physical culture classes.[3]

In her role as assistant matron, Josie was a constant factor in the daily activities of the girls, and the trust and respect she earned there carried over to her classes in the gym. Josie expected the best from each of her students. She paid due attention to their work in all areas of gymnastics—from club swinging to barbells—though basketball remained her passion. She introduced all incoming students to the rudiments of the game, but only those who showed special aptitude or expressed strong interest in playing were invited to evening practices where shooting, dribbling, and passing drills were interspersed with an occasional scrimmage.

Emma Sansaver's speed on the court, plus her obvious delight in shooting and passing a basketball, caught Josie's attention at once. What Emma lacked in height she made up for in speed and agility.[4] She was soon a part of the evening sessions with the girls who had been playing under Josie for more than a year—Lizzie and Nettie Wirth, Mattie Hayes, Belle Johnson, and Katie Snell, plus the irrepressible nine-year-old Genevieve Healy. While Gen had a tendency to work as hard at getting a laugh as she did at getting a basket, her lighthearted banter helped ease ruffled feelings in hotly contested practice games.

~

Emma Sansaver had more than basketball on her mind during her first year at Fort Shaw. Frequent letters from her sister, Mary, kept her apprised of matters back home. The news went from bad to worse. By late January Mary had concluded that their mother was hopelessly addicted to alcohol—and to Joseph Rondo, who was more belligerent and abusive with each passing day. When Isadore had stepped in front of his mother during a particularly brutal attack, Rondo had buried a knife in the boy's arm. Shortly thereafter, with Isadore's help, Marie Sansaver fled the camp and Rondo—only to take up with a Canadian Cree named Hunting Dog, a jealous man rumored to be even more abusive than Rondo. The two took off for parts unknown, leaving Isadore at the mercy of ever-present, ever-dangerous Rondo.[5]

As the guardian of her three younger siblings, Mary contacted Dr. Winslow, explaining the situation and asking that he accept fifteen-year-old Isadore at Fort Shaw in the fall. She also asked that Emma and Flora be allowed to spend the summer at her home in Havre. Winslow acceded to both requests. With her mother's whereabouts still un-known, Emma looked forward to this reunion with Mary.[6]

~

Unknowns of another nature lay ahead for all Fort Shaw students—as well as for the citizens of Sun River Valley for whom William Wins-low's leadership had been a major factor in their growing support of the Indian boarding school. After six years at Fort Shaw, Winslow was ready to move on. Hard as it was to leave the school he had founded, his legacy there was assured and other opportunities awaited him. He had been offered a position as surgeon in a hospital in Kansas, and the chance to return to the practice of medicine was too much to resist. There were family considerations as well. While his wife had supported his work at Fort Shaw and had adjusted reasonably well to Montana winters, she wanted her three little ones to grow up knowing their grandparents, aunts and uncles, and cousins. A change in venue would have advantages for all of them.[7]

Determined as he was to leave Fort Shaw in capable hands, Dr. Win-slow had taken an active role in the search for his replacement. He had watched with admiration as F. C. Campbell turned the struggling agen-cy school over at Fort Peck into a model for other reservation schools. He had been particularly pleased with the young administrator's reac-tion to the Fort Shaw program during that afternoon Campbell had spent on campus last fall—and by Campbell's presentation at the na-tional Indian teachers' institute down in Utah just this past summer. Lingering over dinner one night at that conference the two men had discussed their respective views of Indian education. Winslow had been encouraged to discover how similar those views were, and it was then that he had shared the news of his pending resignation with Campbell. With Winslow's strong recommendation—and on the basis of Camp-bell's own record in the service—the commissioner of Indian affairs had appointed the tall, ruddy Scotsman as the new superintendent at Fort Shaw.[8]

Campbell had accepted the appointment at once, pleased to be promoted to superintendent of an off-reservation school, especially one considered to be among the best in the system. The move would also be a good one for his family, for Ella Campbell had seen Fort Peck as an isolated outpost far from many things dear to her heart. She was looking forward to enjoying the social amenities of the Sun River Valley and to being within a few hours' buggy ride of the city of Great Falls with its shaded avenues, stores, library, and even the Grand Opera House.[9]

∼

A change of command. The news traveled fast in the valley. The way some folks in Sun River saw it, it was asking a lot of them to accept some new fellow at the school, just when they were feeling comfortable with what Winslow had done with the place. But there were just as many who thought they should give this Campbell a chance before making any judgments. After all, Winslow had highly recommended him. And they knew they could trust Winslow. He'd made good on every promise, hadn't he? A few runaways, that was about the only excitement those Indians had caused in the last five years. And when the parents had come through town on their way to closing exercises, had there been any trouble? None.

Why not count the benefits the school had brought the valley? So far, the merchants had known nothing but profit from having that school in their midst. And there was no denying that the womenfolk were enjoying Fort Shaw's literary programs, the music, the recitations, the socializing. Truth be told, that Indian school was something to be proud of. So give this new superintendent a chance. If anything changes, well, then we'll see.

∼

Although Emma Sansaver had enjoyed spending the summer with her sister's family in Havre, she was eager to get back to the campus at Fort Shaw—and away from the talk on the streets about her mother, especially from the comments made by her all-knowing former neighbors, the residents of the Métis camp, when they came to town. The more judgmental among them implied that wherever she was, Marie

Rose Sansaver had only herself to blame. The more sympathetic observed that she was likely better off than she had been with Joseph
Rondo. Some were certain she had been headed toward Havre to pay
off a debt when she was waylaid and left for dead. Others said she had
been murdered by Rondo; still others pointed to Hunting Dog. Some
claimed she had started walking down the frozen Milk River to seek
refuge with relatives camped farther east but had fallen through the ice
and been swept under. A cold and watery grave. But who could know
for sure what had happened to Marie Sansaver?[10]

No more able to answer that question than anyone else, Isadore
Sansaver packed up his few belongings and joined his sisters on their
return to school that September of 1898. Fort Shaw would henceforth
be haven as well as home for Isadore, Emma, and Flora. No one at the
school was likely to have heard anything about what might or might
not have happened to their mother. That was one advantage of being
a landless Indian. The "moccasin telegraph" operated only within reservation circles. And there was no need to worry about anyone seeing an article in the *Havre Plaindealer*, for what would be newsworthy
about the disappearance of a drunken Indian woman who lived with an
abusive man? Without a body, there was no crime. Marie Sansaver had
likely chosen to move on, and who could say—and who would care—
where she had gone?[11]

~

Arriving almost simultaneously with the returning Sansaver siblings
that September were the new superintendent, Fred Campbell, his wife,
Ella, and their three children, Mead, eight, Fred, five, and baby Freda,
six months. Ella found the warm greetings of the faculty and staff reassuring, and she appreciated, in particular, the help of several young
Indian assistants who unloaded the crates she had brought from Fort
Peck, especially since her husband was already off to the administration
building in the company of Dr. Winslow, who had stayed over a few
days after seeing his wife and children off at the Great Falls depot.[12]

Grateful as he was for Winslow's solicitude, and attentive as he was
to the man's suggestions for meeting some of the problems that would

invariably arise with the new school year, Campbell could hardly wait to get his hand on the tiller. At last he had an off-reservation boarding school under his command, and he intended to prove himself worthy of that challenge. He had the confidence born of eight years of good, solid work in the Indian School Service, he was proud of what he had just accomplished in rescuing the floundering agency school over at Fort Peck and turning it into something everyone was praising. He had every reason to think that at this stage of Fort Shaw's development, his administrative style, while different from that of Dr. Winslow, would be just as effective.[13]

Whatever hopes the new superintendent brought with him for an easy entry into life in the Sun River Valley were dashed by an outbreak of measles in late September. A few isolated cases quickly exploded into a full-blown epidemic that ravaged the school. By November some two hundred pupils, roughly two-thirds of the student body, were under the care of Dr. Wittke, the newly assigned school physician. Classes were cancelled and only the essential kitchen, workroom, and livestock chores were carried out. During the worst two months of the siege, "the school was practically a hospital," Campbell told his superiors in Washington, with teachers and staff relieved of their normal duties and assigned nursing shifts in the dorms and infirmary. The epidemic did not let up until mid-January, by which time faculty and staff were as exhausted as the students.[14]

With Belle Johnson, Flora Lucero, and Nettie Wirth among those confined to the infirmary, the promising basketball program begun by Josie Langley was at a virtual standstill—a particularly bothersome state of affairs, since there were rumors that other schools in the state were now showing an interest in the game.[15]

A November 1898 article in the *Exponent*, the student newspaper of the Montana Agricultural College in Bozeman, announced that the school's coeds were practicing basketball twice a week in the campus drill hall. The Women's Athletic Association had invested in "the necessary outfits for basket ball," and W. J. Adams, a senior from Butte with a keen interest in the new sport, had offered to form and coach a women's team. His offer was quickly accepted. Now it was only a matter of finding competition.[16]

That turned out to be easier said than done; there were no teams to be found, even in the state's larger cities—Butte, Helena, and Great Falls. Most disappointing of all to Billy Adams was the lack of a team at the state university in Missoula, archrival of the college in Bozeman. Intramural games would have to suffice for the "Farmerettes," but Adams wondered how long that would sustain the young women's interest. About to graduate and return home to Butte, he could only hope the fledgling program he had begun in Bozeman would survive. Perhaps he could generate interest in basketball among the high school girls in Butte. Perhaps soon enough he would be scheduling competitive games between the high school girls and the college women.[17]

⁓

At Fort Shaw that very same spring, just as the campus began to come back to life after the fall and winter measles epidemic, the school was hit by a new wave of illnesses. Influenza, dysentery, pneumonia, and conjunctivitis took their toll among children still weak from the ravages of the measles. Superintendent Campbell and Dr. Wittke began to make judicious decisions as to which children were likely too sick to survive and to make arrangements, when possible, to send those children home. Their decisions were not made totally for the sake of the child or of the child's family. No, every superintendent in the system sought to avoid having to report an on-site death to the Indian School Service. A death on campus was not only demoralizing for fellow students, it was also a black mark in a school's "sanitary records" and viewed with disfavor in Washington. Yet, despite the superintendent's and the doctor's best efforts to save the children they couldn't send home—and protect the institution's reputation—by the end of the spring semester there were seven new graves in the old military cemetery at Fort Shaw.[18]

While the families of faculty and staff suffered no fatalities, they were not immune to the infections, and many of them, including Ella Campbell and her two boys, became Dr. Wittke's patients. Josie Langley, who had worn herself out taking care of students the previous semester, was confined to the infirmary with an ulcerated leg from January until March. At that point, Dr. Wittke recommended a leave of absence, and Josie went home to Birch Creek. She would not return to the campus until the following October.[19]

With Josie's hospitalization and subsequent sick leave, the girls' physical culture program would likely have lapsed altogether had it not been for the presence of twenty-seven-year-old Sadie Malley, who had joined the faculty in January, just as the measles epidemic of the first semester was waning. Miss Malley, who had developed an interest in club swinging, barbells, and other gymnastics exercises during her schooldays back in Illinois, willingly added supervision of physical culture classes to her teaching duties. Superintendent Campbell was especially appreciative of her willingness to assume that extra assignment at such a crucial time, for he was a firm believer in the restorative powers of physical exercise for those debilitated by sickness.[20]

~

Across the country, another educator who was an equally strong believer in the benefits of rigorous exercise was defending the sport she had helped to popularize against ongoing attacks from those who insisted the game was harmful to women. Senda Berenson, who had once been too frail to continue her studies as a concert pianist, was living proof that exercise was an effective restorative, a healer of mind and body. And to her way of thinking there was no better form of exercise for girls and women than the game of basketball. *Mens sana in corpore sano*, the "sound mind in a sound body" concept, had become her credo, and passing on that concept had become her passion.[21]

In the classroom, on the platform, and in articles in professional journals, she urged abandoning the Victorian ideal of a "small waisted, small footed, small brained damsel who prided herself on her delicate health, who thought fainting interesting and hysterics fascinating" in favor of a new ideal—woman as a "glowing, happy creature with confidence in her intellectual and physical capabilities." Her personal goal was to alter the way her students perceived themselves. And she found no better way of doing that than through the game of basketball. As she saw it, basketball taught them the value of teamwork, of playing to one another's strengths in order to achieve a common goal. And most important, it fostered a sense of joie de vivre, a passion for living life to the fullest.[22]

Not everyone agreed with her on that point. Influential leaders in the fields of education and medicine voiced the opinion that women did not have the strength or endurance to play rigorous sports, that such exercise could even cause "permanent injury to beauty and health." To one observer, "There was something disquieting in the grim and murderous determination with which young ladies chased each other over the court."[23]

In the face of such opposition, Berenson called for moderation. At a national conference in Springfield, Massachusetts, in June 1899, she offered "a set of rules for basket ball for women," rules that would "suit women's needs." For the most part, these were the same guidelines she had first proposed five years earlier. The two important changes were the division of the "playing field" into three equal zones—front court, center court, and back court—with players assigned to each zone, and the prohibition of "snatching or batting" the ball from the hands of another player. In essence, these two rules alone, she felt, would encourage teamwork and discourage roughness.[24]

She felt her adaptations would save the sport. Without curtailing the physical action that was so much a part of the game—and so beneficial to the players—they would ensure the future of basketball for girls and women. She knew she was on a crusade, and she recognized the pressure. She would not be able to change the world overnight. Just one young woman at a time.

More to Be Learned
1899–1900

THE PRESSURE HAD AGENT YEARIAN AT THE BREAKING POINT. WAS there was no one in Washington who understood what life was like on the Lemhi Reservation? Was there no one who appreciated the Herculean task he faced in persuading these people to allow their children to attend the agency school right here on the reservation? Apparently not, or the BIA would not continue to pressure him to send students to schools beyond the borders of Idaho. He would do his best, he responded each time, knowing full well how slim his chances were: Only one parent on his entire reservation had consistently expressed an interest in having his children attend a non-reservation school.[1]

In response to yet another recruitment letter from Colonel Pratt back at Carlisle, Agent Yearian sent word that this one parent—William Burton, his tribal interpreter—would very much like to send his two youngest children east to school. While Yearian highly recommended fifteen-year-old Minnie, "a splendid girl," he characterized her younger brother Willard as "not very bright." But he had five other very suitable boys whose parents might allow them to go east, if Pratt could provide their passage—along with a round-trip ticket for Burton himself to accompany the seven children. Rightly assuming that these other Lemhi parents would never allow their sons to leave the reservation, Pratt replied that he would not be able to pay round-trip passage for a chaperone accompanying only two students—or actually only one, since Yearian's characterization of Willard Burton as "not very bright" had led Pratt to decide the boy was "too young" for Carlisle.[2]

Once more Minnie Burton's dreams of attending Carlisle had been dashed. All because her father refused to allow her to make the trip to

Pennsylvania on her own—despite Colonel Pratt's insistence that she would be perfectly safe as long as she was given "a ticket through and a lunch and . . . a letter to railroad officials."[3] That was fine for Colonel Pratt to say, her father had told her. *He* was not the one whose daughter would be traveling all the way across the country without a chaperone. Perhaps sending her to a school whose superintendent seemed to be more concerned about his travel budget than about the welfare of his students was not such a good idea after all.

Perhaps her father was right, but since he had been the one who had wanted his children to go to Carlisle in the first place, Minnie knew he must be at least as disappointed as she was by this turn of events. You must wait for the moment, Grandmother reminded her. Life has many lessons. There is still more to be learned here with us. Minnie wished she could be as sure of that as Grandmother was. If she thought about it—and as with everything Grandmother said, she thought about it a lot—maybe Blind Maggie was the reason she was not supposed to leave the reservation yet. A lot of things had changed since her father's new wife had moved into their home. Maggie Burton kept house and prepared meals with the skill of a sighted woman. She was an artist with a needle and thread, and Minnie was learning a lot about sewing from her. Blind Maggie was also teaching her to bead, and the more adept Minnie became at beading, the closer she grew to Maggie. Perhaps Blind Maggie was why Minnie couldn't go to Carlisle.[4]

∽

Colonel Pratt was not the only one interested in gaining Shoshone recruits. The Lemhi and the Fort Hall reservations both fell within Fort Shaw's sphere of influence, and Superintendent Campbell was well aware of that fact. While he concentrated his own recruiting efforts on the Montana reservations, Campbell began dispatching Lillie Crawford, the school's new matron, to Idaho to talk with agents and parents about the benefits of a Fort Shaw education. Crawford, who had come to the school from her native Pennsylvania in the fall of 1898, was an effective representative, and the results of her efforts were soon apparent, although more so among the Shoshone and Bannock of Fort Hall than among the Lemhis, where Chief Tendoy remained a powerful influence against capitulating to the white man and his ways.[5]

Crawford's warm, quiet demeanor appealed to the parents and children of Fort Hall, and perhaps no one was more taken with the kindness shown by Miss Crawford than Rose LaRose, the teen-aged daughter of tribal policeman Fred LaRose and Nettie Kutch, his Bannock wife. If Miss Crawford was what the teachers at Fort Shaw were like, then that school was where Rose wanted to be. But she was the oldest in the family, and she knew her mother needed her at home to help with the six younger children. Even so, Rose was flattered that Miss Crawford spent so much time talking with her parents and encouraging them to give her and her brother, Leonard, a chance to go to Fort Shaw.[6]

~

Superintendent Campbell was pleased by Miss Crawford's report. He could use all the good news anyone had to offer as fall semester of 1899 got under way. His first year at Fort Shaw had been a veritable disaster, even though he could hardly have been blamed for the chaos and tragedy that had immobilized the school and taken its toll on students, faculty, and staff. There was no use looking back; he had done all he could to bring the school through the crisis. The majority of his students had remained on campus through the summer, and every effort had been made to see that they got fresh air, exercise, and fresh vegetables, along with eggs and milk produced by their own farm animals.

The students who *had* gone home on vacation had returned by now, and for the most part they seemed to have recovered completely from the illnesses suffered the previous year. There were still a few stragglers who had not yet returned to campus. There always were. But by and large most were present and accounted for. Spirits were high, and the students seemed as glad to have the last year behind them as he was.

Energies on campus that fall of 1899 were centered on the public performance of virtually the entire Fort Shaw student body. When the city of Great Falls began planning a parade to honor Montana veterans returning from the Spanish-American War, the organizers approached Superintendent Campbell with an invitation to enter the school's now-famous Cadet Band and four marching units, two companies of boys and two of girls, comprising some two hundred students in all. Campbell seized the opportunity, and according to the *Great Falls Daily Tribune*, next to "the boys in blue," the Fort Shaw squadrons were far and away the parade's most popular attraction.[7]

The publicity generated by such a showing was everything Superintendent Campbell could have hoped for. But it only whetted his appetite for more exposure for his students. From the success of Carlisle, Fred Campbell knew that fielding superior athletic teams could go a long way toward building the image of any institution. The Fort Shaw baseball nine and newly formed football squad were already drawing the attention of sports fans in the area. It was time to see what he could do with Josie Langley's fledgling basketball team.[8]

Although Josie's ulcerated leg had healed sufficiently for her to return to campus in late October, she was not yet able to resume her practices with the basketball girls. Even so, in her frequent visits to the gym, she learned what they had discovered in her absence. Miss Malley had arrived at Fort Shaw with more than a rudimentary knowledge of the game of basketball. The young teacher had watched with interest the development of interscholastic play between girls' teams in her native state of Illinois and in neighboring Missouri. She had particularly followed a girls' team from St. Louis High that was winning games against colleges and high schools in both states. Serendipitously, her assignment at Fort Shaw had given her a good excuse to learn more about the sport, and she was reading everything she could find about the game.[9]

In early spring 1900, Superintendent Campbell sought out the opinions of Sadie Malley and Josie Langley on the future of basketball at Fort Shaw. Did they think there was potential to build a competitive girls' team, he wanted to know. Malley quickly assured him that she was sure of it—and that she was ready to move ahead with the program, provided she had his permission to ignore the "girls' rules" that had been put forth at a Springfield, Massachusetts, meeting of physical educators the previous summer. One look at those rules convinced Campbell that Miss Malley was right. Why should the girls learn a new way of playing just as they had begun to master the sport as it was originally designed? Especially since it seemed the new rules would slow the game and probably lessen their interest in it—and since, as Miss Malley said, those rules would likely be ignored by most of the teams in this part of the country.[10]

With that issue settled, the superintendent and the two women reviewed the names of the girls who had been in the program from its beginnings. Some of those veterans were superior athletes, seemingly born to bounce a basketball. Then there were those whose determination and hard work made up for their lack of talent. The one thing all the girls had in common was their enthusiasm for the game—but how much longer could that enthusiasm be sustained without the opportunity to test their skills against an outside team?

Campbell had recently heard that a group of young women in Great Falls had expressed an interest in forming a squad, and apparently plans were under way for summer games. Private games, from all accounts. This group seemed to be something akin to a club for young society women and not a group likely to want to play a team of Indians. Perhaps he could generate interest closer to home. He would contact families he knew in Sun River. He felt sure he would be able to find young women there who would be interested in playing against the girls from Fort Shaw. He would talk it up and see what happened. But that might be jumping too far ahead. First he had to be sure he had a team strong enough to represent the school well, for his whole purpose was to show to advantage the athletic abilities of Indian girls who had been taught to play a "white man's" sport.[11]

Over the next few months, Superintendent Campbell found more and more time to visit the gymnasium whenever basketball practice was scheduled. He liked Miss Malley's flamboyant approach to coaching. She made hard work enjoyable, and her praise of the girls built their confidence and kept their spirits high. By late spring, Josie Langley was not only helping Miss Malley in coaching but was also playing center in afternoon scrimmages. Her leadership on the court was invaluable, as was her knowledge of the personalities, as well as the abilities, of many of the girls. Some of the most talented players—Lizzie and Nettie Wirth, Mattie Hayes, Katie Snell, and Belle Johnson—had been under

Josie's watchful eye from their earliest years on campus. But she knew the others just as well. There was Emma Sansaver, a quiet presence in all her classes but a sparkplug on the court, and that irrepressible little eleven-year-old, Gen Healy, a fierce competitor when she got serious about the game. Then there was that brand-new recruit from the Crow Agency in southeastern Montana. Minnie Scoldbear was strong, athletic, and definitely interested in playing basketball. Minnie could be Lizzie's replacement when Lizzie left, as scheduled, for Carlisle come fall.[12]

But Josie couldn't help worrying about Flora Lucero. Flora's thoughts were obviously elsewhere, certainly not on basketball or on her classwork. And Josie knew there was good cause. Flora had lost her little sister Emma to pneumonia that last summer, and Rosa, her half sister, she of the lovely voice, whom Flora had admired so much, had scandalized the campus by getting herself into trouble, the kind of trouble the matrons were always warning the girls about. Rosa had delivered a baby girl in a Great Falls hospital this very spring. Although Rosa had been dismissed from Fort Shaw, Flora and her younger brother Lawrence were left at school in the midst of the unending gossip. Josie did everything she could to comfort the siblings and ease their embarrassment, and still she knew that they both would need time to heal.[13]

Soon Josie had reason to be concerned about Belle as well. The superintendent had asked Josie to be with him the evening he called all of the Johnsons—Mary and Belle and Ida, Charlie and William and James—out of the dining room to tell them that their mother had passed away. The news was unexpected, stunning. Their mother had been the center of their lives, and Jenny Johnson's children were in shock for weeks thereafter. Their only consolation was the fact that at least they were all together there at Fort Shaw, and nothing would separate them. For a while, William and James even gave up all talk of heading home. For now there was no home.[14]

∿

As pleased as he was to see the almost daily improvement of the fledgling basketball team, Superintendent Campbell made no mention in his year-end report of his hopes for his athletic program. At this stage, they might sound too frivolous to the bureaucrats back in Washington. He would wait until he had some successes to report. Instead, he emphasized his public outreach, his untiring efforts to alert Montanans to the importance of the work being done at Fort Shaw. Because the "isolated situation of the school" severely limited his potential draw for student performances on campus, he had begun to expand his horizons. The time and money invested in getting students and exhibits to and from civic celebrations and county and state fairs had already paid dividends beyond his expectations. A year of public exposure had led to more invitations for student appearances than he could possibly accept. Next year would bring even more opportunities to showcase the academic, artistic, and vocational achievements of his students.[15]

And, in due time, their athletic achievements as well.

Gateway to a World's Fair
1900

June 4, 1900. Dusk was settling over the city by the time David Francis managed to make his way through the crowd gathered in celebration at the Southern Hotel in downtown St. Louis. Out on the street, he broke into a run to catch the last westbound streetcar. Then, still a bit out of breath—and still exhilarated by the news of the day and by the high spirits of those who had been streaming into the Southern since mid-afternoon—he settled into his seat and willed himself to relax. As the soft click of the wheels replaced the cacophony of clinking glasses, bursts of applause, and incessant chatter, the reassuring words that had been hovering in the back of his mind all afternoon rose to the fore: To everything there is a season, and a time for every purpose. With today's congressional approval of a $5 million appropriation for the 1903 Louisiana Purchase Exposition, the time had finally come for a world's fair to be held in St. Louis.[1]

As chair of the exposition's executive committee, Francis had been toasted more times than he could count during the past few hours. And with good reason. His eloquence and persuasiveness—plus what his Kentucky relatives would have called good ol' stick-to-itivity—had been vital components of his city's bid for this honor. But Francis had special reason to appreciate, and publicly acknowledge, the hard work, dedication, and perseverance of the many organizations and individuals whose combined efforts had been equally essential to the success of this enterprise.[2] Some lessons are never forgotten, especially those learned the hard way.

David R. Francis had learned the hard way a dozen years earlier that it took more than single-minded determination, more than eloquence and persuasiveness, to land a world's fair. The lessons he learned in losing the 1893 Columbian Exposition to archrival Chicago had been brought to bear in his campaign to win this exposition for St. Louis. This time around, the man who had built a successful business, then leapt from the mayor's office to the governor's mansion to the president's cabinet, all before the age of fifty, had set about doing it the right way.[3]

Four years after Chicago had closed its fair and only a few months after his return to St. Louis from a two-year stint as secretary of the Interior under Grover Cleveland, Francis had once again immersed himself in plans for a world's fair, one built around the centennial of the Louisiana Purchase of 1803, an event integrally tied to the history of his city. With a stroke of a pen—and $15 million—Thomas Jefferson had effectively doubled the size of the United States and provided enough growing room for carving out thirteen new states, including Missouri. The Lewis and Clark Expedition, the epic journey that mapped the new territory, had been launched from right here in St. Louis. The Louisiana Purchase merited an international exposition. And there was no more appropriate place for such a celebration than the city acknowledged to be the gateway to the West.[4]

Thus Francis had found his centennial event—and he applied the lessons he had learned from the past. Landing a world's fair was not a personal quest. It had required building an invincible coalition, forging public and private alliances with people in high places, bringing in millions of dollars, securing the support of foreign dignitaries. It had been an epic journey in its own right, one shared by his old friend Pierre Chouteau. Scion of one of the area's earliest and most famous fur traders, Chouteau embodied the city's heritage. He was well known and well liked.[5]

The two men had taken their case before a group of city fathers. A planning committee with Chouteau as general chair and Francis himself as executive chair had begun fundraising efforts. A conference of governors from the other states that lay within the boundaries of the Louisiana Purchase had garnered outside support. Pledges from wealthy friends and organizations, the state of Missouri, and various departments in Washington were obtained. Trips to Asia and Europe yielded assurances of participation in the fair from scores of foreign nations.[6]

Closer to home, businessmen, politicians, and influential women's groups had taken up the cause, giving countless presentations and producing a barrage of pamphlets and newspaper articles citing the many ways in which hosting a world's fair would be a major step toward solving the health, housing, and transportation problems that made the nation's fourth-largest city a less-than-ideal place in which to live. A proud heritage was not enough to make up for some serious failings. It was time to look to the future, to move into the twentieth century. In this "New St. Louis" there would be clean drinking water, a state-of-the-art sanitation system, improved streets, expanded rail and trolley service, and educational and cultural facilities worthy of an emerging metropolis. The reformers were tireless, their points well taken, and their campaign successful.[7]

That very spring the City of St. Louis had passed a bond issue in support of the fair. On April 29, Francis had graciously accepted the presidency of the newly incorporated Louisiana Purchase Exposition Company. Today's congressional appropriation would trigger contributions by a number of individuals, corporations, and agencies that had been wary of putting their money on the table before Uncle Sam had done so. Slowly but surely, the pieces were following into place.[8]

The vision was large. The St. Louis fair was to be "the grandest, most magnificent exposition in the way of buildings, architectural effects and landscape gardening the world [had] ever seen." The tasks were legion—from locating and procuring the fairgrounds to finding the men who would take charge of turning the idea of a world's fair into a reality worthy of the city that had worked so hard to host it. The time was short, for April 30, 1903, the centennial of the signing of the Louisiana Purchase treaty, was only two years and nine months away. And President McKinley had specified that the government funding appropriated today was contingent upon the fair's opening on that anniversary date.[9]

David R. Francis needed no such presidential edict to stay on course.

He had his own reasons for keeping this fair on schedule. His disappointment over losing out to Chicago a dozen years earlier had been tinged with bitterness. Now that he had a fair of his own, he could afford to be gracious. Indeed, with the passage of time he had found it easier and easier to give that city its due. Yet on one point Francis would not give an inch: While there was no denying that Chicago had put on a credible show, it had missed the whole point. "Columbus sailed the ocean blue in eighteen hundred and ninety-two." The Columbian Exposition celebrating the four-hundredth anniversary of that historic event took place in eighteen hundred and ninety-*three*. Chicago's inability to have the Columbian Exposition up and running on the appointed date was a blot on the brilliance of the White City itself. Failure to open a fair on the anniversary of the occasion it celebrated was, in a word, unconscionable.

There would be no such failure on the part of David R. Francis.

George Catlin sketch (ca. 1835) of Santee Dakota women playing double ball.

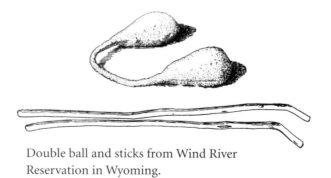

Double ball and sticks from Wind River
Reservation in Wyoming.

Fort Shaw gymnasium, physical culture class. The girls are drilling with Indian clubs. This photograph was taken sometime after the turn of the century, when the gymnasium had been "modernized," with a raised ceiling and a wooden floor.

Students in formation on the Fort Shaw parade grounds, with school buildings in background.

The Johnson sisters, in a
photo taken at Fort Shaw.
Left to right: Belle, Ida, and
Mary.

Jenny Johnson and five of her six children. Charles, far left and barely discernable, is squatting in front of the horses. Standing, left to right, are William, Belle, Jenny and Mary; in the wagon are James and Ida.

Outdoor basketball drill at Fort Shaw. Because the
girls are wearing school uniforms rather than bloomers, it is likely this drill took place during a physical
culture class.

Fred C. Campbell, superintendent of Fort Shaw Indian
Boarding School and team coach, ca. 1902.

Fort Shaw girls' string orchestra, ca. 1907. Katie Snell and Sarah Mitchell are the two girls (with guitars) at the very right of the top row; Genevieve Healy (violin) is at the far right in the bottom row. The 1904 mandolin club that went to the world's fair featured four different stringed instruments: the mandolin, guitar, violin, and cello.

WHY OUR GIRLS LOST

SCORE
INDIANS - 15
HS — '9

After the Basketball Game Was Over Last Night the Indian Maidens Sprung the Fact That They Had a Mascot Along in the Shape of a Little Red Warrior—How Could the High School Girls Expect to Win Against Such Odds.

Cartoon printed in *Butte (Mont.) Inter Mountain*, November 28, 1902, the morning after a Butte High School loss to the Fort Shaw team. The child depicted in feathers represents the Fort Shaw "mascot," ten-year-old Louis Youpee.

The 1903 team. Standing, left to right: Nettie Wirth, Belle Johnson, Minnie Burton, Genie Butch; seated, left to right, Delia Gebeau, Josephine Langley, Emma Sansaver.

Josephine Langley as assistant matron at Fort Shaw.

School Spirit
1900–1901

OUT IN MONTANA FRED CAMPBELL READ WITH INTEREST THE news coming from Missouri. A world's fair in St. Louis. He would have to plan a vacation around that fair. Ella and the children would be excited about a trip home to Kansas, combined with perhaps a week in St. Louis. He might even make it a surprise and not say anything yet, for three years would be a long time for the boys to wait.

In the meantime, there were more pressing things to attend to. For instance, if Fort Shaw athletics were ever to be showcased, the school would need a new gymnasium. He had emphasized that need—along with the need for a new hospital and two new dormitories—in his year-end report to D.C. But those requests had fallen on deaf ears, again. There would be no new gymnasium, although there would be new equipment. Washington had approved the money for extra barbells, dumbbells, and Indian clubs for the physical culture classes as well as for uniforms and gear to equip the football team that Mr. Sargent had pronounced as ready to play. Next year's budget, Campbell promised himself, would have an item for the purchase of the material and patterns for the uniforms that would be needed when the girls' basketball team came into its own.[1]

When, not if, for the girls were coming right along. Lizzie Wirth's leadership would be sorely missed, but Campbell could hardly begrudge such a talented young woman the opportunity to continue her education at Carlisle. Josie Langley would once again be the heart of the program, and the other girls who had shown such promise last spring would no doubt continue to improve. Most of them had stayed on campus and maintained their practices over the summer—with the exception of the troubled young Flora Lucero. Her mother, pregnant and still in mourning, had asked that Flora and Lawrence be allowed to spend the summer at home, and Campbell had not had the heart to deny the request. He could only hope they would choose to come back in the fall, but he was by no means certain that they would.[2]

~

September 1900. Duty to their mother had kept the Lucero siblings in Choteau that summer, but now Flora was literally pacing the floor. She had worried for weeks that her father would not come home in time to get her and Lawrence back to Fort Shaw for the beginning of the fall term. Whenever he sat down to that poker table in the Dupuyer saloon, she knew he gave little thought to any responsibilities at home.

Getting back to Fort Shaw was uppermost in Flora's mind. And not only because she was eager to return to her friends, her sewing classes, and basketball practices. Getting back to the campus had become a matter of self-preservation. Over the summer months the arguments between her parents had become more violent each time her father returned home, and Flora had begun to look forward to his increasingly long absences. But now that she really wanted and needed him to come through the door, days had passed without his reappearance. School had started more than two weeks ago. How much longer could she and her brother afford to wait?

No longer, their mother decided. Lawrence would hitch up the horses and drive the wagon up to Dupuyer. She would pack him a lunch and dinner. He could stop overnight at the Bynum store and be in Dupuyer in the morning. If he had to drag his father out of the saloon, so be it. No matter how drunk he was, a ride on the floor of the farm wagon would shake the whiskey right out of him. And by the time Lawrence got him home, she could fill him up with coffee and point him in the direction of Fort Shaw.[3]

This was not the way Flora had envisioned her trip to school that fall. But at least she would get there.

With Lawrence on his way, Flora slept well for the first time in days, little knowing the scene that was building at Dean's Saloon in Dupuyer.

All through that night of September 25, Philip Lucero was drinking his way through hand after hand of poker. Mostly the cards kept falling his way. By 4 A.M. everyone else had folded, leaving only Lucero and Baldy Smith, the bartender, at the table. By late morning, a small crowd had gathered as men who had given up on waiting out the game the night before began drifting in to see how the action had gone. Lucero's chips and Smith's silence told the story. It was time to fold and go home. Then two kings fell. An accusation was thrown, a knife was drawn, and Smith fled the bar.[4]

The game and the night were done.

Stiff-arming the saloon's double doors, Lucero stepped out onto the boardwalk and breathed in the crisp morning air. A shot rang out. Then another. Philip Lucero went down.

According to the *Dupuyer Acantha*, Philip Lucero, "known as Philip the Spaniard, was shot and killed instantly" by David P. "Baldy" Smith following a dispute over a poker game. The paper laid the blame solely on the Spaniard. Lucero had "been on the war path" all night, calling Smith "vile names," and threatening him with a knife. The reporter failed to note that Lucero's nine-year-old son had arrived at the saloon in time to see his father fall.[5]

As quickly as Lawrence could get the body home, the family shut themselves off from the rumors that swirled up and down the corridor from Dupuyer to Choteau. They did not even read the article in the *Acantha* that spoke of the "sympathy of the entire community" that went out to them in the wake of their loss, but they did receive word that a hastily summoned coroner's jury had found Smith "criminally responsible" for the death of Philip Lucero, and he had been summarily escorted to jail.[6]

With her father dead and buried, Flora knew the guilt that comes from wishing someone would never come back again—only to have that wish come true.

It would be another full month before she and her brother felt ready to go back to Fort Shaw, by which time everyone had heard of the shooting in Dupuyer. Anxiety engulfed the campus. Emma Sansaver's brother, Isadore, by now one of Superintendent Campbell's most trusted Indian assistants, was sent to Choteau to pick them up. Though Isadore had seen his own share of loss and violence, he kept his feelings to himself and his eyes on the road ahead, never once looking over his shoulder at the children who rode in silence behind him in the wagon bed. But there were warmer welcomes awaiting the two at school. The superintendent himself was on hand to greet them. Josie Langley and the basketball girls took Flora off to the gym. They could easily fit in a scrimmage before it was time to freshen up for supper. And Mr. Parker led Lawrence off toward the band room where the boys were working on a new march for the upcoming football game.[7]

~

The band was as ready as the football team itself when the boys from Great Falls High arrived to take on the Fort Shaw Indians on the roughed-out field abutting the parade grounds. The band—as well as the entire student body and a few of the valley families—lined the field on the afternoon of November 10, cheering the Indians to a 58 to 0 rout of the visitors. Undaunted, the Great Falls coach challenged Fort Shaw to a rematch at the city's Black Eagle Park.[8]

On Thanksgiving Day, November 29, 1900, the two teams met again for "the first game of Rugby football" ever played in the city of Great Falls. School spirit ran high on both sides. The Fort Shaw team was led onto the field by "a number of girls carrying bright banners," and their fans greeted them "with a series of school yells." Fort Shaw was again victorious, this time by a score of 21 to 0. The "superior playing of the Indians was cheered vociferously," and the *Great Falls Tribune* commended the boys for their "most gentlemanly" conduct. The girls were commended for the gaiety they had added with their banners, their songs, and their cheers. And F. C. Campbell was delighted by the enthusiastic support of the Great Falls fans.[9]

With Great Falls seemingly under the spell of his students, Campbell determined to win over the other major cities in the state. As he had hoped, Butte, the largest city of all, agreed to host a football game in early December. To his surprise, the townspeople of Butte rolled out the red carpet, not only meeting the boys at the station upon their arrival the evening before the game but also entertaining them that night with a minstrel show. Although the fifteen hundred fans in attendance at the game the next day saw the Fort Shaw Indians go down in defeat 15 to 0, Campbell considered the experience a rewarding one for his students and his school. As for his own expectations of the team? His boys might not be on a par with that Carlisle eleven that was making national news for toppling some major teams in the East, but Carlisle had been building its program for a while and the Fort Shaw program had just gotten under way. There would come a time, Campbell felt, when Fort Shaw would rise to the top of the sports world too.[10]

There was no way the superintendent could yet know that in a few short years it would be his basketball girls, not his football boys, who would fulfill his expectations.

~

A little more than two weeks after the game in Butte that closed the school's brief football season, Fort Shaw students, staff, and faculty gathered in the chapel for a Christmas program. Later that day the entire school enjoyed a bounteous holiday feast of turkey, stuffing, cranberries, rutabagas, potatoes, bread, and pies. Each student was given a stocking filled with candy, nuts, and an orange, along with a small gift. An afternoon of taffy pulling, games, and caroling brightened the holiday, despite the homesickness that made the celebration bittersweet for those children accustomed to spending Christmas with families now far away.[11]

Nettie Wirth, who had not celebrated a single Christmas at home since arriving at Fort Shaw as a six-year-old, was not thinking of home but of Lizzie, for the two sisters had never spent a Christmas apart. Sensing Nettie's loneliness, Josie Langley shared reassuring memories of Christmas at Carlisle. There was snow. There was a tree with candles. And Lizzie would have a stocking with candy and nuts and an orange in Pennsylvania, just as Nettie had in Montana. But Lizzie did not have Nettie. And Nettie did not have Lizzie.

There was no way around it. The holidays were tinged with loneliness for almost all of Fort Shaw's students. Yet over time, for those who had found some kind of contentment and purpose there, the school had become a home away from home. And for Nettie and Flora, Emma, Belle, and Katie—and for Mattie Hayes and Gen Healy and Minnie Scoldbear as well—friends had become almost sisters, sharing dreams and hopes, good news and bad, and hours of racing up and down the dirt floor of the old dance hall, passing and dribbling and shooting a basketball. Their pairing up into teams and playing against one another had strengthened, not lessened, their sense of unity. There was the ongoing challenge of shuffling the lineups, of creating squads so evenly matched that the outcome was unpredictable and victory hard-won.

But the girls were beginning to long for the chance to test themselves against another school and in front of a crowd. They had gotten a taste of what that kind of excitement meant on that windy November afternoon when they ran onto Black Eagle field, banners waving, the football team close on their heels, the crowd cheering. Accustomed as they were to winning the applause of an appreciative audience during the school's various entertainments, the applause at those events was entirely different from what they had experienced at Black Eagle Park. During programs the audience always waited politely until a given number was over. During games the crowd yelled in the midst of the action, becoming an integral *part* of the action. The football team had enjoyed that kind of applause. Now it was their turn.

Josie Langley shared the sentiments of her younger teammates, but as a member of the staff as well as the team, she felt obliged to seek the middle ground, championing their cause while offering them advice about how to go about achieving their objectives. Tact and diplomacy would be required. They would do well to plan their strategy carefully, choosing exactly the right moment to broach the subject with Superintendent Campbell.

For Genevieve Healy the right moment came on a February afternoon when Josie was late to practice. As soon as Miss Malley entered the gym, Gen accosted her with the question uppermost in everyone's mind. It had been almost a year since Superintendent Campbell had first talked about organizing a girls' team at Sun River so they could play against someone other than themselves. Just when could they expect that to happen?

And what about the uniforms he had mentioned last fall? They would need bloomers and stockings and middies. They could make everything but the stockings, if the school would just give them a pattern and enough material to work with. Considering how much had been spent on the helmets, padded uniforms, shoes, and everything else the man from Spalding had said was required for interscholastic football competition, was a little wool serge and a Butterick pattern too much to expect?[12]

Somewhat taken aback by Gen's outburst, Miss Malley reminded the players that while she was proud of the team spirit they had developed, team spirit must always be secondary to the *school* spirit they had displayed in supporting the football team last fall. The boys on that team had already proven themselves and would be the school's primary athletic ambassadors next year. So how, Gen demanded, could the basketball team ever prove *themselves* if they were never allowed to compete against another school in the first place?

Sending the girls back out onto the floor, Miss Malley promised to ask the superintendent to look into the matter of forming a Sun River team as soon as possible, although she doubted the young women of the town would be able to field a squad that would offer much competition. After all, they had had very little, if any, experience with the sport. She sounded one other cautionary note. Sun River was one thing, but she held out little hope of scheduling any games outside the valley. At least not any time soon. But with continued hard work and a little patience, who knew what the future might hold for the basketball girls from Fort Shaw Indian School?

New Connections and Old
1901

On the Lemhi Reservation in southeastern Idaho, Agent Yearian was waiting for word from Washington. He was sorely in need of a replacement for the school seamstress, who had left abruptly in early March. An accomplished Indian girl would be perfectly acceptable for the post, and he had recommended one of his own students. Sixteen and "large for her age," Minnie Burton, the interpreter's daughter, was healthy, strong, "competent and thoroughly qualified for the position." Yearian had no doubt whatsoever that she would "do better than almost any girl" who might be sent from Carlisle or Haskell. Hiring Minnie Burton would also inspire some of her classmates to devote themselves to their studies in hopes of rising to similar heights. There was one other consideration. This would likely be Minnie's last year at the agency school, given her age and the fact that she had already met— or exceeded—all requirements for completion of her schooling there. And Yearian feared that unless she was given this position or decided to transfer to an off-reservation school, this exemplary young woman might well "go back to camp life" at the end of the term.[1]

The smell of spring was in the air as fourteen-year-old Rose LaRose watched Miss Crawford make her way around the semicircle of parents and grandparents who had brought their children into the agency compound at Fort Hall to begin their rail journey from Idaho to Montana. She approached each family group with an air of genuine kindness, reassuring them that although they would miss their children, they were doing the right thing to allow them this opportunity to study at one of the finest off-reservation schools in the country. Then she waited patiently as her words were repeated in Shoshone by the interpreter.

Miss Crawford was the main reason Rose LaRose had begged to transfer to Fort Shaw that April of 1901. Not once in the three years since this teacher had begun visiting the reservation had Rose ever heard her raise her voice, even though there had been many parents who had turned their backs and walked away, saying things Rose had been glad Miss Crawford could not understand and the interpreter chose not to convey. She, of course, understood exactly what those parents were saying, and she understood their fears that children sent so far away from home for such a long time would forget their own language and the ways of their people.[2]

Rose herself was glad to have learned the English language first at home and then at the agency school. Her father had encouraged her efforts, since his experiences as tribal policeman had shown him how useful the language could be. Useful. But hardly easy. Even after knew English fairly well, she found it exhausting to try to think and speak in a language so different from her own. She had always looked forward to the times she was allowed to visit her family, times when she could communicate her thoughts with ease, using the words she had grown up with. Now that she was going so far away, those times would be fewer and farther between. She might not be able to come home again until she was eighteen and done with her studies. By that time would she, like Miss Crawford, be unable to understand her own people?

What exactly *was* "the language of her own people"? Rose's mother, Nettie Kutch LaRose, had grown up speaking Bannock, the language of her mother, and English, the language of her father. Rose's father, Fred LaRose, spoke Shoshone, the language of his mother, and the Métis mix of French, Chippewa, and Cree that his father had spoken—plus the English in which he and Rose's mother sometimes conversed and the language he used when talking with the agent and other reservation officials. If her parents could hold onto so many languages at once, she and her brother Leonard ought to be able to do the same. Rose vowed

then and there to make sure the two of them found someplace private
to use Shoshone at Fort Shaw.[3]

~

Pleased as he was by the arrival of the new students from Fort Hall
that April, Superintendent Campbell was grappling with a problem that
seemed to escalate each year with the coming of spring. Runaways. This
time Katie Snell's fifteen-year-old brother Richard and Gen Healy's ten-
year-old brother Willie had somehow managed to make it all the way
back to their homes on the Fort Belknap Reservation without being
caught. Worse yet, neither James Snell nor Colonel Healy seemed to
be in any hurry to send the boys back. Then there was Belle Johnson's
younger brother James, a chronic runaway. And now that his mother
was dead, Campbell had all but given up on getting James returned to
Fort Shaw.[4]

Having long puzzled over the wide spectrum of attitudes toward
boarding school life exhibited among his students, Campbell had found
those differences among children from the same family the most difficult to explain. The Snells, the Healys, and the Johnsons were perfect
examples. Jennie, Katie, and little Daisy Snell were model students, while
their brother Richard had become increasingly discontented. Similar
differences were apparent in the Johnson siblings. Mary, Charlie, Belle,
and even young Ida, were campus leaders. For Willie and James there
had been nothing but turmoil.

None of the Healy children had adjusted easily to the rules and rigors
of boarding school life. Even after five years at Fort Shaw, Gen remained
as mischievous as ever, but her contentment with all her classes, her
friendships, and her love of basketball had allowed her to focus her
energies in positive ways. Conversely, eleven-year-old Willie, on edge
from the moment he first set foot on campus, had habitually defied authority, incurring punishments that only fueled his resentment toward
the school and its teachers. Gen and Willie Healy had come to Fort
Shaw at the same time. One had settled in. The other had not. Why?

For whatever reasons, boys from all three of these families had followed the example of other malcontents and run away from a life they found intolerable. How could he reach these children—and others who stayed in place, even when their longing for home and family made campus life something to be endured rather than enjoyed. The answer eluded Campbell. He could only push the question aside and concentrate on educating the reachable ones.

If there were problems as the school year moved toward an end, they were hardly apparent at a most impressive end-of-the-year event. Superintendent Campbell had managed to convince U.S. senator Paris Gibson to come over from his home in Great Falls and inspect the government boarding school that was practically in his own backyard. In honor of the visit by Senator Gibson, the *Great Falls Tribune* devoted the entire front page of its May 26 edition to coverage of what its feature editor hailed as "one of the largest and best of the Indian boarding schools."[5]

This was the first time Senator Gibson and his colleague from the House of Representatives, Caldwell Edwards, had ever been on campus, and they were more than favorably impressed by the exemplary behavior of the students. According to the reporter, they marveled at the ability of only "30 employees and teachers all told to control" the 316 children in their charge, especially since most of those children had "come from the tepees of savage parents . . . and ha[d] ever been free to go and come when they chose." The elaborate precision drills performed on the parade ground by the boys' and girls' battalions gave further evidence of the regimentation and discipline under which the students lived and worked. And a look at their essays and other classroom work had led the visitors to conclude that academically these children were "much further advanced than [Montana's] white children of the same age." The reporter summed up the day's tour by noting that "to say that the statesmen and those who accompanied them were astonished" by all they observed would be "putting it mildly."[6]

F. C. Campbell could not have been more pleased by all that transpired on that day. His yearly report to the commissioner of Indian affairs dwelt on "the honor" paid the school by a visit from Senator Gibson and Congressman Edwards. Both gentlemen appeared to be "very much in favor of the education, on industrial lines, of Indian youths," and Campbell predicted that their influence in Washington would be of great benefit not only to Fort Shaw but to "Indians and Indian schools generally."[7]

~

Leaving the superintendent to follow through on his promise to create enthusiasm for basketball among the young women of Sun River, several of the girls on Fort Shaw's nascent team went home that summer of 1901. For some it was the first visit home since enrolling in the school. Almost nine years had passed since Nettie Wirth and her sister Louise had seen their family, and Nettie found it hard to imagine what "home" would be like, given all that had changed in her absence. The half sister she had never seen had returned to the reservation. Her mother had left her father and married another man. Her father, too, had married again and moved into what he described as a fine house in Poplar, where he worked as the baker at the agency school. All of this Nettie knew only through his infrequent letters. Now, finally, she was going home to see things for herself. Her mother she did not worry about. Susan Wirth was a strong woman, as her Indian name would imply. Lizzie had always said the Wirth sisters had been shaped from birth by the influence of Woman That Kills Wood. But Nettie *did* worry about her father.[8]

That summer visit only reinforced Nettie's worries. Jacob Wirth was not doing well at all. In fact, he had just resigned as the agency school baker. On consecutive visits, the government inspector had found the bakery wanting in every way. According to his reports, the baker was "a . . . filthy old squaw-man . . . whose example for cleanliness cannot count for much among the children." Major Scobey, the Indian agent at Poplar, had defended Wirth. The building in which the baker worked was "almost beyond repair." If a new bakery could be built—perhaps closer to the kitchen so Wirth would, in effect, "be under constant inspection"—then all would be well. Wirth's bread was tasty, and it was clean enough to suit him and the children. And where, pray tell, would he be able to find another baker to replace Wirth?[9]

But Agent Scobey's defense had come too late to salvage Wirth's pride. Lodging a scathing rebuttal to the inspector's criticism in a letter to Washington, Wirth had resigned his position, and by the time Nettie arrived in Poplar, her father was unemployed, depressed, and living with her stepmother in a shack Agent Scobey described as "an absolute disgrace to any halfway respectable Indian."[10]

Nettie's vacation turned into an ordeal to be endured. At least her mother seemed happy with Grasshopper. But Nettie knew that neither her mother's home nor her father's would ever truly be *her* home again.

~

For Belle Johnson and her little sister, Ida, who had not been back to Heart Butte since the death of their mother, there was also no going home. They spent the summer of 1901 with their uncle, their mother's brother—once known as Sleeping Wolf, now known as Charles Martin—on his ranch in the northern reaches of the Blackfeet Reservation. Uncle Charles and his wife treated Belle and Ida as their own and assured the girls they could come back to the ranch any time and stay as long as they wished. There were fields to wander, good food to eat, and cousins to play with. Yet by summer's end, Belle found herself looking forward to getting back to Fort Shaw and scrimmaging with her teammates once again.[11]

~

While Belle and Ida Johnson spent their vacation on their uncle's ranch near the Canadian border, Emma and Flora Sansaver were in Havre again, at the home of their sister Mary Sansaver Dubois. It was not the way Emma would have preferred to spend her summer. She would much rather have stayed at Fort Shaw, as she had the two previous summers, helping Mrs. Campbell with the housework, looking out for the boys, and tending little Freda. Havre was tainted by painful memories of the Métis camp—and by cruel comments about her mother's mysterious disappearance. She would rather not have those old wounds reopened. But Flora was lonely for Mary, and Emma could hardly have turned down the chance for the three of them to be to-gether again. It was good to see Mary's happiness in her marriage, and it was fun to play with her lively youngsters. But Emma missed her team-mates. Could they possibly be as eager as she was to get their hands on a basketball again?[12]

~

Katie Snell's summer at home was not what she had expected it to be. This was to have been the summer she would have bounced her new baby sister on her knee, carried her on her back while she worked in the garden, rocked her to sleep in the twilight. But tiny Alice had died within two months of her birth. Katie was concerned for her mother. Not only did Fanny Black Digger have the care of the house and her huge garden to fill her days, it seemed as if three-year-old George was always clinging to her skirts. *And* she was expecting yet again. Katie dedicated the summer to trying to ease her mother's workload, doing everything she could to help her get through the hot summer days and get ready for the fall when the baby would arrive and there would be no household help. With Jennie, she canned and dried fruits and vege-tables and filled the shelves in the root cellar. With Daisy, she kept little George entertained and out of his mother's way. And in between, she showed off her baking and sewing skills by turning out loaves of bread and berry and custard pies for family dinners and stitching up work shirts for her father and Richard.

In the evenings, when they were all together, she and Jeannie would talk with Richard, trying to understand his discontent at Fort Shaw. How could he not enjoy such an exciting place? Often as not, Jennie grew angry with him and walked away from the argument, but Katie really wanted to understand. She could only hope that her patience would pay off. By the time she and Jennie and Daisy left for Fort Shaw late that August, Richard was promising her that he would think about returning to school, once he had finished helping their father with the harvest.[13]

~

Superintendent Campbell, still buoyed in spirits after Senator Gibson's visit to the campus, now turned his attention to fulfilling his promise to start a girls' basketball team at Sun River. He had gotten to know the community and its residents quite well, and having enlisted the support of the school principal and the town's most influential citizens—all of whom seemed delighted with the idea of having a team represent the Sun River Valley—he began the search for possible players. As was the case in most rural areas, girls who had completed the eight grades offered at the local school generally stayed on in the vicinity, at least until they married. Several of those graduates—most notably Edna Blossom and Norma Robertson, daughters of Main Street proprietors, and Blanche Ish, whose father was a freighter—seemed eager for the chance to socialize as well as exercise with a group of other young women. Within days a skeletal team began to shape up.[14]

Having set the plan in motion, Superintendent Campbell went back to the business of running Fort Shaw School, leaving Josie Langley in charge of tutoring the Sun River girls in the rudiments of basketball. Josie was not entirely alone in her work. Mattie Hayes, Minnie Scoldbear, Flora Lucero, and a few other girls who were spending the summer on campus were eager enough to join their future opponents in drills and scrimmages, all the while looking forward to the return of their Fort Shaw teammates.

Staking Out the Fair
St. Louis, 1901

High noon, September 3, 1901. David Francis stood in the midst of the directors of the Louisiana Purchase Exposition Company—the LPEC. In his hand was a stake of polished oak. In his mind was a vision of something much grander than this weedy patch on the western edge of Forest Park. He saw stately colonnaded buildings, cascading fountains, terraced flowerbeds, and hundreds of thousands of people from all parts of the globe strolling the grounds of the grandest fair ever mounted.[1]

But all great journeys must begin with one small step. And today the LPEC was taking one small step. As the *Globe-Democrat*'s photographer pushed closer, Francis nudged the stake into the soggy ground, at about the center of where the fairgrounds, as yet nothing more than architects' renderings, would rise. Then he stepped back, and William Thompson, chair of the committee on grounds and buildings, brought the head of an axe down on the stake, driving it into the sodden ground. The directors, the reporters, even the photographer broke into applause.[2]

No one enjoyed ceremony quite as much as David Francis, and yet this day he would just as soon have been back at his office. There was so much to be done, perhaps too much. Eighteen, nineteen months between now and April 30, 1903? One could think of that as a generous stretch of time. But Francis knew what had to be accomplished between now and the opening day of the St. Louis World's Fair, and it was beginning to keep him up nights.

Not that much hadn't already been done. For instance, the very fact that they were standing here in Forest Park on this late summer's day meant that the site of the fair had finally been determined. It would rise on the very best location St. Louis had to offer. The park's gently rolling terrain would yield locations of special interest for the ground plan Francis and his architects envisioned. Just as important, the site lay on the western edge of town, next to residential areas where the affluence of the city's bourgeoisie was most in evidence, where visitors from across the world would come face to face with the city's expanding energy. The choice of Forest Park had not met with universal approval. There were many citizens who objected to the destruction of parkland and the loss of hundreds of majestic old trees. Letters to the editor complained that no matter how many silver maples might be brought in to line the fairgrounds' walkways and plazas, they could not replace the natural beauty of the groves of Forest Park.[3]

Then there was the challenge of rerouting the River Des Peres, of bringing water, gas, and sewer lines to this rugged, undeveloped site. And the 657 acres of Forest Park that had been set aside could not possibly support the size of an exposition such as the directors of the LPEC were touting to the public, not to mention to the federal government and the governments of the many foreign nations that had committed their resources to this endeavor. And the engineers had not yet even brought in their estimates of the costs involved in site preparation for the land they already had.[4]

Francis tried to push these worries aside as he exchanged hearty congratulations with the men who had gathered to celebrate this driving of the first stake. He himself, uncharacteristically, waved aside an invitation to say a few words, but others stepped into the breach. Isaac Taylor, newly appointed as the fair's director of works, whose concerns should have matched Francis's own, was upbeat. He reminded the onlookers of President McKinley's invitation to "all the Nations of the Earth" issued barely two weeks earlier. Francis tried to tap into Taylor's enthusiasm. It was unlike him to see a glass half-empty. He should be taking as much pleasure and pride in this day as the others were. After all, McKinley himself had noted that this fair in St. Louis would be the greatest of expositions. It would demonstrate America's progress in the century since the Louisiana Purchase. It would promote friendly relations with the peoples of the world. And while this went unspoken by the president, it was of great significance to Francis: the St. Louis World's Fair would dwarf Chicago's Columbian Exposition in size and scope.[5]

Scope. It was not just the choice of location that had finally been decided. The directors of the LPEC had, in all their wisdom, also settled on a unifying theme. The fairgrounds would constitute, in essence, a "University of the Future." Every exhibit, from the palaces to the Pike, would be designed to educate the fairgoer, and the department of anthropology—the first department to be so designated—would be at the heart of that educational mission. It would present a "Congress of the Races" that would clearly illustrate the virtues of Progress versus Primitivism.[6]

The members of the fair's anthropology committee had already consulted with WJ McGee, preeminent anthropologist and most recently the head of the federal Bureau of Ethnology. McGee had proposed an exhibit that would provide a stark contrast to the modern marvels on display in the fair's majestic halls and palaces, enabling the exposition as a whole to convey a sense of the march of progress "from the dark prime to the highest enlightenment, from savagery to civic organization, from egoism to altruism." For his part, McGee proposed transporting representative groups of indigenous peoples to the fairgrounds and establishing them in replicas of their "natural setting," thereby creating a living exhibit designed to show fairgoers "something of [the] upward course of human development."[7]

The anthropology committee had agreed that McGee's exhibit could have great visitor appeal and could easily be the most notable feature of the fair. The committee members had shared his ambitious vision, including his projected budget, with Francis. The exhibit would cover one hundred acres and could cost upwards of $2 million. It would also take a minimum of two years to mount.[8]

This exhibit would clearly set the St. Louis World's Fair apart from any other. Yet the figures had stunned David Francis. And he could not shake them from his thoughts this September day.

The Team Takes Shape
1901–1902

FIFTEEN-YEAR-OLD GENIE BUTCH ROSE EARLY, SLIPPED INTO THE blue denim jeans and striped shirt she had worn all summer, tugged on her boots, and headed out to do all her usual chores. Although her father had offered to do them for her, she wanted this morning to unfold like any other September morning. By the time she returned to the kitchen, her stepmother, Susan, was frying strips of bacon. A sprinkle of flour at one end of the table suggested the biscuits were already in the oven. She should have known this would not be an ordinary breakfast. There was too much love in this kitchen to let the day go by unmarked.[1]

There always had been plenty of love in this house, even when she and her father had been there alone after her mother died and her sisters, Josepha and Rosa, had gone away to the agency boarding school at Poplar River and then on to Fort Shaw. Too young to go so far away, Genie had been allowed to stay home and ride the range with her father, keeping him company and learning all the skills she would need when the place became hers. And there had still been enough love to go around after her father brought home a second wife, another full-blood Assiniboine called "Steps On" by her own people, "Susan" by Genie's father, and "Steps On *Joe*" by both her people and his, once it was clear Joe Butch would no longer be running his household—or his life—all by himself.[2]

By that time Genie herself was enrolled at the rebuilt Fort Peck agency school, and the school's then-new superintendent had quickly singled her out for her strong academics, high energy, and hard work. In fact, sensing her envy of the chores assigned to the boys, Fred Campbell had given her the special privilege of grooming his own team of horses and taking care of his buggy and tack.[3] He had also urged her father to think of allowing her to transfer to Fort Shaw. After his own move to the school in the Sun River Valley, Campbell had kept up the pressure on Joe Butch, although until now neither Genie nor her father had been ready for her to go so far away. Even that very morning, over what was supposedly her last breakfast at home, her father had told her there was still time to change her mind and stay on at the agency school.

But in Genie's own mind the matter was settled, even though she asked to be excused from the table to take one last ride along the bluffs above the river. As she drew near the familiar grove of alders, she reined in her cow pony, slid from his back, and tied the reins to a sapling. Then she made her way down the narrow path to her secret place on the Missouri, the spot where the ice had given way as A-nin ta-tca'n-gu Wa-ka'n was crossing to the other side of the river on a November day almost nine years ago. It was the spot Genie had visited every fall to say goodbye to her mother before leaving for the agency school. This time she lingered a little longer than usual before climbing back up the bluff, mounting her horse, and heading toward home at a gallop.[4]

Her father was waiting. There would hardly be time to wash up, change into her long muslin skirt and blouse, tuck in a few stray strands of hair, and make the wagon ride down to the railhead at Nashua, at a point only a few miles from her secret place on the bluffs above the Missouri. Superintendent Campbell and the students he was taking to Fort Shaw had caught the Great Northern at Poplar and were already moving west. Genie would be joining them at this station closest to home.

Home. But not home any longer.

This year there would be no waiting until October so she could help with fall roundup before returning to the agency school. This year there would be no way for her father to bring her home for Thanksgiving or Christmas, no chance to pull on her jeans and boots and ride her pony down through the coulee. This year there would be no spring branding, no long summer gallops toward an ever-receding horizon.

This year there would be only Fort Shaw.[5]

~

Despite the warm greetings from Superintendent Campbell, Genie Butch was subdued for the first hour or so of the journey west. That last glimpse of her father, waving to her from the platform, had renewed her misgivings about leaving home. She was still struggling with those thoughts when the train pulled up to the siding where students from the Fort Belknap Reservation were waiting to step aboard for their own journey to Fort Shaw.

There was no more time for quiet contemplation once Gen Healy paused in the aisle, caught sight of the Assiniboine stranger who looked to be as uncomfortable in a skirt as she was, and plopped down in the seat beside her. Eager as she was to share her summer adventures, Gen barely introduced herself to Genie Butch before plunging into stories about how she had finally proved to Ponley—whoever this "Ponley" might be—that she had learned her way around the kitchen and how she had finally convinced her father's wranglers that she still knew her way around a corral, and how she had done her best to convince her brother Willie that he needed to go back to Fort Shaw with her, but to no avail. Having spilled out her own story, Gen leaned back and prodded Genie. What had her summer been like? How did she feel about transferring to Fort Shaw? There was no escaping Gen Healy. Genie Butch began to open up. And long before the train pulled into Great Falls, Gen had convinced her new friend that she should learn to play this game called basketball.

~

Gen and the rest of the girls were no sooner back on campus that September of 1901 than Josie Langley gathered them around her in the gym. Word was that Josie had a surprise for them. First there was the introduction of the new girl. Genie Butch. She had never played before, but she was ready to give the game a try. Then came the real reason they had been called into the gym. Over the course of the summer the Sun River team had been formed, drilled, and readied for a game sometime within the next month or so. Now it was time to begin to figure out a Fort Shaw lineup that would show the school to best advantage.

The promise of the beginnings of interscholastic basketball play was the good news. The bad news was that football would remain the primary focus of Fort Shaw athletics again that fall. Superintendent Campbell had received a unique invitation. Would the Indians be willing to represent Great Falls in the newly formed Montana football league? Fort Shaw had a superior squad but lacked a suitable playing field and offered no lodging for visiting teams and fans. On the other hand, Great Falls had a fine field and numerous hotels and boardinghouses. But its high school team was far from ready to play against the top scholastic, college, and industrial teams in the state. Would the Indian boys be willing to form the heart of the Great Falls team? Would they be willing to wear the gold, royal purple, and red of Great Falls High?[6]

Campbell hesitated. He polled the team. This might well be their only chance to play against the best teams in the state because, for reasons he could only guess at, Fort Shaw had not been included in the newly formed, if still unofficial, league. But as Indians wearing Great Falls uniforms, they could prove their prowess and have a shot at the state championship. The decision was theirs, Campbell told them. And their response was unanimous. What did it matter whose colors they wore? It was time to show what Indians could do—even incognito Indians.[7]

That fall the boys put on a show that anyone would have been proud of. The Great Falls fans took them into their hearts. In an abbreviated season, the Fort Shaw/Great Falls club defeated the university in Missoula and the high school in Helena, played to a scoreless tie in a rematch against the capital city boys, and lost by a touchdown, 7 to 0, in front of 1500 spectators in a late November game in Butte.[8]

~

While the boys from the Butte High and the Great Falls/Fort Shaw teams were being royally entertained on the evening before their November 29 meeting on the gridiron, Coach W. J. Adams was over at Butte Auditorium, leading the basketball girls of St. Patrick's to an impressive win over Butte Business College. While this was but one of several games played between teams in the Smoky City since Billy Adams's return to his native town after graduating from the agricultural college in Bozeman, all those previous matches had been played behind closed doors at the high school gymnasium. This was the first basketball game played in a public arena, and reporters had taken due notice of that fact, alerting their readers to the upcoming contest and then describing the landmark game in sufficient detail to generate interest for future matches.[9]

According to the *Anaconda Standard*, "the sight of 10 graceful girls, gowned in short skirts [bloomers] with dainty feet skipping over the smooth floor, earnestly endeavoring to throw a huge inflated leather ball into baskets that are suspended high above their heads" would be ample reward for the spectator. The fans were indeed entertained by the game that evening, inspiring Billy Adams to organize more matches between city teams before taking his "Parochials" from St. Patrick's on the road. He had already invited the team from Bozeman's Business College to come to Butte to play his girls in December, and he was orchestrating a road trip to Dillon for a contest between the teachers' college and a hand-picked team from the best of Butte High School's players. He hoped to use this kind of momentum to build the basis for a statewide basketball league.[10]

~

Press reports of Billy Adams's activities did not escape Fred Campbell's notice. In the gym, as Josie and her teammates mingled with the Sun River players after the second of their scrimmages over the Christmas holidays, he voiced his concerns to Sadie Malley. These girls were obviously ready for much stiffer competition, but who knew that beyond the people in the valley? Now he was reading about teams in Butte and Bozeman, Missoula and Helena that were already scheduling interscholastic games. And his girls were not in the mix. Had his failure to heed their pleas for extracurricular games and for uniforms cost Fort Shaw the edge it had gained in being the school that first introduced Montanans to this game of basketball? He was going to rectify that. He was going to build a basketball program that would make W. J. Adams over at Butte sit up and take notice.

~

February at the Lemhi Agency School had been a distressing month for Minnie Burton. Until then, she had immersed herself in her work as seamstress, spending extra time with students who needed more help in learning new stitches and with those who were eager to learn everything she had to offer them. And all the while she was doing her best to avoid being part of the faculty squabbles that had long been endemic at the school. Yet suddenly she found herself caught up in a furor, pulled in because of her first-hand knowledge of dormitory life. She had, indeed, been living on the campus when, according to Agent Yearian's report, "several camp Indians had . . . been making regular visits to the girls' dormitory and had debauched all of the girls indiscriminately." To Minnie, Yearian's claim that *all* the girls in the dormitory had been involved was just the kind of exaggeration one might expect from a man who invariably characterized the Lemhi people as "entirely destitute of principles, morals, and common decency." Yet as a student among students, she had not challenged the agent.[11]

But this new crisis had roused her to action. This time Minnie Burton dared to speak out against Yearian's blanket condemnation of her people. Her protests fell on deaf ears. As much as she enjoyed teaching, she saw no way to repair the rent between cultures that seemed to be worsening day by day. She had declined the invitation of the Fort Shaw recruiter each time Miss Crawford had visited the reservation over the last two years, convinced as she was that Grandmother was right, that she should wait for the moment, that perhaps she had more to learn here at home. But now it seemed to her that moment had come. Only further schooling, away from the Lemhi Reservation, would give her the credentials—and the power—to come back home and change things for the better. She tendered her resignation to Yearian, announced her intention to transfer to Fort Shaw, and went down by the river to share the news with Grandmother Pea-boa.

On April 20, 1902, in the company of six other students from the agency, Minnie Burton began her journey to the school in Montana's Sun River Valley.[12]

Her timing would prove fortuitous.

~

By late spring of 1902 Superintendent Campbell had become Coach Campbell, joining Miss Malley and Josie Langley in their attempts to turn an enthusiastic group of Indian girls into a competitive basketball team. The new girl, Minnie Burton, immediately drew Miss Malley's attention in gymnastics class for her strength and coordination, and she invited her to join the girls' basketball practices. But Minnie declined. She had never played the game, she said, and if she were to give extra hours to anything, she thought she'd do better to concentrate on her classes and other required activities. At least at first. Perhaps over the summer months she would have the time. Miss Malley admired the girl's maturity, even as she alerted Coach Campbell to the fact that they had a promising recruit in the wings.

The superintendent was glad to get such news; he intended to make sure that Fort Shaw found a place on this full slate of interscholastic games that Billy Adams was scheduling for the upcoming school year. There was some risk involved. Campbell wanted nothing but excellence from his students in their public performances, and this girls' basketball team of his was untested. He could not know for sure how they would measure up, say against those teams from Butte. Or from Missoula, where the women at the state university were engaging in intramural games with regularity and were anticipating "match contests" against other teams as soon as the new gymnasium was completed. The agricultural college in Bozeman had been playing the game for some time now—thanks to Billy Adams's efforts during his senior year on that campus—and Helena High had also entered the competition.[13]

Superintendent Campbell was determined to give his girls the chance to test themselves against the best. More scrimmage games with the Sun River girls, perhaps outdoors in front of Fort Shaw students and folks from the valley, would be a good thing. But there was likely more to be gained from intramural games, given the strength of his bench. Plus daily drills on the basics, right through summer break. His team should be more than ready for the challenges that lay ahead. Whatever those challenges might be.

"Basket Ball Is the Thing"
Fall 1902

❦

BY SUMMER'S END COACH CAMPBELL HAD ALREADY COME TO THINK
of Minnie Burton as a likely starter. She added the height he had been
looking for. She handled the ball as if she had played the game all her
life. She seemed to intuit the flow of the action, was quick to the ball,
and could set up a play faster than any of the others. Her teamwork was
exceptional, perhaps because of her years playing double ball, perhaps
because the veteran players trusted her from the start. Minnie Burton
was the key to Campbell's plans to put Billy Adams and his Butte girls
in their place.

∼

But the basketball season, however it would develop, would not begin until late in the term. The first order of business for the 1902–1903
school year, as it had been for the opening of every year before, was
preparing the Fort Shaw exhibit for the Cascade County Fair. There
would, of course, be the customary display of student work from all
areas of the curriculum, work that had netted numerous blue ribbons,
earned the accolades of local reporters, and helped convince visitors of
the importance of all that was being accomplished at Fort Shaw.[1]

Yet there was always room for improvement, and this year Superintendent Campbell was adding a new component to the school's exhibit,
a component William Winslow would no doubt have deemed inap-
propriate, since it flew in the face of the basic tenets of Indian education. Indian boarding schools, had, after all, been designed to break
tribal loyalties, eradicate cultural traditions, and move children away
from their past and toward a more promising future. Now, a mere

four years after Superintendent Winslow's departure, Superintendent Campbell had devoted much of his summer to working with reservation agents and the families of his students in accumulating authentic examples of ceremonial attire and traditional crafts, tools, and musical instruments—even weapons typical of those once used against the soldiers at the military post out of which Fort Shaw School had sprung. And he intended to make those artifacts of the old way of life the highlight of the school's exhibit at the county fair.

The idea was not original with Campbell. In fact, he was only following the lead of the country's new superintendent of Indian education, Estelle Reel, who saw the traditional arts and crafts as a source of livelihood for indigenous peoples, particularly indigenous women. Reel had even once called for the creation of "emporiums for the display and sale of hand-wrought Indian goods."[2] Campbell was not yet prepared to give precious time and scarce resources to teaching students things they could always learn once they returned to their reservations, if that's what they chose to do. But he saw this exhibit as an opportunity to improve the self-esteem of students who had otherwise been taught to be ashamed of the traditions revered by their families. It might also, by way of no harm—and this was never far from Campbell's mind—draw record numbers of fairgoers to the school's display.

A buckskin dress trimmed out in elk's teeth; a breastplate made of porcupine quills; cradleboards; and a pair of beaded moccasins made by Blind Maggie, Minnie Burton's stepmother, were only a few of the items in the elaborate array of articles from the tribes represented within the Fort Shaw student body. And the exhibit did, indeed, draw record crowds. True to form, the local press weighed in on the event. A reporter for the *Great Falls Tribune* applauded the "Indian relics" in the school's display, which he judged the best ever mounted by Fort Shaw—and by far the best exhibit of the entire fair.[3]

Campbell could only wish that Miss Reel had been there to see it. She would have been as pleased as he was by the public's response. She would, in fact, be pleased with many other ways in which his school was beginning to make changes in line with her *Uniform Course of Study*. And then there was her outspoken advocacy of athletics for women.

Yes, it was time to entice the superintendent of Indian education to visit his school in the Sun River Valley.[4]

~

Superintendent Reel's support of athletics for women seemed like a mandate to Superintendent Campbell. He could hardly ignore the head-lines on sports pages around Montana that fall of 1902. "Basket Ball Is the Thing" trumpeted one Great Falls daily. Girls' basketball. Butte and Helena each had one year's interscholastic play behind them, and the university at Missoula and the college at Bozeman were boasting teams as well. Even so, Campbell had enough faith in his girls' potential that he worked toward arranging a series of matches against these more ex-perienced squads. Finally, in early November, he received confirmation of a Thanksgiving Day game against Butte High, the team with the best record in 1901–1902, followed by a game the next night against Helena High, the only team to defeat Butte in that abbreviated first season.[5]

With Fort Shaw's girls having had no experience other than intramu-ral games and a number of scrimmages against the Sun River team, the quality of their play remained unknown. It was obvious Billy Adams fully expected that Butte High would trounce the Indian girls, just as Butte's football team had defeated the Indian boys in their encounters. Adams's confidence in his girls was matched by his confidence that cu-riosity about an Indian girls' basketball team would help pack the Butte Auditorium—and bring in significant revenue for the high school's athletic program. A skilled promoter himself, Fred Campbell offered to bring along his mandolin club and gymnastics drill team for a pregame concert and exhibition, since several of the basketball girls were also members of those two groups. And the deal was struck.[6]

Now came the task of solidifying Fort Shaw's lineup. Which of his players should Coach Campbell choose as his starting five? The easiest choice was captain and center Josie Langley. Now in her late twenties, she was at least ten years older than most of the teenagers with whom she played. She would obviously lend both experience and leadership to the club. She brought one other advantage. As the heaviest girl of all the candidates, Josie knew how to use her body on the court. The Butte girls played a rough game—so rough that parents and high school officials over there were threatening to ban basketball, upset as they were by the hard-driving nature of the sport and the rowdy behavior of the fans. Josie was Campbell's best bet to counter Butte's aggressiveness.[7]

There were a number of good candidates for the two spots at forward, but Campbell favored Belle Johnson and Emma Sansaver. Belle had been barely eleven when she sat on the sidelines watching that first exhibition of "basket ball" at the closing ceremonies of June 1897. In the years since, she had developed into one of the steadiest players on the court, and the joy she took in playing, plus her diligence in practices, made her a clear choice for the team that would go to Butte. For her partner at forward, Campbell looked to the "Little One." Although less than five feet tall, Emma Sansaver made up in quickness what she lacked in height. Her swift and accurate passing, her dribbling skills, and her ability to decide in a split second whether to take a shot or pass the ball off made her virtually unguardable.[8]

Except by Minnie Burton. In addition to giving the team the height it needed, Minnie was the ball hawk, the one who could snare a pass the minute it left an opponent's hand, then turn and start the ball moving in the opposite direction. Her relative lack of experience aside, she was an obvious choice at guard. For the other guard spot Campbell favored Nettie Wirth. Nettie, like Belle, had been drawn to basketball from the day Josie Langley brought the game home to Fort Shaw. While not as tall as Minnie, Nettie was blessed with long arms and a vertical leap that enabled her to block shots that might otherwise go sailing through the hoop.[9]

Now to the substitutes. According to the rules, a team could carry only two substitutes, and they could enter the game only in the event that one of the starting five was injured. Even with such a limited role, they would still need to be as strong and talented as the members of the first team. Gen Healy was among Campbell's most eager and capable players, but at fourteen, she was also one of the youngest and she still tended to lose her composure in the thick of the fray. She was learning restraint, but she was still too unpredictable for this first outing. Katie Snell, tall and serene, had yet to develop the kind of aggression Campbell considered essential in games against experienced teams like Butte and Helena. If some of Gen's feistiness could be swapped for some of Katie's cool-headedness, those two could move up in the ranks. But not yet.

Then there was Mattie Hayes, who had come from Fort Peck with the first contingent of students back in 1892. Over the last few years Mattie had been one of his steadiest and most reliable players. And, at eighteen, she would give some maturity to the team, but Campbell did not see her as a well-rounded player. Not yet. Minnie Scoldbear's height could be an asset but she did not move as quickly as some of the other girls. Campbell also considered Genie Butch, whose all-out play made her a logical choice for the team. But there were others who came closer to the starters' level of play.

Including a newcomer, fifteen-year-old Delia Gebeau. A member of the Colville band of the Spokanes, Delia was a new transfer from St. Ignatius Mission School, where she had lived and studied since the age of six. She had barely arrived at Fort Shaw when she turned out for practice, and it was immediately obvious to Campbell that she brought a good deal of basketball experience with her. Querying her about this, he discovered what he might well have guessed. She had learned the game from her nephew Joe, who had been at Fort Shaw for two years now, had been playing on the outside court with his friends during their free hours, and had taken the game home to his brothers and cousins. Scrambling with the boys—older boys at that—had given Delia confidence on the court. Like Genie Butch, she moved easily back and forth between the forward and the guard positions. If she continued to improve, she should soon be ready to back up the first string.[10]

Still not quite sure of his choices for the traveling squad, Coach Campbell decided to ask for advice from the acknowledged authority on basketball in Cascade County, Fred Preston.

～

The cofounder of Great Falls Commercial College, Preston was a man for all sports. Having tried—and failed—to build a Great Falls football team capable of playing against some of the larger schools in the state, he was the one who had come up with the idea of asking the boys from Fort Shaw Indian School to don the colors of Great Falls High and become that school's team for the 1901 season. And he was disappointed when their success did not muster enough interest among the boys of Great Falls High to field a football team of their own in the fall of 1902. He had been similarly disappointed in not being able to entice the girls of the high school to take up basketball.[11]

Thus when Campbell called him and invited him to come out to the valley to help prepare the Fort Shaw girls for their late-November games in Butte and Helena, Preston jumped at the chance. Come on Friday night, November 14, Campbell said, and that will give you the entirety of Saturday to work with us.[12]

At breakfast that Saturday morning, the girls eyed Professor Preston with a mixture of anticipation and apprehension. With Coach Campbell—and with Josie and Miss Malley—they had always known where they stood. Professor Preston was an unknown factor, a stranger brought in to pass judgment on their abilities and help make final decisions as to who would make the traveling squad. He would also be introducing a number of plays with which they might or might not be comfortable and which they might or might not be able to execute. Little wonder the girls were unnaturally quiet as they warmed up in the gym. What does a business school teacher know about basketball anyway? Gen Healy grumbled.

Plenty, as it turned out. The well-muscled stranger walked onto the court, motioned for the ball, dribbled twice, and sank a shot from far beyond the foul line. Following his shot to the basket, he pulled the chain that let the ball fall free, scooped it up, and headed for center court, motioning for Josie Langley and Nettie Wirth to join him in the circle for a jump ball. Like James Naismith of old, Preston then signaled every girl in the gym to take the court. No teams or positions were assigned. The girls covered their confusion and scrambled for the ball that Nettie tipped to Belle. Belle passed it to Emma, who passed it back to Belle, who arched a shot over Genie Butch's outstretched arm. The ball missed the basket, careered off the backboard, and bounced out of bounds. The girls, frozen in place, looked to Preston.

That was the last time they stood still and watched as a ball missed its mark. Professor Preston's scowl was enough to tell them that he expected them to get untracked and start playing basketball. Quickly he singled out ten girls, seemingly at random, with no concern as to whether he had chosen guards or forwards or centers. Dividing the ten into two teams, he waited for Josie to hand out white armbands to five of the players, identifying them as one team, then stepped to center court, and called two girls, one with an armband, one without, to the center's position.

Ten minutes of action. A whistle. Another seemingly random juggling of players—including a couple pulled from the sidelines as substitutes—a quick exchange of armbands, and then another scrimmage. A whistle, a different pairing up.

The rest of the morning was spent refining the matchups, and by the time the girls were released to go to their dorms to wash up and head for the dining hall, there was no doubt in their minds as to why Coach Campbell had decided to bring in Professor Preston. Although not allowed to talk at table, the excitement in their eyes told the story.

The afternoon session found Preston choosing the same lineup Coach Campbell himself had first chosen: Josie at center, Minnie and Nettie at guard, and Emma and Belle at forward. His second team was as scrappy if not as strong, with Katie Snell at center, Genie Butch and Delia Gebeau at guard, and Minnie Scoldbear and Mattie Hayes at forward.

After a brief warm-up session, Preston bought out a slate and called the girls into a huddle around him. While Coach Campbell and Miss Malley watched from the perimeter of the circle, Preston began to sketch the first of several plays he would introduce that afternoon. Playing smart, he told the group around him, was as important as playing hard. It was more important, even, since running up court with no plan of attack yielded confusion, not points. With that, he pointed to two circles on his slate representing Minnie and Nettie, then drew in more circles. In staccato tones, he set everyone's position, everyone's role. Here, here, here, here, and here, his finger pointed from the slate to the floor to the slate again.

And then the girls were on the court, executing the play as well as they could, then speeding it up on the next try and the next before returning to Preston and his slate. Another play was sketched out, executed, polished, and then once again the chalk scratching across the slate.

They had the skill and the talent, he said, as the long session drew to a close. The strength, the endurance, the teamwork. And the choice. Would the Indians be the victors or the vanquished?

The answer lay in their hands, not his.

~

New plays were not the only thing the team needed to make a good showing in Butte and Helena. There was also this matter of uniforms. It was one thing to have played in makeshift bloomers and tops when Sun River was the opponent. But playing in two of the state's largest cities before crowds that could number in the hundreds or more, playing against teams whose girls would be wearing the very best uniforms and shoes Spalding had to offer was another thing altogether. Despite Josie's constant reminders, Superintendent Campbell had put off ordering the pattern—the Butterick's pattern from which teams all across the country now fashioned their uniforms—and the bolts of navy wool serge until he felt absolutely sure the games were in place.[13]

Now the girls raced against time. A week before game day, they received permission to be excused from their morning classes to spend those hours in the sewing room. Measurements were taken—waist, bust, inseam, sleeve—and Minnie pinned pattern pieces on dark wool, using white chalk to outline the extra inches Josie's measurements required. As soon as a sleeve or cuff had been cut, the pattern piece was handed back to Minnie, who began the process all over again, expanding or slimming, lengthening or shortening, adapting the pattern to fit the seven girls chosen to make this first trip.

Under the watchful eye of Mrs. Parker, each girl took charge of assembling some part of the outfit. Belle, Emma, and Nettie turned out the loose-fitting, tightly cuffed bloomers. Rose, Genie, and Gen produced the middy blouses to which Josie and Katie stitched collars and cuffs trimmed in white piping. Red-and-white striped dickeys came from the machines of Mattie Hayes and Minnie Scoldbear. And finally, Flora

Lucero and Delia Gebeau drew the best assignment, the final touch: monogramming the white "F" and "S" on either side of the wide sailor collars. Long black stockings that hid the ankles and lower legs from view and rubber-soled shoes turned out in record time by the boys in Mr. Goings's cobbler shop completed the outfits, the seven uniforms that would be worn proudly by the five starters—Josie, Minnie Burton, Emma, Nettie, and Belle—and the two substitutes, Minnie Scoldbear and Mattie Hayes.[14]

Over in Butte, Billy Adams was building the crowd, encouraging the press to play up the clash between races as a drawing card for the event. "White Girls against Reds" blared the Sunday morning headline in the *Anaconda Standard*. A basketball team of white girls was in itself quite "an attraction," the reporter noted. "[W]hat, then, may be said [about] a team of Indian girls?" They were not only "strong and lithe," but "very comely," and the reporter could only predict that "a great number of white boys will cheer for the dark-complexioned maidens." He went further, employing the vernacular of the day: "Three members of the team," he pointed out, "are full-blooded Indians and the others are half-breeds."[15]

A cartoon that appeared that same day in the *Butte Inter Mountain* depicted the Butte players dressed in uniforms worthy of a Gibson Girl and wearing the upswept hair style of the day. Sketched in at the edge of the cartoon was a handyman holding crutches and behind the girls stood a stretcher marked "High School Property." The promise of physical play and a touch of racism should be enough to guarantee a capacity crowd.[16]

Back home at Fort Shaw, the "dark-complexioned maidens," now only days from their first interscholastic game, could hardly wait to get their hands on the Sunday *Anaconda Standard* Coach Campbell had ordered delivered to the school. Elated as they were to be front-page news and accustomed as they were to the way white people talked about Indians, they had difficulty in dismissing the label of the "half-breed" and the reporter's confusion of their tribal affiliations. And how did he know whether they were "very comely" or "very homely," since they could not recall ever making his acquaintance?

Coach Campbell watched their reactions with interest, for this was their first exposure to reporting by writers who cared more about sensationalism than accuracy. Heretofore all the press releases coming out of Fort Shaw were in his words. From now on, he would have no control over what other coaches, other journalists might say. Now that he had moved the girls into the world beyond the Sun River Valley, they would have to take whatever the press handed out. It would be a hard lesson, and he hastened to point out the compensations. Consider all they had to look forward to in Butte—including the reception that would be held in their honor. Yes, the game itself would likely be just as competitive as the paper predicted. But once that final whistle blew, hostilities would be left on the floor and courtesy would rule. They could count on that.

Perhaps, but Gen Healy, who would be making the trip as a member of the mandolin club and the gymnastics team, even if she wouldn't be suiting up for the game, would not let go of the reporter's words. As the girls walked back to their dorm, she muttered, "They're going to see how half-breeds play basketball."

Testing Their Mettle
Thanksgiving 1902

ON NOVEMBER 26, 1902, THE DAY BEFORE THANKSGIVING, THREE farm wagons pulled away from Fort Shaw on their way to the railhead at Sunnyside. Harvey Liephart, the school baker and a would-be beau of Josie's, drove the lead wagon, wherein rode Coach Campbell and the team—plus a multitude of trunks and valises containing their basketball uniforms and the skirts, blouses, and scarves for the girls of the mandolin club to wear in performance. The second wagon, driven by Isadore Sansaver, carried Misses Malley, Crawford, and Patterson and the members of Miss Patterson's musical group. Gen Healy, disappointed not to be playing basketball but excited to be traveling with the team, waited until the two wagons were approaching Sun River before she pulled out her mandolin—which should, of course, have been packed with all the other instruments—and began to play. Many of the citizens of that little town had gathered on the street to watch the students pass by, and at the sound of Gen's mandolin and the chorus of girls' voices, they broke into applause.[1]

They were still clapping and waving when the third wagon, driven by Indian assistant John Minesinger, came into view. On the seat beside him sat ten-year-old Louis Youpee, who for the weekend would be known as "Lone Calf," the team mascot. In a carefully packed box behind the two lay the ceremonial dress of a boy chief, in addition to the outfits in which he would deliver two humorous recitations during the entertainment portion of the evening. As they drove along, Minnesinger, an experienced orator himself and a mentor of sorts for young Louis, listened as his protégé recited his "pieces," prompting the boy when he missed a word and cautioning him to anticipate audience reactions to some of his funniest lines and wait for the laughter to subside before continuing his recitation. Not too long. Just until the laughter begins to fade, then pick it up again.[2]

Behind the two boys, the box containing Louis's outfits lay alongside boxes of Indian clubs, barbells, and musical instruments wrapped in thick blankets, secure against jostling.

~

After the tedious pace of the wagons, the miles flew by as the entourage rode the "Turkey Trail" from Sunnyside to Great Falls, where Isadore and John joined Coach Campbell in transferring their cargo, while the other travelers boarded the Montana Central for the trip through Helena and on down to Butte. They had the car to themselves, and Louis Youpee, Lone Calf, stepped into the aisle and went through his recitations, complete with gestures and bows and exaggerated pratfalls each time the train rounded a curve and sent him sprawling. Not to be outdone, Gen Healy joined him in an impromptu dialogue. There was laughter and chatter, and plenty to talk about. But plenty to worry about, too. How would they be received? As the train rolled along from Helena toward Butte, the travelers fell into periods of quiet talk, then periods of pensive silence. These weekend games were getting a lot of newsprint around the state. The girls knew they had a lot to prove in these next few days—about themselves, about girls' basketball, and about their school.[3]

~

Whatever their anxieties, the Fort Shaw girls felt like champions when they stepped off the train to find Coach Adams and the Butte High team waiting to greet them. While exchanging pleasantries—and a few giggles—with their opponents, they tried to hide their reactions to the cityscape that spread out before them. No one had prepared them for the sight of smelter stacks belching a dark fog into the sky, or the sulphurous smell that rose from the open roasting pits. Their eyes burned from the acrid soot, and they were taken aback by the ugliness of Montana's largest city. As they made their way by streetcar toward their hotel, Miss Crawford assured them that Butte was not always like this.

She had stopped over on her many recruiting trips to Idaho and knew there were times when the smoke lifted, blown up and away, clearing the atmosphere and revealing a hazy blue sky. She wished they could see the other face of Butte—the city's mansions and the famous Columbia Gardens, with all the flowers and trees, the pavilions and carousel.[4]

The next morning, after Thanksgiving services at the Presbyterian church, Campbell gave the team a few hours to wander the streets in the vicinity of the hotel. Because of the holiday, those streets were far quieter than usual, and even at that, the atmosphere was foreign to anything the girls had seen before. Streetcars rattled past, disgorging their passengers in front of three- and four-story buildings. Department-store windows displayed the latest fashions; colorful awnings graced the entrances to saloons and restaurants; brick steps led up to multiple-family apartment houses.

After a mid-day meal in the hotel dining room, Campbell brought the girls' focus back to what lay ahead. One more round of rehearsals. First, the mandolin club, which would lead off the evening's entertainment. Miss Patterson took the girls through the program once, then turned the baton over to Nettie Wirth. It would be the first time Nettie would lead the group in public, but Miss Patterson had full confidence in her and in the eleven other musicians. Then Miss Malley put them through their Indian club drill, telling them to think of this as being no different from a physical culture class back at school. While the girls were engaged in these rehearsals, Miss Crawford joined John Minesinger in still more work with Louis Youpee, this time practicing not only his delivery but also the quick changes he would make from his boy chief's regalia to the baggy pants and shirt he would wear for one recitation and then into the tailored suit and black parson's hat he would wear for his final number.[5]

Then the girls headed over to the auditorium for their first look at the court. After a brief warm-up and a round of shooting from the free-throw line, the team gathered around Coach Campbell. The game they would play that night was no different from all the hard-fought intramural scrimmages they had played over the months they had worked together, he reminded them. Only the environment would be different. Butte was known for its partisan fans and their loud cheering and stomping. The girls would need to keep their eyes on the ball, stay steady in the midst of all the chaos, and concentrate on the game, not the crowd. It was a matter of trusting themselves and their teammates.

~

Despite the jitters, Nettie and the mandolin club performed flawlessly, with every number drawing a round of applause. The club-swinging and barbell drills were equally well executed, and the crowd's enthusiastic response reassuring. Then, while Lone Calf clowned his way to center stage in his preacher's garb, the girls on the team retired to the assigned dressing room to don their brand-new uniforms.

At eight o'clock sharp, they reentered the auditorium to a sound unlike anything they had heard before. The roar that echoed off the walls, the shouting and clapping and horn-blowing, were deafening, and for a moment all the girls could do was stare at the hundreds of people who had risen to welcome them. Since their performance no more than a half hour earlier, the crowd seemed to have doubled in size. There were people everywhere, in the hallways, in the galleries, and arranged in rows around the court itself. Across that court the girls from Butte were already shooting baskets, going through passing and dribbling drills, loosening up for the game. It could have been an intimidating sight, but Coach Campbell called his players to attention. He tossed a ball to Josie and watched with satisfaction as she set her teammates in motion—Belle and Emma, Nettie and Minnie—plus substitutes Minnie Scoldbear and Mattie Hayes. Campbell smiled. Seven Indian girls in their navy-blue bloomers and middies, moving with the grace and confidence that told him they belonged in this place on this night.[6]

Just before the whistle, Coach Campbell motioned the girls to his side. This game, he told them, was theirs for the taking. True, they had never seen Butte High in action, but Butte High had never seen them in action either. The only thing the people in Butte knew about the girls from Fort Shaw Indian School was what they had read in the paper. And with that he pulled out the clipping from last Sunday's *Anaconda Standard*. He pointed to the words he had underlined: "It is said that

. . .[the Indian girls] are fast and quick with the ball and they play the game with a vim and dash that are lacking in many girls' teams." Now was the time to show that quickness, that "vim and dash," he said, glancing around the group—the vim and dash of champions.[7]

The fans who filled the auditorium to capacity that evening were rewarded with what the local press described as "one of the best and most fiercely contested basket ball games ever seen in the city." There was no denying, however, that the first half was marked by ragged play on the part of Fort Shaw. Perhaps the Indians were, as one reporter had predicted, a bit "disconcerted" by the size and noise of the crowd. Their play was as rough as it was ragged. First, Vera Ledwidge, "the crack basket thrower of the high school," was knocked to the floor. Then forward Jesse Hickox, "severely handled" by the Fort Shaw defenders, "retired in favor of Miss Lee." This no-holds-barred, shove-and-tussle sort of play seemed to be the Butte brand of basketball, and the partisan crowd was warming to the Indians. As the first half came to a close, two "flying throws" by Belle Johnson drew cheers that were "fully as vociferous and spontaneous as when the local girls [scored]." Little Lone Calf, "adorned in the full dress of a chief," kept the crowd involved, dancing up and down the sidelines. Yet cheers and dancing seemed to be in vain as the "steady, sure" pressure of the Butte girls brought the rally to a standstill and enabled them to hold onto a two-point lead, 7 to 5, as the first half ended.[8]

While the Butte High band entertained with music and Lone Calf rendered another of his recitations, Coach Campbell settled his girls down. They could control the game by keeping to their hard-driving play but avoiding the fouls. They could outrun, outshoot, and outhustle the city girls. They could outwit them too. Yet here they were falling back into old habits, charging down court with no plan of attack instead of running the plays Professor Preston had set up for them. This game was a long way from over. All they had to do was to play *their* brand of basketball, not Butte's.

At the center jump, Josie tipped the ball to Nettie, who set up the play that gave the girls the first score of the second half. Butte had no answer for the sense of purpose with which Fort Shaw now worked the ball from one end of the court to the other, nor could they maintain the pace set by the Indians. If they couldn't outhustle the visitors though, they could outmuscle them, and the physical play that had marked the first half intensified in the second. Vera Ledwidge engaged Nettie Wirth in several fierce tussles for the ball before being knocked unconscious when a collision sent both girls hurtling out of bounds and into the dressing-room door. With their best player out of the game, the Butte team faltered as the Indian girls exploded for six points. Unable to stay on the bench any longer, the indomitable Miss Hickox returned to the game and "distinguished herself by throwing a basket from long range." But Belle Johnson answered with two points, and the contest ended in a decisive 15 to 9 victory for Fort Shaw.[9]

In celebration, the two Minnies, Burton and Scoldbear, hoisted little Chief Lone Calf to their shoulders, to the delight and amusement of the packed house. The triumphant scene was depicted in a *Butte Inter Mountain* cartoon the next day, and the *Anaconda Standard* reported that the girls from Fort Shaw Indian School attributed their come-from-behind victory to the presence and spirit of their spunky little mascot.[10]

All the competitiveness of the contest was left behind when the girls from Butte High gave their visitors "a royal good time" at a postgame reception at Pythian Hall. Butte's high school orchestra provided the music for dancing, and onlookers seemed surprised that "the red girls . . . could dance as well as play ball."[11]

One surprise at a time, the girls from Fort Shaw School were challenging assumptions about the capabilities of Indian youngsters.

~

Morning came early for the Fort Shaw entourage, for chaperones, students, bags and baggage had to be at the station to catch the one train that would get them to Helena in time for their evening game. The group was exhausted physically and emotionally. Dancing into the night had helped relieve some of the tension of the fiercely fought game, but settling down and going to sleep had been difficult when minds were racing with memories of an exciting evening.

But that was last night, Coach Campbell reminded his sleepy contingent at breakfast. Tonight they would face the only team to defeat last year's state champions. Tonight they would have to prove themselves all over again—first and foremost on the court , but also by repeating their stellar performances with their guitars and mandolins and their Indian clubs and barbells. There would barely be time to check into the hotel, have lunch, and run through rehearsals for the program that would be given tonight *after* the game rather than before. There would be a light and early supper. The entire day would be grueling, but Campbell assured his students they would muster the energy to make this night as memorable as the last.

Sure enough, spirits were high when the team was greeted by a "crowd of many hundreds," all of whom had heard of Butte High's embarrassing loss to a little Indian school from somewhere near Great Falls. The most prominent area of the auditorium, the elevated stage, was "filled with rooters who were resplendent in the scarlet of the high school." And at center stage, decked out in matching scarlet suits, sat "two small gentlemen of color aged 5 and 6 respectively"—Helena's answer to the inspiring and entertaining little chief from Fort Shaw Indian School.[12]

From the opening whistle, it was obvious that the girls from Fort Shaw had left their game in Butte. There were moments when the teams seemed evenly matched. The lightning speed and smooth passing of the Indian forwards several times moved the ball "the entire length of the hall in less time than it takes to tell it." Yet it seemed that "in front of every blue clad visitor there flashed the scarlet uniform of a high school girl" ready to deflect the ball as it arched toward the basket. On the other hand, the Helena forwards "managed to elude the lithe forms and outstretched arms in front of them" and make their shots count. At the half, Helena led, 9 to 2.[13]

As the orchestra played and Helena's little "gentlemen of color" pitted their dancing against the comedy routines of Chief Lone Calf, Coach Campbell did his best to energize his girls for the second half. He reminded them of how many times they had come close to scoring. If they continued to execute their plays, the ball was bound to begin falling their way. Minnie and Nettie had to run a little faster, jump a little higher, and show some of the aggression they had shown against Butte. And Josie needed to do her part at each end of the court. She was the strongest girl on the team, if not the fastest. She could take up the slack for Minnie and Nettie if she could pick up the pace a little.

If. If. If.

The whistle blew and the two teams took the floor. Josie's tip sent the ball to Emma, and she and Belle set out to turn the second half into a new game. A quick basket, followed by a second, cut the lead to three points before the magic ended and the Indians went into a slump. Once again their speed and passing got them down court, but time and again their ball handling went for naught, while Helena continued to make shots that "brought the audience to their feet in a pandemonium of cheers and braying horns."[14]

The final score stood 15 to 6. The girls from Fort Shaw Indian School had been handed their first defeat.[15]

There was no time for that hard truth to sink in. The team had barely wiped the sweat from their faces before they found themselves back on the floor, joining Gen and Genie, Katie and Mattie and Minnie Scold-bear in a series of exercises with the barbells and Indian clubs. The applause was deafening. It was as if the audience had been waiting for the opportunity to cheer for the girls from Fort Shaw. For them and only them. While Lone Calf delivered his "Nothin' 't All" piece, the girls changed into skirts, blouses, and scarves and took the floor again to perform with the mandolin club—with Nettie again conducting. Then followed dancing with the Helena boys, who eagerly sought the hand of this girl or that, and the night was over.[16]

The train trip home the next day was subdued. That morning's *Montana Daily Record* had carried a front-page story of the game. The article was accurate in its coverage and more than generous in its commendation of the efforts and talents of various members of the losing team. Losing team. Not a title the girls from Fort Shaw had wanted to earn. But this game was over and done with. Facing the classmates and faculty who had sent them off with such great expectations would be hard, but life would go on. As much could be learned through a loss as through a win, Coach Campbell reminded them. He had already begun to analyze what had gone wrong and why. And he was negotiating for a rematch with Helena. They could avenge this loss and move on through the season like the champions they were. Or they could give up and spend the rest of the season losing games and feeling sorry for themselves.[17]

They would have a chance to redeem themselves many times over. He guaranteed it, for just that morning the Helena coach had confirmed the rumor Campbell had heard over in Butte. Plans for a girls' state basketball league were under way. The press coverage of these two games and the enthusiasm shown by the standing-room-only crowds had now given Billy Adams just what he needed to turn plans into action. A select number of teams would be offered a place in the league, and there was every reason to think Fort Shaw would be among that number.

~

Within a matter of weeks, the high schools in most of the state's "principal cities"—as well as the college teams in Missoula and Bozeman—confirmed their interest in joining the proposed basketball league. As Superintendent Campbell had predicted, the organizers extended an invitation to Fort Shaw to participate. Helena High was eager to sign on, for on the basis of its single game that fall—the victory against Fort Shaw—the school board saw girls' basketball as "a great drawing card." That game had attracted "an enormous crowd to the Auditorium and netted a good sum for the Helena High Athletic Association."[18]

However, the school board and parents of Butte High School had followed through on their plan to put an end to girls' basketball. What they had seen in the Fort Shaw game had heightened the concerns raised by the roughness of games played the previous season. Basketball was not an appropriate sport for their daughters. Having anticipated this objection, Billy Adams began concentrating on the team he had organized from among St. Patrick's High School students. And he set about arranging a schedule of games for his "Butte Parochials"—beginning with a New Year's Day contest against the girls from Fort Shaw Indian School. If Butte High was no longer in a position to avenge the city's

earlier loss to the Indians, Butte Parochial was ready to put those up-
starts in their place.[19]

This was a must-win game, Coach Campbell told his girls at a Christmas Eve practice. They could not afford a second defeat on the heels of
their loss to Helena. In pondering the reasons for the girls' inability to
score against the capital city team, he had been thinking of juggling his
lineup. With Professor Preston's approval, Campbell now moved Nettie
to center, with Josie taking her place at guard. A center with a vertical
leap like Nettie Wirth's could lend a major advantage to a team. And
wherever she played, Josie's leadership—and her size—would still work
to Fort Shaw's advantage.[20]

This reconfiguration, plus several new plays devised by Professor
Preston, seemed likely to surprise the Parochials sufficiently to allow for
some quick points. There would be no surprises in terms of substitutes,
however, for once more Mattie Hayes and Minnie Scoldbear would be
ready to take the place of an injured teammate. Even so, Preston suggested that before season's end Campbell might want to consider moving a couple of the more promising younger players onto the bench.

Samuel McCowan's Indian Exhibit
December 1902

SAMUEL MCCOWAN, SUPERINTENDENT OF CHILOCCO INDIAN SCHOOL, laid the telegram aside and pushed back in his chair. Although his glance was drawn out the window, he saw nothing of the bleak Oklahoma landscape beyond the frosted panes. This message from the commissioner of Indian affairs had made everything official. He could now proceed with the assurance that he was indeed to head the Indian exhibit on the fairgrounds of the Louisiana Purchase Exposition.[1]

For the last two months, ever since Commissioner Jones had first discussed the idea with him, McCowan had been mulling possibilities for the design and execution of such an exhibit. He wanted it to be dynamic, something that would capitalize on the current interest in the traditional ways of the "vanishing Indian." At the same time it would need to demonstrate the effectiveness of the government's Indian education policy. He was sure both things could be done within one exhibit, although no world's fair of recent memory—Chicago, Buffalo, Omaha—had yet succeeded on either front. But might not those seemingly disparate goals be achieved by mounting a display of items representing the housing, foods, crafts, and weapons of the old way of life against a display of the products of today's Indian youth? Better yet, could there be a display of real, live "primitives" juxtaposed against a display of real, live Indian students? The traditional Indians would be shown living in replicas of their own villages, whereas the youth would be shown living in some kind of a model Indian school.[2]

McCowan knew something about Indian schools. From his earliest post as superintendent of the agency day school on the Rosebud Reservation in South Dakota, he had moved steadily upward in the service, becoming superintendent of Albuquerque Indian School, and then of the off-reservation school at Phoenix, before accepting the superintendency at Chilocco. He now led one of the largest schools in the service; the nine-thousand-acre complex was home to some seven hundred students and more than seventy employees. It was also one of the most prestigious. What if he could create, in microcosm, such a school on the grounds of the world's fair?[3]

Fortunately, Commissioner Jones had kept him up to date on developments in St. Louis. First, and perhaps most important, the BIA had set aside forty thousand dollars for the Indian exhibit at the Louisiana Purchase Exposition. If anything had handicapped Indian displays at fairs in the previous decade it was the lack of financial commitment from the BIA. It seemed that would not be a problem here. Then too the LPEC had recently announced the acquisition of an additional six hundred acres on the western edge of the fairgrounds. Some one hundred of those acres were for the use of the anthropology department, including the thirty allotted to McCowan's Indian exhibit. And, finally, in one of their most difficult decisions to date, especially for David R. Francis, the directors of the LPEC had announced that, of necessity, the opening of the St. Louis World's Fair was to be pushed back for exactly one year. April 30, 1904, looked a bit more realistic to McCowan than April 30, 1903. He would have time to gather his resources. But barely.[4]

Before he did anything else, he had to bring forth a solid concept for the exhibit out of the vague idea he had been entertaining. The only mandate he had from Commissioner Jones was to create a display that would demonstrate the progress of the American Indian and avoid any "objectionable features" such as those that marked the Wild West shows of the era—in other words, no Indians dressed in loincloths and war bonnets attacking immigrant trains and cavalry units. The commissioner wanted something compelling, something educational and entertaining—"something to remember."[5]

That was exactly what McCowan intended to give him. But he needed to get to St. Louis as soon as possible to meet with this Frederick Skiff, the LPEC's director of exhibits. Skiff could be an important ally in terms of avoiding any problems with WJ McGee, who was only a pen stroke away from becoming the director of the fair's anthropology department. By all reports, McGee was ambitious, proud, and eccentric, a man sure of his own ideas and all too eager to impose them on others. Nor was he above funneling any available monies into his own projects. Well aware of McGee's reputation, the BIA had secured some degree of autonomy for Samuel McCowan by insisting on his appointment as *assistant* director of the fair's anthropology department. It might not be easy to work alongside a fellow who had an ego the size of McGee's, but McCowan would have to find a way.[6]

"Like Lambent Flames . . .
across the Polished Floor"
Winter 1903

NEW YEAR'S EVE, 1902. THE BLUE SKIES, BARE GROUND, AND MILD temperatures of the last few days had been a minor miracle in the middle of a Montana winter. It would be an easy trip to the railhead at Sunnyside, and there would only be one wagon. The other members of the traveling troupe—the mandolin club, the gymnastics drill team, and little Chief Lone Calf—were not going along this time. Superintendent Campbell could not justify taking so large a group, considering what he had invested in the Thanksgiving trip.[1]

Once again they traveled the "Turkey Trail" into Great Falls, then transferred to the Montana Central, heading south and west to Butte. The route was the same, but with their reduced numbers—and without Gen Healy and Louis Youpee—much of the excitement of that previous journey was lacking. There was no anticipation of that first glimpse of the Smoky City, and no festive greeting by their opponents at the station, either. At least one thing had not changed. As Miss Malley reminded them, a hot meal, a warm bath, and soft, snug beds awaited them at the hotel.

But if the magic was gone for the girls, was it gone for the city as well? Would anyone show up for the game?

Would anyone even think of missing such a game as this promised to be? This was Montana. This was Butte. And this was girls' basketball.

On New Year's evening the auditorium was packed with spectators who were as interested in seeing the new team Billy Adams had put together as they were in getting another look at the girls from Fort Shaw

Indian School. On the other hand, the enthusiastic greeting the Fort Shaw team received as they made their way through the crowd and onto the edge of the court made it seem that many of the fans had come out just to cheer the Indians to victory.[2]

From the first play those renegade fans knew they had put their faith in the right team. In less than a minute the Indians had taken the ball downcourt and Belle had made her first field goal of the night. The fans quickly noted what the *Anaconda Standard* reported the next day: Fort Shaw had "a better knowledge of the fine points of the game" than they had shown in that earlier game in Butte. And with the revamped lineup, with Nettie at center and Josie at guard, there seemed to be a new energy to the team. The girls were quick to the ball with their steals, blocks—and rebounds. Their rebounding merited a column-inch of print: "Whenever a throw was made for the Indians' basket, the Indians were prepared for a miss and were always under the ball when it fell and would toss it up again before the local girls could realize that a miss had been made." Those tosses did not always yield points, so the score bounced back and forth. At the half the teams were tied, 5 to 5.[3]

With the Parochials playing "a fast and snappy . . . game" that matched the speed and rebounding of the Indians, the contest was in doubt to the very end. The fans appealed for a last grand rally by the home team, but "as the minutes passed by and the seconds began to be counted, the shouts of encouragement gave way to despair." The final score was 13 to 11. The *Standard*'s reporter singled out Belle as the star, but he was quick to add that she "was closely pressed for honors . . . by every other member of the team."[4]

Having pulled to within two points of a win, the Parochials had played a creditable game, and Billy Adams was satisfied with their performance. His hat was off to the Indians. "[They] beat us fair and square," he told reporters. Coach Campbell accepted the gracious concession for what it was and readily agreed that the Parochials deserved a rematch. Before he and Adams left the auditorium that evening they had even set a date—January 15, two weeks hence—and agreed to a change in venue. Fred Campbell was about to bring basketball to Great Falls.[5]

Assuming, of course, he could convince the city of the advantages of hosting home games for his basketball club. If Great Falls would provide the court and other amenities, Fort Shaw would provide the team. It was as simple as that. Fortunately, the years of good will built up through the participation of Fort Shaw students in entertainments and parades in the city, not to mention the willingness of the school's football team to don Great Falls' colors, gave him a basis upon which to mount a successful campaign. Before the first week of 1903 was out, he had rented a hall for the game, negotiated room rates for the visiting team, and worked with newspaper editors, city officials, businessmen, and women's clubs to assure the capacity crowd he needed—at fifty cents a head—to cover expenses for his team and the visitors. And there would be enough left over to build a fund for the basketball program at Fort Shaw.[6]

The most crucial aspect of Campbell's plan for transforming Great Falls into a basketball city was generating extensive pre- and postgame press coverage. Thus far both the *Tribune* and the *Leader* had been curiously apathetic about girls' basketball. Now, through interviews and carefully timed announcements, Campbell provided plenty of incentive for editors to keep the upcoming event before their readers. Mention was made of the possibility of games with Helena High, with the university team from Missoula and with the college team from Bozeman, provided that turnout for this initial game was sufficient to guarantee good crowds for future contests. Out-of-town fans held the promise of income from overnight stays, meals, and visits to local attractions. Civic pride was also at stake, for those cities, along with Butte, had "gone wild over the game," and they would be paying close attention to what happened in Great Falls on January 15.[7]

Both city papers took Campbell's prodding to heart. To pique the interest of fashion-minded women—and of gentlemen curious to see young women attired in something other than corseted, bustled, full-length dresses and skirts—the *Great Falls Leader* offered descriptions of the girls' uniforms. The Fort Shaw Indians would be wearing "blue bloomer suits trimmed with white," while the black-trimmed-in-blue "bloomer suits" of the Parochials would be set off by matching "short skirts." The game would begin promptly at 8:30 and be over an hour later, leaving plenty of time for a concert by Fort Shaw's mandolin club, followed by dancing to the music of the school's orchestra. There would, it seemed, be something for everyone on the evening of Thursday, January 15.[8]

Luther Hall, a high-ceilinged dance hall, would serve as gymnasium. For the benefit of readers who might not be familiar with the sport, the *Great Falls Tribune* published a brief summary of the basics of the game. The official "round inflated leather ball" was "about twelve inches in diameter." Two goals—net baskets "suspended from an iron ring hung about 10 feet from the floor"—had been placed at either end of the hall. The object of the game was to "throw or toss the ball" into the opponent's goal, while the opponents attempted to block the throws. Lines "traced upon the floor with chalk" outlined the court, "the outer boundaries being the first row of very excited spectators," and players were "not supposed to play outside those boundaries." The game would consist of "two twenty-minute halves with a ten-minute intermission."[9]

A few days before the contest, Campbell released the lineups. The starting five for both teams would be the same as had taken the floor two weeks earlier at the Butte Auditorium. However, Genie Butch and Delia Gebeau had replaced Mattie Hayes and Minnie Scoldbear as substitutes.[10]

Campbell's carefully orchestrated press releases had the desired effect. Spectators began filing into Luther Hall early that Thursday evening, hoping to get a seat despite what was predicted to be a standing-room-only crowd. Well before 8:30 the hall was packed. The crowd stilled as the referee—Butte coach W. J. Adams—walked to center court. Raising his hand for silence, he explained that instead of playing two twenty-minute halves, as stipulated by the rules, the teams had agreed to play "three twelve-minute thirds," for the girls from Butte "did not feel equal to longer periods of play after their journey from the smoky city." Coach Campbell had indeed agreed to this last-minute rule change, though he, as well as his players, had some trouble reconciling the previous performance of the rough-and-ready girls from Butte with this plea to accommodate their inability to play a regulation-length game.[11]

Referee Adams blew the whistle, Nettie Wirth squared off against Stella O'Donnell for the tip-off, a scuffle ensued, and within moments the whistle blew again. Holding called against Fort Shaw. The game's first score, a free throw by the Parochials. Were the girls going to get a fair shake from the ref? Well, what could not be helped must be dealt with, and under Josie's leadership the girls from Fort Shaw settled down. From that free throw onward both teams picked up the pace, and "the nimble maidens played like lambent flames back and forth across the polished floor." Yet quickness and grace were not enough to garner points, and the first period ended with the score still 1 to 0 in favor of "the Smoke-Eaters."[12]

During the brief pause allotted under the unaccustomed format, Coach Campbell told the girls that he was inserting Genie at Minnie's place at guard. No, Minnie had not been injured, but since rules could apparently be bent at will in this particular game, there was no reason not to give Genie a chance to see what she could do in a real game.[13]

Determined though Genie was to show herself to advantage, neither she nor her teammates could do anything to stop the Parochials' offense. In the second period "the little maids from Butte" made "five goals from the field." As one-sided as the game was to this point, there was no lack of excitement, for despite the rule against playing "outside the boundaries," more than once "the daring girls dash[ed] into the spectators on the side lines in a wild scramble to recover the sphere." On one such occasion, "the fat black ball . . . shot into the crowd, and the two opposing players who dived after it upended a small boy." No damage done. And the crowd reveled in the "zest" such plays added to the contest.[14]

Zest but no points. At least not for the Fort Shaw girls, who could not sink a basket. And still, as the *Leader* reported, the crowd was with them all the way: "[Emma Sansaver] fires the fat ball for her fishnet and as it misses dropping in, the crowd groans 'A-a-aah!' in a tone which would indicate that the fishnet has been guilty of a personal affront." Finally, in the waning minutes of the second period, in the midst of yet another melee in which half a dozen players managed "to smash a chair, upset a fat man, [and] break an electric light globe," a long pass "thrown by an Indian girl" was caught by "another dusky maid" who "deftly tossed it in the goal." Scoring their first two points—and hearing the crowd's applause—put new life into the team, although their momentum was broken by the whistle that ended the second period of play. Butte opened the final period with yet another basket, but that score was to be their last as "the Indians went on the warpath," hurling "the leather globe . . . as fast as a ping pong ball."[15]

To no avail. When time ran out, the score stood 15 to 6 in favor of Butte Parochial.[16]

As had been the case in Helena, the Fort Shaw girls had no time to deal with their disappointment. Quickly donning their skirts and blouses, they took up their mandolins and guitars and joined the other members of the mandolin club to show their supporters a different side of their talents. Then the evening belonged to the Fort Shaw orchestra, which played an opening number as chairs were cleared for dancing. There were those who danced and those who continued to replay the game long into the night, arguing among themselves as to the reasons for "their" team's loss. Reflecting the partisanship already evident among the fans in Great Falls, the *Tribune* reporter noted that "the short periods of play probably afforded the Butte players some advantage," since the Fort Shaw girls had "more staying power than their white opponents." The *Leader* suggested that while the officiating was fair, there was an inherent conflict of interest any time one team's coach was also the referee.[17]

Despite the loss by the hometown team, basketball was a hit with the fledgling fans of Great Falls. "Talk about excitement!" wrote the reporter for the *Leader*, who apparently felt a need to give stay-at-homes some indication of what they had missed. "Two wrestling matches, a football slaughter, three ping-pong tournaments, a ladies' whist contest, a pink tea, and one Schubert musical recital combined would fall short in comparison with one game of basket-ball." When final figures were tallied, the 540 people who "paid cash at the box office," plus those who had bought tickets in advance, brought the total number of spectators to 700, only 400 of whom were lucky enough to find seats. The size and enthusiasm of the crowd, plus the profits cleared, left no doubt as to the city's readiness to support a full slate of games.[18]

Superintendent Campbell promptly went into action, finalizing plans for two more "home" games, the first a January 30 clash with the girls from the state university in Missoula, the second a February 7 rematch against Helena High. And still more games were in the offing, as teams from Kalispell High and the agricultural college in Bozeman expressed an eagerness to come to Great Falls to play the Indians.[19]

If Great Falls was ready for basketball, Luther Hall was not. Coach Campbell was well aware of the problem noted in virtually every newspaper account of the game against Butte Parochial—the hazards of playing basketball on the polished floor of a dance hall. While no one had been seriously injured during the game, the hard falls taken by players on both teams and the dangerous slides into chairs and spectators might serve to bolster the claims of those who felt that basketball was not a proper activity for women and girls. And there could be no home-court advantage for Fort Shaw if the slippery nature of that court made his players tentative. Once again Campbell called on Fred Preston, for as much influence as the Fort Shaw superintendent had in the city of Great Falls, it did not compare with that of the founder of the Commercial College, who in any event was in a much better position to handle this problem.[20]

The problem could be eliminated, Fred Preston assured Campbell, by covering the playing surface with canvas—an expense that could be justified on the basis of expected gate receipts over the remainder of the season. He had already begun discussions with those in charge of maintenance and scheduling at Luther Hall, had elicited the support of several businessmen and city officials, and had put out bids for the kind of heavy canvas that would be needed. He was also making arrangements for the purchase of another hundred chairs for the hall.[21]

Preston had another suggestion. Still rankled by Billy Adams's request for a game of three twelve-minute periods, he suggested that henceforth competing teams should come into Great Falls a day early, thereby preventing any real or imagined disadvantage caused by travel fatigue and eliminating any worries about delays due to inclement weather. For instance, arriving in the city on January 29 would allow both the

Missoula and Fort Shaw squads to get a good night's rest at the Park Hotel and engage in light scrimmages on the new canvas floor the next day. As for the added expense of putting up the girls from Fort Shaw as well as the visiting team, Preston felt certain he could persuade local boosters to provide affordable—perhaps even gratis—lodging for "their" team.[22]

~

Fred Campbell clearly saw that his girls' success at basketball afforded him a prime opportunity to promote the programs offered at Fort Shaw Indian Boarding School. And he was not one to let such an opportunity pass. His press releases rarely failed to point out the importance of music and athletics in adding to the "social, moral, and physical welfare" of his students. Participating in these programs was, he said, not a right but a privilege; in order to take part in these activities a youngster had to exhibit both "proper deportment" and the ability to "keep up to grade."[23]

If Campbell took pride in his students' accomplishments, he also took pride in what he saw as a noticeable change in the public's attitude toward those students, change he attributed simply to exposure. The citizens of Great Falls might still harbor deep prejudices against Indians—especially against Chief Rocky Boy's Chippewas who had set up camp on the western edge of the city and against the landless Crees, who, according to a *Leader* editorial, were "accustomed to roam about in the vicinity of the city."[24] But the Indians who represented Fort Shaw were accepted as "good Indians." Take Emma Sansaver and Louis Youpee as just two examples of what such children could become, given the proper guidance. They had achieved what many a citizen's child had not. What ten-year-old boy in Great Falls had the social graces young Youpee displayed in mingling with audiences after his public performances? Or the mental acuity to memorize and recite such long set pieces? What teenage girl in Great Falls could hold her own on a basketball court with Emma? Or write an essay that was a part of a blue-ribbon exhibit at the Cascade County Fair?

As much as he relished the public acclaim for the work being done at Fort Shaw, Superintendent Campbell would be the first to say that these children came to the school with inherent abilities and sound character. The training they received at Fort Shaw could be credited with enhancing their abilities and strengthening their character, but he himself would never claim that these particular students were solely the products of the government's education policy.

By now, the citizens of Sun River didn't know whom to credit for the good things that had happened in the valley since the school had opened at Fort Shaw. But they liked the results. Their daughters did too. The young women who had formed the valley basketball team knew that the girls at the school were now in a league of their own, so to speak, but they still felt a special link to those who wore the Fort Shaw blue. And they readily accepted Josie Langley's invitation to come up to the campus one January afternoon, shortly after the Helena game, to watch a practice in the old gym and stay on for supper. In return, the girls from Fort Shaw were to be their guests at Sun River's upcoming Friday night social.[25]

~

Professor Preston was on hand for the Indians' workout in Luther Hall the morning of their game with the women from the university in Missoula. He liked the polish with which they were running their plays now, and he approved Coach Campbell's brand-new configuration of the lineup. Moving Minnie Burton to forward meant the team could take advantage of her height. And Belle Johnson had quickly adapted to Minnie's old slot at guard. Belle really didn't care where she played, just as long as she played. Confident as he was in this new lineup, Campbell knew the advantages that accrued to being the underdog and told reporters the Indian girls—having lost to the Helena team over which Missoula had posted an easy victory—"could hardly expect to win" but would give the crowd their best. Over in Missoula, C. P. Hargraves, the university coach, was not about to cede the underdog's role and announced that *his* team was hoping for an upset. He was encouraged to see that interest in the game was running high in Missoula, and a sizeable entourage of supporters planned to accompany the team to Great Falls.[26]

The game-day edition of the *Great Falls Tribune* featured a three-column article about the Fort Shaw team and a photograph of the seven girls who would be suited up that evening, giving Great Falls readers their first opportunity to get to know their adopted team as more than just "the Indian girls from Fort Shaw." Brief biographical sketches alluded to the diverse backgrounds and personalities of the players and provided physical descriptions to help fans identify the girls during games. There were some errors in the sketches—tribal affiliations and reservations were mixed up, and not for the first time. Yet the reporter did not once resort to such terms as "dusky maiden," "warpath," and "squaws." He might well have been describing the players on a white team.[27]

The article did, however, err in another respect—in promising that there would be accommodations for all. Instead, Luther Hall was so crowded "that had it been twice the size, it would undoubtedly have been taxed to its capacity." People were turned away at the door, while those who could find no seats inside were glad enough to stand, eager as they were to see a Fort Shaw victory. They were not to be disappointed. From the opening tip the game was hardly a contest. Although the women from Missoula played with determination, they could not match the "fearlessness" with which the Indian girls played. Despite taking a few hard falls—canvas was obviously not the perfect solution to slips and tumbles—the girls stayed focused on moving the ball up and down the court.[28]

A "number of brilliant plays" by girls from both teams marked the game, most notably a "double play" by Nettie Wirth who, after missing an attempt from the foul line, "caught the ball as it bounded from the . . . rim of the basket and successfully tossed it into the net," despite the "struggling mass" of university women surrounding her. Throughout the game the Indians' rebounding made a difference. As did their teamwork. Indeed teamwork was cited as the primary reason "the Indians ran up the score over that of their white sisters." And run it up they did, with the newly configured front line of Minnie, Emma, and Nettie combining for six points in the first half, then exploding for thirteen more in the second, for a final score of 19 to 9.[29]

Not wishing to be any less hospitable than the people of Butte or Helena, the citizens of Great Falls joined the girls from Fort Shaw in hosting a postgame meal for the visiting team. In addition, early on the morning following the game, members of the university team and their chaperones climbed aboard a carriage drawn by four horses for a drive to Rainbow Falls on the Missouri. Then, after their somewhat chilly early morning tour, the group from Missoula caught the ten o'clock train for home.[30]

At the Saturday evening meal back on their own campus, the Indian girls were applauded by all and praised by their coach for their exemplary behavior as well as their excellence on the court. Then Josie stepped forward to announce that the team had been given "many pounds of candy" by friends and supporters in Great Falls, and they wanted to share the spoils of their victory. Applause broke out as the girls went from table to table, distributing the confections. Superintendent Campbell had a surprise of his own. The older boys and girls were to adjourn to the gymnasium, where the orchestra would provide music for a dance in honor of the team. This was a rare enough treat, since the teenagers were not often allowed the privilege of social interaction on this order. It was only fitting that team captain Josie Langley should be the first on the floor, and she and Harvey Liephart led off, followed by many of her teammates and their escorts for the evening. Mr. and Mrs. Campbell enjoyed a waltz as Emma Sansaver twirled around the floor with five-year-old Freda Campbell. It was a memorable evening in every way, and ten o'clock came all too early for students, faculty, and staff alike.[31]

~

After the gaslights were extinguished in the big girls' dorm, classmates clamored for the team's own version of their time in Great Falls. They listened breathlessly to the story Belle told of Josie's shoelace getting caught on the button hook of a spectator's shoe as she plunged into the crowd after the ball. According to Belle's version—Josie, of course, was not there to verify or deny the story—Josie was so intent on getting the ball back into play, and so unaware of her entanglement, that she simply dragged the man off his feet and onto the floor. When the fellow was finally disengaged and able to return to his seat, Josie whispered to Belle, "The next white boy who becomes so closely attached to me will not escape so easily." The stifled giggles eventually faded into drowsy yawns.[32]

Next door, in the little girls' dorm, Matron Stark walked in on another version of the game of basketball. Tams stuffed with straw were the balls, and the windowsills were the baskets. Miss Stark simply closed the door behind her. What damage could be done—except for the wear and tear on the tams? These pseudo-games provided her young charges with good physical exercise *and* the mental challenge of devising strategies to overcome the limitations of their "court."[33]

Meanwhile, in the dorms across the way, several boys—among them twelve-year-old Lawrence Lucero and seventeen-year-old James Johnson—were devising strategies of their own, strategies that would free them from Fort Shaw Indian Boarding School. Some of them had tried to escape before, only to be tracked down, herded into wagons, and brought back to face the consequences. Some—like the Piegan boys who had slipped away the weekend Superintendent Campbell was in Great Falls for the girls' game against Butte Parochial—had even made it all the way home, only to be handed over to the school disciplinarian by tribal police. But there were those who had managed to escape and remain on their reservations or disappear into the various Métis settlements from which they had come. Those courageous few were the heroes these boys sought to emulate. The success of the girls' basketball team had little to do with them.[34]

"Like a Wall of Fire
through a Cane Break"
Winter 1903

❦

BASKETBALL REIGNED AT FORT SHAW. SUPERINTENDENT CAMPBELL was eager to put the newly formed boys' team on the court in front of the citizens of Great Falls. In order to ensure a good turnout for the city's first look at the boys, he decided on setting up an intrasquad exhibition game of two ten-minute halves as a bonus attraction for those attending the February 6 girls' game against Helena High, and he sent the notice to the city papers. "The boys play the game so fast and so hard," the *Leader* said, that before the opening tip-off "all the ladies and children . . . will be asked to take seats back of the first row in order to save any chance for accidents."[1]

The promise of the boys' game, coupled with a game in which the girls from Fort Shaw Indian School would be seeking to avenge their earlier loss to Helena High guaranteed a packed house. In anticipation of that, the boys in Mr. Merrill's carpentry classes were working long hours making benches and putting together "five dozen small round top stools" to be used that coming Friday night, and at all future basketball games in Luther Hall. With new "seats sufficient for 200 people," the hall should be capable of accommodating all spectators comfortably.[2]

There was every reason to think the game would draw a sell-out crowd, for up to this point Helena had lost only once—to the university women from Missoula. And although Fort Shaw's recent defeat of Missoula would seem to have evened the odds, there were other factors to consider. Since Helena's loss to the university team, they had "secured a young lady who is reputed to be the best center in the northwest," perhaps even the best center "west of Chicago." As Coach Campbell read this special release, he made up his mind to keep this kind of publicity from his girls as long as he could. It would be of little use for Nettie to read of the reputation of her opposing center. Perhaps the least flappable member of the team, she was, nevertheless, only sixteen, and Campbell did not want to risk having her confidence shaken by the press this Kate Merville was getting in the Helena papers.[3]

In accordance with Campbell's new plan to bring the team into Great Falls a day ahead of the scheduled game, the Fort Shaw contingent arrived at the Park Hotel on Thursday, February 5. Ella Campbell traveled with the team as an honored guest this time, and she and her husband made the experience a special one for the girls by taking them to the opera house that evening to see *Corianton*, an extravagant touring-company production featuring a cast of forty.[4]

Early on game day, soon after the team had finished a light scrimmage and at about the same time the Helena team was boarding the train for Great Falls, a crew of young carpenters from Fort Shaw arrived at Luther Hall to set up the benches and stools they had built. For their reward, they would be allowed to stay over to see the exhibition game between their friends on the boys' Red and Black teams as well as to see, for the first time, their celebrated classmates on the girls' basketball squad in a "real" game. Those classmates were now resting following a game-day routine Coach Campbell had drawn up right after their loss to Helena. Rehearsals were run through in the morning, while afternoons were reserved for hot baths, rubdowns, and an hour's rest before a light meal.[5]

By early evening all was in readiness for the arrival of the Helena team—and the expected crush of eight hundred fans. But by the time the first three hundred had paid their fifty cents and were seated inside the hall, word arrived that a burned-out bridge on the Montana Central line from Helena had left the visiting team stranded a scant fifteen miles shy of Great Falls. While everything possible was being done to see that they made it into town safely, there was little hope that they would arrive in time—or in any shape—to play basketball.[6]

F. C. Campbell took the floor inside the hall to give the disappointing news. He extended his apologies and those of the Helena coach and announced that the game had been rescheduled for the following night. He assured the assembled fans that they would get a full refund of the ticket price, though they were welcome to stay on and see—gratis—the boys' intrasquad game. He repeated the announcement to the people waiting in line outside the hall and invited them to move on into the building for a full-length game between the Fort Shaw Red and Black teams. Disappointed as they were to miss the girls' game, the fans were treated that night to "a rattling game of basket-ball." The contest, won by the Reds by a score of 20 to 14, "kept the crowd up on their toes for the entire time." Before the evening was over, Superintendent Campbell was able to assure the fans that the Helena girls had arrived safely at the Park Hotel and were enjoying a late meal. They were exhausted and somewhat traumatized by their experience, but they looked forward to a quick recovery and an exciting contest the next evening.[7]

While Campbell had taken the only honorable course by refunding admission, the additional expense of keeping his entourage in Great Falls for another night had essentially doubled the expenses of the game against Helena. But besides the added expense, would the rescheduled game draw as large a crowd, and therefore as large a gate? He had been hoping to build a treasury to cover the costs of a trip that would allow the girls to accept challenges from two teams in the state of Washington, with anything left over going toward "making a court . . . and putting in a gymnasium apparatus" at Fort Shaw. Such plans now seemed unrealistic in light of the extra expense of this weekend.[8]

Despite his worries, Fred Campbell was his usual gracious self the next morning as he and Ella and little Freda, the Helena coach, and both teams climbed aboard the trolley for a tour hosted by one of the city's women's auxiliaries. Pleased as always by the social interaction between his Indian students and white students from other schools, the superintendent relaxed into the ride "over the car lines" to Black Eagle Falls, where the party crossed the river "by the suspension bridge" and then returned to the city.[9]

When it was time to get down to the business of playing basketball that evening, social graces took a backseat to competitive fire. "[T]ime and again the girls went into a heap, and two would arise, both hanging on to the ball." But the Indians "brought more method to their play," and at the half the score was 13 to 4 in favor of Fort Shaw. Nettie, who was easily outplaying her highly touted counterpart, had accounted for seven of those points, while Minnie had added the other six. In the second half Minnie exploded, sinking five baskets. Eight hundred voices began to chant, "Shoot, Minnie, shoot!" As the score built up against their team, the hopes of Helena rooters gradually faded until finally "those wearing the red ribbons felt disposed to hide them and cheer for the Indian maidens as the big sphere dropped, time after time, into the basket." Fort Shaw claimed a resounding 28 to 10 victory. Minnie alone had contributed sixteen points, and the reporter for the *Leader* claimed that the fans had been treated to "the prettiest, fastest and most enthusiastic" basketball game ever played in Montana. That painful loss to Helena High had been avenged.[10]

The following morning, the girls from Fort Shaw Indian School returned to the campus, where they were met with much fanfare and regaled with questions about all aspects of their victory. But the season was not over. Billy Adams was pushing for a rubber match between the Parochials and the Indians—at home in Butte. The challenge was tempting, but Campbell was wary. Given Adams's status as the founder of the "league," given the fluidity of the scheduling, and given the lack of any rule as to the length of the season, Campbell wanted some assurance that this game, which would supposedly decide the state championship, would be played in Great Falls.[11]

⌒

With details of the proposed game against Butte still to be worked out, Superintendent Campbell turned his attention to his boys' team. The press coverage they had received in their exhibition game at Luther Hall must surely have raised sufficient interest in boys' basketball to draw crowds and raise money for the school's athletic program. With that hope in mind, Campbell scheduled games against the newly formed Great Falls club, headed by player/coach Fred Preston; the hastily organized Boston & Montana Smelter squad; and two capital city teams, Helena High and Wesleyan College.[12]

Despite all the publicity, boys' basketball proved a disappointing draw. The *Leader*'s reporter pointed out the obvious: As far as basketball was concerned, the boys had "the lesser drawing capacity . . . as compared with school girls." Less obvious were the reasons for this discrepancy. Perhaps Montanans, accustomed to seeing physical strength as the key to success on the gridiron, found it hard to accept basketball as a worthy sport for men and boys. Perhaps the fact that boys' basketball was almost an afterthought and had never been given the same attention that such boosters as W. J. Adams and F. C. Campbell had given girls' basketball had something to do with this discrepancy. Perhaps the novelty of seeing girls clad in bloomers display the kind of athleticism once thought of as limited to males made the difference. Perhaps it was the girls' infectious enthusiasm for this liberating activity that drew the public's attention. Or, most likely of all, it was simply that Naismith's new game had been introduced to Montanans by girls and was therefore seen as a girls' sport. For whatever reason, men and women, boys and girls, flocked to see the girls play the game, while the boys played in near-empty auditoriums. Campbell conceded. Barely breaking even on some games and going in the hole on others, he decided to cut his losses and bring the boys' basketball season to a close.[13]

Campbell now turned his full attention to the girls' team, the team whose popularity had raised Fort Shaw's visibility and bolstered its reputation. The girls' basketball program had given the players and the performers "the advantage of travel" and had put the people of Montana in "closer touch" with Indian children. Letters such as the one he opened in late February from C. P. Hargraves only proved his point. "Our girls have not yet ceased to sing your praises," the Missoula coach wrote, "and there is a very friendly feeling in our university toward Fort Shaw." Hargraves noted that in all his years of coaching, both in the East and West, he had never had a "more thoroughly enjoyable" experience than his encounter with the Fort Shaw girls. He wanted to return the hospitality and hoped to bring the Indians to Missoula some time in March, if he and Campbell could find some mutually satisfactory date.[14]

Close on the heels of this invitation came a telegram from the coach at Montana Agriculture College in Bozeman. The Farmerettes would like to come to Great Falls to test themselves against the Indians. Campbell immediately checked the availability of Luther Hall for that very next Friday night—March 13—and wired the Bozeman team to "come on."[15]

With a storm moving in, the Fort Shaw contingent set out by wagon early Thursday afternoon. Huddling under woolen blankets, the troupe rode into Sunnyside through blinding snow and arrived at the Park Hotel cold and exhausted. Meanwhile, the state college team, traveling through the same storm, stopped overnight in Helena and arrived in Great Falls the next morning. Having rested up at their hotel, the college women appeared at Luther Hall in early evening, ready to pit their talents against those of the Fort Shaw team.[16]

Because of the short notice and the inclement weather, only five hundred fans were on hand to greet the teams. Outnumbered as they were, a dozen or so supporters of the college girls waved their blue-and-gold streamers and stomped and cheered for their team. But as the *Bozeman Chronicle* reported, "the white girls . . .were never in the game at all." They were overwhelmed by quick and accurate passes. And superior shooting. Fort Shaw scored "basket after basket . . .which the Palefaces could not block." A reporter for the *Exponent*, the college newspaper, gave his readers the flavor of the action in Luther Hall: "Promiscuous heaps of navy blue mingled with gold and white stripes, shoe strings, [and] hair ribbons," he wrote, "midst cries of 'Shoot, Minnie, shoot!'" By the start of the second half, with the score already 16 to 4, "the little tin horns, bedecked with the . . . college colors were hidden away and never again brought to light." The college women played hard, even "when they knew that defeat was inevitable." But they were no match for the smooth performance of the Fort Shaw team. Nettie and Minnie scored most of the points in the 36 to 9 rout, though Belle "furnished the excitement under the basket, backed up by Emma Sansavere [*sic*] and sturdy Josephine Langley."[17]

As had become the custom, the visiting team was entertained by the victorious Indians at a banquet and dance following the game. The college girls were so impressed by the hospitality shown them by the Fort Shaw girls, along with their "fairness and courtesy" on the court, that they were eager to bring the team to Bozeman for a rematch. They hoped to make a better showing on their home grounds.[18]

Meanwhile, Billy Adams resumed his pressure to schedule a rubber match for the state's top two teams. He contacted Campbell, offering March 20 as a possible date—at Butte Auditorium. Although he had initially vowed that the next game against Butte would take place in Great Falls, Campbell saw some advantage to Adams's proposal. It actually dovetailed nicely with an idea he had been entertaining. A late March, early April road trip around the western part of the state would allow his girls to demonstrate their skills—and the worth of the Fort Shaw experience—to a broad audience of Montanans. Missoula and Bozeman had both expressed an interest in hosting the Indians, and arranging to play those two teams, plus the Butte Parochials—and perhaps one more team in that part of the state—over, say, an eight-day stretch, would enable him to minimize expenses and maximize exposure. With his own timetable in mind, Campbell countered Adams's proposed date with a suggested date of Friday, March 27, the game to take place in Butte. Billy Adams accepted, and the remainder of the tour fell quickly into place.[19]

~

Ella Campbell was packing her bags. Freda was dancing around the floor with her doll, singing a made-up song about riding on a train. Ella smiled. It took so little to make the child happy. In fact, it also took very little to make *her* happy: an invitation to join her husband on a tour that included two college towns she had never visited, the promise of comfortable accommodations and good food, even the possibility of attending one or more dances. What more could she want?Though she should not expect too much, F. C. had warned her, for this was to be a bare-bones trip. Not even the scrimmage squad would be boarding the train with the girls. Having made no money at all on the boys' games played in February, the superintendent was stretching his budget just to cover ten travelers—the five starters, substitutes Genie Butch and Delia

Gebeau, Sadie Malley as the player chaperone, and himself and Ella, with Freda going along at no extra expense.

~

On Thursday, March 26, as the girls climbed aboard the wagon to begin the first leg of their week-long, four-game road trip, they were given a splendid send-off by the Fort Shaw band and the boys' and girls' marching squads. After a medley of marches and snappy maneuvers by the drill teams, the students sent up a rousing rendition of the cheer that had first been heard at the big game at Black Eagle Park, back in the days when football had been "the thing":

> Bum-a-ling! Bum-a-ling!
> Bow-wow-wow!
> Ching-a-ling! Ching-a-ling!
> Chow-chow-chow!
> Bum-a-ling! Ching-a-ling!
> Who are we?
> Fort Shaw! Fort Shaw!
> Rah! Rah! Rah!

Even though the old school cheer had been replaced of late by the cry of "Shoot, Minnie, shoot!" it had never before seemed more inspiring.[20]

The basketball girls needed all the inspiration they could get, for they had been pushing themselves to the limit in order to be ready to avenge the loss the Butte Parochials had handed them in their first "home" game in Luther Hall. There would be no band to play for them as they squared off against their old rivals, only the echoes of the cheer that had sent them off that morning.

"These teams are conceded to be the best in the state and the battle between them for supremacy should be a royal one," the *Anaconda Standard* predicted on Friday morning, March 27. Yet the moment the girls from Fort Shaw Indian School stepped onto the court at Butte Auditorium, they knew this night would be theirs. From the opening tip-off when Nettie sent the ball into Emma's hands and a pass brought a basket by Minnie, the Indians never looked back. Still, the enthusiasm of the hometown crowd never waned. This time there was far too much at stake to inspire the crowd to applaud even the most spectacular plays by the visitors. After all, the girls from Fort Shaw were no longer the exotic "dusky maidens," no longer a novelty. They were the only team that stood between the Parochials and the state's first championship, and Butte was not a city that liked to lose. But lose they did, by a score of 18 to 8, a win so impressive the *Anaconda Standard* announced that the "Indian school team clearly showed its superiority over the local[s]." Before a thousand people Minnie and Nettie had led the way, "making all kinds of pretty plays and sensational throws and catches." The competition over, both teams were treated to a "bountiful spread at the Grotto cafe."[21]

With their greatest challenge out of the way, the girls from Fort Shaw took the Saturday morning train to Boulder for a game that evening against the girls from Jefferson County High. It was hardly a contest, with Fort Shaw crushing the newly organized team 37 to 6. With one tough game and one almost embarrassing "scrimmage" behind them, Coach Campbell and his girls headed out on Sunday morning for their clash with the Farmerettes, checking into the Bozeman Hotel for a good night's rest in anticipation of a full day of activities planned by their hosts.[22]

That Monday the Fort Shaw girls were the toast of the campus at Montana Agricultural College. They were welcomed at a morning assembly by the college president, James Reid. Predictably, F. C. Campbell used the occasion to speak briefly on the federal policies behind Indian education in general and the programs at Fort Shaw in particular. After the assembly, the guests were given a tour of the campus, followed by a luncheon prepared by members of the domestic science department. At the meal each of the Fort Shaw girls was paired with her counterpart from the college team, giving the players "a good opportunity to get acquainted." The "modest and ladylike conduct" of the Indian girls "made a fine impression" on faculty and students alike."[23]

In late afternoon, after their accustomed ritual of warm baths and rest, the girls made their way down Main Street from their hotel to Story Hall, the only place in town capable of holding the anticipated crowd. Inside they were welcomed by the cheers of some eight hundred spectators, many of whom had never before seen a game of basketball. From the beginning of that night's contest it was clear that the visiting team had left their "modest and ladylike conduct" back on campus. The girls took the floor with confidence and gave "one of the largest audiences . . . ever assembled in Story Hall . . . one of the finest exhibitions of basket ball ever seen in the state." There was little difference between the contest in Story Hall and the one played earlier in Luther Hall. The Farmerettes were hopelessly outclassed. While scoring eighteen points themselves, the Fort Shaw five denied their opponents a single basket. It was "a clean shut-out . . . the first in the basketball history of the state."[24]

Their embarrassing loss did nothing to diminish the hospitality extended by the college women. As soon as the crowd dispersed, the basketball court was transformed into a dance floor and, according to the *Bozeman Chronicle*, "the dusky bell[e]s had no cause to complain for a lack of partners among the gallant college boys."[25]

The next morning Miss Malley and the team rose early, dressed for their trip to Missoula, and hurried down to the hotel dining room to join the Campbells. It had been a short night's sleep for all, but little Freda was as lively as ever, and Superintendent Campbell was beaming. Professor Preston had just telephoned from Great Falls to extend his congratulations and report that, according to an article in that morning's *Leader,* the girls from Fort Shaw Indian School were moving through the state "like a wall of fire through a cane break." The quaint phrase did seem an apt description of the team's accomplishments thus far, but winning one game—or even three in a row—did not guarantee winning the next one. The university women at Missoula had been working hard since their defeat in Luther Hall, and this time the Indians would be the ones coming into town after a long day on the train to take on a well-rested team playing on its home court. Catching a few winks right after boarding the Northern Pacific might be a good idea for them all.[26]

Arriving on sea legs after the long train ride from Bozeman, the team was more than ready to get to their hotel and begin the afternoon ritual to which Coach Campbell attributed their strength as a road team—a bath, a rubdown, a nap, and then a "light meal."[27]

The university women no doubt expected to see a travel-weary Indian team walk into the Union Opera House that night. Instead they saw a group of girls as well rested and ready to play as they had been the night of their first meeting in Great Falls. Missoula fans had turned out in full force for this game, hoping their team could pull off an upset. Every seat in the house was taken—even those in the balcony—and "every foot of standing room . . . between the walls and the players" was occupied. Among those present was a delegation from the Flathead Reservation who had come to see the Indians—including their own Delia Gebeau—and had arrived early enough to claim seats in the first and second rows. That night they discovered just how rough-and-tumble a game of girls' basketball could be, even for the spectators, as time after time the ball bounced out of bounds into the crowd, only to be recovered by one of "the athletic girls who shouldered their way into the audience in their rush for the sphere." The contest was hard-fought, but the outcome predictable. The Indians won 17 to 6. The university women scored but a single field goal, four free throws accounting for the remainder of their points. Nettie and Minnie split the scoring between them—nine from Nettie and eight from Minnie.[28]

As promised, the university team returned the hospitality extended to them in Great Falls, treating their guests to an informal reception after the game. Superintendent Campbell seized the opportunity to thank their hosts for "such an enjoyable evening" and to announce his intention of challenging the champions of Utah, "the Mormon girls of the Latter Day Saints' university at Salt Lake," to a series of games that would determine an "interstate champion." The sportswriter for the local *Missoulian* was confident that the "superior ability" of the girls from Fort Shaw would acquit them well in representing Montana.[29]

McCowan in St. Louis
April 1903

❦

F ROM THE MOMENT OF HIS ARRIVAL IN ST. LOUIS, SAMUEL MCCOWAN, recently appointed as head of the Indian exhibit for the 1904 World's Fair, had been shown every courtesy. Frederick Skiff, the fair's director of exhibits, had hailed him as he descended the streetcar at the Wabash Station. Indicating the buggy that stood waiting just a few paces away, Skiff took McCowan's valise from his hand and guided him carefully through the mud and construction debris toward the hack. Once the men had settled themselves on the padded leather seats, Skiff pulled from his briefcase a map of the grounds and handed it to his visitor. This very spot where we sit, he said, pointing at the same time to a large X on the map, will be the main entrance, ultimately a magnificent archway through which all will enter this magical world. Then, with a sweeping gesture back toward where McCowan had just alighted from the streetcar, Skiff continued his glimpse into the future: Visitors will debark from cabs or streetcars at that Wabash Station, he said, then enter the grounds and board cars that will speed them along an intra-mural railway linking the most significant exhibits on the grounds.

With that, Skiff nodded to the driver and the buggy began to roll slowly through the mud and ruts along the northern border of the fairgrounds. As they rode along, McCowan studied the map, matching what he saw on paper to what his host was describing along the way. All around him he could see elegant structures rising, some of them complete and standing ready for Dedication Day. But what was most apparent was how unready these grounds were for the ceremony that would take place in just three weeks to mark the centennial of the signing of the Louisiana Purchase treaty.

David Francis and the directors of the LPEC had barely managed to persuade Congress that dedicating the fairgrounds on April 30, 1903, would satisfy the mandate tied to the federal appropriation to open the fair on that date. Still, it was clear that much, much more would need to be done in the year between Dedication Day and Opening Day. For every building that stood complete, there were ten that were still merely frameworks and another ten that were hidden by scaffolding as workers swarmed to place the staff, the lightweight material that formed, or would form, the facade of every structure on the grounds.[1]

At long last the buggy bumped its way to the very western border of the fairgrounds, the proposed future home of the Anthropology Department's Indian exhibit. McCowan, a visionary long accustomed to seeing what was not yet in place, could not have been more satisfied with the location if he had picked it himself. "Prominent, semi-exclusive, and a half mile from the Midway," the thirty-acre site offered sufficient seclusion and yet an elevation that would make it easy for fairgoers to locate it. Furthermore, because Skiff had placed the forty-seven-acre Philippine Reservation—sure to be one of the most popular venues of the entire fair—just beyond the Indian exhibit, a steady stream of visitors to his own site was all but guaranteed.[2]

Morning had moved well into afternoon when Skiff ushered his visitor into the dining quarters of the fair's administration building. Over a leisurely lunch, he apologized for being so forgetful as to not have immediately extended greetings from David Francis, explaining that the president of the LPEC would certainly have joined them on the day's tour had he not been at that moment on his way home from London. The conversation then turned to something McCowan had heard often enough since accepting the post of assistant director of the anthropology department. WJ McGee could be a difficult man to work with, Skiff said, although he had made it quite clear to McGee that, according to his arrangements with the BIA, McCowan would have sole responsibility for the Indian exhibit. Anything outside that would fall under

McGee's jurisdiction. Mind you, the man hadn't even been officially appointed head of anthropology yet, but Skiff wanted the division of labor clearly understood from the outset. McCowan nodded, grateful—and relieved—to hear that he would have a free hand.[3]

~

At the entrance to the three-story apartment building that would house visiting dignitaries as well as persons who, like himself, would be creating and overseeing various exhibits before and during the fair, McCowan insisted on going in alone. He had only a valise to carry, his trunk would be brought in from the station in due time, and for now he would be fine on his own. Perhaps he would accept a sandwich, if Skiff insisted on having one sent around later, but nothing more.

Skiff apologized for his insensitivity to McCowan's need for rest. He must be exhausted after traveling so far, then plunging right into the business of meeting officials and touring the grounds. A good night's sleep would serve him well.

Yet it was not sleep but solitude that Samuel McCowan needed, along with a pencil and paper and the files he carried in his valise. He spread a clean sheet of paper on the table and began to draw in broad strokes. Location and layout fit hand in glove. His model school would sit at the top of the hill, the encampments would spread out on either side of it. The school building would house 100, maybe 150, students representing the 29,000 children enrolled in the country's Indian boarding schools. The encampments would be built and lived in by people, families even, chosen from fourteen or fifteen different western tribes, say, Kickapoos in their bark huts, Pawnees in their earth lodges, Sioux in their tepees. And then there were the "exotics" that McGee planned to bring in—the Patagonians from Argentina, the Ainus from Japan, and the Pygmies from the Congo. They would put up their own dwellings. He would leave all those arrangements to McGee.[4]

The school, a two-story, classic revival-style structure with a hint of the parapets of an old fort or mission, would blend beautifully with the architecture he'd seen on his tour today and still be distinctive. The front entrance, porch, and balcony would overlook a broad plaza and parade grounds. The auditorium would accommodate conferences and concerts and serve as a chapel on Sundays. A wide hallway would dominate the main floor, running the length of each wing and separating a row of open classrooms and workrooms on one side from a row of stalls on the other. The children would live, study, and work in the school. The traditional Indians would live in their camps but come to the school each day to ply their "primitive" crafts. In the stalls opposite the children's classrooms and workrooms, they would shape pottery; weave baskets and rugs; carve flutes and other musical instruments; and fashion tools of stone, flint, and wood. It would be a dramatic display, one intended to leave the public with a lasting impression of the contrast between the old ways of life and the new. Old ways and new. The march of civilization. The very theme of the fair itself.[5]

The sun had long since set, and still the sandwich that had, indeed, been sent over by kindly Mr. Skiff, sat untouched. But McCowan had firmed up his plans. He could hardly wait to put them in front of Skiff in the morning. If they met his approval—and McCowan had full confidence they would—there were myriad tasks to see to as soon as he was back in Chilocco. He would have to contact the agents on the various reservations, laying out his expectations and asking them to select and send their most trusted and talented Indians to the fair.

And then there was the matter of finding the students and a corps of teachers for the model school. Before he went much further, even while he was looking for a contractor, he had to be about the business of looking for his students. He wanted those who had "best prepared themselves, in all ways the most deserving." He knew he could find a good number of those children among the seven hundred youngsters at his own school in Oklahoma. But he wanted representation from other schools in the Louisiana Purchase Territory. He would contact the superintendents at Haskell and Genoa. That would be a good start. Perhaps he could fill out the ranks of the student body right there. But he should probably look farther west.[6]

Perhaps as far west as Montana, where a small school was earning a big reputation. Hadn't he just read that Edwin Chalcraft, inspector of Indian schools, had pronounced Fort Shaw "the most important institution of the kind under government support"? He had even tried at one time to entice the school's superintendent to come to Chilocco. It was probably time to get in touch with Fred Campbell again.[7]

Montana's Champions
Spring 1903

❦

OVER IN BUTTE, W. J. ADAMS WAS NOT ABOUT TO LET FRED CAMPBELL call his Indians the champions of Montana and claim the right to represent the state in a series of games against the champions of Utah. Not yet. Campbell and his party were no sooner home from Missoula than Adams contacted the superintendent with a proposal for a two-out-of-three-game season finale that would determine the state's champion team "once and for all." This business of settling the title "once and for all" was getting a bit tiresome, but if Adams wanted a showdown, Coach Campbell and the girls were willing to give it to him—on the condition that the first two games be played in Great Falls. A "championship playoff" should pack Luther Hall and raise enough funds for the proposed trip to Utah. There would be no need for a third game back in Butte Auditorium. Campbell was certain of that. He dashed off a note to Adams proposing the second weekend in May for two games in Luther Hall. The note did not specify a date for the third game.[1]

⁓

Campbell had other proposals to deal with as well on his return from the trip. Gen Healy found him in his office as he was catching up with the week's accumulation of paper on his desk. Perhaps she had acted out of turn, she said, but since he and Miss Malley and Josie were all gone, there was no one else to meet with Edna Blossom, the Sun River captain, when she had come up to the campus. In brief, Edna wanted to arrange a game with Fort Shaw's "scrimmage squad"—although Gen called it the second team. Edna thought the Sun River girls could be competitive in a game against the second stringers. Gen had explained to Edna that she, Gen, couldn't accept the invitation for Fort Shaw, but she was sure Coach Campbell would, once he was back.

It was not the first time that Gen Healy had caught the superintendent off guard. But it didn't take him long to see her point. He had been increasingly aware that any one of the girls who scrimmaged with the team—Genie Butch, in particular, but Gen Healy, Katie Snell, Flora Lucero, and Rose LaRose as well—could hold her own against his starters. It was probably time to give them a chance to play. He knew that Delia Gebeau had lost interest in the game and would be returning to the Salish-Kootenai reservation at year's end. She had been an exemplary student and an unselfish member of the team and she would be missed. But he still had five strong candidates for a second team. Maybe it was time to formalize *two* Fort Shaw teams. In that way he could create a traveling troupe that would take the gospel of basketball and Indian education on the road, playing exhibition games in towns around Montana that had no teams of their own. Games between these two evenly matched Fort Shaw teams could be as entertaining as the interscholastic matches played all season.[2]

And Edna Blossom—and his own Gen—had just given him the chance to put his "second team" on the floor in a match game in front of a crowd. Before Gen left his office, he suggested that she tell Mrs. Parker and Minnie that the basketball girls would be needing some extra uniforms.

~

The excitement had been building in the valley in the week since the young women of the Sun River team had announced that Fort Shaw had accepted their invitation to meet on the evening of Monday, April 13. The valley girls were a much stronger team than the group Josie Langley had coached on the rudiments of the game almost two summers ago. Perhaps they were still no match for the team that had just stormed its way through Butte, Boulder, Bozeman, and Missoula, but they would be testing themselves against Fort Shaw's "second team." Wouldn't it make for an evening's entertainment to show family and friends their talents on a court—without, they hoped, embarrassing themselves?[3]

By the weekend, there was talk of little else around town. Some folks had been on the Fort Shaw campus that day in spring '97 and had seen that first-ever exhibition of basketball. And now to think that these few years later their own daughters and granddaughters would be playing the teammates of the state champions. There were even some side bets made in Billy Devine's Saloon. You couldn't get many people to bet on the Fort Shaw girls, but that had more to do with local pride than with common sense. As steadfast as they had been in supporting the Indian school in the last few years, there was no question as to where the towns-peoples' loyalties would lie in this game. There would be plenty of other opportunities to root for the Indians. On Monday night their cheers would be for the valley girls. Better be there early, the locals warned one another, just to be sure to get a good seat.

No one in Sun River, not even the oldest citizen, could remember when Murray Hall had been that packed. On Monday night, valley residents were out in force, early enough to watch the girls from both teams warm up on the improvised court on the second floor of Murray Hall. And early enough to give Superintendent Campbell some good-natured ribbing when he took the floor in his referee's shirt and whistle.

Edna Blossom and her girls got off to a fast start, while Gen Healy and her teammates could not seem to get themselves untracked, eager as they were to prove themselves, too eager perhaps. As "the leathery sphere wound its way to Sun River's basket," the fans "yelled themselves hoarse." Overwhelmed by the feisty underdogs, the Indians made only three field goals, giving Sun River a 10 to 6 lead at the half.[4]

The second half, however, was a reverse of the first. As the Indians began sinking baskets, the valley girls grew so flustered that they went to "wild playing" and scored not a single second-half point. The final score was 22 to 10. Although the Fort Shaw girls were victorious, it was actually seen as a triumph for both sides. The Sun River team had "gone down with colors flying," while the second team had proved worthy of wearing Fort Shaw's colors—and proved to Coach/Referee Campbell that they were ready to take the floor in front of a crowd against any competition, including even their good friends on the starting five.[5]

With the game concluded, chairs and benches were stacked at the side of the hall, bets were settled—or were brushed aside with a "we'll settle up after the next game"—and the Fort Shaw orchestra swung into music for dancing. At midnight, the women of Sun River hosted a supper at the Largent Hotel down the street from Murray Hall. The long evening wound to a close with neighborly good-byes. Relations between the valley's white settlers and the Indian children in their midst had come a long way in ten years.[6]

⁓

As the date for the early May showdown between the Butte Independents—"formerly the Parochials"—and the Fort Shaw Indians drew near, the *Great Falls Tribune* made clear to its readers that, according to "the basis on which championships are decided"—that is, the percentage of games won and lost—"the Indian maidens are entitled by all odds to the championship in basketball." Their record of nine victories in eleven games, a percentage of .818, ranked them above any other team, including the Independents, who had won five of seven, an inferior .714 percentage. If one considered total points scored and points against, then the Indians were clearly superior, having scored 242 points while holding their opponents to 98. The numbers for the Butte team: 87 and 60. No contest. And yet still Billy Adams was not ready to concede.[7]

While fans speculated over the outcome of the meeting, the citizens of Great Falls prepared for game day. "A number of the ladies of the city" were planning a lavish postgame banquet in honor of the two rivals. Senator Paris Gibson and Mayor James Freeman had been invited, and the names of businessmen who had donated cash and supplies were published in the paper. Obviously basketball had a social as well as an athletic impact in Great Falls. And the girls from Fort Shaw Indian School had, without a doubt, become the city's "favorite daughters."[8]

On Thursday, May 7, Superintendent Campbell met the travelers from Butte at the depot and accompanied them to the Park Hotel, where he and his wife and daughter were also staying. His players were already resting, having experienced a hair-raising ride from Fort Shaw to the railhead at Sunnyside. Temperatures had been well below freezing and the wind unrelenting.[9]

Cold winds and shivers were forgotten by the time the teams walked into Luther Hall the next evening. Indeed, a blast of cold air would have been welcome, for the hall was "packed to suffocation" with well over eight hundred fans anticipating a game worthy of this fierce rivalry. Fort Shaw's starting lineup, pictured on the front page of the morning paper, was the one that had carried them through the season, although there were new faces among the Butte Independents who stepped onto the court. Their center and captain, Stella O'Donnell, was familiar enough, and as she and Nettie Wirth positioned themselves in the center circle for the tip-off, a hush fell over the crowd, as if every spectator had taken a sudden breath in anticipation of the opening whistle.[10]

That collective breath exploded as the ball was tapped to Butte but almost instantly stolen by Emma, taken down court, and tossed into the basket for the first score of the game. Three more field goals by the Indians came in quick succession. Elbows flew and bodies became tangled as the Independents did their best to slow the pace of the game. To little effect. At the half, the score stood 22 to 4.[11]

The action did not let up in the second half, as "the ball was first at one end of the hall and then the other." In "one of the prettiest throws of the evening," Minnie launched the ball from "nearly 20 feet . . . and sent [it] into the basket." Cheer after cheer greeted the efforts of both teams, but there was little question as to the outcome. At the final whistle, the score stood Fort Shaw 35, Butte Independents, 6.[12]

Fort Shaw supporters had much to celebrate that night, and though Senator Paris Gibson was not on hand to offer a toast, Mayor Freeman paid tribute to the visitors as well as the triumphant Indians. Not surprisingly, while the *Great Falls Tribune* devoted several columns to a play-by-play description of the game, the *Anaconda Standard* offered few details, citing only Butte's "failure to work in harmony."[13]

Apparently the idea of another one-sided game—even one featuring their home team—minimized the turnout the next night, and Luther Hall was only half full on Saturday evening. Reduced gate receipts were a disappointment for Superintendent Campbell, for he had announced earlier that "the net revenue above expenses" for this series of games would go toward a fund for "the purchase of a large covered vehicle to be used in bringing the girls from Fort Shaw on future occasions." The great discomfort experienced by the travelers two days earlier—and all too often before that—would not be repeated, not if the superintendent could help it.[14]

Although small in number, the crowd that gathered for the Saturday night rematch was noteworthy for the conspicuous presence of Chief Rocky Boy and his band of Chippewas, who were attending as the special guests of Superintendent Campbell. For some of the group, who were "sporting the gayest kinds of colors," it was their first glimpse of basketball. Even so, as had been the case for those Great Falls fans who had come to that first "home" game a scant four months ago, the Chippewas' unfamiliarity with the game was no handicap to their enjoyment of it. They had come to see the Indians play, and they were engaged in the action from the first.[15]

Fort Shaw got off to a shaky start and seemed "out of form" early in the game. Perhaps their lackluster play was due to the "fiercer fight for victory" the Independents were putting up. Fierce indeed: The referee kept a lid on the game by calling multiple fouls on both sides. Still, there were bruising collisions. When Emma and an opposing player went to the floor after a loose ball, the little forward took a blow to the jaw that knocked two of her teeth loose. Unwilling to leave the game, given the closeness of score, Emma played on without complaint. Even at the halftime break, with Fort Shaw ahead 8 to 7, she managed to hide the extent of her injury.[16]

The Indians were able to open a more comfortable lead in the second half, though the Independents gave no quarter. When the game was finally called, the scoreboard told the story: Indians, 17; Independents, 12. There would be no third game in Butte. There would be no more contesting the title of Montana's champions.[17]

Taking the Gospel Back Home
June 1903

❦

AT THE CONCLUSION OF THE SERIES WITH BUTTE, SUPERINTENDENT Campbell announced that he had engaged the girls, the two full squads, in an exhibition tour of the northeastern part of the state. It was time to take the gospel of basketball and Indian education on the road again.[1]

On Sunday morning, June 7, a party of some twenty students, plus Coach Campbell and Miss Malley, departed the campus to begin the tour of towns along the "High Line," the Great Northern rail route across northern Montana. The twenty students were a versatile lot, for the ten basketball players were joined by a handful of "club swingers," with whom they would perform calisthenics exercises, and another handful of musicians, who would join them for the musical part of the program to be given each evening. The first stop on this seven-site tour was Great Falls, always a welcoming venue. But the other six sites—Fort Benton, Havre, Chinook, Harlem, Glasgow, and Poplar—were communities whose citizens had likely never seen a game of basketball. Those sites had been chosen with care; holding games and entertainments in these small towns would provide parents, grandparents, and friends of some of these students with their first opportunity to see them in action. The championship series in Great Falls had turned out to be nothing more than a prelude to more exciting things to come.[2]

The game at Luther Hall on Monday, June 8, was the only time on the tour the Fort Shaw starters were slated to play against another school's team—and the first time they had ever faced the newly formed Great Falls Grays. Since the Grays had struggled against the Sun River team just weeks before, Coach Campbell proposed a handicap game. Fort Shaw fielded only four players, while Great Falls fielded six. Yet Fort

Shaw's victory was so convincing that the *Tribune* suggested the Indians could have come out winners if the Great Falls girls had been allowed to put ten players on the floor. Even without Minnie to supply firing power, Nettie, Genie, Belle, and Emma held their opponents to one point while scoring forty-five themselves.[3]

Since raising money for his athletic program was one goal of this tour, Superintendent Campbell was keeping expenses to a minimum. The troupe would move from town to town along the Great Northern, traveling in the daylight hours and arriving at each site in time to give an evening exhibition, sleep over at a local hotel, then move on to the next town the following day. Fort Benton was their first stop after Great Falls, and their intrasquad game at Green's Hall was "a grand success, socially and financially." All the players "acquitted themselves admirably," according to the local *River Press*, but "Misses Emma Sansavere [*sic*] . . . and Belle Johnson, a former resident of Highwood, were the favorites of the audience."[4]

As the train moved toward Havre, Emma was thinking ahead to the reunion with her sister. Mary Dubois and her husband and children were bound to turn out for the game, and Emma wanted to play her best for them. Yet she had a sense of foreboding as the cars clattered past the Fort Assinniboine siding. This was as close as she wanted to come to the place where she had spent her early years, the place she had last seen her mother alive. She could only hope advance publicity for the game would not draw Joseph Rondo and others from the life she had left behind.[5]

But the news that greeted Emma Sansaver when the train pulled into Havre was worse than she could have imagined. Mary hailed her from the platform and took her aside. Their uncle had ridden in from Maple Creek, Alberta, the previous evening, drunk, angry, and bent on organizing a new search for the body of his sister—their mother—Marie LaFromboise Sansauver. The story had not yet hit the local paper, but many of their kinspeople knew about the furor. Whether due to the unfortunate juxtaposition of events or to genuine interest in seeing one of their own play basketball, it was a given that Emma would recognize a good many faces when she entered Swanton Hall that night.[6]

And indeed she did. But there was no time to worry about whether these people had come to cheer or to gawk. As soon as the whistle blew, Emma was lost in the familiar give and take, the running, dribbling, passing, shooting. Matched up against Gen Healy, she could not afford to give attention to anything but doing her job on the court. Partly because of her intensity, the Blues, the first team, fought their way to victory, despite the impressive teamwork and shooting of the Browns. The final score mattered little to the large and appreciative audience, most of whom had never seen a game of basketball and none of whom had ever had the privilege of watching "the Indian girls [who] exemplify the sport." The audience enjoyed the performance of the gymnastics team and the orchestra almost as much as they had the game itself, and a dance closed out the evening.[7]

For Emma Sansaver, being one of the honored guests at a dance given by white citizens who had heretofore shown nothing but disdain for residents of the "breed camp" south of town should have been a pleasant, if ironic, experience. But by the time the dancing began, the opiate provided by her focus on the game had worn off, leaving only the pain and embarrassment of knowing that her family's violent history was the talk of the very people hosting this social event. Even the boys who asked her to dance must have been well aware that they were dancing with the daughter of "a half-breed Cree Indian" who had been murdered by a jealous lover. Was there a bit of bravado involved in choosing to waltz around the floor with the niece of a man the papers termed "a drunken breed"? Somehow Emma got through the evening, said her thanks to those who had hosted the postgame festivities, and retreated to the hotel room she shared with her teammates.[8]

If only she had been able to spend the night at Mary's house! There had barely been time for a hug and a whispered exchange prior to the game, only enough to learn that officials seemed to be giving some credence to her uncle's story that he had proof that Hunting Dog, a Canadian Cree, had killed Marie Sansaver, tossed her body into a well behind Devlin's slaughterhouse, then fled north across the Medicine Line. But even if Hunting Dog was dragged back down to Montana and dropped on the boardwalk in front of the marshal's door, Emma doubted the authorities would bother to reopen the case. Aside from having her world turned upside down all over again, nothing had really changed. She had long since given up hope that her mother might be alive.[9]

Accustomed as they were to weathering news of various illnesses, accidents, and deaths within their own families, Emma's teammates were at a loss as to how to comfort her. Only Flora Lucero had experienced having a parent's murder appear in the headlines of her hometown newspaper, and even she had no words of wisdom to offer. Whatever was said or left unsaid by her traveling companions, Emma realized she had little choice but to move forward with her own life. Day by day. Or mile by mile, as it were, for she and her friends left Devlin's slaughterhouse and all the rumors behind them as the Great Northern moved out of Havre and rolled on toward Chinook. The distance was less than twenty miles, the relief immeasurable.

The next night the Fort Shaw Blues and Browns again played before "a very good and appreciative audience," even though, according to the *Chinook Opinion*, the crowd was "not as large as it should have been." Superintendent Campbell made his customary comments on the education of Indian youth, and the evening concluded with a dance that continued "up till the early hours of Friday." A few hours' sleep, then four stops and twenty-four miles later, they were in Harlem, the closest depot to Fort Belknap Reservation, home to Katie Snell and Gen Healy.[10]

Unlike Emma, Katie and Gen were overjoyed to have this chance to perform in front of people who knew them and their families. As Superintendent Campbell had hoped, the crowd that gathered that night numbered many Assiniboines and Gros Ventres. The Snells were there, with Jimmy, Katie's little brother, the toddler she had never seen, who was clinging to Fannie Black Digger's skirts. Colonel Healy, more crippled than Gen had ever seen him, and as irascible as ever, had come up with Ponley, leaving behind William, the runaway, who sent his sister his best but said the last thing he wanted to do was get close enough to Superintendent Campbell to be dragged back to Fort Shaw.[11]

Predictably, the Blues toppled the Browns that night in Harlem, 25 to 10. But the second stringers were improving with each outing. Besides, the score was really not the important thing. It was the fun of seeing the girls in action. At game's end, the old colonel was beaming, and the Snells could not have been prouder if their Katie had been declared the star of the game.[12]

Gen and Katie were still in high spirits as the train made its way toward Glasgow the next morning—where the Fort Shaw ambassadors were met by a group of Glasgow's most influential citizens, including General Coleman, proprietor of the hotel in which the visitors would be lodged. Their fame had preceded them, and the basketball girls played to a standing-room-only crowd that night in the Valley County courthouse. Among those crammed into the confines of the largest hall in town were Genie Butch's father, stepmother, and two older sisters. The ranch Genie had been so reluctant to leave was only a dozen miles away, and seeing her family, even for so short a time, made her all the more homesick. She resolved that night to spend the summer on the Little Porcupine, if she could get permission. The cry of the killdeer in the marsh at the bend of the creek, the sight of antelope leaping the coulee that split the back quarter of the ranch, the smell of a horse lathered up from a gallop across the dusty plains—and her secret place down by the river—were all calling to her. Some things were more important than basketball.[13]

Apparently on that particular night the citizens of Glasgow felt there was nothing more important than this exciting new game. The evening's entertainment—from the high-scoring intrasquad scrimmage to the club swinging, to the dance music provided by the Fort Shaw orchestra—was so well received that an invitation for a second appearance at the hall on the team's return trip was immediately extended and immediately accepted. Those who had not been able to get into the packed hall on this night would be given preference for tickets to an exhibition on Tuesday, June 16. There was no possibility of staying over another night now, not when the town of Poplar was awaiting them.[14]

Poplar: Superintendent Campbell's first home in Montana and a town that held a special place in his heart. The warm feelings were apparently mutual, as that Sunday afternoon Campbell and his students were met at the train by a large crowd, many of whom had known the superintendent well during his years at the Fort Peck Agency School and many others who had come to see their children and grandchildren perform—so many, in fact, that Campbell agreed to have his group stay over for a repeat performance on Monday night, a decision that would allow him to linger among old friends and former students.

After playing six games in as many nights, the girls were exhausted that evening in Poplar, but once they walked out onto the court the roar of the crowd restored their energy and they played one of the most tightly contested games of the entire tour. Among those in the hall that evening were Woman That Kills Wood and her new husband, Grass-hopper, as well as Jacob Wirth and his wife, Lydia. In a brief visit before the game, Nettie's father pressed her to come home for the summer—at least part of the summer. Although she had mixed feelings about that prospect, Nettie promised to try.[15]

That first night Superintendent Campbell held to his practice of charging admission, for having this tour pay for itself was imperative. But he announced after the match that there would be no charge for Indians attending on Monday, and among the others who crowded into the hall for the second game were David Mitchell and his youngest daughter, Sarah. Too young to go to Fort Shaw at the time her sisters were sent there ten years earlier, Sarah had begun her studies at the Fort Peck Agency School when F. C. Campbell was its superintendent. In the years since, despite Campbell's repeated entreaties and her own pleas to join her sisters at Fort Shaw, David Mitchell had insisted on keeping his youngest daughter home. Yet something shifted during the few days the Fort Shaw students spent on the reservation that June. Perhaps seeing Nettie Wirth, Sarah's idol, play basketball, perhaps seeing the girls' accomplishments with Indian clubs and musical instruments gave Mitchell a firsthand look at the opportunities Sarah was missing. Whatever the cause, he was softening. Sensing the change, Superintendent Campbell approached him yet again on the matter of allowing Sarah to transfer to Fort Shaw. She was bright. She was strong and athletic. And, at fourteen, she was mature enough to handle the transition. David Mitchell finally agreed. Sarah would go to the Indian school in the Sun River Valley.[16]

The next morning, as the team was boarding the train, Sarah sought out Nettie to share the exciting news. Nettie immediately promised to put her through some basketball drills that very summer. *If* she could get permission to come home, she would bring a ball with her, rig up some kind of basket, and teach the game to the agency girls who had never played. With this idea foremost in her mind now, Nettie toyed with the idea of approaching Coach Campbell on the ride back to Glasgow, hoping to get his permission while he was in such a relaxed mood. But once on the train, the superintendent seemed distracted. Nettie knew this was not the time to put her question in front of him.

It was a wise decision. As the train moved toward Glasgow, Campbell was mulling the telegram from Billy Adams that had been handed to him in Poplar. It carried the Independents' challenge to another two games, preferably on June 26 and 27, preferably in Great Falls. Campbell hesitated. He was still haunted by the vision of a half-empty Luther Hall just a month earlier. Dare he risk losing the interest and support of his most ardent fans? Except . . . What if he provided the fans of Great Falls with yet another "first"? How about an outdoor game—or games—at Black Eagle Park? An exchange of telegrams with Professor Preston during the team's second engagement at Glasgow assured him of the feasibility of his proposal. As the train rolled on westward, Campbell presented the idea to his players. And from Fort Benton he wired Adams that Fort Shaw accepted the challenge. Both games would be played in Black Eagle Park, the last weekend of the month, immediately after closing exercises on campus.[17]

By the time the train rolled into the station at Great Falls on Wednesday, June 17, the *Tribune* had already announced that Fort Shaw fans were about to see basketball played in the out-of-doors. Many of those at the depot cheered as the girls, the musicians, club swingers, and chaperones stepped onto the platform. The welcoming crowd was as eager to hear details about the upcoming games with Butte as about the tour from which the group was just returning. Both games would be played in the cool of the evening, Campbell explained. The court would be "brilliantly lighted," and the view of the game would be as good or better than "if seated in a crowded, hot hall." He expected that "at least 1,000 spectators" would be drawn to the spectacle.[18]

But all of this should in no way lessen the impact and importance of the tour from which they were just returning, he said. Not only had his girls carried the gospel of Fort Shaw—and of the federal Indian policy—across the High Line, they had carried the gospel of basketball. Indeed, Superintendent Campbell predicted that in the wake of the tour, girls would be organizing their own teams in every town visited. Fort Shaw was spreading basketball fever across the state.[19]

Josie Langley waited until the tour was over and the girls were back into some kind of routine at school before telling her teammates what their coach already knew—her playing days were over. She was twenty-eight years old. And she confessed to an ill-kept secret. She was considering a proposal of marriage from Harvey Liephart. She would always be there for them, but from now on Genie Butch would be permanently replacing her place at guard. As this tour had proven, Genie was more than ready to fill her shoes.[20]

"In All Ways Most Deserving"
Summer 1903

TUESDAY, JUNE 23, 1903. F. C. CAMPBELL WAS IN HIS ELEMENT. Some six hundred visitors "from all over the county" had arrived on campus for the year's closing ceremonies. The weather was glorious, "an exceedingly bright morning" having enticed people to drive out for the big event. By eleven o'clock, "All of the stable room had been taken up [by] in the neighborhood of 175 teams." At noon, Superintendent Campbell officially welcomed the visitors, urged them to make the most of this opportunity to better understand "the workings of the institution," and announced that he and his wife were going to spread their picnic blanket and enjoy the box lunch provided by the Ladies Aid Society of Sun River. He hoped his guests would feel free to do the same. Within minutes the six hundred visitors and over three hundred students and staff were scattered about the parade grounds and the grassy stretches beyond, a mosaic of colors and patterns and people backed by the phalanx of tepees lining the banks of the Sun River. Campbell could not recall a more animated and amiable year-end gathering than this one.[1]

Indeed, the superintendent found himself almost reluctant to move on with the program. His students seemed to be at ease in the midst of so many strangers, and those boys and girls whose families had come were clearly enjoying their company. But the afternoon program had to go forward. An hour of guided tours of classrooms and shops, an hour of battalion drills, and "an hour's literary program, consisting of talks and recitations, interspersed with musical selections by the band and mandolin club" followed. Promptly at 4:30—for promptness had ever been a trait of Indian school education—the Blues and the Browns who had so recently played their way across the northeastern part of the state gave a demonstration of basketball on the grassy field where Josie Langley had first directed the school carpenter to devise two poles to which baskets could be attached.[2]

The last event of this crowded afternoon was the highlight of the day, as Campbell had planned it would be. Calling Josie to the front of the crowd on the parade grounds, he handed her a steel case within which had been placed items that the faculty, staff, and student body had decided were emblematic of Fort Shaw School as of June 1903. This time capsule was to be buried the next morning within the cornerstone of the new boys' dorm that would rise on the quad over the summer. Asking Josie to describe each item within the steel case, Campbell stepped aside.

Confidently, proudly, Josie read off a list of the capsule's contents: the current roster of students and employees; a wood carving by Elmer Ellsworth and a hand-drawn calendar by Charles Feather to exemplify the artwork of the students; the *Great Falls Leader* of May 28, 1903, and the *Great Falls Tribune* of June 1, 1903; and, finally, a photograph of Montana's state champions, the 1903 girls' basketball team, along with a typed copy of their season record.[3]

~

The superintendent was finding it hard to let this day go. As he walked his wife and little girl to their quarters after supper, he peeled off at the administration building, promising Ella that he would be home as soon as he'd seen to one more detail. In truth, it was more than a detail. It was a decision he'd been mulling for some time. And now he'd made the decision, and it was time to tell the girls.

Catching sight of Josie walking toward the dorm, he hailed her and asked her to assemble the basketball girls in the gymnasium in half an hour. Stifling her curiosity, Josie went off to round up the team. In the quiet of the office, Campbell picked up the letter from Superintendent McCowan once again. How many times had he read it since his return from the trip across the High Line? Read it and reread it, and yet he had taken his time before responding, for his answer would have a major effect on some young lives, and his decision had to be a well-considered one. It was. If Samuel McCowan wanted a delegation from Fort Shaw for his Model Indian School at the world's fair next summer—say, seven to ten students who had "best prepared themselves, [who were] in all ways the most deserving"—then Campbell had the perfect group for him.[4]

His basketball girls were leaders in their classrooms and workrooms, in the dorms and certainly on the playing field. If, as McCowan said, he wanted students with special talents in some area—music or recitation or domestic or manual arts—they fit the bill there too. McCowan had not specified athletics as a field of accomplishment, but why not? If the state of Montana was intrigued by their success in basketball, how would an international audience respond to a group of young Indian women playing a sport that was barely a dozen years old?

His choice seemed almost foreordained. The basketball girls were, without doubt, mature enough, responsible enough, to take advantage of this once-in-a-lifetime opportunity, to rise to the challenge in the same way they had faced every other challenge. It was time the idea was put in front of them, and depending on the girls' reaction, in front of their parents.

~

The gymnasium still held the heat of the day when the nine girls, plus Josie, who could not stay away, gathered in a circle around the superintendent. For once they could not read his expression. He looked somehow more serious than usual. Just how important could this meeting be? It didn't take long to find out. Holding up an envelope, Campbell told his girls that he had here an invitation from the superintendent of what was going to be a "model Indian school" on the grounds of next year's world's fair in St. Louis. This man wanted a group of students from Fort Shaw to live and work and study in this school for the duration of the fair—from the end of April to the beginning of December. There would be about 150 students all told, from all parts of the West. This student body would be a "living exhibit" of the success of the government's educational program. Having given a lot of thought to the matter, he had decided that the students he wanted to represent Fort Shaw were the very students gathered in front of him now.

Campbell paused. Silence. The girls glanced from one to another, too stunned to know what to make of the matter. You are my chosen delegation, Campbell said, because of how you've conducted yourselves in all your public appearances, because of how you've proved yourselves in classes right here on campus. Because of your talents. Our "talents"— this from Gen—what do you mean? Talents on a basketball court primarily, he responded, but you have talents to spare in the domestic arts and in performance as well. It all depended on how Superintendent McCowan, the man who sent the invitation, thought he could best use them. There was obviously lots more to learn about their possible roles at the model school, and he intended to explore all that—as soon as he knew what they thought. *He* thought this was a marvelous opportunity, but it was their decision. If they were interested, he would let McCowan know, and then he would get in touch with their families.

Again silence. And then one head nodding, then another, and then the contagion swept around the circle. A world's fair! A summer in St. Louis, Missouri! All of us together!

It was only as the group walked back to the dorm that Gen expressed what perhaps some of the others were thinking. Does this man ever come through with his grand plans? Are we going to Utah? No. Are we going to Washington? No. But this is different, Emma said. He really wants this to happen. You can just tell. And, Belle added, this Superintendent McCowan wants it happen, too.

~

On Wednesday evening, June 24, the girls from Fort Shaw Indian School once more squared off against the girls from Butte. The Independents had a new look, with a lineup that boasted "some of the Smoky [C]ity's crack players." Coach Adams had promised that this team was far superior to the one the Indians had faced before. Yet the girls from Fort Shaw had the confidence born of experience that they could prevail against any lineup Butte might put on the floor. Their fans in Great Falls were equally confident, and the novelty of seeing an outdoor game played under the lights was as much a drawing card as watching yet another match between the state's top teams.[5]

According to the *Tribune,* the "field of battle was a large area of leveled ground in front of the grand stand," with the playing area "illuminated with six electric 'arch lights.'" On three sides of the field were "double rows of settees for the spectators," but the majority of spectators filled the grandstand. While Campbell did not get the crowd of a thousand he had hoped for, some seven hundred people did turn out, and their applause, while less audible than the applause echoing off the walls of Luther Hall, was no less enthusiastic.[6]

The hometown fans had plenty to cheer about, as the Indians scored six goals in the first half and threatened to turn the game into a shutout. The attack was balanced, with Nettie, Minnie, and Belle making two field goals apiece. The second half moved slowly, marred by frequent fouls. When time was called, the score stood 13 to 5. The girls from Fort Shaw Indian School had once again proved their superiority. The former substitute, Genie Butch, had turned in an "excellent" performance, "little Emma Sansavere [had covered] all parts of the field at once," and the cries of "Shoot, Minnie, shoot!" had rung out across the park throughout the game.[7]

The Butte papers held out hope that the second game might see improved play by the Independents. But it was not to be, for the Indians went after them "like tigers," guarding their opponents so closely that the Independents failed to score. "The bronze-skinned maidens clearly outclassed their pale-faced opponents" from the opening tip-off. "Little Emma Sansavere made her usual lightning charges" and rifled passes to Belle, Genie, and Nettie, each of whom contributed a field goal to the cause, and all of whom helped get the ball to Minnie, who sent the leather through the net nine times, six times from the field and three times from the free-throw line. The final score was 21 to 5. Minnie's steady hand had carried the day, and in their exuberance, several of her teammates attempted to hoist her to their shoulders, but Minnie "was built too much" and toppled down almost as quickly as she had been lifted up. Laughing and hugging had to suffice.[8]

The game and the season were finally over. Billy Adams had nothing more to offer, and the Great Falls fans were now convinced that "the little Indian maidens can defeat any team on earth—no holds barred." Campbell seized the opportunity. Never one to keep good news a secret, he announced that very night that his girls might have a chance to prove that boast, for it was possible that the team from Fort Shaw Indian School might well be demonstrating the game of basketball next summer in St. Louis at the world's fair, the Louisiana Purchase Exposition. It was still only a possibility at this point, "nothing definite," Campbell cautioned. Skeptics took those words to heart, as aware as his players that nothing had yet come of the trips to Washington and Utah he had so frequently mentioned earlier in the year. Yet, given Campbell's determination to give his girls a larger stage for their talents, there were those who thought that this time his ambitious plans just might work out.[9]

~

Superintendent Campbell was faced with a moral dilemma of sorts. Given his growing conviction that by this time next summer his basketball girls would be playing before an international audience in St. Louis, his temptation was to keep them playing right through the next two months. But was it fair to them or to their families to ask them to stay on campus this summer when they would possibly, even probably, be spending all of next summer in St. Louis?

And then there was the matter of burnout. He thought back to his college days when he played semi-pro baseball all through the summer after a full season of intercollegiate games in the spring. He could remember how much he had looked forward to a fall reprieve. His girls had been playing basketball almost nonstop since October. Perhaps time away from the game and the school was what they needed right now. He had already granted Nettie's request to spend the last part of the summer at home. And Genie Butch could already hear the pounding of hooves and feel the rush of the wind back home. Gen Healy and Katie were both eager for home visits after seeing their families so briefly during the team's visit to Harlem. He didn't know about Emma. He knew that her sister Mary wanted her to come to Havre for a few weeks, but he also knew how close Emma had grown to his own family, how she enjoyed spending the summers working for Mrs. Campbell, caring for Freda, keeping an eye on Freddie and Mead, who would soon be home from boarding school.[10]

But this summer Emma would choose Havre. It was probably time to be with Mary again. She needed to talk with her sister. She admired Mary's strength, and she needed to get close to that, needed time to go back over the painful memories associated with their mother. With that, Campbell made up his mind. It would probably benefit *all* of his girls to have time with their families.

~

The officials back in Washington who read Superintendent Campbell's year-end report of August 1903 must have been impressed. It spoke enthusiastically of plans to expand the irrigation system, increase the herd of range cattle, and complete the new boys' dorm. In its entirety it was a comprehensive survey of the school year, ending with the customary hope that Congress would "see fit to provide liberally" for the maintenance and improvement of Fort Shaw Indian School.[11]

A comprehensive survey. Yet within this report there was not a single word about the time, money, and energy devoted to developing and showcasing Montana's basketball champions. The superintendent offered not a single word about the team, although there was a strangely oblique reference. "Some of the pupils . . . had the privilege during the year of visiting all of the State educational institutions as well as many of the city high schools," Campbell wrote, adding that he felt these visits had helped to develop a "mutual acquaintance . . . that will eventually be helpful to the Indians as well as to the State."[12]

Not a single word about the team. And yet F. C. Campbell intended to do all within his power to see that "some of the pupils" from Fort Shaw Indian School would have the privilege of visiting educational institutions far beyond Montana's borders on their way to and from a summer's sojourn at the Louisiana Purchase Exposition in St. Louis.

Looking to the Future
Fall 1903

Although his year-end report made no mention of the possibility of the Fort Shaw girls' basketball team spending the following summer in St. Louis, Superintendent Campbell had that goal uppermost in his mind in August 1903, and a series of press releases from Louisiana Purchase Exposition publicists fueled his resolve to turn possibility into certainty. Competitive games were to be an official feature of the world's fair, and James Sullivan, secretary of the Amateur Athletic Union (AAU), would be the fair's chief of physical culture. His would be a decidedly complex assignment. St. Louis had managed to edge out Chicago as host city for the first modern Olympic Games to be held on American soil since their revival in Greece in 1896, and Sullivan would be in charge of local arrangements for the Games of '04 in addition to handling the AAU, YMCA, and interscholastic competitions associated with the fair.[1]

Those interscholastic competitions were billed as open to "all the preparatory . . . and high schools in the country," and Fred Campbell resolved that the girls from Fort Shaw Indian School would have their shot at the girls' basketball championship. Confident as he was that Mc-Cowan would see the great advantage of having girls from his Model Indian School meet and defeat the top high school teams in the country, Campbell was determined to sign up his girls the minute Sullivan issued the call for entries.[2]

Meantime, he had other things to attend to. The death of fifteen-year-old Alice Pandoah, a Lemhi student who had come to Fort Shaw with Minnie Burton, had sent shock waves through the school. Alice was to have accompanied Minnie on the trip home that summer, but she was confined to the infirmary with blood poisoning in late June, and Minnie was obligated to go home without her. The girl's condition worsened over the summer, and in August pneumonia set in. On the fourth of September Alice Pandoah was laid to rest in the school cemetery.[3]

Two days later, Superintendent Campbell set out for Idaho to gather up new and returning students from the Lemhi and Fort Hall Reservations. It was with some trepidation that he made this trip, knowing that his letter would have reached Agent Yearian and news of Alice Pandoah's death would have gone out across the Lemhi Reservation. Would the tragedy keep families from allowing their children to go to Fort Shaw? To his relief, the number of students—new and returning—who gathered at the Lemhi rail siding met expectations. He greeted each one in turn, all the while keeping an eye on Minnie, who stood apart from the others, silent and inscrutable.[4]

There would be time to talk during the rail journey to Fort Hall, Campbell told himself. Yet once they boarded the train, Minnie moved to the back of the car, the set of her shoulders warning against intrusion. And so he let the matter go—all the way down to Fort Hall, where excited greetings seemed to lift spirits. But a hush quickly fell over the car as some of the Lemhi returnees whispered the news of Alice's death to friends from Fort Hall, while Minnie continued to stare out the window. To Campbell's relief, when the chatter resumed, Rose LaRose moved back to sit beside Minnie, taking her hand but keeping her silence. And F. C. Campbell continued to keep his distance. All the way to Fort Shaw. There were students and staff on campus with whom Minnie might be more willing to share her feelings. In particular, Josie Langley.

As Minnie Burton and Rose LaRose were settling into the dorm, five of their teammates were en route to Fort Shaw from their homes in eastern Montana. The long train ride gave them time to share their summer adventures. True to her word, Nettie Wirth had recruited enough girls to organize two teams at Poplar, and having worked one-on-one with fourteen-year-old Sarah Mitchell, Nettie knew the girl was ready to battle for a place on Fort Shaw's second team. The moment Genie Butch stepped on the train, Nettie began singing Sarah's praises. At Harlem,

Katie Snell and Gen Healy had barely settled into their seats before Nettie introduced Sarah as their new teammate. By the time Emma boarded the train at Havre, Sarah was practically in uniform.[5]

There was, of course, more to talk about than Nettie's new protégée. First there was the exchange of news about home, about families. And since Emma talked only of the fun she'd had with her nieces and nephews, her friends assumed there was no further news as to her mother's whereabouts. Then there was the question to which there was no easy answer. Everyone but Emma had heard about Alice Pandoah's death. Everyone knew how close she and Minnie had been. No one knew exactly what they would say to their grieving teammate.

As the train rolled on, the mood lightened, and conversations turned to the exciting prospects of the summer to come. Nettie's father had done his military training in St. Louis when he first came over from Germany, and he was full of stories about the city. He didn't know anything about world's fairs, but he knew St. Louis, and he knew Nettie would have a grand time there. In fact, no one knew anything about world's fairs. Not yet. They knew something about Indian schools, but not about *model* Indian schools. Not yet. It was going to be awfully hard to wait until April.

On the short ride from Great Falls to Sunnyside, thoughts went back to the difficult moment when they would have to acknowledge Minnie's loss, and the mood shifted yet again. As it turned out, hugs and tears seemed to be enough.

That evening the basketball girls joined their fellow students in the dining hall for the back-to-school supper. Then boys and girls alike dispersed to their dorms, eager to catch up with one another's activities. Highlights of the experiences of those who had spent the summer at home were exchanged for news of what had transpired at Fort Shaw during their absence. On the part of summer-school students, accounts of the picnics and hikes that had broken the monotony of campus life were postponed as they shared their memories of the death and burial of Alice Pandoah. Then talk of that tragic event faded with the call for lights-out. The rules of boarding school life were once again in force.

Beginning the very next morning several of the basketball girls—

Emma, Belle, and Minnie—joined Josie Langley and a number of Indian assistants in escorting new students to the various classrooms and workrooms in which they would spend the largest portion of each day. Sarah Mitchell took it all in, wondering if she could ever accomplish all that seemed to be expected of her. Returning to the Fort Peck Agency School each fall had meant walking into familiar rooms filled with familiar faces. There she had been a leader; here she was a stranger lost among three hundred strangers. Yet Nettie assured her she would be feeling right at home in a day or so. And once they were all playing basketball, she would remember why she had come to Fort Shaw.[6]

∼

The rhythms of the new year were hardly established when Superintendent Campbell announced that W. J. Adams—Coach Billy Adams of Butte—was coming to the Sun River Valley to serve as Fort Shaw's athletic director. The locals assessed the news. What could have induced that swashbuckling young coach to leave the Smoky City and cast his lot with Fort Shaw? Certainly not financial reward, considering the salaries of Indian School Service employees. And as far as anyone knew, there was no official position for a coach at the school, much less an "athletic director." Perhaps Billy Adams only wanted to hitch his star to the girls' basketball team that had stomped his Butte Independents. That might be so, but word had it that Campbell had brought him in to revitalize Fort Shaw's ailing football program. Might be good to see those Indians take on the big boys from Butte and Missoula again. It had been a couple of years since the heyday of Fort Shaw football. Been some lean years in between; not much to get excited about. Maybe Adams would have the answer. Still, it was a tall order.[7]

∼

While the valley chatter went on, Campbell welcomed Billy Adams to Fort Shaw. Fall meant football, and Campbell was, indeed, intent on reviving Fort Shaw's fortunes on the gridiron. And he felt he had the right man. Even before his arrival on campus in late October, Adams had arranged two games for the boys, a November 14 contest against the university team at Missoula and a Thanksgiving game against Butte High, two teams considered the best in the state. Adams obviously held high hopes for Fort Shaw football, and he brashly predicted he would soon have "an all-star aggregation which will be able to show any of the Montana teams a good time." The prediction flew in the face of those who insisted that no team he could field this year would approach the squad that had stormed the state three years earlier.[8]

Fort Shaw fans continued to have far more confidence in the girls' basketball team than in the boys' football team, provided last year's starting five remained in place. Certainly the lineup had undergone major change with Josie's retirement, but that change seemed to have gone smoothly. Genie Butch had made an easy transition into Josie's guard position on the exhibition tour across the High Line and in that final series with Butte. The girls had chosen Belle as their new captain. But would Josie's loss be more keenly felt once the new season was under way? And what about the second string? Would there be changes there?[9]

With Superintendent Campbell traveling on business much of that fall—to Chicago, to Olathe, Kansas, and to St. Louis—it fell to J. E. Mountford, Fort Shaw's farmer, to issue a statement designed to dispel any such concerns. "The girls' basketball team is . . . unbroken," he assured a reporter from the *Leader*. They were practicing frequently, well aware that they would be star attractions at the "enormous school" being built on the fairgrounds at St. Louis.[10]

~

The football season, which was inaugurated with such high hopes in late October, was concluded by late November. In the wake of three losses, Billy Adams heaped praise on the efforts of his players and talked of "next year."[11]

The end of the football season allowed the athletic director to turn his attention to his real interest—basketball. It had been understood from the first that Adams would not preempt the coaching duties of F. C. Campbell and Sadie Malley. Rather, his job was to "manage" the team, scheduling the games, making the travel arrangements, handling the press releases. But nothing could keep Billy Adams out of the gym, and in late November, he began dropping by to watch the drills and scrimmages. He noted with approval the changes Malley had made over the last two months, changes that had strengthened the second team. With Genie Butch's promotion to the starting five, Katie Snell had taken charge of the Reds—the erstwhile "Browns." Miss Malley had placed her in the center's position and had paired Rose LaRose with Gen Healy at forward. Flora Lucero, a little scrambler, was a natural at guard. The other guard slot, the position vacated by Delia Gebeau, had been the question.

At Nettie's insistence, Miss Malley had given Sarah Mitchell a serious look. She had the speed and endurance. She was also increasingly accurate from the field and from the free-throw line. She and Rose worked well together, and to Nettie's delight, when the two-team roster was posted, Sarah's name was listed at guard. The Fort Shaw squads were set. For the moment. But Miss Malley had warned the players that Superintendent Campbell would have the final say when he was home and able to turn his attention to basketball.[12]

In answer to the other big question, Miss Malley said, they would have to be patient and wait for the superintendent to talk to Mr. Adams about the schedule of games for the upcoming season.

Much as they liked working under Miss Malley, the girls missed the attention they had once had from Coach Campbell. And then, one late November afternoon, their long-absent leader walked in on their practice as casually as if he had never been away at all. They rewarded him with a fast-paced, hard-fought scrimmage. He watched with obvious satisfaction. The two teams were playing each other with as much skill and intensity as the first string had displayed in interscholastic games the previous season. When Miss Malley's whistle ended the scrimmage, Campbell gathered the girls around him. Commending them for their play, he told them that he had just come from St. Louis, where he had visited with Superintendent McCowan, the head of the Indian school that was just beginning to rise on the fairgrounds. The two of them had walked the construction site. He had seen the architect's renderings, and he could assure the girls it would be a beautiful building. Superintendent McCowan was still hoping to have his chosen students—including those from Fort Shaw—in residency by April 30, the opening day of the fair.[13]

It was all but certain that the girls would be going to St. Louis come next summer. But first they had to prove themselves worthy in every area of school life—classroom and workroom as well as on the court—if they expected to represent Fort Shaw at the Louisiana Purchase Exposition.

Belle seized this moment to assure their superintendent that they would prove themselves worthy of his trust, both during this school year and during their summer in St. Louis. Nine other girls nodded solemnly in agreement. But when would Mr. Campbell be announcing their schedule of games for the coming season? The superintendent had no news on that front, but never mind, he said. He had some exciting news from his visit to St. Louis. He and Superintendent McCowan had discussed at some length exactly what would be expected of the Fort Shaw girls. Exhibition basketball games, of course, and Coach Campbell had assured the man that his girls would be more than ready to dazzle the crowds at the world's fair. But Superintendent McCowan had reiterated his earlier requirement for enrollment in the Model Indian School: Every student would be expected to take on more than one assignment. Furthermore, despite Campbell's praise for the academic and vocational strengths of his girls, McCowen had decided to assign the classroom "literary work" to a cadre of students he was bringing from Chilocco. He also planned to have his Chilocco girls demonstrate the "domestic sciences" in kitchen and laundry, while girls from the Haskell Indian School in Kansas would be demonstrating the "domestic arts"—sewing, tailoring, millinery.[14]

The disappointment this announcement evoked in Minnie and Flora, Gen and Nettie, was hardly surprising. Minnie's and Flora's needlework was the pride of Fort Shaw, and both girls had wanted to demonstrate their skills in St. Louis. And Gen and Nettie had looked forward to working in the state-of-the-art kitchen "laboratory" at the Model Indian School. If not classroom or sewing room or kitchen, then what exactly would their responsibilities be—besides basketball?

The performing arts, Campbell said, finally coming to the point. Superintendent McCowan was counting on the ten young women from Fort Shaw to demonstrate their performing-arts skills: from club swinging and barbell exercises, to music, dance, recitation, and pantomime.[15]

Disbelief, anxiety, a sense of betrayal—all were apparent on the faces of the ten young women. This man McCowan expected them to perform in public as gymnasts and musicians, as dancers and actors? What had Coach Campbell committed them to? All of a sudden the excitement went out of this trip to St. Louis. And fear crept in. Then came Gen Healy's outburst. Club swinging and barbell exercises? Music? Pantomime? She demanded to know, did he expect them to master all that in seven months?

Campbell was ready for the question. Let's just take them one at a time, he said. They had been using Indian clubs in their physical culture classes since the day they came to Fort Shaw, he reminded them. In fact, they had given club-swinging demonstrations all during last year's championship season. Miss Malley would now be introducing them to a few new maneuvers performed to music. There was nothing to worry about in that area. The whole routine would last no longer than ten minutes, and their movements with Indian clubs would soon be as smooth as their movements with a basketball. Miss Malley would also be helping them to hone their skills with barbells. They would be learning some new, sophisticated routines that involved manipulating the bars in concert with a partner rather than individually. Again, there was nothing to worry about. There was no group more adept at working in tandem than the girls sitting right there in front of him.[16]

The primary musical contribution expected of the girls, Campbell continued, would be mandolin concerts. Most of them were already members of the mandolin club, and most of them had performed at Fort Shaw entertainments over the last two years. In that regard they were seasoned musicians. Their music teacher, Miss Evans, would be developing a suitable repertoire for performance in St. Louis. She would hold thrice weekly rehearsals with them all spring and would offer extra lessons to those who needed the help.[17]

Nettie glanced over at Sarah, well aware of the effect Campbell's words must be having on her. Of all the girls in this little group, Sarah had to be the most intimidated. She had been on campus a scant two months. She had come with no background in gymnastics and little more in music. Catching Sarah's eye, Nettie knew she was right. Sarah was on the verge of tears. Nettie nodded to her teammate, a reassuring kind of nod. The mandolin was Nettie's instrument, and she was sure that if she spent extra time with her, Sarah would quickly master it. Nettie wished so much, and not for the first time, that Lizzie were here—not far away at Carlisle—for Lizzie would be the one to take Sarah under her wing.

Gymnastics and music. Belle looked around. Maybe she and her teammates were ready to concede that they did have some experience and expertise in club swinging and mandolin playing. But dance and recitation and pantomime? She, for one, had never done any public speaking and could not recall that any of her teammates had either. Would they be expected to dress up in funny clothes and speak funny little pieces like Louis Youpee did? Now, without elaborating, Mr. Campbell was telling them that Miss Crawford would instruct them in these new areas. She would expect them in the chapel at four tomorrow afternoon for their first rehearsal.

Well, isn't this Jim Dandy, Gen muttered as the girls left the gymnasium to ready themselves for supper. Recitations in the chapel. What about basketball? Here it was, the end of November, and Coach Campbell had not yet scheduled a single game. What were they going to do all spring? Dance and play the mandolin?

~

Dance they did. But in slow motion. When the girls arrived in the chapel at four o'clock the next afternoon, Miss Crawford explained that they would be learning precise movements to accompany the recitations they would deliver as a group, blending their voices into one. They would be presenting stylized pieces featuring mature subject matter, not pieces like those recited by Louis. For example, their first number would be "The Famine" scene from Longfellow's *Hiawatha*, a piece sure to meet with the approval of Superintendent McCowan and to impress all those for whom it was performed.[18]

Provided, of course, that they spoke from their hearts. Because their movements would interpret the lines they spoke and convey the spirit of the scene they were describing, their first task would be coming to understand the passages they would be reciting. At that point Miss Crawford handed out pencils and paper and instructed the girls to copy the lines she had written out on the blackboard. And yes, they would be memorizing those lines. With Christmas holidays right around the corner, they would concentrate on "The Famine." The other pieces would have to wait.

There would be no waiting where mandolin practice was concerned. Before December dawned, Miss Evans had shaped the girls into a ten-piece club. Nettie, who had served as the student director of the long-standing, larger Fort Shaw mandolin club, would fill the same role here. She would also be first mandolin, with Gen Healy and her beloved "tater bug," right behind her, joined by Belle, Minnie, Genie, and Sarah. Flora and Katie were assigned the guitars. Rose, who had been fiddling tunes alongside her father since she was little, would be the group's violinist. Six mandolins. Two guitars. One violin. And Emma, an exemplary pianist who had mastered every stringed instrument in the music room, was handed the school's new cello. The "Little One" would play the mandolin club's largest instrument.[19]

All through December the hour that had once gone to scrimmaging in the gym was divided instead between practices with Miss Evans and rehearsals with Miss Crawford, for the girls' first performance would be part of a gala three-day holiday celebration over the Christmas weekend. The highlight of that celebration was to be the wedding of their former captain and teammate, Josephine Langley. The event warranted a two-column formal announcement in the *Great Falls Leader* under the headline, "Basketball Team Captain to Wed." The groom was "Mr. Harvey Lephart [*sic*], a white employee of . . . the Fort Shaw School." The entire campus—especially Josie's former teammates—was looking forward to a wedding.[20]

And beyond. Just before Christmas, the girls learned that the St. Louis newspapers had published a challenge issued in their names by Samuel McCowan. He had a team of Indians coming from out west, he announced, who would play "any girls' basketball team in the world—bar none." In effect, they would be going "against all comers" for the world's championship in girls' basketball.[21]

"A Great Thing for Girls' Sport"
Fall 1903

❧

When James Sullivan, director of the physical culture department, was not engaged in overseeing the construction of the gymnasium and stadium that would be the setting for the many athletic events connected with the St. Louis fair—including the Games of the III Olympiad—he was busily arranging tournaments in such sports as baseball, basketball, football, golf, and tennis. Some of these would be restricted to college and "scholastic" entries, others would determine national AAU and YMCA championships. These events, like all others under his direction, would be designated "Olympic events." And in all cases, the competition would be open only to men and boys. According to custom.[1]

But customs were changing. And as the world's fair approached, Sullivan began receiving requests from women's colleges and organizations seeking parallel competitions. He was trapped between his own long-held sensibilities about women and sports—especially team sports—and the increasing pressure from female athletes seeking their own place in this hitherto all-male realm. He offered a double-edged response. "The idea [of women's competitions] is an excellent one," he said. "Our girl athletes . . . are not only becoming more numerous yearly, but the records made at some of the college meetings . . . are really surprisingly good." And then came his hedge: The problem, as he saw it, arose from the fact that these events were, and always had been, "not for the eyes of the public," whereas all competition held in conjunction with the world's fair had to be staged in a public arena before mixed crowds. Whether the prejudice against allowing women to compete in front of male spectators could be overcome remained to be seen.[2]

Sullivan held out little hope that it could be, given the entrenched attitudes concerning the propriety of female participation in sports. But, assuming such "objections" *could* be overcome, he would be happy to arrange a women's athletic meet. "It would be a great thing for girls' sport," he declared, "and . . . would prove a drawing card at the Fair." He would be especially open to scheduling "several women's basket-ball games," provided the entrants were willing to play in a public arena.[3]

That was all Campbell needed to hear. In his meeting with Samuel McCowan in St. Louis, he had pressed the point. He would gladly contact James Sullivan on behalf of his athletes—whose games had always been open to the public—but perhaps the offer should be made by the superintendent of the Model Indian School. Campbell left it in McCowan's hands, although he helped McCowan draft the letter to the head of the department of physical culture, advising him that a basketball team of "full-blood" Indian girls from the West stood ready and willing to challenge all comers for the championship of the fair.[4]

If Sullivan wanted "a drawing card," he had just been handed one.

Getting Ready
Winter 1903–1904

BACK AT FORT SHAW, THE HOLIDAY SPIRIT REIGNED. THE CELEBRATION began on Christmas Eve when 320 students assembled in a dining hall decorated with boughs and bows and two large Christmas trees. A dozen large laundry baskets laden with treats—candies, nuts, and oranges—were passed around, and children's voices blended in carols.[1]

At high noon the next day, in the school chapel, Josephine Langley and Harvey Liephart recited their vows in front of the entire student body, faculty and staff, and a number of friends from the Sun River Valley, Great Falls, and the Blackfeet Reservation. Superintendent Campbell escorted the bride, "prettily gowned in white," to the altar to the strains of Mendelssohn's wedding march. At the close of the ceremony the bride and groom led the way to a small reception held in the parlor of the employees' quarters, and at two o'clock an elegant wedding banquet was served.[2]

That evening everyone reconvened in the chapel for "a musical and literary entertainment," including a performance by the ten-girl mandolin club. The holiday festivities were concluded the following day with an exhibition match between the Fort Shaw Blues, captained by Belle Johnson, and the school's newly configured Reds, captained by Katie Snell. Honored guests for that game were Mr. and Mrs. Harvey Liephart.[3]

Finally, there was basketball news. At a New Year's Day exhibition game and dance at Sun River, Superintendent Campbell announced to the friends and neighbors who had gathered in Murray Hall on that snowy night that Billy Adams was working toward a late-January or early-February series of games for the girls against Chemawa Indian School in Salem, state champions of Oregon. A series of eight games featuring the two championship teams should attract capacity crowds and would, Campbell predicted, result in the girls from Fort Shaw being crowned as champions of the Northwest. Half the games were to be played in Oregon and half in Montana—two at Great Falls, one in Helena, and one at Sun River. Confident that gate receipts at each venue should more than pay for transportation and lodging for both teams, Campbell stood ready to open the series by taking his girls to Chemawa.[4]

At almost the same time, Spokane's *Spokesman Review* was reporting that the Fort Shaw, Montana, Indian girls' basketball team planned a series of games "from Butte to the coast," including a game against Spokane High. It was easy to get caught up in Coach Campbell's announcements, yet memories of his equally enthusiastic plans, laid out the previous spring, for a game against the University of Utah team were still too fresh to allow the starting five to put their hopes on going west.[5]

With so many hopes having been raised and dashed, it was sometimes hard to believe that there would even *be* a Model Indian School at the world's fair, much less that they would be pupils at that school. But the girls found it reassuring that Miss Evans and Miss Crawford and Miss Malley never seemed to waver in their belief in the summer that lay ahead, nor did they let up in preparing the girls for the "entertainments" they would give in St. Louis.

In late December Campbell provided a Great Falls reporter with yet another news release, this one describing in detail the Model Indian School rising on the fairgrounds in St. Louis and noting that of the thousands of students enrolled in "the fifty-three Indian schools" that lay within the boundaries of the Louisiana Purchase, the ten "quiet little ladies" who made up Fort Shaw's basketball team would be counted among the school's elite student body. In addition, one member of the Fort Shaw band, trumpeter Lewis Snell, eighteen-year-old half brother of Katie Snell, had been invited to become part of the Indian School Band in St. Louis. And John Minesinger and little Louis Youpee would be going along to perform their popular routines before an international audience.[6]

According to the *Leader*, Fort Shaw's having been allotted "such a large proportion of students" was due to the overall excellence of the school, the amazing accomplishments of the girls' basketball team, and the fact "that Superintendent F. C. Campbell is perhaps the best all round hustler, as well as the most enthusiastic [leader] . . . of a school in the United States." Enthusiastic indeed. And Campbell's enthusiasm never failed to infect his hearers, even jaded newspaper reporters. "The Famine" scene from *Hiawatha*, a recitation being perfected for St. Louis by the girls, would be given "in full Indian costume," the *Leader* proclaimed, costumes "not to be seen more than once in the ordinary man's lifetime."[7]

Locating "full Indian costume[s]" for young women who had grown up on reservations where wearing traditional clothing was discouraged or forbidden turned out to be more difficult than Superintendent Campbell and Miss Crawford had anticipated. The girls were eager enough to comply, especially since this was a rare opportunity to show the distinctive regalia of their respective tribes. Their families were equally enthusiastic about locating or replicating the buckskin dresses, moccasins, leggings, breastplates, and other adornments appropriate for such an occasion. But sometimes finding something like that meant going generations back. For instance, Emma's earliest memories of celebrations in the Métis camp of her childhood involved bright cotton blouses and shawls and dark skirts. Yet her sister Mary was able to find—or fashion—a beautiful buckskin dress whose beadwork recalled her Chippewa foremothers and whose fleur-de-lis designs at the hemline bespoke her French ancestry.[8]

The most difficult task Superintendent Campbell faced was locating suitable regalia for his star, Minnie Burton. In early January 1904, he sat down to draft a letter to Agent Yearian of the Lemhi Reservation: "Minnie Burton . . . will be one of the representatives from this school at St. Louis during the Exposition. She takes a prominent part . . . . I am very [desirous] that she have an Indian dress, Buckskin, with any Indian decorations, leggins [sic] and moccasins complete." The dress, which should "represent the work of her tribe," was needed for a concert recitation of "The Famine" scene from *Hiawatha* and would be needed in time for Minnie to join her teammates in a publicity photo in late January.[9]

The request posed a dilemma for Agent Yearian. Minnie's father, William Burton, had been among the first of the Lemhis to comply with edicts from the commissioner of Indian affairs concerning the abandonment of traditional dress for "white man's" clothing. By 1904 most of Minnie's people had given in to the agent's demands rather than lose their food subsidies. Both Yearian and Burton "tried in every possible way to prepare the articles desired," but by mid-January they had only managed to come up with "an ordinary cloth dress, a pair of moccasins, necklace and earrings." Yearian promised to send those items off at once in hopes that they "might do for the picture." In the meantime, he would continue his search for a buckskin dress and a pair of leggings and hoped to get them to Minnie before the girls departed for St. Louis.[10]

Indeed, by the time the photographer arrived to take the formal portrait, Minnie Burton was wearing a fringed buckskin dress. Coach Campbell had achieved his primary purpose: there was enough variety in the colorful breastplates and necklaces to suggest the diverse tribal backgrounds of his basketball players. Seeing ten beautiful young women dressed in their ceremonial best reciting lines associated with "the noble savage" would have tremendous effect on those who longed to see "real Indians," not just dark-skinned teenagers wearing school uniforms reflecting the white world they were being trained to enter.

Miss Crawford's sessions with the girls who would soon be performing the scene from *Hiawatha* in public took on new pressures. Memorizing Longfellow's lines, in part by reading them over and over as a group, turned out to be relatively easy. Learning to recite those lines as if in one voice was another matter altogether. Carried along by rhythms as steady as drumbeats, the story told in "The Famine" lent itself well to choral reading, but only if every girl enunciated every word in the same way. Indeed, Belle Johnson, who had been chosen to recite the refrain, found her solo performance easier than her participation in the responses voiced by all ten girls. The earliest efforts were so crude that Miss Crawford herself became discouraged. Yet before long the ten girls had surpassed her "most sanguine expectations." All the hard work was paying off, for having mastered the elocutionary aspects of the performance—and having internalized the feelings evoked by the passage—they had little difficulty in adding the gestures and poses Miss Crawford taught them. Horror, supplication, discovery, mourning—all had their specific movements, and the girls had soon enough perfected them.[11]

As pressured as the ten young women were in keeping up with classroom and workroom requirements and spending extra hours learning and perfecting the entertainments they would perform in St. Louis, basketball practice at eight o'clock each evening was a welcome release of energy as well as a welcome return to the familiar. They knew the game. They knew its rhythms better than they knew the rhythms of their stylized choral recitations. Dribbling, passing, moving the ball from one end of the court to the other, always intent on getting it to the player in best position to score. This was their world, their game.

∼

In January 1904 the Montana teachers' organization formalized the constitution for an interscholastic athletic association whose mission it was to "systematize athletics throughout the state." Though long rumored, the announcement that only accredited colleges and high schools would be allowed to join the new association sent shock waves through the sports community. The *Great Falls Leader* went to print with an article that conveyed the essence of the ruling. It appeared under the heading, "Fort Shaw Shut Out."[12]

Emma Sansaver picked up the news in a paper lying on the Campbells' sofa when she was tending Freda one January afternoon. There it was in black and white: "The Fort Shaw Indian School will not be eligible [for] membership in the association." Having all but memorized the article, Emma carried the news to practice that night. The girls were shattered. But Belle figured that Superintendent Campbell must have seen this coming, for how else to account for his continuing to stall in scheduling games against Butte and Helena, Missoula and Bozeman, while arranging any number of games outside Montana? The girls looked for some explanation for their exclusion. The league was to be limited to accredited high schools and colleges. Fort Shaw Indian School was not an accredited high school. Pure and simple. But was that their fault? Miss Malley pointed out that schools in the league would probably not be disqualified for playing against excluded teams like Fort Shaw. But there was little consolation in that. What would other teams gain by playing against—and losing to—the Indians? What point was there to playing games that were nothing more than fund-raisers for elite association schools?[13]

~

Putting the disappointment behind them, the girls threw themselves into preparations for the exhibition schedule Coach Campbell now laid out for them. The Chemawa tour had, as anyone could have predicted, fallen through. But Billy Adams had arranged a series of in-state appearances that would allow them to polish their intrasquad play and hone the various entertainments they would be taking to the world's fair. And because these events were being billed as the last chance for Montanans to see the girls in action before they left for St. Louis, they should draw capacity crowds and go a long way toward defraying expenses associated with the world's fair adventure.[14]

Miss Malley, Miss Evans, and Miss Crawford were consulting with one another almost daily. Miss Malley, as expected, had nothing but praise for the girls' expertise at barbells and club swinging. They had easily learned the thirty-five movements with the clubs that she had worked into a ten-minute routine. Miss Evans could not have been more pleased—nor could Nettie—with the way Sarah Mitchell had picked up the mandolin. And Emma was mastering the cello as quickly and easily as Miss Evans had thought she would. The musical part of their entertainments was falling into place.[15]

There yet remained the question of the recitations. A dress rehearsal of "The Famine" scene, performed for their schoolmates, had gone exceedingly well. Miss Crawford could now put that piece aside in order to concentrate on their pantomime of "Paradise and the Peri." This verse tale, like "The Famine," was a portion of a longer work, this one by the nineteenth-century Irish poet Thomas Moore. This time no memorization would be required, for Miss Crawford would recite the piece they would pantomime. Even so, their first task was to read and reread the text that would be the basis for their movements. Understanding the setting and situation described in the narrative poem was a crucial first step toward preparing for their danced interpretation of the story. In essence, this "Peri," an elfin miscreant, was denied entry into Paradise unless she followed the angel's injunction to "Go...and redeem thy sin."[16]

As strange as the setting for this Persian folk tale was to the girls, it was no stranger than the movements Miss Crawford now introduced as background for the recitation. Miss Crawford was confident the girls would come to enjoy the "dance." She was even more certain they would love the flowing Grecian tunics in which they would perform it. The piece was perfectly suited to an international audience such as the girls would find in St. Louis. One need not understand the English language to understand the feelings they would be conveying in their interpretation of "Paradise and the Peri."[17]

Perhaps it was that element of the exotic that made her students so receptive to Miss Crawford's idea. Perhaps it was the opportunity to create empathy for a guiltless outcast. Perhaps it was simply the freedom of movement the routine allowed. For whatever reason, the girls became fully engrossed in their practices. In late January, with some trepidation, Miss Crawford invited Superintendent Campbell to observe this work-in-progress. To her relief, Campbell, never one to shy away from pushing limits himself, was enthusiastic. This work was bound to be one of the most impressive in the girls' repertoire. And he immediately authorized the purchase of the materials needed to create costumes so different from the school uniforms, the basketball bloomers, and the buckskin ceremonial dresses already gathered for the team's performances at the fair.

But time was a factor. The bolt of material was ordered from Great Falls. Minnie Burton and Flora Lucero, under the watchful eye of Miss Holt, the school's seamstress, began designing the pattern from the illustrations Miss Crawford had collected, and the girls most skilled with needle and thread spent hours in the sewing room, placing the patterns on the filmy cloth and cutting and stitching. Nettie and Katie volunteered to create the coronets they would wear, wrapping silk ribbon around carefully molded wire.[18]

On Friday, January 29, all preparations came to a halt as Superintendent Campbell, his basketball girls, and Miss Crawford loaded their school uniforms, the precious buckskin dresses, the mandolin club's instruments, and the Grecian tunics onto the train and headed toward Cascade and the first of the series of in-state exhibitions Billy Adams had arranged. The girls were nervous. Not about the game. Not about "The Famine" scene. But about "Paradise and the Peri." They had not yet perfected the synchronized movements. Yet Miss Crawford insisted there was nothing to be lost and everything to be gained by trying the piece before an audience, especially one that had likely never heard of, much less seen, a performance in pantomime. Her prediction proved correct, for although the basketball game had been billed as the feature of the evening—with band music and a dance open to the public being an added draw—the people of Cascade were "surprised and delighted" by "Paradise and the Peri."[19]

Heartened by their experience in Cascade, the girls returned home eager to perfect their performance. But all the confidence gained in Cascade began to slip way as the train made its way toward the city. Why had they thought they were ready to perform this piece in front of a Great Falls audience? Yet there it was, the second item on the program. Placing this unconventional entertainment early in the program, Miss Crawford assured them, meant they would have little time to be nervous. Time enough, Gen Healy interjected.

Showcase Season
February–April 1904

FEBRUARY 5, 1904. THE FRIDAY MORNING EDITION OF THE TRIBUNE trumpeted the arrival of the Fort Shaw Indians: The evening's entertainment had been "prepared specially for the St. Louis Exposition, and nothing like it [would] ever again be seen in Great Falls."[1]

That night there was standing room only in Luther Hall. For all the girls' anxieties concerning the premiere of their pantomime, their rendition of "Paradise and the Peri" was deemed "beautiful," their interactions, "past perfect." The reporter was even more effusive in his praise for "The Famine" scene that followed, perhaps because it was something more familiar to both him and the audience. In any event, the applause started the moment the "bronze Minnehahas" walked into the hall. Their buckskin dresses were "the finest ever seen . . . in the city." One dress was reputed to weigh fifteen pounds, simply because of the beadwork. Another was estimated to have an "intrinsic worth . . . greater than [that of] many a white bride's trousseau." The array of finery was not the only thing to be noted, for it was the unity and fluidity with which the girls spoke and moved that so impressed the audience.

> All the earth was sick and famished;
> Hungry was the air around them,
> Hungry was the sky above them,
> And the hungry stars in heaven
> Like the eyes of wolves glared at them!

The somber phrases rolled through the hall. Miss Crawford and Superintendent Campbell could not have been prouder as "the girls were applauded to the echo."[2]

If Fred Campbell had any doubts as to the overall effectiveness of his proposed St. Louis program, the response of the Great Falls audience erased them. For the price of a fifty-cent piece, the six hundred spectators also enjoyed a violin solo, "The Blue Danube Waltz," performed by Miss Evans, and a recitation by "a full-blood Indian who blacked up and dressed as a negro preacher and gave an 'Alphabetic Sermon' by reciting the alphabet over and over with the different intonations and motions that a negro camp meeting preacher would use." That "full-blood Indian" was John Minesinger, once a student and now a member of the Fort Shaw staff, who would be one of the chaperones on the St. Louis trip. Minesinger's special charge would be the boy who stole the show this February night in Great Falls.[3]

"Mr. Louis Youpee Came to Town!" the *Leader* headlined the following afternoon. This eleven-year-old with a natural bent for comedy had been scheduled for a single recitation, but his performance of "Nothin' 't All" prompted call after call for encores. "He had the crowd going from the start," the paper reported, and Superintendent Campbell kept bringing him back onstage, not only pleasing the fans but also providing extra minutes in the dressing room for the girls, who were finding that it took more time than anticipated to change clothes and hairstyles between their performances. All in all, the diminutive Youpee, his "three-foot form" clad in baggy pants, recited eight pieces, "becom[ing] famous in a single evening." A modest little fellow, Louis dismissed the crowd's adulation. "That ain't nothin' to speak like that: I got dozens more like 'em," he was quoted as saying before leaving the hall that night.[4]

As Youpee took his last bow, the ten girls reappeared, this time in their basketball uniforms, to perform their new club-swinging and barbell exercises. The exhibition game followed, with a relay race as the half-time attraction. The race featured four girls from each team, with each runner taking the handkerchief of her team—red or blue—and "dashing full tilt down the hall, swinging around a young buck seated on a stool and rushing back to pass the handkerchief to another runner." The Blues won the contest "by about 10 feet," though the result was actually as irrelevant as the score of the exhibition game itself, since that game "simply show[ed] what an excellent team Fort Shaw has to pit against the crack teams of the east at the Fair."[5]

While the girls basked in the praise, the *Leader* was going to print with the unsolicited comment of one of the valley's earliest settlers. Robert Vaughn, a member of the audience at Luther Hall that night, noted that "the old pioneers can realize more than others the progress that has been made . . . by the aborigines." Hearing the "plain English" spoken by the girls and listening to the boys in the brass band playing "our national airs" had made Vaughn aware that "education and civilization have done wonders in Montana" in the thirty years since soldiers posted to Fort Shaw were securing the protection of citizens like him from hostile Indians.[6] Intended as highest praise, the words stung. "Old pioneers" and "hostile Indians." Would this game never play itself out?

~

With confidence gained from their performance in Great Falls, the troupe from Fort Shaw Indian School took their show on the road. On Leap Day, they set out on a five-site, six-day tour that would take them to Craig, Helena, Butte, Anaconda, and Dillon. Snow clouds were gathering as they set out in open wagons for Craig before dawn that Monday, and the winds were rising by the time they reached the rail platform there. Fortunately, the local hotel, which their party filled to capacity, was less than a block away, and even so they were chilled to the bone by the time they walked into the lobby. But this was Montana, and a blizzard in late February was hardly surprising. Nor was the bitter cold reason enough for the fans to stay away. Few citizens from Craig had ever made the forty long miles up to Great Falls to see the girls from Fort Shaw in action, and knowing this might be their one and only chance to do so, they overflowed the little hall.[7]

Body heat from the crowd made the place as cozy as could be, and by the time the entertainments were over and the game under way, the girls had forgotten all about the weather outside. Later, glowing from the enthusiasm of their new fans as well as from the exertion of so much energy, they walked out into the growing storm, tucked their heads against the stinging, blinding snow, and laughed their way back to the hotel. Their good spirits and high energy held as they slid between cold sheets. But Katie, whose bed stood against the outside wall, found it difficult to get to sleep as fierce winds rattled the boards, and she snuggled next to Nettie, her bunkmate, grateful for shelter from such a storm.

Going to bed fueled by inner warmth had been easy compared with crawling out from beneath the thin wool blankets and touching feet to freezing floorboards the next morning. Wasting no time, the girls pulled on wool dresses, stockings, and shoes and hurried down to the dining room to warm themselves around the welcoming fireplace. They could linger over their hot oatmeal and cups of steaming coffee, their superintendent told them, for the storm had delayed the south-bound train, and they had his permission to stay right there by the fire until they heard the engine's whistle.

Warmed as much by their chatter about last night's performance as by the flaming logs on the fire, the girls were more than ready to be on their way to Helena by the time the train arrived. With the wind dying down, the snow subsiding, and visibility improving, the engineer was able to make up for some of the time lost to the blizzard, and they arrived in the capital city only an hour behind schedule. There was still time to enjoy the warm bath and massage they had come to associate with overnight stays in fine hotels, although their afternoon naps were cut short by Miss Crawford's polite but persistent knocking at their doors. She wanted a quick run-through of both "The Famine" scene and the pantomime. The girls were glad enough to comply, since tonight's audience would be far more sophisticated—and likely more critical—than the audience in Craig.

Excellent work, Miss Crawford said as she dismissed them for the light supper awaiting them in the dining room below. There were more than pre-performance jitters to talk about at table; soon after they were seated, Superintendent Campbell came in with a copy of that morning's *Anaconda Standard*. The paper carried an item that would be of some interest to them, he said, and opening to the page in question, he began to read aloud: Fort Shaw's "famous girls' basketball team" was coming to town. "The team has not been playing much throughout the state this year," the article said—and here the superintendent paused and glanced around to be sure he had everyone's attention—"for the reason that there is no girls' team in the state that can give them anything like a tussel [*sic*]. They stand alone and unrivaled," he continued. "This may not be good reading for the white girls but it is true."[8]

With that, Campbell passed the paper to Belle. His point had been made. Belle could read the rest of the article to her teammates as they finished supper. The star of the show that was coming to town, the *Anaconda* reporter said, was "a little Indian named Louis Youpee . . . a born actor. . .a wonder in moccasins." This was too much for Gen, who immediately assumed the slouch and shuffle affected by Louis, hitched up a pair of imaginary oversized trousers, and launched into her own rendition of "Nothin' a 'Tall." Louis began to match her, line for line, hitch for hitch. In the midst of the laughter, none of the students noticed that Superintendent Campbell had slipped away from the table, having been summoned to the front desk to receive a telegram.[9]

Sometime between that moment and the troupe's departure for the Helena auditorium, the superintendent caucused with the adults in the entourage—including John Minesinger. Consensus was reached. The news he had just received in the telegram from the school would be withheld for now. It would be hours before another north-bound train came through Helena. And only the late train to Great Falls connected with the "Turkey Trail" that would take the students back to the school. There was no point in imparting such devastating news until he could take them directly to the station, for he knew their first instinct would be to get home to Fort Shaw. Under the circumstances, there was every reason to let the day unfold as scheduled in hopes of keeping them occupied and in high spirits for as long as possible. The show would, indeed must, go on.[10]

And quite a show it turned out to be. The entertainments were a smashing success; the fans were almost as enthusiastic about the game between the Fort Shaw Blues and Reds as they had been about the interscholastic matches between the Indians and the Helena High players, all of whom had front-row seats in the crowded hall. The game was hard-fought, with the Blues edging out the Reds, 12 to 10, but the real victory was audience appreciation of all the events of the evening. Indeed, the applause might well have gone on much longer had Superintendent Campbell not signaled the director of the high school orchestra to lift his baton and get the dance under way.[11]

The girls had been looking forward to the dance as a chance to visit with friends they had come to know from previous games with Helena High. But there would be no dancing for the young performers from Fort Shaw that evening. Miss Crawford and Miss Evans had packed up their clothes and instruments the moment their literary and musical entertainments were finished, then hurried back to the hotel to pack up all the clothes and other items the boys and girls had left in their rooms. Miss Malley and John Minesinger had whisked away barbells and Indian clubs even before Nettie and Katie met at center court for the opening tip of the exhibition game. And although the girls were too involved in the action to notice, no one from Fort Shaw except Coach Campbell stayed to watch the game, as trunks and boxes were quietly taken out of the auditorium and down to the train station.

By the time the troupe was herded out of the hall, all was prepared for the emergency rail journey home that Superintendent Campbell had managed to arrange. The news could be held back no longer. Katie Snell's little brother George and his cousin Fred Kuhnahan, both seven years old, had run away sometime yesterday afternoon and been caught in last night's blizzard. Mr. Mountford had alerted neighbors and organized search parties as soon as the two were reported missing, but as night fell and the blizzard closed in, the search had to be called off until morning. By then it was too late for Freddy, who had died of exposure. Somehow George had managed to survive, though "badly frozen." According to what news Campbell had received from the campus, George would likely make it through, although his hands and feet, his cheeks and ears, had been severely frostbitten.[12]

Katie pushed for more information. Why had the boys set out with a storm coming in? Had they been upset about something? Had one of them been punished that morning? George was still too disoriented and exhausted to offer much of an explanation, Superintendent Campbell told her, but according to Mr. Mountford, he and Freddy had been inspired by the successful Sunday night escape of Freddy's older brother

Dan and four other boys. The teenagers had slipped out of their dorm well ahead of the incoming storm and in plenty of time to hitch a ride into Great Falls, hop a freight, and be well on their way toward Fort Belknap before the blizzard hit. But the little boys had not planned so well, nor moved so quickly. They had been out in the open all night and had gotten no farther than the Sun River crossing when they decided to turn back toward school. When Freddy dropped from exhaustion, George had covered his cousin as best he could and pushed on. By the time he reached school and gave directions to the rescuers, Freddy "had succumbed to the terrible cold" and his frozen body had been carried back to the campus.[13]

Katie was beside herself. There she was in that hotel in Craig last night, listening to the wind and thinking only of her own discomfort. She should have taken better care of her little brother. She had known George was homesick. Why hadn't she taken more time to be with him? If she had not been off playing basketball, would he have stayed on campus? Not necessarily, her teammates hastened to tell her. Gen and Belle and Flora had all been right there on campus when their siblings ran away. Flora's brother had made his bid for home three times in a single year. At least George, like their own siblings, had lived through his attempt for freedom, although he would likely feel responsible for his cousin's death for the rest of his life. For now, all the group could do on their way back to school was to pray the doctor was right in predicting that George would survive the ordeal.[14]

~

The train heading north seemed to crawl, and the wagon ride from Sunnyside was interminable. At Sun River most of the houses were dark, though one woman was up and walking her fretful baby when the two wagons clattered through town on the frozen road in the early morning hours. Drawn to the window, she pulled aside her parlor curtain. Yes. These were the students who had passed through so gaily on their way to Craig not thirty-six hours earlier. But now there was no merriment in the wagons. She opened her door and peered out into the darkness. Accustomed to hearing the laughter and chatter of student celebrants returning from their various adventures, she was struck by the eerie quiet. This was not the silence of sleep. She could hear muffled sobs. These had to be the schoolgirls returning to the tragedy at Fort Shaw.[15]

~

That first week of March was given, not to a triumphant tour, but to yet another funeral. Yet another procession to the little cemetery just west of the school. Yet another period of mourning for the students of Fort Shaw Indian School.[16]

But it was also a time of decision for the basketball team, even if none of the girls felt much like giving thought to the future. Within a week of the tragedy, Coach Campbell assembled his players and shared with them Superintendent Samuel M. McCowan's latest proposal. The girls stared at him in disbelief. They knew that McCowan was not only the head of the Model Indian School in St. Louis but was also the superintendent at Chilocco. It made sense that he would return to Oklahoma after the fair was over. But why would this man they had never even met think they would want to follow him there? How could they even consider such a thing? Even if they transferred to Chilocco as a unit, all together, as Superintendent McCowan requested, it would still mean leaving "home." They had already done that once in their lives. They were not ready to do it again. Not yet. St. Louis, yes. That was enticing, but that meant a summer's adventure, not a wrenching departure from life at Fort Shaw. They would go to the fair, they would come home. Home to Fort Shaw. As a team.[17]

"Since receiving your letter I have called the Basketball girls together and . . . laid your proposal before them," Superintendent Campbell wrote to Superintendent McCowan. "At the present time they are not willing to agree to it." It was with no little pleasure that Campbell wrote those words. Admittedly, McCowan's "proposition" had not come at a good time. But had it come at any other time, Campbell found it difficult to believe that the decision would have been any different. "However," he added as he closed the letter, "later developments may change the situation." He hoped his phrasing would soften the message, for he certainly did not want to offend this fellow, who had over the last few months come to be a friend as well as an important ally in the Indian School Service. And Samuel McCowan would, after all, be an important figure in the girls' lives during their residency at the Model Indian School. But the motivation behind the invitation, gracious as it was, was transparent. Anyone could see what Samuel McCowan would gain by enticing the Fort Shaw team to transfer to Chilocco. And no one knew better than Fred Campbell himself how much he, as well as his school, had to lose if his girls had decided to go there—or anywhere else.[18]

~

Time to be on the road again, to complete the tour so recently aborted: Butte on March 24, Anaconda on March 25, and Dillon on March 26. Katie was reluctant to leave her little brother, though George was now out of the infirmary and back in his classes. There was certainly little danger of his running away again. Even so, the group was subdued as they pulled away from the school. Not even this chance to show off their skills to their erstwhile opponents on the high school teams raised their spirits. Still, once they entered the hall and began to perform, they played to the crowd and left the tragedy behind them.[19]

The trip from Butte to Anaconda the next morning was full of anticipation, for this would be their first visit to that city, and the paper had warned the residents not to miss "a performance that in many respects is more entertaining than many . . . traveling shows." The reporter for the *Standard*, who had covered their games against Butte High and the Butte Independents in earlier days, promised his readers that if they showed up Friday night in Turner Hall they would see "an exhibition of how the exciting game [of basketball] should be played." This, he said, was the team that had "much to do with making that game so popular in Montana."[20]

At Dillon they had yet another chance to see a new town and perform and play before a new—and most appreciative—audience. Having begun on such a somber note, the three-site tour ended on the upbeat, with the group already talking about their next adventure, another fund-raising tour that would begin the very next Tuesday night with an exhibition game at Fort Benton and take them all the way to Williston, North Dakota, for a match game against that city's high school team.[21]

A trip as far east as the North Dakota border, of course, held out the promise of stops at the Fort Belknap and Fort Peck Reservations. The Fort Belknap performance gave Katie her first opportunity to see her family since her brother and cousin had been caught in the deadly blizzard. And at Poplar Nettie was happily reunited with her sister Lizzie, who had returned home in February after four years at Carlisle. When all the excitement had died down, Superintendent Campbell found time for a few quiet minutes with Lizzie. Having long admired her leadership abilities, as well as her athletic talents, he now pressed the young woman to join the group on their way back through Poplar after the game at Williston. She could be of great help to Miss Malley, he told her, in honing the girls' Indian club and barbell routines. And, having learned her basketball under Josie Langley Liephart and sharpened her skills at Carlisle, she could also fill a crucial role in taking the floor should one of the girls be injured or take sick. Perhaps most important of all, Campbell told Lizzie Wirth, he saw her as the ideal chaperone and role model for his girls, and he would like her to accompany them to St. Louis. With her concurrence, he would ask Superintendent McCowan to add her to the list of Fort Shaw travelers.[22]

With the brand-new energy gained in Poplar, the girls crushed Williston High 27 to 0, and they returned home, with Lizzie on board, to prepare themselves in earnest for the departure for St. Louis. They were actually relieved at that point to hear that the departure date had been postponed until the first of June. Even though the delay meant they would miss the grand opening of the fair, the girls were road-weary, and they looked forward to two months of little more than campus routine and the comfort of being with friends for a while.[23]

"Open, Ye Gates! Swing Wide, Ye Portals!"
April 30, 1904

❦

SATURDAY, APRIL 30, 1904. DAVID R. FRANCIS AWOKE TO AN EARLY-morning drizzle. The weather was the one thing he couldn't control on this opening day of the Louisiana Purchase Exposition. But the forecast promised bright sun and blue skies by late morning. Turning from the window, he resolved to put his faith in the meteorologist.[1]

Six long years of dreaming, planning, and building would culminate in this day that would showcase not just the world's largest-ever exposition but a city's can-do attitude. Francis had never thought of himself as a proud man, but by god, he was proud of what this day meant. If waking to gray skies didn't discourage too many, he had every reason to believe that somewhere in the neighborhood of 200,000 people would turn out for the biggest event St. Louis had ever witnessed. Adjusting his frock coat, he glanced at the notes he had prepared for his welcoming remarks. Then hurrying downstairs, he called to his wife that he was on his way to pick up Secretary Taft and would see her later at the fairgrounds. She had her official pass, right? He would meet her at the reviewing stand on the Plaza of St. Louis in two hours. And please, he threw back over his shoulder, don't be late.

By the time David Francis and William Howard Taft, secretary of war and President Roosevelt's representative for the occasion, arrived at the fairgrounds, bright sun was greeting the thousands pouring in through the Lindell Avenue entrance. Finding his wife exactly where he had asked her to wait for him, Francis ushered her to the seats reserved for special guests. Then, taking Secretary Taft's elbow, he steered him up the steps of the platform at the foot of the Louisiana Monument.

All was in readiness. And Francis was most eager to get the ceremonies under way. Back in Washington, the president, members of his cabinet and of the diplomatic corps, as well as the chief justice and congressional leaders were all gathered at the White House, ready to participate, long-distance, in this historic event. At exactly 12:15 P.M. President Theodore Roosevelt would be prompted to touch the golden telegraph key that would signal the opening of the world's fair. Francis had to move the program forward with all due haste in order to meet that deadline.[2]

As he stepped to the front of the dais, the great crowd hushed. Introductions and brief comments from the dignitaries on the platform followed. Francis's remarks too were brief. Brief, but calculated to give dramatic context to the dream that on this day was becoming reality. "So thoroughly does [this fair] represent the world's civilizations," he intoned, "that if all man's other works were by some unspeakable catastrophe blotted out, the records here established by the assembled nations would afford all necessary standards for the rebuilding of our civilization."[3]

The microphone now belonged to the secretary of war. While Taft was speaking, Francis's thoughts drifted to all that lay before him—not just the scene there in the Plaza of St. Louis, but behind the scene, where in some ways the fair was still a "work in progress." He had read the letters to the editor—some within the last week—that had described "mud" as the only completed work on the fairgrounds. Well, the skeptics be damned. Taft was concluding his remarks, and Francis signaled the telegrapher to notify Washington.[4]

Back at the White House, with barely a moment's delay, President Roosevelt pressed the key that opened the great exposition out in St. Louis. "Open, ye gates," cried Francis. "Swing wide, ye portals." At that moment, the cascades sprang to life, fountains erupted, and flags of all shapes, sizes, and colors were run up their poles. The assembled multitude cheered. And John Philip Sousa struck up the band.[5]

Threatening weather and unfinished exhibits aside, the ceremonies had gone as well as David R. Francis could ever have hoped.

~

Superintendent McCowan was as impressed with the opening ceremonies as was anyone else in that crowd. But as he hurried back to Indian Hill the celebratory spirit gave way to some nagging thoughts. Three weeks earlier he had notified the Bureau of Indian Affairs and the LPE committee that neither the Model Indian School nor the Native encampments surrounding the school would be ready for the public by opening day. And while he could take some comfort in the fact that at least a third of the other exhibits were no more ready than his, he would be hard put to have the Indian exhibit up and running by his new target date of June 1.[6]

Between now and then, he could only hope that he would have a full complement of "traditional" Indians living in their encampments. Their arrival had to be perfectly timed, however. He couldn't have too many coming in at once, for then he would have no place to lodge the teenage boys he had brought in from Chilocco and Haskell to do the finish work on the interior of the school building. Until the building was completed, or they were dislodged by incoming Sioux, Pueblos, Wichitas, and others—whichever came first—the boys were camping in tents set up on the plots reserved for the traditional Indians.[7]

Back on the Hill, McCowan wandered through the empty shell of the school building, checking on the most recently installed plumbing and noting that the interior walls were going up quickly now as the boys' skills improved almost daily. He would have to congratulate them on their progress when they returned to the campsites that evening. There was no doubt in his mind that they had deserved this holiday in order to witness the opening ceremonies and recharge themselves for the month of work that lay ahead.

"Everybody Is Going"
May 1904

"Everybody Is Going" read the caption for a cartoon appearing in the *Great Falls Leader* the first week of May, and that one line told it all. Montanans were indeed excited about the fair and about their representation in St. Louis. A year earlier, the state legislature had appropriated $50,000 for the Montana exhibit, and Governor Joseph K. Toole had appointed a thirty-one-member committee to oversee the design, erection, and furnishing of the Montana Building that would rise proudly on the "Plateau of States" on the eastern edge of the fairgrounds. Now, before the month of May was out, reports were already coming back from St. Louis that the Montana building was "one of the prettiest on the grounds, . . . [was] handsomely furnished, and . . . a popular resort for Montanans" at the fair.[1]

The women's auxiliary committee had worked hard to come up with artistic displays for the building's interior that would show to advantage the products that Montanans were proudest of—symbols of the state's agricultural, horticultural, industrial, and cultural heritage. It was that final category that had brought Mrs. T. R. Carson to Fort Shaw in early January in search of student work to display alongside traditional Indian artifacts in the Montana Building. Josie Liephart and Isadore Sansaver had spent the good part of a day taking her into classrooms and workrooms and helping her select the needlework and beadwork, leather tooling and wood carvings that would sit in glass cases next to arrowheads and cradleboards. In sending Mrs. Carson off that evening, Superintendent Campbell had smiled to think how closely the "Indian exhibit" in the Montana Building would resemble the prize-winning exhibits he had sent over the years to the Cascade County Fair.[2]

~

At Fort Shaw preparations were well under way. At an exhibition game at Sun River in late April, the girls broke in their new uniforms, complete with red-and-white-striped dickies for the Red team, blue-and-white-striped for the Blue; their new stockings and bows; and their new regulation rubber-soled canvas shoes. The uniforms were new, and their game was good. They were ready.[3]

Then Lizzie Wirth, always one to think of contingencies, made a suggestion. Practices should be moved out-of-doors. She was concerned that the team had become too accustomed to playing on hardwood floors and anticipated, correctly as it turned out, that their games in St. Louis would far more often be played on grass "courts." It was time for the girls to get reacquainted with the outdoor field where Josie Langley Liephart had first introduced Montana to the sport of "basket ball." The players were indeed some time in getting used to the art of running and dribbling on a grassy surface that was less than uniformly level—and sometimes slick from spring rains and a few snow flurries. The challenge was equal to that they faced in earlier days when playing on the polished floors of ballrooms. But it was just one more challenge, and the girls soon enough developed the skills to compensate for unpredictable court conditions.

While his basketball girls prepared themselves for outdoor competition, Superintendent Campbell was finalizing matters with Superintendent McCowan. It had been agreed that McCowan would make the arrangements for the transportation of eleven young women and three young men—John Minesinger, Louis Youpee, and Lewis Snell—from Fort Shaw to St. Louis. The Misses Crawford, Evans, and Malley would be included in the official party. Campbell's passage would also be covered, although he had advised McCowan that he himself would make the arrangements whereby Mrs. Campbell and the children, who were all currently in Olathe, Kansas, would join him at the fair. Now Campbell received confirmation from McCowan that round-trip passage for the party from Great Falls to St. Louis had been arranged via the Northern Pacific, with a change to the Rock Island at St. Paul. The $53.35 cost of each ticket provided stopover privileges to allow the team to play the series of whistle-stop games Billy Adams had scheduled across Montana and North Dakota.[4]

With that settled, Campbell now verified the equipment and materials that McCowan would expect the travelers to bring with them. Per earlier communications, Campbell verified that the group would be packing two blankets, six sheets, six pillowcases, and one towel for each student, in addition to their clothing and costumes. They would also be bringing basketballs, Indian clubs, barbells, and musical instruments. McCowan confirmed the inventory as more than adequate and asked Campbell, as a cost-saving measure, to bring everything as luggage rather than sending it ahead as freight.[5]

Closing exercises that spring of 1904 coincided with the traditional Memorial Day observance, even though the school would not officially close for another month. Campbell had rearranged the schedule in order to allow the basketball girls and the others in the St. Louis entourage to take part in the exercises. The morning opened with the customary address in the chapel. Then, to the band's slow dirge, students, staff, and guests formed a solemn procession to the little cemetery that held the graves of twenty-two Indian children. Katie Snell held George's hand as he placed a bouquet of wildflowers on the grave of his cousin Freddy. Minnie Burton, with characteristic stoicism, laid a single flower on the grave of her friend Alice Pandoah.[6]

With the luncheon interval helping to break the morning's solemn mood, Fort Shaw students went through an afternoon program featuring a band concert, battalion drills, and a literary program in which the girls ran through their newly polished pantomime of "Song of the Mystic," which Miss Campbell had chosen for the St. Louis repertoire as similar to but possibly more appropriate than "Paradise and the Peri." Then "Mr. Louis Youpee, the 10-year-old [*sic*] comedian with the bronze complexion and the misfit clothes," performed his "pieces." The day closed with a moment of silence, after which the band struck up the "Star-Spangled Banner," and a young cadet lowered the colors.[7]

The 1904 team. *Standing, left to right:* Nettie Wirth, Katie Snell, Minnie Burton, Sarah Mitchell; *seated, left to right:* Genie Butch, Belle Johnson, Emma Sansaver.

The girls in the buckskin dresses in which they performed "The Famine"
scene from Longfellow's *Hiawatha*. *Left to right:* Emma Sansaver, Nettie
Wirth, Katie Snell, Belle Johnson, Minnie Burton, Sarah Mitchell, Rose
LaRose, Genie Butch. *Not pictured:* Flora Lucero and Gen Healy.

(Facing page, left) Detail of Lizzie Wirth from
St. Louis team photo.

(Facing page, right) Indian clubs belonging to
Lizzie Wirth. Used in exercises at Fort Shaw
and in St. Louis, the clubs remain with the
family today.

The girls in performance of "Song of the Mystic." *Top row, left to right,* Emma Sansaver, Rose LaRose, Sarah Mitchell; *middle row, left to right,* Katie Snell, Belle Johnson, Minnie Burton, Genevieve Healy; *bottom row, left to right,* Nettie Wirth, Genie Butch. This photo appeared in the *St. Louis Republic* of September 12, 1904. *Not pictured:* Flora Lucero.

The team in St. Louis. *Standing, left to right,* Rose LaRose, Flora Lucero, Katie Snell, Minnie Burton, Genevieve Healy, Sarah Mitchell; *seated, left to right,* Emma Sansaver, Genie Butch, Belle Johnson, Nettie Wirth.

The Model Indian
School on the grounds
of the 1904 St. Louis
World's Fair.

Samuel McCowan, superintendent of
the Model Indian School, ca. 1904.

Minnie Burton

Belle Johnson

Genie Butch

Sarah Mitchell

Nettie Wirth

Katie Snell

The team before their first game against the St. Louis All-Stars, Kulage Park, St. Louis, September 3, 1904. The girls are pictured with their temporary coach, Jesse McCallum of Genoa (Nebraska) Indian School, who filled in for Fred Campbell after he returned to Montana. Kneeling in back, left to right: Nettie Wirth, Coach McCallum, Katie Snell, and Minnie Burton; seated in front: Genie Butch, Belle Johnson, Emma Sansaver.

Fort Shaw team halftime huddle on the plaza in front of the Model
Indian School, October 8, 1904, championship game against the
St. Louis All-Stars. The mound-like structure immediately behind
the crowd is the top of the Navajo hogan in the Indian Village. The
fair's 264-foot Ferris Wheel can be seen in the far distance.

St Louis Mo.
Nov. 5th, 1904.

Dear Emma —
Remember the times
we have had at the fair and
dont forget this evening the
band boys went away for their
journey to Chilocco it is sad
but cheer up little girl.
Your friend Etta

St Louis. Missouri
Nov 6 1904.

Darling Emma — J.
All I ack of you is to
remember N. J. and I as long as
can. Dont forget the good times
we have spent in St Louis.
Your Friend as ever
Genevieve N Healy

Pages from Emma Sansaver's memory book. Inscriptions by Fort Shaw teammate Genevieve Healy and by Etta Loafman, a fellow student at the Model Indian School, were among those gathered by Emma during her last weeks at the world's fair.

Cup made of ruby flash glass, with memory book and locket. The cup and memory book were brought home from the fair by Emma Sansaver and are still in the family's possession.

The silver trophy brought home from St. Louis.

"Something to Remember"
June 1, 1904

SAMUEL MCCOWAN SANK BACK IN HIS CHAIR. IT HAD BEEN AN exhausting day, but such a good one. The official opening of the Model Indian School might have been delayed by a month, but no one could fault him for not doing things right. The school had opened only after everything was in place. Wednesday, June 1, from 8:00 A.M. until the supper bell rang at 6:00, the lobby and the main hallway had been jampacked. Ten thousand people had wandered through the building on this first day. Among the most impressed of those visitors were David Francis himself and Alice Roosevelt, the twenty-year-old daughter of the president. Not a bad start. And it all redounded to the great benefit of the Indian School Service. First thing in the morning, he would compose his report to the commissioner of Indian affairs, assuring him that the exhibit in St. Louis fulfilled all expectations: It was, indeed, "something to remember."[1]

But for now, he intended to enjoy the moment, here in the quiet of his office. Taps had sounded just minutes ago, and as far as he could tell from the silence emanating from the dorms upstairs, the students were as exhausted as he was. With good cause. They had done well to adjust to the routine so quickly after their arrival in St. Louis. Of course, that "routine" was very similar to what they were familiar with in their boarding schools back home. But the pressure of performing their assigned tasks in front of ten thousand people? There was nothing routine about that.

As each group of students had arrived over the last week—from his own Chilocco, from Haskell, from Genoa and Sacaton—Superintendent McCowan had reiterated his expectations of them. As in their home schools, they would be wearing uniforms and would speak only English. Reveille each day, even Sundays, when the fairgrounds were closed, at 6:00 A.M.; then all students would assemble on the plaza in front of the school at 6:45 for the flag salute. Breakfast would be served in the downstairs dining room at 7:00. From 9:30 to 11:30 on weekdays the teenagers were to engage in the various individual activities for which they had been brought to the fair. That meant that the forty boys who made up the Indian School Band would be giving concerts—on the broad porch at the main entrance to the school or in the auditorium, depending on the weather.[2]

One group of Chilocco girls would form the seventh-grade "literary" class held in an open classroom on one wing of the main floor, and a second group would be demonstrating modern techniques for handling laundry work in an open area next to the classroom. Young men from Chilocco would be running the print shop that produced a daily paper, *The Indian School Journal.* Boys from Haskell would be building wagons and displaying the work of their blacksmithing shop, and girls from Haskell would be demonstrating the domestic arts of sewing, tailoring, and millinery. Genoa boys would be fashioning harnesses—all in first-floor workrooms. And under the supervision of a professional chef, girls from Chilocco would be demonstrating baking and meal preparation in the "domestic science lab."[3]

In giving these instructions, McCowan made clear to the students that across the hallway from their classrooms and workrooms, visitors would be looking in on booths where "traditional" Indians dressed in Native costumes would be plying their ancient arts. Navajos would be weaving blankets and fashioning silver jewelry, Apache women would be weaving baskets, Pueblo artists would be shaping pottery, Lakota Sioux would be demonstrating their expertise in beadwork and pipestone carving, and Pomos would be making stone tools and crafting musical instruments. Geronimo, the legendary Apache chief, would have a booth to himself. Although he was technically a federal prisoner at Fort Sill, Oklahoma, the old fellow had become quite accustomed to being a major attraction at these fairs, and he would enjoy any attention the students gave him.[4]

After the noonday meal in the downstairs dining room, the band would reassemble at 1:30 to offer another two-hour concert, and at 2:00 the other students would be expected to return to their classrooms and workrooms. By 4:00 each afternoon the students' workday would be over, and they would be free, if they wished—and if they weren't performing themselves—to join the general public in enjoying the late afternoon musical and "literary" programs of their classmates. The flag salute and dress parade were scheduled each evening at 5:30, supper at 6:00, and taps at 10:00.[5]

In addition to their performances, classes, and demonstrations, students would be required to attend to their assigned housekeeping duties. Boys would sweep the hallways and porches and girls would help in the downstairs kitchen and laundry. After dinner, there might be a lecture in the auditorium, but more often there was free time for studying, visiting among themselves, and writing to their families.[6]

After summarizing the daily schedule, the superintendent emphasized that there would also be opportunities for all of them to enjoy the fair. They would go in groups to visit the major "pavilions." There would be regularly scheduled visits to the Pike, the mile-long midway on the northern boundary of the grounds. There would be free time for simply wandering the fairgrounds, people-watching, perhaps revisiting favorite sites or amusements—properly chaperoned, of course. Or they could ride the Intramural Railway that ran the full perimeter of the grounds or take the "auto/bus" along the concourses connecting the various exhibition halls. Flexibility within an ordered, tightly structured environment. This was Samuel McCowan's vision of life at the Model Indian School.[7]

The superintendent could only wish he could impose at least some sense of order in the encampments of the older Indians. The agents had, for the most part, acceded to his request to choose the most cooperative adults among their reservation populations and dispatch them to St. Louis on schedule. But as of this moment, the Apaches were still at home in Arizona, negotiating with their agent for per diem payments as well as transportation. At least the Rosebud Sioux, Pueblos, Wichitas, Pawnees, Arapahos, and Comanches were all on site and, under the watchful eye of the public, were putting up their tepees, hogans, and earth and grass lodges on the perimeter of the Indian compound, where the tents housing the boys who finished out the school building had so recently stood.[8]

Once the Indians had completed their camps, McCowan could only hope that prospects for selling the items they crafted would be enough to entice them to spend every day at work in the open booths across from the classrooms and workrooms in his school building. The Indians who had plied their trades before the lines of people crowding into the hallway on this first day seemed pleased by the interest visitors showed in their work and the compliments they offered. In fact, visitors to the school had thus far seemed more enthralled by the work of the colorfully attired "old" Indians across the hallway than by the formal demonstrations being given by the uniformed students on the other side of the corridor. Disconcerting as that might be, there was no denying the public's fascination with the "exotic" and their desire to see "real Indians"—like Geronimo.[9]

McCowan was not about to end this day dwelling on this one discouraging note. It had otherwise been a glorious, auspicious beginning for his Model Indian School. Turning off the light and moving toward the stairway to the second floor and the modest quarters he shared with his wife, he smiled to think that public preference might well shift with the arrival of this celebrated basketball team from out in Montana. They had just begun their rail journey to St. Louis, a trip punctuated by well-advertised whistle-stop games and entertainments that were bound to generate interest in his Model Indian School.[10]

What a publicity opportunity the team's arrival at the fair, after this unique cross-country journey, would provide! He would send out press releases that very week, plus photographs of the girls and the time and location of the first of the many musical and literary programs they would be giving during their summer on Indian Hill. A few days later he would ring up his contacts at the *Globe-Democrat* and the *Post-Dispatch* to let them know exactly when the Fort Shaw group was expected. And then he had it. The ultimate touch. If he wired Superintendent Campbell somewhere along his route east, perhaps he could arrange for the girls to step onto the platform at the Intramural Railway stop in front of the school wearing their fine buckskin dresses. Now that would be a sight no reporter would want to miss.

The Adventure Begins
June 1904

JUNE 1. FORT SHAW INDIAN SCHOOL. THE BASKETBALL GIRLS WERE awake well before reveille—thanks to Gen Healy's having made the rounds, shaking shoulders and tugging braids. She had news for them: A glance outside had confirmed what Mr. Mountford, the school's weatherwise farmer, had predicted—wind and rain. Still in bare feet and long flannel gowns, the girls rushed to the windows and surveyed the wet world below. Their adventure would not have the sunny beginning they had imagined.[1]

Even so, there was certainly no lack of excitement in the dining room at breakfast. And although the pelting rain scuttled plans for a festive all-school send-off, the cheers of classmates shouted down from dorm and classroom windows were sufficient sign of their support. Peering out from beneath the hoods of their new slickers, the basketball girls continued to wave and call out their goodbyes, even as they were signaled to climb into the wagon and pull up the tarpaulins that would be their only shelter against the ongoing downpour.

In the wagon behind them, tarpaulins also protected the trunks and crates that would accompany them to St. Louis. Packed away among the customary outfits and uniforms, the basketballs, musical instruments, Indian clubs and barbells, were the bed and bath linens Superintendent McCowan had requested they bring, as well as boxes filled with the finest beadwork, needlework, and leatherwork of their classmates, all to be displayed in the grand entry hall of the Model Indian School.[2]

For all the excitement of the journey, the entourage and equipment went no farther than Great Falls that first day, for that city was the first stop on their journey east. Their game and program that night would be a tribute to the loyalty of the fans whose unfailing support had brought them to this moment. As the *Leader* noted, the girls from Fort Shaw Indian School could "fill any hall in the city to the limit on a day's notice," and true to form, the citizens of Great falls packed the house that night.[3]

They were treated to a program quite similar to the one fans had seen some three months earlier, save for the substitution of "The Song of the Mystic" for "Paradise and the Peri" as their rhythmic pantomime routine. The evening concluded with a "rattling" good game of basketball. House receipts lived up to Superintendent Campbell's expectations and provided a good financial cushion against those times when expenses might exceed income at some of the whistle-stop venues Billy Adams had arranged.[4]

The rain had let up by the time the troupe—and their considerable baggage—departed the Grand Hotel the next morning and headed for the depot, where there were more good-byes to be said between those heading back to Fort Shaw and those on their way to the fair. The reporter for the *Leader*, who for two years had kept them in the public eye, was on the spot once more. "The Fort Shaw Indian School basketball team left for St. Louis this morning," he wrote, "accompanied by Supt. F. C. Campbell of the school, Miss Crawford, Miss Malley, and Miss Fern Evans." Also bound for St. Louis were Nettie Wirth's older sister, Lizzie, leader of club and barbells exercises; Katie Snell's older brother, Lewis, cornetist; John Minesinger, singer and performer; and little Louis Youpee, who was eager to "make medicine for the audiences."[5]

And, lest the public confuse the mission and motives of this group with those of numerous Indians who would be part of the midway shows at the fair, the reporter emphasized Superintendent Campbell's oft-repeated message: His Fort Shaw students were not going "as an exhibit or anything of that sort, but as pupils of the Indian School which the United States government will maintain at the exposition."[6]

Reading this statement in the *Leader* the next morning as the Montana Central carried them toward Bozeman, the girls shook their heads. How could their superintendent stand in front of a reporter and repeat that time after time? Especially since, when he had first asked them if they wanted to go on this adventure, he had warned them that they would be "a living exhibit" in St. Louis? They respected this man and were grateful for all he had done for them. But did he, or anyone else, really believe that they were not on exhibit every time they took the court or stage? Was that not the whole point of the programs they had been giving around the state for the last year? But did that fact diminish their enjoyment of playing basketball and giving entertainments to the applause of crowds all across the state of Montana? Not one whit, they all agreed. Nor would their being "on exhibit" keep them from enjoying their months in St. Louis.

Of course, at this point the girls had no way of knowing the full extent to which their lives and their actions—and the lives and actions of their classmates at the Model Indian School—would be on display. Every single moment of every single day. And had they known, would that have lessened their enthusiasm? Not likely, for being on exhibit was a part of the bargain by which they would be spending the summer on the grounds of the world's fair. They would honor that bargain and do all that was expected of them. Their families back home, even those parents and grandparents who had, at first, been reluctant to allow them to travel so far, were proud of their having achieved this honor. And without a doubt the girls themselves were ready to see all there was to see, learn all there was to learn, and enjoy to the fullest all that lay ahead of them.[7]

~

In Bozeman, Campbell was handed a telegram from Billy Adams, who had gone on ahead to secure dates for games in Minnesota. The schedule across Montana and North Dakota was solid. Tonight's game at Bozeman would be followed by one at Big Timber, June 3, and Billings, June 4, with a Sunday layover, as dictated by law and convention. Following a Monday night game in Miles City, they would travel on to Glendive for their last Montana appearance. Scheduled North Dakota games included Mandan, June 8; Valley City, June 9; and Fargo, June 10. The game in Valley City against "the champions of North Dakota" would probably be the girls' toughest, Adams said. He still had hopes for two Minnesota games—Little Falls on June 11 and Minneapolis on June 13—but he had not yet firmed them up. He would let Campbell know about them as soon as he could.[8]

The route to the fair was filled with its own rewards. In Bozeman they attended college commencement ceremonies prior to their own performance at Story Hall. Crowds in Big Timber and Billings welcomed them warmly. The local paper in Miles City urged its readers to come to the opera house and see this group of young Indians who "have become versed in the ways of the white man" and who play basketball "in a particularly entertaining way."[9]

It was in Miles City that Coach Campbell received a second telegram from Billy Adams. The game he had most anticipated, the match-up with the North Dakota state champions, had been canceled. Rather than risk his squad's reputation by playing a seemingly invincible team, the Valley City coach had evidently decided to take his team to Fargo, where he would combine his best players with members of an All-Star team there. In place of the game at Valley City, there would be two games in Fargo, played on consecutive nights. The reporter for the *Miles City Independent*, in announcing the change, predicted that, having seen for themselves the excellence of the Fort Shaw team, plenty of folks there in Miles City would be willing to "go a long way to witness" a game between the Indians and "a picked team from all over the state of North Dakota."[10]

This would not be the test Campbell had wanted for his girls. But he characteristically put the best face on the news, and his enthusiasm was contagious. One game, one performance at a time, he reminded the girls. And they turned their energies to the coming game against the local team in Glendive, a town reported to have a good case of "basketball fever." Despite the enthusiasm of the Glendive five, the Indians won the game by a wide margin. The result was as expected and did nothing to dampen the crowd's enjoyment of the evening.[11]

The Northern Pacific car rolled on, carrying the Fort Shaw contingent into Mandan, North Dakota, for a Wednesday, June 8, engagement in the opera house. In spite of heavy rain, a large crowd was on hand to greet the visitors. The various entertainments resulted in "numerous encores." Fort Shaw's exhibition game was so impressive that it was with some trepidation that a team of local high school girls took the floor thereafter against the visitors for a challenge game. Although clearly outclassed, the Mandan team "forced the Indians to play their best." The hometown fans—-and the players themselves—could find consolation in that.[12]

Mandan could afford to be gracious in defeat. Their younger, less-experienced high school girls had not expected to beat the Indians; they were glad enough to have been given the chance to play such a famous team. But in Fargo the mood was decidedly different. From the moment the Fort Shaw troupe stepped off the train and onto the virtually empty platform, they sensed something was wrong. Accustomed as they had become to being welcomed by town officials, they were a bit embarrassed for their superintendent when his request for directions to their hotel met with a mumbled response and a vague gesture toward a building whose second story was visible a block or so away. As they crossed the street and walked toward their hotel, were they imagining things, or were people on the sidewalk staring—maybe even glaring—at them?[13]

Even the desk clerk's demeanor suggested something was wrong. Up in their rooms the girls exchanged theories as to what was going on. Apparently this town did not like Indians. Or maybe they just didn't like Indian girls who could play ball better than white girls. Emma, for whom stepping off that train had been like stepping back into her childhood in Havre, kept her counsel but resolved to be sure Fargo never forgot the girls from Fort Shaw Indian School. Belle, feeling her responsibility as captain, cautioned her teammates that anger could only hurt their game. Their best course of action was to forget about the slights they might, or might not, have suffered and go out there and play like the champions they were.

Maybe things would lighten up, Katie suggested, once they walked out in their ceremonial dresses and won over the crowd with their recitation of "The Famine." Assuming, of course, this was a crowd who would know or appreciate Longfellow's *Hiawatha*. At least, Lizzie assured them, their club-swinging and barbell exercises should go over well. And who could resist Louis Youpee's charms? Or John Minesinger's "Alphabetic Sermon"? All they had to do was go out there and perform. That armory full of wary strangers could not help but be impressed.

The armory was only *half* full, as it turned out. The girls had long since discovered that their energy was in direct proportion to the energy reflected by their audience, and all through that evening's program, they had the sinking feeling that their performance was only half as good as it should have been. Not even Louis Youpee's antics seemed to break the ice. The North Dakota All-Stars sat in the front row during the entire entertainment, suited up for the game and seeming to pay very little attention to what was going on in front of them.[14]

That was disconcerting enough, but it was the sneers they received as they moved past their opponents on the way to change into their uniforms that set off the Fort Shaw girls. The sneers and the comments. When Belle heard one of the All-Stars say the word "squaws" and another mutter that Indians are too "heavy and slow" to play basketball, she forgot that she had earlier preached forgiveness. Usually the calm one in a storm, she goaded her teammates as they pulled on their middies. There would be no quarter given in this game. The Fargo girls may have ignored the Indians up to this point, but they would have a hard time looking past them now.[15]

Later that very night a proud and happy Superintendent Campbell filed a report with the hometown papers. "You can imagine what Bell [*sic*] would do under such circumstances," the coach wrote. "Her fighting mood was up [and] it was worth more than the price of admission to see her alone." From the opening tip, Belle had come out "strong as a lion and quick as a panther." The spectators, who had been so confident that the Indians would be played "off their feet in the first five minutes," were quickly taken out of the game. Sparked by their captain's energy, Fort Shaw moved up and down the court like "cyclones," while their opponents "might just as well have been wooden figures." Genie Butch was everywhere at once. It was her finest performance yet. It was, in fact, the finest performance of the team as a whole. Fort Shaw, 34; All-Stars, 0. The slurs had been answered.[16]

The report that appeared in the next morning's Fargo paper contained no racist undertones. "The Fort Shaw Indian Girls of Montana gave an entertainment last evening to a small but appreciative audience," the article began. The club swinging was "one of the prettiest drills ever seen in Fargo." In fact, the entire entertainment was inspiring. The people of Fargo "may never again have an opportunity of witnessing [such an event]." The phrasing heartened the Fort Shaw troupers. Perhaps their performance the evening before was better than they had thought.[17]

The game itself was given short shrift: "A spirited game of basket ball between the Fort Shaw girls and a local All Star team . . . was won by the Fort Shaw girls." No score was given. Even so, the reporter knew excellence when he saw it and urged his readers to come out for the rematch that night. "No basket ball enthusiast should fail to witness this game," he said.[18]

The second evening drew a much larger crowd. The program was slightly different. The girls performed "Song of the Mystic" rather than "Paradise and the Peri," and Louis Youpee drew some new recitations from his vast repertoire. But there was very little difference to note in the basketball contest, or at least in its result—another overwhelming victory for the Indians from Montana. A professor from the University of Minnesota who witnessed the contest confided to Campbell afterwards that, to his mind, there was "not a team in the United States that can touch these girls at the game."[19]

Billy Adams, who had rolled into town from Minnesota in time to see that second game, was of the same mind. He was on his way home to Butte, and he assured Campbell that he would make sure the newspapers across the state knew how well the tour was going. Or *had* gone. In effect, Adams said, the tour had just ended; he had not been able to line up anything in either Little Falls or Minneapolis. The news was almost a relief to the weary travelers. And whatever might have happened in Minnesota could hardly have topped the success that had been theirs in North Dakota.[20]

It was time to move on to St. Louis and the world's fair.

"A Veritable Fairyland"
St. Louis

JUNE 14, 1904. THE GIRLS FROM FORT SHAW INDIAN SCHOOL
could barely contain their excitement as the train pulled into Union
Station on that Tuesday morning. Although they had been on the
road for two long weeks of basketball and entertainments, weariness
gave way to wonder at the sights and sounds that greeted them as they
stepped down onto the platform and into the stream of fellow passengers. They had been prepared, to some extent, for the excitement
of the city. Even so, their abrupt entry into the hustle and bustle of the
largest and busiest railroad terminal in the world was overwhelming.
Travelers, porters, and hawkers pressed in on them from all sides—and
their leader and guide was apparently abandoning them to their fate.
After directing Miss Crawford, Miss Evans, and Miss Malley to move
the girls down the platform and into the waiting room of the station,
F. C. Campbell strode off toward the baggage car, with Lewis Snell and
John Minesinger in his wake and an unusually subdued Louis Youpee
in tow.[1]

Once inside the station, the girls formed a tight group around their
three teachers. Awestruck by the grandeur and size of the Grand Hall,
the height and breadth of its vaulted ceiling, and the press of still more
people, they turned this way and that, examining their surroundings.
They nudged, pointed, and exclaimed over one sight after another. All
but Emma. Having spotted the magnificent stained-glass window over
the terminal's main entrance, she stood in silence, transfixed by the way
the sunlight intensified the hues and sent a stream of color across the
upper reaches of the room. Following her gaze, Minnie pointed out

how closely the Grecian robes of the three women in that massive window resembled the flowing white robes they had created for their pantomime. A good omen, according to Flora, who had spent long hours sewing those robes.

But who are they? Emma wanted to know. She had seen saints, lambs, Jesus, and the Holy Family in church windows back home, but never any figures like these. And never any windows so perfectly crafted. Miss Crawford, who had come to St. Louis well prepared to teach as well as chaperone, explained that the three women represented the cities with the three largest rail stations in the country—St. Louis, New York, and . . . and San Francisco, a passerby filled in. The window was the work of Louis Tiffany, Miss Crawford continued, one of the country's finest stained-glass artists.[2]

A loud, but familiar voice interrupted Miss Crawford's lecture and caused the girls to turn as one, to see their tall, red-headed superintendent, hatless, but otherwise very much his dignified, take-charge self, motioning them to follow him. He had, with the help of Lewis and John, completed the task of counting their trunks and crates and valises as they were being unloaded. Given Superintendent McCowan's warning about the dangers of having their baggage lost during transfers, Campbell had taken extra care to see that everything was accounted for. Now, having gathered his group, he led the way to the Market Street exit, explaining that two redcaps had loaded their tagged items onto handcarts for transport to the fairgrounds and the Model Indian School.

Only as they broke out onto the street did Miss Crawford realize that two of their number were missing. As if on cue, John Minesinger appeared, trailed by Louis Youpee, who was munching the first of the untold number of hot dogs he would consume during his time in St. Louis. Seeing the looks on the faces of the girls, Coach Campbell promised there would be dinner awaiting them at the school, and he planned to have them there well before noon. Besides, he said, with a pointed look at the mustard smears on the face of the youngest member of their troupe, Superintendent McCowan would definitely *not* be expecting a bunch of painted Indians.

Hunger was forgotten as Miss Crawford pulled out a map of the city to help the girls get their bearings. So this was St. Louis, lifted from map to reality. A city whose buildings stretched as far to the east as they could see, all the way to the Mississippi River, a mile away. There were hundreds of historic old buildings down there by the river, Superintendent Campbell informed them. This city had been a fur-trading settlement back in the late 1700s, and two of the earliest traders were the Chouteau brothers. Yes, as in Choteau, Montana, he said, catching Flora Lucero's eye. These traders—and trappers and soldiers—had come up the Missouri, had settled in Montana and the Dakotas, and had married Indian women. He halted, mid-sentence, aware that he was speaking to a group of young women whose families had lived this bit of history.

Sarah Mitchell was, at that very moment, trying to picture her grandfather's life in this place fifty years earlier. It was one thing to know that her grandfather, David Dawson Mitchell, Indian agent for all western tribes, had been a powerful man in St. Louis. It was quite another to stand in his city and finally *feel* some connection to this person she had never known. How strange to think that this city and its tall buildings were a part of her heritage as surely as were the unending plains of the Fort Peck Reservation. A *part,* but such a small part. She needed more time to think about these connections.[3]

The Wirth sisters were joined in their own reverie, poring over Miss Crawford's map as Lizzie traced the route south to Jefferson Barracks. So near and yet so far. They simply must find a way to see this post where their father had begun his military training. Overhearing their murmured exchange, Coach Campbell reminded them, gently, that they were here first and foremost as students at the Model Indian School. Anything else would be lagniappe.

Lagniappe. The word leaped out at Emma, taking her back to a time and place her mind seldom traveled. She could barely remember her father, yet suddenly she was seeing him coming home from the trading post, a bolt of gingham under his arm and three narrow silk ribbons in his hand. She could remember him tying those ribbons, one by one, onto the braids of his three daughters. She could remember her mother fussing about his wasting money on such foolishness—until he whipped out a fourth ribbon, tied it onto his wife's dark braid, then kissed the top of her head. It was then he had winked at his girls and said that magic word: *lagniappe.* A bonus. Something unexpected. Like having a long-buried memory conjured by a single word, *lagniappe.* Like ending up here in St. Louis.

But Campbell's thoughts had long since turned from history to the practicalities of the present—specifically, keeping his group close at hand while watching for their chance to board one of the "trains" designed to shuttle the thousands of incoming visitors from Union Station out to the fairgrounds five miles to the west. This was all new to him, for only the Wabash line had served the city on his first visit to the fairgrounds just seven months ago. Now, in the crush of people at this time of day, their only hope of all boarding one car seemed to be positioning themselves, en masse, at the platform's edge and moving forward, en masse, the minute the way was cleared.[4]

Then the train was pulling in, the doors of the car directly in front of them were opening, and they were stepping into the car, with barely time to fall onto their seats before they were moving down the rails. Campbell relaxed now, though he kept his eyes on his group, anticipating their reactions as the cityscape gave way to more open space, landscape dotted with houses and churches, a brick schoolhouse or two. Suddenly, there were no more houses, only acres and acres of trees. They had entered Forest Park. No one had said there would be a *real* forest. Belle was the first to comment, remarking on how different these trees were from those back home. Trees are trees, Gen said, and she, for one, was glad to see something other than buildings.

Yet with the suddenness with which they had entered the forest, they moved from its canopied shade into sunlight glinting off buildings, buildings unlike any they had ever seen. They had come upon this "veritable fairy land" one Montana reporter had written about. Yet the magical landscape abruptly disappeared as the train jerked to a stop, the doors slid open, and they were swept out of the car and onto the platform of the Wabash terminal, beyond whose walls, Miss Crawford told them, lay the main entrance to the fairgrounds.[5]

The lines at the ticket booth were long, and people were pressed together so tightly the girls were unable to see anything but the backs and heads of those directly in front of them. It was hard to even breathe. And no one in that phalanx of figures seemed to be moving. Except for Superintendent Campbell, who had shouldered his way over to one of the uniformed cadets—a member of the Jefferson Guard, Miss Crawford whispered to Lizzie—and was showing the young man the blue pass he had been sent by Superintendent McCowan. Since they were to be admitted as a group, he explained, he saw no need for them to take up valuable room by standing in line when the guard could so easily escort them through the gate and assist them in boarding the Intramural Railway that would take them to the Indian exhibit.[6]

Indian. Campbell knew how to use the word to his advantage, and the moment he gestured toward the Fort Shaw contingent, the young cadet followed his gaze. One look at the pretty young women immobilized by the crush roused his sense of chivalry, and a short blast on his whistle brought a second guard to his side. The two gallants parted the crowd as easily as Moses had parted the Red Sea, and Louis, the girls, and their chaperones were escorted through the grand arch and onto the Intramural Railway. Katie would later confess that she had been so flustered by the attention of the handsome young soldiers that she had entirely missed the sweeping view of the plaza and the Festival Hall beyond. Miss Crawford's attempts to point out the various buildings to their immediate left—there was the Palace of Varied Industries, and beyond it the Palace of Electricity and Machinery—went for naught. Her charges sat, unhearing, mesmerized by the seemingly endless array of massive ivory buildings that reminded Emma of the paintings of heaven she had seen at St. Paul's Mission School. She had come through the pearly gates into a shining city.

For some the spell was quickly broken by the cacophony of sounds emanating from the other side of the tracks. Those who turned in that direction were treated to a glimpse of the fabled Pike. The shrieks of people flying down a railroad track full of twists and turns and dips and climbs riveted their attention. Gen nudged Genie, goading her to ask Coach Campbell to let them ride that thing, maybe even this very afternoon. Ignoring Gen's prod, Genie instead pointed to a line of cam-

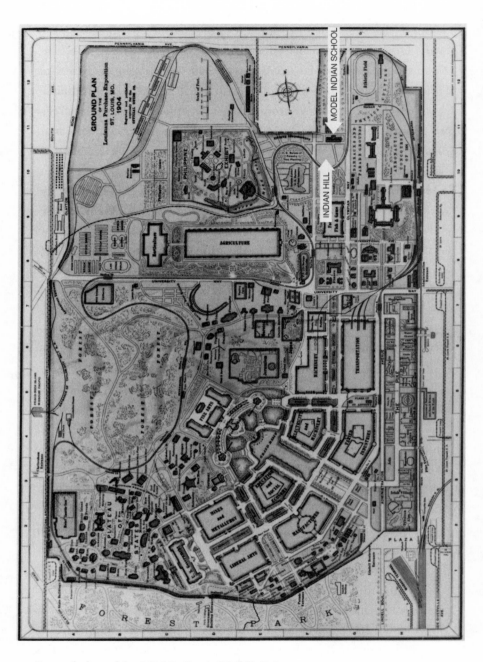

Ground plan of the 1904 St. Louis World's Fair.

els being ridden by a group of young ladies carrying parasols. Along the Pike, barkers lured customers into the Streets of Cairo, the Tyrolean Alps, the wonders of Constantinople, places some of the girls had heard about but never expected to see. They would see it *all,* Miss Crawford promised. They would do everything they had been brought here to do, but they would also take advantage of everything else the fair offered. This was, after all, the University of the Future—and of the past and present as well.

The minute the train stopped to let off passengers at the Palace of Transportation, Louis caught sight of what he had been looking for ever since they entered the fairgrounds. There it is, he sang out, his finger jabbing the window. Everyone in the car followed his gaze. There, beyond the New York Building and the Japanese Gardens rose the Ferris wheel. Gigantic beyond description. Dwarfing anything they had ever seen or would ever see again. Louis turned in his seat to be sure that Mr. Campbell was looking at the wheel. He didn't say anything more, couldn't say anything more. He just wanted to be sure Mr. Campbell had seen it too.[7]

Beyond the palaces and the Pike, the Intramural Railway looped through the Physical Culture complex. The superintendent pointed out the stately gymnasium in the distance and the athletic field that was only yards away from the tracks on which they traveled. Then, with a suddenness that caught even Campbell off guard, the train jerked to a halt to disgorge yet another carload of passengers—including, this time, the entourage from Montana.[8]

Fred Campbell was almost as stunned as the rest of the party, for no more than seven months ago he had slogged his way through the mud, doing his best to keep up with Sam McCowan, to the top of the hill where the outline of the school was marked off by string and stakes. Now the series of circles and squares on a piece of paper that drizzly November day had become this line of tepees and lodges and huts making up the Indian village here below.

As quickly as they alighted from the cars, the Fort Shaw troupe was surrounded by a mix of villagers and tourists, for news of their arrival had spread quickly through Indian Hill. A trio of reporters fired a barrage of questions at the girls, all the while scribbling away without even looking down at their pads. Catching one newsman by the elbow, Campbell steered him toward the walkway that led up to the plaza in front of the Indian school and motioned his group to follow along behind. Finally free of the crowd, the girls were able to see what they should have seen the moment they stepped down onto the platform at Indian Station. The Model Indian School.

The stately building before them featured red-roofed turrets at all four corners and on either side of the main entry. Wide steps led up to the broad, columned portico in front of the main entrance. On those steps stood a sizeable crowd of students and staff who had gathered to greet them. But the girls were hardly aware of the greeters, stunned as they were by the beauty of the building in front of them. They had seen so many grand buildings that day—from Union Station to the array of palaces they had just passed. None of those buildings, like none of the grand homes of Butte and Great Falls, had anything at all to do with *them*. But this castle was to be their home. And there was no quarreling with Katie Snell's assessment: This school they had waited so long to see was like no Indian school they had ever heard of. Even Carlisle, according to Lizzie, seemed shabby by comparison.

As the Fort Shaw contingent walked across the plaza, Samuel Mc-Cowan stepped forward from the crowd of strangers on the porch and hustled down the steps to offer a hearty handshake to Fred Campbell. Campbell returned the warm greeting, expressed his pleasure at being in St. Louis once again, then introduced Misses Lillie Crawford, Fern Evans, and Sadie Malley, plus his Indian assistants, Lizzie Wirth, Lewis Snell, and John Minesinger. Louis Youpee, the pint-sized charmer, in-troduced himself with a tip of his cap. Then came the basketball girls McCowan had waited so long to meet. Though they had not, after all, arrived in their buckskin finery, they were no less striking, standing before him in their navy polka-dot, ankle-length dresses, their hair swept up in the Gibson Girl style of the day. Each introduced herself in turn, feeling a little shy, even insecure, under McCowan's steady gaze—feeling, as Genie Butch put it later, a bit like a newly delivered string of

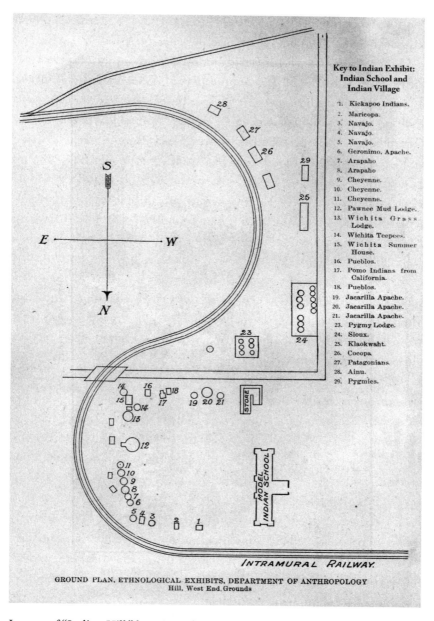

Key to Indian Exhibit:
Indian School and
Indian Village

1. Kickapoo Indians.
2. Maricopa.
3. Navajo.
4. Navajo.
5. Navajo.
6. Geronimo, Apache.
7. Arapaho
8. Arapaho
9. Cheyenne.
10. Cheyenne.
11. Cheyenne.
12. Pawnee Mud Lodge.
13. Wichita Grass Lodge.
14. Wichita Teepees.
15. Wichita Summer House.
16. Pueblos.
17. Pomo Indians from California.
18. Pueblos.
19. Jacarilla Apache.
20. Jacarilla Apache.
21. Jacarilla Apache.
23. Pygmy Lodge.
24. Sioux.
25. Klaokwaht.
26. Cocopa.
27. Patagonians.
28. Ainu.
29. Pygmies.

GROUND PLAN, ETHNOLOGICAL EXHIBITS, DEPARTMENT OF ANTHROPOLOGY
Hill, West End, Grounds

Layout of "Indian Hill," location of the Indian exhibit at the St. Louis World's Fair.

horses being examined by a rancher who wanted to be sure he'd gotten his money's worth.[9]

The formalities over, McCowan beckoned the group to follow him up the broad steps of the building, through the double doors, and into the grand lobby where he turned and pointed back with pride to the motto hanging over the lobby entrance: "Indian nature is human nature bound in red." Belle and Emma exchanged a quick glance, and before Gen could open her mouth, Lizzie glared her into silence. Dropping into his tour-guide mode, McCowan launched into his monologue. The items in the glass cases and those displayed on the walls were representative of the best work from Indian schools west of the Mississippi. The empty case in the far corner would soon be filled with the items that had traveled with the group from Fort Shaw.[10]

Shepherding his flock to one side of the crowded entryway, their new superintendent explained that the school's main entrance faced east, toward the palisades and palaces beyond. The lobby in which they were standing was the central segment of a hallway that ran north and south the entire length of the building. No visitor could walk that hallway, end to end, without realizing the extent to which government Indian schools were transforming the lives of their pupils. The young people were the exemplary products of a system designed to move the aboriginals of this country into modern living. . . . As the superintendent went on, the girls were aware of the aroma of oatmeal cookies wafting through the corridor. Somewhere down that hallway there was a bakery. They were getting hungrier by the minute.

". . . The traditional Indians across the corridor . . . " The superintendent droned on. There was much more to this recitation, the girls were sure of it, but they were saved by the bell that signaled the end of the morning sessions. There would be no time—or space—for touring the hallways now, Superintendent McCowan conceded, not with the students and the old Indians moving out into the already crowded corridor.

For now, he said, his wife—and Emma McCowan appeared at his side just as she would appear at just the right place at just the right moment

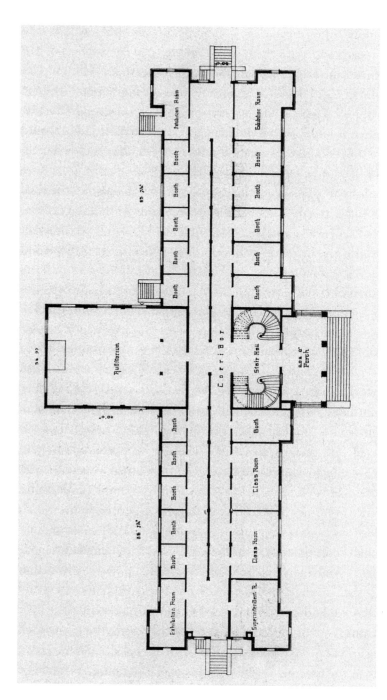

Superintendent McCowan's initial floor plan (first floor) for the Model Indian School.

so many more times during the course of the summer—would take the girls upstairs and show them the room they had been assigned. Mr. McCallum, he said, catching the man's sleeve as he passed on his way to the central stairway, Mr. McCallum would take the boys up to their part of the dormitory. There would just be time enough for them to freshen up for dinner. If Superintendent Campbell and the three ladies would follow him down to his office for a briefing session, they could all meet up again in the dining hall downstairs.

Like the school as a whole, the dormitory was unlike any the girls from Fort Shaw Indian School had ever seen. And with good reason. For as Mrs. McCowan explained, the public would be allowed to visit their otherwise private space—but only during their midday break and only under escort of a member of the staff. If they didn't want visitors at that hour, they could close their door, she hastened to assure them—though the Chilocco girls had found that a closed door was no guarantee against being disturbed by the school's most curious visitors.[11]

The basic floor plan upstairs matched that of the main floor. There was a girls' wing and a boys' wing, as well as some extra rooms for the boys—since they outnumbered the girls—at the inner edge of the girls' hall. Which boys, every girl in that group in front of her wondered, though not even Gen asked. The Fort Shaw girls could not have been more pleased with their own quarters. Their room was airy and light, since they were lucky enough to have one of the arched windows that faced east and allowed them to look down on the parade grounds, on the semicircle of homes in the Indian village, and beyond to the buildings and lagoons of the fairgrounds. Now, for the first time, they noted the basketball goals that stood on the north and south ends of the parade grounds. And there in the distance stood the Ferris wheel that would take them to the top of the world and back again.[12]

Before they could do more than get their bearings, choose their cots, and check out the foot lockers at the end of their beds, the dinner bell was tolling and Mrs. McCowan was leading them back down the stairs, all the way to the basement, where they were caught up in a stream of students flowing down the hallway and into a dining room filled with long tables covered with cloths like those they had made in the sewing room back at Fort Shaw. Here, like at home, girls and boys had separate tables, though as Gen later observed, there was no formal marching to meals, just an easy stroll that allowed time for visiting along the way. Dinner was not unlike the noonday meals at Fort Shaw, basic but tasty food, no doubt prepared by students under the supervision of the cook who presided over the school kitchen.

Just as they were finishing up the roast chicken and mashed potatoes, Superintendent McCowan joined them. There would be plenty of time tomorrow for touring the rest of the school and all of Indian Hill. Since it would be hours before their luggage arrived from Union Station, there was no need to wait around to unpack. After so long a journey, would they like to get out and stretch their legs? A little bird had told him—and at this he glanced toward Miss Crawford, who blushed and looked down at her plate—that someone wanted to see the Pike.

Within a half hour the entire group from Fort Shaw, including Superintendent Campbell, was wandering the midway. Because there was far too much to see in the few hours they had, Superintendent McCowan suggested they break into groups and choose one attraction for this first day. Gen and Genie, with Mr. Campbell close behind, headed off to see Jim Key, the educated horse. Miss Malley took a group through Hagenbeck's Zoological Paradise and Animal Circus. The boys chose the Temple of Mirth, and Miss Crawford, Belle, Emma, Katie, and Sarah visited the Baby Incubators. Reconvening at the appointed time, they were asked what they would like to do with their last hour on the Pike. By consensus, the entire party chose to end the afternoon with a ride on the Scenic Railway—a thrill of a ride that took one's breath away as the cars slid up and down the rails, around curves, twice around before that final terrifying dip and then a gentle climb back to the starting point.[13]

The exhausted travelers returned to the school in time to see the 5:30 dress parade, ending with a salute to the flag that flew from the parapet above the school's main entrance. Then supper, unpacking the trunks, and falling into bed. It had been a full day. And tomorrow they would have to be at their best, for Superintendent McCowan had told them at supper that their first entertainment, including their first exhibition game, was scheduled for the next afternoon. Their program would begin at 4:00 in the auditorium, their game at 4:45 on the plaza. The news brought them up short. Eager as they had been to take the stage here in St. Louis, it was hard to imagine how they would have the energy to perform for the hundreds of strangers who would be the first to see the girls from Fort Shaw Indian School in action.[14]

"Eleven Aboriginal Maidens"

REVEILLE. NETTIE OPENED HER EYES. SIX O'CLOCK. JUST LIKE THE first reveille that had shattered her sleep as a six-year-old at Fort Shaw nearly a dozen years ago. Her teammates were already on their feet, slipping out of their gowns. Why rush? Nettie wanted to know. This might be the one and only morning when there was no schedule to meet. Fortunately, old habits prevailed, for just as they had finished putting on their new uniforms and were ready to make their way to the dining room, a light knock came at the door. A group of girls from Chilocco, clad in the very same uniforms, stood in the hallway, a welcoming committee of ten, eager to meet their new dormmates. Motivated by curiosity as well as hospitality, the visitors had come armed with all sorts of questions about Fort Shaw School and life in Montana. In turn, the Fort Shaw girls had plenty of questions about life here at the model school, about other people on Indian Hill, about how often they were allowed to leave the Hill. There was instant camaraderie and nonstop chatter. Only the breakfast bell caused them to move toward the stairs. Lizzie lingered a moment longer, taking one more look at their room before closing the door behind her. Yes, their neatly made beds, well-ordered trunks, and clean-swept floor would pass muster with Matron McCowan.[1]

More introductions were made on the stairs and in the lower hallway. Names filled the air, bouncing about like bits of summer hail. Smiles mattered more than words at this point, for smiles lingered on, while names slipped away more often than not. The easy conversations of the hallway trailed off, and the students assumed a more formal air as one by one or group by group they took their accustomed places at table.

For the girls from Fort Shaw, their table of yesterday would, it seemed, be theirs through the summer. There would be no dining with girls from other schools. Belle, for one, thought keeping the troupe together would have its advantages. Of course, the boys in their group—John Minesinger, Lewis Snell, and little Louis Youpee—would forever be on the other side of the room—and there they sat, with the boys from the band to whose table they had been assigned yesterday. There were three more tables filled with boys in those handsome band uniforms. All strangers. No, Emma said. Just friends we haven't yet met. Gen groaned. That was just like Emma. And were the girls and boys grouped by schools or by duties? Or both? They wondered. So much to be figured out. One big puzzle—and they were right there in the middle of it all.

Miss Crawford's sudden appearance ended their speculations. As soon as they were dismissed from breakfast, she and Miss Evans wanted to show them the rest of the basement complex—the laundry, the sleeping rooms for visiting students and staff, and Mr. McCowan's office quarters. The tour was no sooner under way than Mr. Campbell came down the hall, waving a copy of the morning's *St. Louis Republic* that carried the article announcing their arrival at the fair. "Eleven aboriginal maidens from the Fort Shaw Reservation," he began. No, the group in front of him chorused, no, it doesn't say that.[2]

That and more, their superintendent said, well aware that even garbled publicity was better than no publicity at all. The girls could only cringe, hearing that Nettie was identified by the reporter as Mattie Wirth, and that Rose LaRose and Sarah Mitchell weren't even named as a part of their group. But the article did note that the newly arrived contingent would be performing at the Model Indian School auditorium at 4:00 that afternoon. Campbell had no sooner read that line than Miss Evans opened the door of a spacious studio off the basement hallway. The room had a piano, chairs, a platform, and a conductor's stand. This was their rehearsal space, she told them. They would share it with other performers, of course, but this was the place they would gather to prepare this afternoon program—after a morning spent touring the rest of the school, including the outdoor exhibits.[3]

Mr. Peairs, the agriculture instructor, had invited them to drop by and see the school garden. Did Miss Crawford hear a groan from some-one? Let that be the last such show of rudeness. This was not an ordi-nary garden, but an irrigated plot designed by Mr. Peairs himself, with the help of some of his older boys at Haskell. This was an operation in which Mr. Peairs took great pride. Courtesy demanded they accept his invitation. Their own curiosity would determine when or whether they chose to return to the site in the future.[4]

Their visit to the school's small farm immediately engaged Katie. Seeing the boys weeding the rows took her back home to "Mrs. Snell's garden," the best on all of the Fort Belknap Reservation. Yet there were things to be learned from this model garden. The crops were differ-ent from the ones Katie knew. Two of the boys were harvesting let-tuce, something her father had never grown. There were also tomatoes, almost ripe enough to be plucked from the vine. Those were an early variety, Mr. Peairs told her. The plants at the far end of the row would come on in July, by which time these earliest ones would be pulled up to make way for another kind that would produce tomatoes right up through early October. Could tomatoes survive in Montana? Katie wondered. She would write her father right away.

Her teammates were getting impatient; there was little enough time now to tour the main-floor hallways before the 11:30 recess. Finally, Miss Crawford suggested that Katie could come back to the farm any time she wished. For now, they should be moving along. Thanking Mr. Peairs and assuring him she would return, Katie ran to catch up with the group that was already moving up the steps to the school and into the lobby.

The girls, like the tourists, found it hard to decide which side of the hallway they should concentrate on: the side featuring the "tradi-tional" Indians working in their booths or the side opposite with the open workshops and classrooms, where they recognized some of the students they had met at breakfast that morning. The wisest course of action, given both the crush of midmorning visitors and the short time left to them, seemed to be to take quick peeks at both sides for now. In the days that stretched ahead, they could take their time in visiting the booths in this corridor.

By 11:15, they had gotten only as far as the booths in the south corridor—the Pueblo weavers, the Pomo basket makers, the Pima potters, the Navajo silversmiths. They had planned to move along quickly, but time had gotten away from them. Perhaps they had spent too much time at Geronimo's booth—but then who didn't? The old warrior was truly fascinating. And he seemed very interested in them, even knew that they were the basketball team from Montana.

Flushed with pride to think that the legendary Geronimo had heard about *them,* the girls lingered on, amazed by the dexterity of those gnarled fingers that fashioned miniature bows and arrows at a remarkable pace. Flora knew that if she took nothing else home from the fair, she would take Lawrence something from Geronimo. For fifty cents, she could have one of these bow-and-arrow sets. Or, for fifteen cents, she could have Geronimo's autographed picture. She would have to see how much spending money she ended up with.[5]

As the bell signaled the end of the morning session, they were caught in the tide of people—visitors, students, and the traditional Indians— moving toward the lobby, leaving them little time to dash upstairs and freshen up for the noontime meal. Coach Campbell told them Miss Crawford was waiting in the studio to go through "The Famine" scene and "Song of the Mystic," although at this point he was thinking they would have to choose between the two if they were to have time to fit in a basketball game as well. Perhaps just "The Famine" scene this afternoon. He'd verify that with Miss Crawford. The mandolin club would need time to go through their numbers with Miss Evans. What concerned him most was the lack of space in which to warm up for the game. He had not thought to tell Superintendent McCowan they would need some place for their basketball practices. Perhaps the superintendent would put up an extra goal, perhaps on the grass behind the school. For today, they could move the folding chairs and run drills in the auditorium, if it wasn't in use. No shooting, of course. Just a workout to loosen them up. They could practice their barbell and club-swinging exercises there as well. He'd talk with Mr. McCowan and then check with them later that afternoon.

Their heads were in a spin. They had never been this nervous before a performance—or before a game, for that matter. Their practice sessions with Miss Crawford and Miss Evans settled them down somewhat. Both teachers convinced them that they were ready to perform. By three o'clock, when Mr. Campbell showed up, they were with Miss Malley in the auditorium going through their gymnastics routines. There would be no time for basketball practice there today, since the auditorium must be set up for the afternoon program. The only warming up they could do was on the court just before the game.

By the time the auditorium had filled to witness the world's fair debut of the troupe from Fort Shaw Indian School, the girls were ready. The mandolin club, under the direction of "Miss Nettie Wirth"—with Lizzie adding a second violin—opened the concert, then yielded the stage to Louis Youpee for his rendition of "Ma's Physical Culture." The girls returned for their barbell exercises, followed by little Louis's "Nothin' t'All"—and then the club-swinging routines. While the girls changed into their buckskins for "The Famine" scene, Fern Evans and Lewis Snell performed a violin and cornet duet, and John Minesinger recited "Songs of the Night." There were gasps from the audience as the buckskin-clad performers filed out of the dressing room and onto the stage. Their "Famine" chorus was as perfect as they'd ever done it before, and the applause continued as they moved down the middle aisle and out into the hallway, leaving John Minesinger, Louis Youpee, and Miss Evans and Lewis Snell to complete the program, while they raced upstairs to change from buckskins to bloomers.[6]

By the time the final notes of the second Evans-Snell duet were being heard in the auditorium, the girls were on the court, shooting baskets and running their plays. The energy was flowing. Alerted to the game by the fair's Daily Official Program, hundreds of spectators, including many residents of Indian Hill, turned out for the event. Early arrivals claimed a place around the chalky borders of the court; latecomers— including those who had just left the auditorium—found themselves several feet back from the action. Those who had never seen a game of basketball were wide-eyed. Even die-hard fans of the sport were surprised by the level of play they observed. The girls were "as streaks of lightning," the sportswriter for the *St. Louis Globe-Democrat* proclaimed. The exhibition game played on the Model Indian School plaza was "the fastest thing of the sort ever seen in this city," and the action on the court had justified the team's title as "undefeated basket ball champions of the north west." This last phrase amused the girls, as they immediately recognized the source. Yes, Coach Campbell had to admit, he had implied as much in his conversation with the reporter that afternoon.[7]

In analyzing the reasons for the "surpassing excellence" of these basketball players, the reporter could only surmise that "the natural agility of the Indian maiden has been developed by [their] training." Coach Campbell put that quote on the table at breakfast. What did the girls think? Their natural agility or his training? Sensing his teasing for what it was, the girls spoke as one. Natural agility. And speed. Indian agility and speed. And Indian teamwork too, Belle added. All for one. And all for Fort Shaw. Their lively banter aside, no one at that table thought of their success on the court in terms of either/or. Everything in their lives had come together to bring them to this moment, a moment that included having their first exhibition game described in the morning edition of one of the leading papers in one of the largest cities in the country. And, no less thrilling, seeing their photograph alongside that article.[8]

~

In very little time, the Model Indian School was hosting thirty thousand visitors a day, Mondays through Saturdays. Just as quickly the Fort Shaw contingent was integrated into life on Indian Hill. Other than Lewis Snell, who was involved with the school's band in public concerts twice a day, the Fort Shaw students had no morning assignments, while their new friends from Chilocco and Haskell and Genoa were in classrooms or workrooms from 9:30 to 11:30 and 2:00 to 4:00. A select group from Chilocco sat in desks in the "literary classroom," demonstrating various aspects of the typical seventh- and eighth-grade curriculum— including writing and reading essays on their tours of the Palaces of Fine Arts, Industry, and Education, plus pieces on the merits of keeping a clean house and the benefits of the education they were receiving.

Girls from Chilocco made pies and cookies in a kitchen equipped with modern appliances, including a deluxe electric stove, while Haskell girls sewed dresses and pinafores on machines as up-to-date as those in the Palace of Electricity and Machinery. Boys from Haskell and Genoa demonstrated the manual arts of carpentry, blacksmithing, wheelwrighting, and harness making. And a group of fifteen boys from Chilocco spent the day in the print shop, turning out the weekday issues of the *Indian School Journal.* [9]

The responsibilities of the contingent from Fort Shaw were afternoon entertainments in the auditorium and twice-weekly games of basketball on the court set up on the parade grounds in front of the school. Originally scheduled to participate only in Wednesday and Friday afternoon programs, they were soon performing three and four times a week in front of audiences "very generous with applause, the recitations of Louis Youpee . . . being especially appreciated." When the auditorium was no longer large enough to accommodate the crowd, a change of venue was announced. Henceforth all musical and literary programs would take place on the porch overlooking the plaza and parade ground, weather permitting.[10]

The girls from Fort Shaw found that much of the time not given to polishing their performance numbers or perfecting new plays for their exhibition games was given to answering reporters' questions. They were also frequently asked to pose for photographs, especially in their handsome buckskins. It was rumored that the beaded dress worn by Belle Johnson had been made by her aunt and was valued at $325. Belle had nothing to do with starting that rumor, but she did nothing to dispel it either, knowing the dress's monetary worth would increase over the next few months—just as its value had crept steadily upward in articles in Montana and Dakota newspapers. How high the price would rise by summer's end was anybody's guess. She had become almost as adept at working the press as F. C. Campbell himself.[11]

With no morning duties of their own, the girls were free to wander the main-floor corridors. If they were early enough, before the size of the crowds made any exchange impossible, they would visit the traditional Indians in their booths and study their art. Minnie was especially interested in the beadwork of the Ojibwa women, which was so different from Blind Maggie's—and therefore different from her own. Mustering all her courage one morning, she offered to show the women her beadwork in the display case in the lobby. Though she couldn't understand their exact words, she knew from their expressions that they liked what they saw—and she took that as high praise.

A favorite stopping place was the kindergarten classroom, where a dozen five-and six-year-olds from Sacaton, Arizona, spent an hour each weekday morning and afternoon learning their lessons. Emma found their efforts to master English endearing and reminiscent of her own struggles with the language in her early years at St. Paul's. For Flora, Rose, and Katie, these little ones were reminders of their youngest siblings, whom they had not seen in a year. Annie Lucero, James and Tom LaRose, and Jimmy Snell were growing up without knowing their big sisters. There was no way to make up for that, but the three girls took advantage of every chance they had—in the hallways and at mealtimes—to seek out the kindergartners, who had never before been away from their families and were always glad to see their new "big sisters." Sometime they walked the little ones down to visit with the families living in the Pima encampment at the base of Indian Hill.[12]

All the girls—and Louis, their welcome tag-along—enjoyed their treks to the village below the school. Some 220 people representing fourteen western tribes, were now in residence there, lodged in homes as varied as their customs and cultures. Although the girls had seen plenty of tepees, this was their introduction to grass lodges, hogans, bark huts, earth lodges, and many of the other structures housing the "primitive" Indians—each structure well suited to the landscape and climate from which these peoples came. Different as well were the lifeways on display, whether it was the Acoma women cooking in their ovens, the Comanche men painting on buckskin, or the Dakota Sioux performing one of their ceremonial dances.[13]

Even more different were the homes and lifestyles of what Superintendent McCowan referred to as "McGee's imported 'exotics'"—the Patagonians from Argentina and the Ainus from the island of Hokkaido in Japan. The camp of the Batwa Pygmies from the Congo still stood empty, but their arrival was anticipated any day.[14]

If they were fascinated by the villagers "on display" at the base of Indian Hill, the girls never lost sight of the fact that they—and all of their classmates—were also on display. Why else were those thousands of people walking through the Model Indian School every day? And what drew the hundreds of visitors to their basketball exhibitions? Curiosity. Not only about basketball, but about how the game would be played by a bunch of Indian girls. But if they were curiosities, they were also celebrities, a status they were enjoying to the hilt. There was no greater fun than seeing Geronimo making his way up the hill to watch one of their afternoon scrimmages. They'd rather play for him than for all the women in bustles and men in fedoras who crowded around the perimeters of their court.

~

With the arrival of his wife and children, Superintendent Campbell had ceased to be a regular presence on Indian Hill. Aware that his time in St. Louis was growing short and determined that his family and his students should experience life beyond the fairgrounds, Campbell took the entire Fort Shaw contingent on a riverboat trip down the Mississippi one warm afternoon. And, yes, the Wirth sisters finally got a glimpse of the Jefferson Barracks that their father talked so much about. The superintendent also treated the group to a performance of *Louisiana*, the new musical that all of St. Louis was talking about. The girls were enchanted with the play—and with the elegance of the newly opened Odeon Theatre on Grand Boulevard.[15]

Such excursions were the exception, however. For the most part, the girls from Fort Shaw stayed close to the school. Even so, their fame spread beyond the fairgrounds, and before the end of June they had received challenges from two of the best girls' basketball teams in the region—the state champions of Illinois, O'Fallon High, and an all-star team made up of alumni and current players of Missouri's perennial state champions, Central High in St. Louis. This was exactly what the girls had hoped for, a chance to test their skills against the best teams in the Midwest. There were those—like James Sullivan, head of the fair's physical culture department—who had dashed their hopes, who doubted that these midwestern teams would play in public, in front of mixed audiences. Sullivan had even said as much to Superintendent McCowan when McCowan had raised the possibility of such matches for the Fort Shaw girls. Yet there were no contingencies attached to these challenges. The Illinois and the Missouri girls offered to meet them any place, any time. The arrangements were to be made as soon as possible. A new energy suffused the exhibition games on the plaza.[16]

~

The last week of June brought some important visitors to Indian Hill. Miss Estelle Reel, national superintendent of Indian schools, arrived from Washington to address the Congress of Indian Educators being held in conjunction with the annual conference of the National Education Association. The same meeting drew William Winslow, Fort Shaw's founding superintendent and now the head of Genoa Indian School in Nebraska.[17] Nettie and Lizzie had been two of Dr. Winslow's first enrollees, and Katie, Belle, and Gen Healey remembered well the superintendent's recruiting visits to their homes. Emma had left St. Paul's Mission School to come to Fort Shaw at his invitation, and Flora had entered school during the last year of his superintendency. In the six years since his departure from Montana, these promising little girls had become accomplished young women. And outstanding basketball players.

When Dr. Winslow joined them at breakfast the first day of the conference, he relaxed into sharing his memories of those earlier years. He began with his first impressions of the run-down fort he was supposed to turn into a school for Indian children—right down to the cows and chickens wandering in and out of the abandoned buildings. He recalled the first time little Nettie stepped up on the platform and gave a recitation in public. No, not Louis Youpee's standby, "Nothin a'Tall." He couldn't remember what it was. Nor could Nettie. This strict disciplinarian had obviously mellowed in age. Or, perhaps the change was within themselves. Whatever accounted for the mood of the morning, they were charmed by the man, and they prodded him for more stories.

Pulling out his watch an hour later, Dr. Winslow begged to be excused in order to make the first conference session of the day. But before leaving, he asked them to please give his regards to Josie and to tell her how glad he was that she had finally persuaded him to order that ball and two baskets she had said she needed. From what he was hearing, both the girls and the game had come a long way since that first "basket ball" scrimmage in June 1897. As to the here and now: he was very much looking forward to their performance in Festival Hall that evening, where Superintendent Reel would also be in attendance.

Again, the butterflies swarmed. The girls were facing one of the most important challenges of their lives. Not only would they be performing in front of the national superintendent of Indian schools, they would be performing in front of the largest audience they would ever likely have, fifteen hundred members of the Indian School Service. They were also without the guidance of Miss Evans, who had departed for her summer break a few days earlier, and they were just beginning to adapt to the teaching techniques of their new music instructor, Ada Breuninger of Chilocco. Although she was not the violinist that Miss Evans was, Miss Breuninger was a skilled pianist, and they knew that her accompaniment behind their "Song of the Mystic" had added a richness to the pantomime.[18]

Not surprisingly, the Fort Shaw performers shone that night. Nettie led the mandolin club in the opening number of the evening, after which the girls demonstrated the "art of club swinging" and presented both "The Famine" and the "Song of the Mystic." The next morning's *Globe-Democrat* called the program "one of the most instructive features of the Congress."[19]

Estelle Reel was as impressed as the reporter, and during the reception after the concert, Superintendent Campbell invited her to visit Fort Shaw on her next trip west. She accepted his invitation and instructed her aide to add the Montana school to her August itinerary. When Campbell mentioned that the evening's performers would still be here in St. Louis while she was at Fort Shaw, she assured him that she would find time to talk with them before she left the conference.[20]

That interview took place the very next evening, just prior to a banquet in Miss Reel's honor, an exclusive affair featuring foods prepared in the model kitchen and served in the model dining room. Though she had only minutes to spare before that event got under way, the national superintendent made her way downstairs to the basement dining hall and asked to be escorted to the table reserved for the girls from Fort Shaw School. She shook hands with each one, then turned her attention to Minnie. Having been alerted to Minnie's desire to teach, she urged her to apply for a position with the Indian School Service. Moved by her encouragement, Minnie shed her shyness and rose to thank Miss Reel, knowing full well that Gen would not let this die without a few taunts of "teacher's pet."[21]

~

With the conclusion of the Indian educators' meeting, it was time for the Campbells to return to Montana to prepare for the coming school year. On the eve of their departure, the superintendent and his wife and children joined the rest of the Fort Shaw contingent and the other residents of Indian Hill—including Superintendent McCowan—for a ride on the Ferris wheel, courtesy of the manager of that famous "moving observation tower." There was plenty of room for all—each of the thirty-six cars held up to sixty passengers. But even with all that room, six-year-old Freda Campbell sought the safety of Emma's lap as her vantage point from which to behold the wonders of the world from 265 feet aloft.[22]

The wonders on this clear summer's afternoon included views not only of the fairgrounds that stretched beneath the wheel but of the countryside for miles around. Not everyone was focused on the "wonders." That old warrior Geronimo would not leave his seat to go to the window; the oscillating motion of the cars unnerved him. On the other hand, his traveling companions, the Patagonians, "howled with delight." From a few of the Fort Shaw students came muffled cries as their car rocked back and forth with each pause to load and unload passengers, but before the thirty-minute ride was over, the awe of the experience had overcome all fears.[23]

Two of their party seemed to be more entranced by each other than by the scene below. Or was she imagining the looks she thought they were exchanging, Katie Snell whispered to her friends as they rode back to the school on the Intramural Railway. Ada Breuninger and John Minesinger had begun singing duets in the afternoon entertainments, and perhaps their hearts, as well as their voices, had begun to blend.[24]

Theirs wasn't the only romance in the offing on Indian Hill. Several of the girls on the basketball team had crushes on some of the boys in the Indian School Band. Under the watchful eye of the numerous chaperones assigned to the school, students were discrete in such matters. No one wished to be sent home in disgrace. And yet, on those warm summer evenings when the crowds had gone and students sat out on the steps of the school, watching the flickering campfires of the encampments below and the lights of the fairgrounds beyond, romances were kindled. What better place to fall in love with love than at the 1904 St. Louis World's Fair?

~

As Superintendent Campbell said his good-byes at breakfast that morning in early July, he pronounced the ride on the Ferris wheel the perfect ending to the time they had shared in St. Louis. Once more he expressed his regrets that he was not able to stay longer, especially to see the girls take on the champions of Illinois and Missouri. However, he was leaving them in the good hands of Superintendent McCowan. Miss Crawford and Miss Malley, like Miss Evans, would be leaving St. Louis one by one as their contracts with Mr. McCowan expired. Miss Crawford would be returning to the fair in mid-August, but in the meantime, John Minesinger was in charge of young Louis. Mrs. McCowan and Lizzie would be there for the girls. Lizzie would also lead their gymnastics routines and take Miss Crawford's role as the narrator in "Song of the Mystic." Miss Breuninger would continue as their accompanist and take charge of the mandolin club. And Mr. McCallum, the instructor from Haskell—with this, Superintendent Campbell looked around the table to see that everyone recognized the name—Mr. McCallum would become the official "coach" of the basketball team, though Belle was their captain and they should trust her leadership.[25]

He would be in frequent touch with Superintendent McCowan. He expected only glowing reports. He knew he would not be disappointed.

The Observers and the Observed

THE ORIGINAL PLAN FOR THE EXHIBIT ON INDIAN HILL WAS FINALLY complete when, on the very day of the Campbells' departure, eight Batwa Pygmies arrived from central Africa and began work on their brushwood home on the southern edge of the village. It was as if they had brought equatorial conditions with them, for with their arrival the temperatures that had thus far been moderate for a Midwest summer began a steady climb.[1]

In spite of the heat, the girls carried on—with afternoon concerts taking place according to the schedule posted daily and with basketball games being played on the plaza every Wednesday and Friday, even on the hottest and muggiest afternoons. They might be invincible on the court, Mrs. McCowan warned them, but they were as vulnerable as anyone else when it came to dehydration. They must drink plenty of water, especially on the days they played basketball. Water, water, water, she preached. But these daughters of the plains found the water of St. Louis unpalatable, especially when compared with all the other beverages available at the fair. Emma's favorite was iced tea with plenty of sugar. Belle preferred the lemonade made by the Chilocco girls. Then they discovered Dr. Pepper, the soft drink that was taking the fair by storm. With each passing week, more and more of their pin money was spent on bottles of that liquid delight.[2]

More and more Dr. Pepper. And more and more basketball games, some of them scheduled as special events. On the Fourth of July that special event was a game against the girls from Chilocco, their classmates at the model school. It was the first match game for Fort Shaw since the girls had arrived in St. Louis, but it was hardly a match in any other sense. Although they had seen many of the Fort Shaw exhibitions, the Chilocco girls had never before played as a team. Their lack of experience showed. Try as they might to make a game of it—and despite Fort Shaw's efforts to keep the score down—the final tally stood 36 to 0.[3]

The game was over quickly enough for the dress parade on the plaza to begin on schedule at 5:30. That scene was "a picture for an artist" in the words of one visitor. As fairgoers crowded the porch and lined the perimeter of the plaza, the sound of a bugle sent the band into "a stirring march," and two companies—one of boys in gray uniforms and one of girls in blue skirts and white blouses—"pass[ed] . . . in front and back of the band and return[ed] to their places." The spectators marveled at the straight lines, at "the grace and ease with which the marchers made the turns, at their erect military bearing, at the manly air of the boys, and the modest, yet self-possessed demeanor of the girls, [and] at the sweetness of the music." As the last strains of that music died, the crowd, "no longer able to restrain its feelings," burst into applause.[4]

It was only then that the crowd's attention was drawn to the figure standing beside the battalion leader, "straight as an arrow and motionless. . . . Broad shouldered and of stocky build, . . . he stood there attired in white man's costume, with a broad brimmed prairie hat, the only suggestion of his race being a single feather on the side." As the Indian School Band broke into "The Star Spangled Banner," this "old warrior, standing in the rays of the setting sun, removed his hat and held it against his left shoulder, in silent salute to the flag he so long defied."[5]

The girls knew Geronimo well enough by now to know that the old man loved to play this role. His transformation from fierce warrior to loyal patriot was, after all, why the government allowed him to leave the confines of Fort Sill and appear at fairs around the county. Having learned the value of the white man's dollar, the Apache entrepreneur drove hard bargains. As his popularity increased, so did his fees. He had told the girls they could make good money playing basketball. People were paying a pretty price to see Indians. Just go to the Pike and watch one of those wild west shows, he said. Yet seeing Geronimo work the crowd on Independence Day was all the proof the team needed of the advantages of "playing Indian."[6]

The day after the Fourth belonged to another performer, Louis You-pee. The school's little showman had been invited to give one of his recitations at the "American Boy Day" celebration at Festival Hall. Louis Youpee, the ultimate American Boy, plucked from the heart of the Indian exhibit. The McCowans saw the twelve-year-old Chippewa as living proof of the transformative powers of the government's Indian schools. To ensure that point was not missed by fairgoers who attended this major event, the couple arrived at Festival Hall in the company of a phalanx of uniformed students. Although he had never before performed in front of two thousand people, Louis spoke his "piece" with the confidence of a professional. When Sarah Mitchell asked him later how he managed to stay so calm, he shared his secret: He had told himself that he was back in Luther Hall in Great Falls. It was as simple as that.[7]

On the afternoon of July 11, the moisture-laden air exploded into a thunderstorm whose torrential rains sent the girls and their friends scurrying up the stairs to move their cots away from under the worst leaks in the ceiling. The tents set up by some of the older boys who had earlier sought relief from the stifling heat of the dorms proved to be no match for the high winds and heavy rains. Several homes in the village below the school were damaged. A bolt of lightning pierced the Palace of Agriculture just east of Indian Hill—yet that exhibit's massive floral clock ticked on, and the building itself survived. Things could have been worse, the basketball girls joked to their friends in the evening calm that followed the storm. They could have been out there on the court, "streaks of lightning" turned into lightning rods.[8]

For all its fury, the storm did not break the heat wave, and four days later, the temperature reached one hundred degrees, where it hovered for days. The heat and humidity were especially hard on the kindergartners, and on July 19, the class was dismissed for what was to have been only a brief vacation. Even with that precaution, sickness broke out. Mrs. McCowan kept careful watch over the little ones who were quarantined in the dormitory, and she checked daily on the children in the village below. But heat and disease were a deadly combination, and when five-year-old Mary Thomas died "of unknown causes," the rest of the Pima kindergartners were taken home to Sacaton. The girls from Fort Shaw were not alone in wishing the decision had been made weeks earlier. Yet that decision, like so many others in their lives, was out of their hands.[9]

Another decision beyond their control, yet affecting their future, was made by a man they had never met and had never expected to. The girls were well aware that while they were playing exhibition games twice a week on the plaza in front of the Model Indian School, a multitude of men's and boys' athletic competitions was taking place in the gymnasium and stadium that were virtually across the street from the school. From May to November teams from across the country competed for trophies in such sports as baseball, football, lacrosse, tennis, roque, and, yes, basketball. AAU, YMCA, college, and scholastic championships were decided in these contests, all of which were deemed "Olympic events" under the rules set forth by the International Olympic Committee. Yet even though crowds of women in bustled skirts and mutton-sleeved blouses looked on with interest, there was not a single female on the field of play.[10]

No one could blame the exposition's director of physical culture for this slight. After all, James Sullivan had cordially offered to add a women's component to the athletic events being held in conjunction with the fair—provided sponsoring schools and organizations would allow women and girls to play in a public arena. Predictably, societal standards trumped any attempt to organize such competition, sparing Sullivan the necessity of making good on his offer. Victims of circumstances beyond their control, the girls from Fort Shaw Indian School listened to the cheers that rose from the stadium across the way but did not have the heart to join the crowds who watched the boys and men compete for the trophies and ribbons they themselves had hoped to win.[11]

This was a new experience for the young women from Montana: They were being excluded, not because they were Indians, but because they were girls. They had no say in the matter, but they did have a choice as to how they responded to the slight. Rather than sulking, they put their energies into hard-driving exhibition games that reminded them of who they were and what they had to offer. If Mr. Sullivan needed verification of his earlier prediction that "girls' sport" might prove to be "a drawing card at the fair," let him drop by the plaza in front of the Model Indian School—a very public arena indeed—and observe the size of the crowds that gathered to see ten girls in bloomers and middies play a heart-stopping game of basketball.

～

Back home, Superintendent Campbell was receiving regular reports from Samuel McCowan regarding his Fort Shaw students, reports he passed along to the local papers. The team was "making a great hit . . . and having a fine time," he told the reporter from the *Great Falls Leader*. They were also "properly study[ing] the many wonderful and interesting exhibits in the buildings and foreign pavilions on the grounds."[12]

The girls were indeed "studying the many wonderful exhibits on the grounds." Mrs. McCowan took them on several excursions into the heart of the fair, where they toured the Palace of Fine Arts, Emma's favorite; the Palace of Education, Minnie's favorite; and, closer to Indian Hill and closer to home for Katie, the Palace of Agriculture, whose giant floral clock ticked off the minutes with the precision and accuracy of a stopwatch. The marvels of electricity, the inventions of Thomas Edison, the dirigible floating above the aeronautic concourse. Everything moved, flowed, pulsed, and surged, as if flying forward could somehow make up for the eons lost in the march toward civilization.

Everything flew forward—except for those "primitive" cultures so prominently displayed in the anthropology exhibit. Harsh innuendoes perhaps, but this was, after all, the University of the Future.

One morning the basketball girls, accompanied by Lizzie, fulfilled a promise to Superintendent Campbell by visiting the Montana Building on the Plateau of States. They were graciously received and treated as celebrities by the volunteers on duty that day. The building, beautiful as it was, was located next to the mining and metallurgy exhibit, and as the girls looked out at the neighboring derricks and smelters, they felt as if they were back in Butte—only without the smoke.[13]

Far different from the Plateau of States was the Philippine Reservation, the largest component of the anthropology exhibit and situated just across Arrowhead Lake from Indian Hill. With Lizzie as their guide, the girls wandered the separate camps of the reservation, observing the dancing of the Igorots and the Moros and the work being done in a "model school" strikingly different from the one up on the Hill. Here adults as well as children cycled in and out of the small classroom at appointed hours, stirring Nettie's memories of the classroom at Fort Peck where her mother had shared her desk and her lessons.[14]

But the girls from Fort Shaw were also "studying" the attractions on the Pike, often after dinner when the temperatures had dropped and the midway was less crowded. With the other residents of the Indian School, they were guests of the management of Hagenbeck's Zoological Paradise and Animal Circus. Man-eating beasts in a jungle setting, talking birds, and elephants sliding down a giant chute into a pool of water. Their letters home were filled with descriptions of these marvelous attractions. On various other evenings, the girls and their friends saw the re-creation of scenes from the Boer War and visited Battle Abbey, a museum offering reproductions of some of America's most storied military engagements.[15]

Intrigued as they were by the many exotic shows on the Pike, none drew their interest so much as Cummins' Wild West Indian Congress, a spectacle replete with the kinds of stereotypical depictions of American Indians that Superintendent McCowan had worked so hard to avoid. Within a huge arena, some eight hundred actors played "cowboys and Indians." Red Cloud and American Horse sometimes made featured appearances, and the most infamous battle of the frontier was played out nightly, with Frederick Cummins himself in the role of General Custer.[16]

Such evenings made the girls aware all over again—as if they could have forgotten—that although they regarded themselves as polished performers and accomplished athletes, they, like the participants in Cummins' Wild West show, indeed like the traditional Indians with whom they shared Indian Hill, were regarded by most fairgoers as a curiosity. That point was frequently driven home by the comments made by people touring the Model Indian School. Visitors spoke their minds as if the students in the workrooms and the adult Indians across the hall were no more capable of understanding what they said than the cattle and sheep in stalls at a county fair.

Gen Healy always seemed to be in the right place at the right time to overhear some of the most insensitive comments, and she made a practice of repeating those comments, with proper intonation and gesture, at night in the dorm. She could imitate to perfection the well-dressed matron who impulsively reached out to touch the hair of a Pomo basket weaver and declared how surprised she was to find it hardly any coarser than her own. And while talking with a Haskell friend who was ironing a tablecloth in the laundry lab, Gen heard a visitor remark to her husband, "It is absolutely amazing what these people can do when properly taught!" Ironing a tablecloth? As Gen reported that evening, "*those* people" had obviously never been "properly taught" common courtesy.[17]

Whether insightful or insensitive, visitors to the Model Indian School continued to increase in number as the days moved on. As one woman put it, "The only mistake Col. McCowan made is that he did not make his building large enough. All the people cannot get in here during working hours." While most of the visitors who filled the hallways were first-timers, many who had been there before returned in the company of friends they felt simply *must* see the place for themselves. Others came back because they could not stay away. "When I leave the hotel in the morning I am just naturally drawn in this direction," one fairgoer told Superintendent McCowan. "When I go home, people will ask me what I have seen and I will have to say, 'Well, I saw the Indian School; then I went to the Philippines [Reservation]; then I went back to the Indian School.'"[18]

Judging from comments overheard or entered in the visitors' book, the girls from Fort Shaw were a major reason for the popularity of the Model Indian School. Time and again their rendition of the Famine scene from *Hiawatha* drew tears as well as applause, perhaps because seeing ten young women in traditional buckskin dresses, leggings, and moccasins deliver Longfellow's lines with such eloquence and feeling moved the poet's romanticized depiction of the plight of the "vanishing" Indian into the world of reality.

Their other entertainments were equally well received. "The 'Song of the Mystic' was grand," one visitor remarked as she exited the chapel one afternoon. "Those girls in the pantomime are [also] champion basketball players," she was informed by a passerby. "And [they] have a fine mandolin club. They surely are versatile." A Boston teacher, obviously familiar with the techniques of Delsarte—and no doubt with the work of mandolin clubs in her area—left her remarks in the visitors' book: "The exercises in the Indian School chapel Saturday afternoon were the finest of the kind I have ever heard."[19]

~

Despite the intense heat and despite their exposure to crowds of strangers, the Fort Shaw contingent was surprisingly healthy—until Sarah, and then Katie, began to complain of toothaches. Lizzie was quick to suggest that the culprit might be the Dr. Peppers or the ice cream cones or the spun sugar known as "fairy fluff." But as Sarah's toothache grew worse, she finally confessed to Mrs. McCowan, who took her into the city to see Dr. Marshall. Three fillings and nine dollars later, Sarah's problems were over.[20]

Katie's had barely begun. Day after day she hid her pain from Lizzie and the others, wanting to delay the trip to the dentist at least until after the approaching game against O'Fallon High. Number six on the Fort Shaw roster, she was determined to be ready to play if needed. However, when the pain became so great she couldn't even jump center without clutching her jaw, Lizzie intervened. On July 25, the Monday before the O'Fallon game, Mrs. McCowan returned to Dr. Marshall's office, this time with Katie in tow. The abscessed tooth, which required a root canal, was treated and prepared for a crown, which was placed the next day. Eight fillings, a root canal, and a crown in two days. Dr. Marshall's bill came to $12.50. And Katie pronounced herself ready to take on O'Fallon High.[21]

Toothaches were easily enough dispatched, but then there was a more serious health problem to be dealt with. In mid-July Louis Youpee suffered a flare-up of trachoma, the eye infection that had plagued him since his first year at Fort Shaw. Realizing the seriousness of the condition, Superintendent McCowan sent him into the city with John Minesinger to see Dr. Shoemaker. The doctor was concerned enough to have Louis return for daily checkups. When he saw no improvement after a week, he advised McCowan that he should probably consider sending the boy home to Fort Shaw. There was always the danger of contagion within the school, and the cooler, dryer climate of Montana would be more conducive to recovery. Reluctantly, McCowan agreed. Placing Louis under quarantine, he notified Campbell and made arrangements for Louis's and John's trip home.[22]

The girls from Fort Shaw tried to put their concerns over Louis aside as they concentrated on getting ready for their game against the Illinois state champions, the team from O'Fallon High. Mr. McCallum had begun attending their exhibition games, and while they appreciated his presence and his support, he was not Coach Campbell. For the most part they relied on Lizzie's guidance—and their own instincts—in preparing for the game. Advance publicity out of O'Fallon claimed its team was ready to "give the Indian girls a taste of the quality of the Illinois girl," and Belle and her teammates were taking the challenge seriously. The game was to be played in Belleville, Illinois, some twenty miles southeast of St. Louis, as a feature of the annual midsummer festival sponsored by that city's YMCA.[23]

On Thursday morning, July 28, the Fort Shaw girls, accompanied by Emma McCowan, Mr. McCallum, the boys in the Indian School Band, and a coterie of fellow students, boarded the train for Belleville. Their car was directly behind the luxury car reserved for the fair's dignitaries— and directly in front of a line of passenger and flat cars conveying "a group of savage Head Hunters from the Philippines," Bedouins from the Pike's re-creation of the ancient city of Jerusalem, and elephants from Hagenbeck's menagerie. The band, "head hunters," Bedouins, and elephants led the parade that opened the festivities in Belleville at 2:00 that afternoon.[24]

The game was not scheduled to begin until five o'clock, but by four the crowd was already so large that ropes had to be used to keep the field of play clear. The "court" was laid out on uneven ground in an open field. The goals at either end lacked backboards. But such conditions afforded no advantage to either side. The starting lineup for Fort Shaw was the one that had carried the team to prominence back in Montana: Minnie Burton, Emma Sansaver, and Nettie Wirth in the front court; Belle Johnson and Genie Butch in the backcourt. By halftime there was little doubt of the outcome. The fast pace of the game and the agility and teamwork of the Indian girls were too much for the O'Fallon team. Even after Emma turned her ankle at the beginning of the second half and had to go to the sidelines, the girls never lost a beat. After months of leading the second team in exhibition games, Katie was more than ready to take Emma's place at forward. Like a racehorse kept too long at the gate, she leapt into action. Her aggressive rebounding and smooth passes energized her teammates, and the score continued to mount right up to the final whistle. Fort Shaw 14, O'Fallon 3.[25]

The Illinois champions accepted their defeat gracefully and offered the winners sincere congratulations. Stepping out of the crowd to offer their own congratulations as well were Philip Stremmel and several of the St. Louis All-Stars, who had come to Belleville to see this western team in action. While the Indian School band escorted everyone from the field, Mr. McCallum slipped away to call Superintendent McCowan, who was waiting by the phone back at the school to hear the results of the game and to ask him to send the news to Montana. Having dispatched that duty, McCallum rejoined the crowd at the bandstand where the boys were treating players, fans, "head hunters," and Bedouins to a lively concert that lasted well into the evening.[26]

Both pleased and taken aback by the applause that greeted them at breakfast the next morning, the Fort Shaw girls looked at once toward Superintendent McCowan and were relieved to see that he was clapping too. Then he raised his arm to restore order. Such an extraordinary accomplishment, he told Lizzie later that day, merited an extraordinary show of the school's appreciation. The news buzzing around the school that day even reached the ears of the president's three sons—seventeen-year-old Theodore Roosevelt, Jr., and his younger brothers, Kermit, sixteen, and Archie, thirteen—who were visiting as special guests of Superintendent McCowan.[27]

Being introduced as a group to the president's sons was thrilling for the girls, who were close in age to the two older boys. Emma, uncharacteristically bold, singled out young Archie and asked for his autograph, not for herself but for Louis Youpee, who had been looking forward to meeting him but was too ill to come down and shake his hand. Archie readily complied, writing his name with a flourish, then extending his hand to Emma, asking her to take the handshake as well as the autograph to her young friend. Louis declared Archie Roosevelt's autograph and handshake the best thing that had happened to him since American Boy Day.

Of course, nothing could dispel his misery over having to leave, even though he seemed resolved not to cry. When the girls gathered to see him off three days after their triumphant return from Belleville, they hugged and kissed him until he begged for mercy. Pulling free, he sauntered down the sidewalk, whistling a little tune and looking for all the world like a lad who had had enough of this muggy weather and was heading home. At the end of the walkway, he spun around, swept off his cap, and threw the girls one of his deep bows. Then he grabbed John's hand and pulled him toward the intramural station. Louis never looked back again, but John's eyes remained on Ada Breuninger until the car pulled away from the platform.[28]

The two boys would be sorely missed, for the Fort Shaw contingent had become a tight-knit group over the summer, each one filling an important role: Louis was everyone's little brother, by turns annoying, by turns adorable. And John was everyone's big brother, someone you could rely on when in need of "big brotherly" advice. Their departure would also have an immediate effect on the school's literary programs. Whose comedy routines could match those of Louis Youpee? Whose voice could blend so sweetly with that of Ada Breuninger? There would be no more duets. But there would be letters. And Miss Breuninger's delight at the receipt of each envelope with a Montana postmark would not escape the notice of the girls from Fort Shaw.

A Silver Trophy

ONE WARM EVENING IN EARLY AUGUST, IN THE COMPANY OF MISS Crawford, who had finally returned to St. Louis, the girls from Fort Shaw enjoyed a huge fireworks display in Francis Field. This was the team's first chance to sit in the stands of that impressive arena, site of many of the summer's "Olympic events" and home to the official games of the Third Olympiad that were fast approaching. As they sat there, watching the breathtaking explosions of color, Minnie dared to ask her teammates whether they too were wondering what it would be like to compete in this stadium.[1]

Even as the girls mulled all the "what ifs," Miss Crawford was well aware that Superintendent McCowan had been working behind the scenes to convince WJ McGee that his basketball team would not only be a colorful addition to the upcoming "Anthropology Days" competition but would also demonstrate the athletic prowess of Indian students—Indian girls at that.

Anthropology Days was the brainchild of WJ McGee, head of the fair's Department of Anthropology, and James Sullivan, head of Physical Culture. The two directors realized that having specimens "from so many primitive cultures so close at hand" provided a unique opportunity to test the purported "natural athletic ability" of "natives from the four quarters of the globe" by pitting these "savages" against one another in such track and field events as the 100-yard dash, the 120-yard hurdles, the 440, the mile, and the shot put, javelin, and broad jump. Other events on the schedule were intended to test the natives at "their own games": throwing stones for accuracy, tree climbing, and archery.

Other contests—tugs-of-war and mud fights—were added as crowd pleasers.²

On Thursday and Friday, August 11 and 12, with virtually no training and little understanding of what they were supposed to accomplish, the men encamped on Indian Hill—Sioux, Cocopas, Cheyennes, Pawnees, Maricopas, Patagonians, Pygmies, and Ainus—plus seven boys from the Model Indian School, Filipinos from the neighboring Philippine Reservation, and Kaffirs from the Boer camp on the Pike, all participated in a two-day track and field meet, dubbed the "Aboriginal Games."³

Although the events themselves seemed to mystify many of the participants, the thousands who gathered in the stadium, "braving the burning rays of the sun" to view the contests, took great delight in the antics of the aboriginals. American Indians, most notably the boys from the Model Indian School, proved themselves far superior in almost every contest they entered. The results could have been predicted, according to the *Globe-Democrat*, because "being educated in American schools, . . . [the Indians] are well acquainted with the American games." Finishing a distant second in aggregate total of points were the Filipinos, followed by the Patagonians. The Pygmies took nothing seriously and finished last overall, although one of their number amazed everyone by climbing a pole, barefoot, to the height of 50 feet in 20 seconds to win the "tree-climbing" contest.⁴

Although the Anthropology Days games would go down in history as "the lowest point of the entire summer," James Sullivan was pleased with the results of what he termed his "special Olympics." As he had predicted, those time-honored tales of "savage peoples' natural athletic ability" had been disproved by contests in which the performance of the "primitives" was hardly the equal of that of "civilized children." McGee argued that most of the contests in this two-day spectacle were not true tests of the natural abilities of his indigenous peoples. In fact, he found the results fell so far short of his own expectations that he pressed for a second "anthropological meet," one that would be preceded by at least a modicum of training for the participants.⁵

While it seems doubtful that either he or Sullivan realized it at the time, McGee's claims that training in the white man's games would show "what brown men are capable of doing" were validated by the stellar performance of a group of young athletes both he and Sullivan had summarily excluded from their two-day meet. As a result of Mc-Cowan's persistence, McGee had belatedly agreed to incorporate an exhibition of basketball as the closing event of the games in Olympic Stadium on Thursday afternoon, August 11.[6]

Alerted by the superintendent at supper on Wednesday, the Fort Shaw girls spent the evening dividing and redividing themselves into teams as evenly matched as possible. By dinner the next day, Belle had made the final choices, and at four o'clock they took the court on the infield of Olympic Stadium with Lizzie Wirth replacing Emma, who was still sidelined with the badly sprained ankle she had suffered in the O'Fallon game. Thus, Lizzie joined her sister Nettie, Belle, Genie, and Rose on the Blues, while Gen Healy, Flora, Sarah, Minnie, and Katie composed the Reds. The game, watched by the thousands drawn to the day's anthropology meet, was hard fought. The natural advantage that should have gone to the Blues, who boasted three of the regular starters, was countered by the determination of the Reds, who had the advantage of Minnie's shooting. And the Reds carried the day by a score of 14 to 12.[7]

∿

By coincidence, Miss Estelle Reel, who had kept her promise to visit Fort Shaw on her tour of western schools, was with Fred Campbell when he received word of the game in Olympic Stadium. Lillie Crawford's wire described in detail the graciousness and maturity with which the girls had handled themselves. And there was no one with whom Campbell would rather have shared the news of such a successful public performance than Estelle Reel. Whatever Sullivan and McGee had hoped to prove by staging this unusual athletic meet—and however it might be viewed in the future—his girls had played in Olympic Stadium before thousands and had performed like champions.[8]

There was cause to be proud.

∿

A week and a half after the exhibition game in Francis Field, in a ceremony held at the Model Indian School, Superintendent McCowan, on behalf of the Physical Culture Department, presented the Fort Shaw team with a handsome silver trophy. Although it came in the wake of the girls' Anthropology Exhibition, it was the same gold-lined, mahogany-based loving cup that was given to the winners of every "Olympic event" held in St. Louis. It symbolized their overall contribution to athletic events at the fair. The inscription said it all:

World's Fair
St. Louis, 1904
Basket Ball
Won by
Fort Shaw Team[9]

The silver trophy was immediately put on display in the lobby of the Model Indian School, where it would stay until it could be taken home to Montana. Lewis Snell joked that he would gladly transport it for the girls when he was called back to Fort Shaw to cover his staff duties in late August, but they begged off. It was going to be hard enough to lose Lewis. They weren't about to give up that trophy too.[10]

Nor were they about to rest on their laurels, for still to be answered was the challenge issued by an All-Star team composed of alumnae of St. Louis Central High, the perennial basketball champions of Missouri.

Champions of the World's Fair

EVEN AS THEY INTENSIFIED THEIR SCRIMMAGES IN ANTICIPATION of their series against the Missouri champions, the girls from Fort Shaw were aware that the "real" Olympic Games were under way in the stadium where they had so recently played. The Third Olympiad of modern times opened in St. Louis on Monday, August 29. Purportedly an international event, the 1904 event was, in truth, an American Olympics. Of the 687 athletes who competed in the standard Olympic events—running, jumping, weight lifting, vaulting, wrestling, swimming, fencing, rowing, boxing, and gymnastics—more than 500 came from the United States. U.S. athletes won every one of the track and field events, save the Canadian victory in the 56-pound shot put and the British victory in the decathlon.[1]

～

On Saturday, September 3—coincidentally, the last day of the Olympic Games—the Fort Shaw team met the St. Louis All-Star team at Kulage Park in the northeastern sector of the city. The girls playing for St. Louis were protecting an unblemished record that stretched back into their school days at Central High, and they had practiced many hours over the course of the summer under the watchful eye of Coach Phil Stremmel. Stremmel himself had scouted several of the Fort Shaw exhibition games on the fairgrounds and had taken some of the members of his team to Belleville in late July to see the game against O'Fallon High. Although the St. Louis girls were awed by the level of play they saw in the Indians' defeat of a very good O'Fallon team, Stremmel had used the intervening weeks to bring his girls to the peak of readiness.[2]

The third of September dawned delightfully cool, a perfect day for basketball. Up until tip-off, it was expected that Katie Snell would replace Emma Sansaver at forward, given Emma's still-swollen ankle. Still, when the girls took the court at 4:30 in front of several hundred onlookers, Emma stood with her teammates—Belle Johnson, Minnie Burton, Genie Butch, and Nettie Wirth. A trolley-load of supporters had followed the girls from the fairgrounds, and as the teams took the court, a cheer went up:

> Bum-a-ling! Bum-a-ling!
> Bow-wow-wow!
> Ching-a-ling! Ching-a-ling!
> Chow-chow-chow!
> Bum-a-ling! Ching-a-ling!
> Who are we?
> Fort Shaw! Fort Shaw!
> Rah! Rah! Rah![3]

According to the reporter sent by the *Post-Dispatch*, any doubt as to the outcome of the game was dispelled within minutes of tip-off. The St. Louis athletes were "not in a class" with Fort Shaw. "The Indian girls were more active, more accurate, and cooler than their opponents" and trounced the All-Stars 24 to 2.[4]

The *Great Falls Tribune* treated Montana fans to a colorful account of the game, courtesy of on-the-spot reporting from Fort Shaw's Lillie B. Crawford. At the tip-off Nettie got the ball and "with some brilliant team work [the Indians] rushed it to the western goal but failed to score—handicapped as they were by the sun shining in their eyes." A member of the All-Stars grabbed the rebound, but in seconds Emma had the ball back and, "dodging here and there with the rapidity of a streak of lightning," displayed a "fearlessness [that] completely nonplussed her opponents." Time and again, "the Little One" managed to get the ball into the hands of the right player at the right time. Most often that was Minnie, who scored two "fine field throws" and two foul shots before the end of the first half.[5]

In the second half, "Nettie made four brilliant field throws," and Belle pulled off "one of the finest plays . . . ever." Genie "was a wonder [at] . . . guard," and the All-Stars could do nothing "but submit as gracefully as possible to the inevitable." Having fully expected to win, Coach Stremmel and his young women had instead suffered "an ignominious defeat." Yet no one seemed disappointed in the one-sided contest. "I stayed over one day to see this game," Miss Crawford quoted one spectator as saying, "and would not have missed it for $50. The playing of those Indian girls is simply marvelous. They can easily defeat any team in the world."[6]

Proud as the girls and their supporters were of their victory, it had been agreed that the championship of the fair would be decided by a best-two-of-three series of games. And so, in parting that afternoon, the two captains, Belle Johnson and Florence Messing, agreed that the second game would take place two weeks hence, on Saturday, September 17, on the plaza in front of the Model Indian School.[7]

There was no cockiness apparent in the girls as they went about their regular activities, plus evening drills and scrimmages after the gates were closed and the plaza belonged to them. By invitation of Superintendent McCowan and their friends from Chilocco, they participated in the celebration of Oklahoma Day at the fair on Tuesday, September 6, once more earning accolades from the *St. Louis Republic.* "One of the delightful features of the [program] . . . was the entertainment given by the . . . girls [who] performed a pantomime of 'Song of the Mystic' with splendid effect," the reporter noted. A photo of the Fort Shaw girls clad in their white robes accompanied the article.[8]

Their white robes. Three months of performances were beginning to tell on the girls' costumes, and none seemed to suffer so much as the outfits worn for "Song of the Mystic." The robes themselves could be spot-cleaned as necessary, but the white stockings were showing irreparable wear by the beginning of September. So shortly after the Oklahoma Day program, Lizzie Wirth asked Superintendent McCowan for permission for herself, Sarah, and Gen to go into town and pick up nine pairs of white stockings. McCowan granted the request, with the stipulation that they be back in time for the afternoon concert.[9]

〜

Because of press coverage of the championship series, basketball exhibitions on Wednesday and Friday afternoons were drawing even larger crowds than usual. But on September 16, the day before the second game of the series was to be played, the St. Louis All-Stars asked for a postponement. Flo Messing, captain of the team, contacted Belle, requesting "a few weeks' delay" but giving no reason. Seeing no other recourse, Belle agreed. So rather than playing a championship game, the girls gave Saturday, September 17, to appearing in two programs, opening the morning concert with a mandolin prelude and demonstrating club-swinging and barbell drills in the afternoon.[10]

The days were growing shorter—and cooler. When they were not in their "performance outfits"—buckskin dresses, basketball uniforms, or Grecian robes—the girls now donned school uniforms made of slightly heavier navy-blue shirtwaist material. Turned out by the Haskell girls in the sewing room of the Model Indian School, the new outfits were a necessary response to the change of season. And Superintendent Mc-Cowan began to consider the possibility of closing the Model Indian School sooner than he had anticipated. The building had no central heating, and the superintendent realized that he could not reasonably expect to house the students through November. In a note to the fair's director of exhibits, he alerted Frederick Skiff to his plan to maintain the Indian School "on approximately the present basis until about October 15, the date of closing to depend on weather conditions."[11]

~

With the end of summer, the number of fairgoers diminished, and the scientists in the Anthropology Building, located just west of the Model Indian School, turned their attention to "scientific measurements" of subjects closer at hand. The state-of-the-art equipment in the anthropometric and psychometric laboratories of the Anthropology Department had been used all summer to take the physical measurements of the fair's visitors, as well as those of the "primitives" on display. In addition to determining strength of grip and measuring height, weight, and lung power, the scientists paid particular attention to facial structure, limbs—even feet—in their dedicated effort to characterize the various "races" represented at the fair. Curious theories abounded: for instance, that the Indian, "along with several of the savage races," had little or no perception of the color blue. A color wheel was part of the scientific equipment installed in the lab.[12]

Now, with the test results on file from thousands upon thousands of "civilized" and "primitive" individuals, the experimenters began to test the students at the school. On Friday, September 30, Emma Sansaver reported on schedule to Dr. Frank Bruner in the anthropometry lab. She was the last of the girls to be called in, and she was eager to have her measurements taken so that she could compare them with the charts the others had already brought back to the dorm. She found the tests interesting and the data predictable: age, 19; height, 4 feet, 11 ¼ inches; weight, 109 ¼ pounds; pulse, resting, 75; hearing, excellent; vision, normal. Defying scientific "expectations," she easily recognized the color blue. Although she wondered what possible significance it could have, she confessed that she liked pink and disliked orange. And she didn't ask why the size of her skull or the distance between her eyes really mattered. Instead, she finished the tests, thanked Dr. Bruner, and hurried back to the school to lay her copy of the chart out on the cot beside those of the other girls.[13]

At about the same time Emma visited the anthropometry lab, the Fort Shaw group shared a frightening experience when Flora Lucero was hospitalized. Since early September Flora had felt weak and listless. Lizzie began taking her place in the scrimmages and often as not in the afternoon performances. By mid-month, Flora had developed a fever and a wracking cough. When tests confirmed tuberculosis, she was taken to Missouri Baptist Sanitarium. Her teammates were not allowed to visit her, but Superintendent McCowan was in daily contact with the doctor, who assured him that he was giving Flora his own personal attention and she was receiving the best in nursing care. Mrs. McCowan relayed these messages to the girls at supper each night, along with her promise that Flora would soon be back at the school, though she probably would not be able to scrimmage with them for a while.[14]

∼

On the first Friday of October—with Flora back from the hospital but still limited in her activities—Belle received the long-anticipated phone call from Flo Messing. The All-Stars were ready to play the second game of the series. Would the Fort Shaw team consider meeting the very next afternoon—Saturday, October 8—on the parade grounds in front of the school? They were ready to play any time, any place, Belle assured Miss Messing. Her only concern was whether there was sufficient time to publicize the game.[15]

She need not have worried. Within twenty-four hours word had spread across the fairgrounds and out into the city. Even had there been time for more extensive publicity, it is doubtful there would have been room for any more fans. At three that afternoon, a cloudy, chilly day in St. Louis, McCowan and the referee assessed the situation. Hundreds of men, women, and children were streaming up the hill to the parade grounds. Realizing the impossibility of keeping the growing mass of spectators from inching onto the playing field, McCowan called in the Jefferson Guard. Within minutes a contingent of soldiers, unarmed except for the ceremonial swords at their sides, marched onto the plaza, formed a protective cordon around the court, and managed to push the crowd far enough back for play to begin.[16]

At precisely four o'clock the captains met at center court. The lineups were the same as in the first game of the series. Once again Fort Shaw's color commentator, Miss Lillie Crawford, wired the *Great Falls Tribune* a full account of the contest from the opening play to the final whistle. At the tip-off as "the leather sphere rose and fell, . . . Nettie made one of her phenomenal leaps . . . and sent it spinning far toward the Indian girls' goal" and into Belle's hands. "Skillfully evading her opponent," Belle got the ball to Minnie, "who smiled as she dropped it into the basket, while the audience went wild with enthusiasm." That enthusiasm never flagged. At the end of the first half, the score was 9 to 3 in favor of Fort Shaw.[17]

Obviously the All-Stars had raised their level of play in the month of practice since the first game in the series, but they could not withstand the onslaught of the Indian girls. In the second half Fort Shaw's teamwork "called forth round after round of applause," applause that seemed to disconcert the All-Stars. They were able to score only three points, all on foul shots. Meanwhile, Nettie made two "magnificent field throws," Emma contributed one, Belle scored in "a play that has never been surpassed," and Genie's work "was par excellence." At the final whistle, the score stood Indians 17, All-Stars, 6.[18]

Coach Stremmel was gracious in defeat. As a team, the Fort Shaw girls "play[ed] a wonderful game," he conceded. "They are so skillful, so fleet, and . . . their powers of endurance are simply marvelous. . . . My girls . . . [were] unprepared to cope with such formidable opponents." Stremmel's players were as gracious as he. Before the next week was out, Superintendent McCowan received a letter from Lillian Randall of the All-Stars congratulating the Fort Shaw girls. The letter was added to the growing collection of souvenirs being set aside for the trip home.[19]

Back in Montana, the girls from Fort Shaw Indian School were more than merely the official champions of the Louisiana Purchase Exposition. In the eyes of their supporters—and the Montana journalists who had followed them for two years—they were "the undisputed . . . world's champions."[20]

~

Even as they basked in the glory of their championship, the girls became the focus of a controversy building around the person of one Charles H. Madison. Reportedly a man of "personal means" and an "intimate friend of President Theodore Roosevelt," Madison was a Presbyterian minister in charge of the People's Union Rescue Mission in Poughkeepsie, New York. Reverend Madison had visited the Model Indian School in late September, praised the work of the students there, and professed a great interest in Indian education. He had attended several of the afternoon concerts at the school and was particularly impressed by the talents of vocalist Katherine Valenzuela, a Pima Indian from Phoenix, and Gertrude Brewer, a pianist from Chemawa Indian School in Salem, Oregon. He invited both girls to return with him to Poughkeepsie, where they would live at his mission and attend Vassar College for further education and training. Emboldened by their en-

thusiastic response, he had laid the plan before Superintendent Mc-
Cowan and received his approval.[21]

Now, in the wake of their recent victories and rising popularity, Madison professed an interest in taking the Fort Shaw girls to New York. He
would pay all their living expenses, see to their enrollment at Vassar,
and set up exhibition games that would introduce their brand of basketball to East Coast fans. McCowan demurred. While Miss Valenzuela
and Miss Brewer were of an age to have made the decision for themselves, the Fort Shaw girls were not. He would have to put the plan in
front of Superintendent F. C. Campbell, who in turn would have to gain
permission from the girls' parents.[22]

And there were more offers put in front of the girls from Fort Shaw. At
the same time he was dealing with the Reverend Madison's entreaties,
Superintendent McCowan received a letter from Ralph Stanion, once
the principal teacher at Fort Shaw and more recently an attendee at the
fair's National Indian Educators conference. Stanion wrote asking that
Rose LaRose be allowed to join him and his family in Washington, D.C.,
as an attendant for the Stanion children. When McCowan approached
her with the offer, Rose immediately declined. She wanted to go home
to Fort Shaw—*if* she couldn't go to New York.[23]

Fred Campbell was upset by the telegrams he was receiving from St.
Louis. He could not possibly contact the girls' parents and obtain their
permission in time for the girls to go east at the close of the fair. And,
generous as Madison's offer sounded, such a decision required careful
consideration. The girls should come home, where he could help them
weigh the advantages and disadvantages of the proposal.[24]

In the meantime, the girls were discussing the advantages, if not the
disadvantages, among themselves. Miss Crawford spoke glowingly of
the benefits in spending a year on the East Coast. Lizzie, too, thought
there was much to be gained by exposure to eastern culture. Gertrude
Brewer and Katherine Valenzuela were already settled in Poughkeepsie,
and Gertrude's letters to Superintendent McCowan told of the comfortable living quarters they shared above the Union Rescue Mission.
They were giving weekly recitals for the benefit of the mission, and
although they hadn't yet started school, they were learning to drive.

This was heady stuff for the teenagers from Montana. Miss Crawford proceeded to change the travel arrangements for the six girls—Emma, Nettie, Minnie, Rose, Sarah, and Katie—who were sure they could get permission to go east.[25]

∽

In mid-October, Helen Keller made a much-publicized visit to the fair. While Keller was already a national figure, she was, in fact, the same age as Lizzie Wirth, and Lizzie had been fascinated with her story ever since first reading about her at Carlisle. Now she shared Keller's story with her teammates: her early childhood, her education, and her crusade for the deaf and blind. They were going to have a chance to see, Lizzie told them, one amazing woman.[26] On Tuesday, October 18, the Fort Shaw troupe was among the crowd gathered in Congress Hall to hear Keller speak. At the close of the lecture, Lizzie and Nettie Worth made their way to the front of the hall and positioned themselves so as to be able to hand Miss Keller an invitation to visit the Model Indian School before she departed St. Louis. Later that night, the girls lay on their cots and talked of the experience. Flora loved Keller's gown "of old rose silk"; Sarah was intrigued by Keller's speech patterns and the way Annie Sullivan interpreted her words for the audience; Minnie appreciated her commitment to education for all, no matter a person's limitations; and Lizzie described, more than once, how Miss Keller had reached out and touched her hand when she gave her the invitation.[27]

Therefore, no one was more disappointed than the girls from Fort Shaw when Helen Keller did not visit the school before leaving St. Louis. Then, a week later Superintendent McCowan called Lizzie to his office and handed her a note he had just received. It bore the return address of Wrentham, Massachusetts. "When I greeted the two Indian girls who held out friendly hands to me," Lizzie read, "I did not know that the envelope they gave me contained such a pleasant invitation or I should have expressed my thanks then and there. . . . By this time you will have learned that it was impossible for me to visit your school. Please give your pupils my kind love, and tell them that in thought I clasp their hands."[28]

∽

As October moved on, McCowan began the process of slowly closing down operations at the Indian school. The encampments of the traditional Indians were all but abandoned now. Geronimo had left the day before the girls' championship game with the All-Stars, but not before they had a chance to tell him how much they would miss having him on the sidelines. In the absence of the old warrior and the other peoples who had given life to the village, Indian Hill became a shadow of what it once was. The student body of the Model Indian School was also thinning out by the day. Emma passed around a memory book to be inscribed by special friends among the many who had shared her adventures in St. Louis. From Lucy, "Remember our World's Fair boys & fun we used to have." From Josephine, "All I ask is you remember me." From Freddie, "Forget me not."[29]

Every good-bye was tinged with sadness, but on November 5, when, for the last time, the boys from the Indian School Band marched down the steps and out onto the plaza, still in the perfect formation that had marked their performances all summer, a pall fell over the Model Indian School.[30]

For the Fort Shaw group, even the possibility of a year at Vassar had lost the appeal it once had. Superintendent Campbell had expressed his misgivings about the Reverend Madison quite openly to McCowan. He just didn't trust Madison, he said. The fellow probably intended to take the girls on the road as a sort of vaudeville show. They would probably be playing games and giving entertainments in eastern cities for the benefit of the minister's mission work, and their schooling wouldn't be at Vassar but at high schools here and there, wherever they happened to stop for any length of time. Miss Crawford, chagrined that she had let her excitement overrule her good judgment, hastened to rearrange once more the reservations she had so impetuously changed just a week earlier. She was only partially successful; while managing to get through tickets to Montana for herself and the six others who had been Poughkeepsie-bound, they would be traveling a few days behind Lizzie, Belle, Gen, Genie, and Flora.[31]

By early November, only a handful of students remained in the dorms. Even Superintendent McCowan was no longer in St. Louis.

Having contracted malaria, he was on temporary leave in Hot Springs, Arkansas, and Emma McCowan had taken charge of the skeletal staff. To all intents and purposes, the Model Indian School was closed to the public. The hallways that had so recently been alive with activity now echoed with emptiness. It was hard to imagine that this same building had hosted over 3 million visitors in the weeks between the first of June and the last of October.[32]

On November 10, the day of their departure, Belle and Flora, Gen and Genie and Lizzie sought out Mrs. McCowan in the superintendent's office. There they thanked her for all she and her husband had done to make their months at the fair so memorable. Mrs. McCowan walked them to the lobby and retrieved the precious trophy from the display case. Handing it to Belle, she wished them all safe journeys.

Then, with one last look at the school, with its flags still flying, and one last exchange of hugs with their teammates and Miss Crawford, the five girls boarded the Intramural Railway at the foot of Indian Hill for the last time, caught the suburban line at the entrance to the fairgrounds, and headed for Union Station. The mood that hung over them now was much different from that evoked by their first glimpse of the city. On June 14 they had been all but overwhelmed by the excitement of the occasion. But on June 14 they had all been together. Now they were subdued, filled with mixed feelings. It might have been different had the entire team been westward-bound, but their separation from their sisters weighed heavily. Lizzie reminded them that, in just five days, the others would follow. Then she shared a secret she had held back for this very moment. Rather than going all the way to Fort Shaw, they could get off the train at Cascade, where they would wait for their teammates to catch up with them. Superintendent Campbell had made all the arrangements. After a grand reunion they could all ride into Great Falls together. Carrying the trophy.[33]

There was much to think about—their future and their past—as the train rolled across the country, through Chicago, the Twin Cities, Bismarck, and Billings. There were layovers in St. Paul and Fargo, but no games, no entertainments this time. They were on their way home.

~

On December 1, two weeks after the departure of the last of the Fort Shaw girls, the city of St. Louis staged the closing ceremonies for the Louisiana Purchase Exhibition. That morning, William Reedy editorialized in his popular magazine *The Mirror,* "[I]t is over—the Fair—yet much of it remains with us, . . . [including] a broader tolerance [and] a keener appreciation of the good in all the world. . . . We have learned to be humble before the achievements of other peoples whom we have fancied we long ago left behind in the march of progress."[34]

Perhaps no other group at the fair had contributed to that appreciation as much as had the students at the Model Indian School, including the young women from Fort Shaw, Montana, who had gone to St. Louis to prove their abilities in the concert hall and on the playing field. Although they were but one small part of the Indian exhibit, they had developed a loyal following among visitors from around the world, many of whom would have agreed with one Montanan's assertion that "the Fair just wouldn't have been the same without them."[35]

"Forget Me Not"
1904–1910

❧❧❧

THE CROWD ON THE PLATFORM BUZZED WITH EXCITEMENT AS THEY waited for the Montana Central to pull in from Cascade. It seemed half of Great Falls had turned out to welcome "their" team. Superintendent Campbell moved through the group, cautioning everyone to stay back from the tracks and motioning the boys in the band into formation as the distant but unmistakable sound of the engine reached his ears. Friday morning, November 18. Five and a half months after their departure, the girls from Fort Shaw were returning home from a triumphant summer in St. Louis.[1]

For this very special occasion, Campbell had invited the siblings of the team members to accompany him to town—Flora and Isadore Sansaver; Nettie and Maude Healy; Leonard LaRose; Lawrence and Lena Lucero; Lewis, Daisy, and George Snell; and Ida Johnson and Mary Johnson Gobert. Others who had a special connection to the team were there as well—Josie Liephart, Louis Youpee, and newlyweds John and Ada Minesinger. And the band. Campbell had brought the band, for this was to be a celebration worthy of returning heroes.[2]

As the train pulled in, the band struck up "El Capitan," the John Philip Sousa march the girls had heard over and over in St. Louis. Miss Crawford and Lizzie Wirth were the first to step from the car to the platform. The cheers rose over the band music as the girls followed, one by one. The last to appear was Belle, holding aloft the gleaming silver trophy. It was an unforgettable moment for all who were at the Great Falls station that afternoon.

∼

As the caravan of wagons approached Sun River, townspeople turned out to line the street to wave and shout their congratulations. The wagons slowed to a stop and Genie and Belle, traveling in the lead wagon, rose to hold the trophy aloft. The cheers were warm and genuine. This triumph belonged to the entire valley.

Back at the school, in the autumn chill of late afternoon, the student body was gathered on the square to welcome the team home. Again the cheers rose as wagons rolled into the compound. Again the trophy was held high, this time by Minnie. Then reunions and celebrations all around until the supper bell. Later that evening the girls had a chance to unpack the souvenirs they had bought at the fair. For her sister Flora, Emma had a miniature vase made of ruby flash glass. Belle had a stereopticon view of the Ferris wheel for Ida; Flora gave Geronimo's autograph to Lawrence; and the team as a whole presented an engraved spoon to Josie, who had been the heart of this squad.[3]

From their arrival back on campus that Friday before Thanksgiving and on through the next week, the girls hardly had time to reorient themselves to school routine. Teachers and staff were patient, allowing the excitement to run its course, knowing that there was probably far more learning going on in the hallways and dorms over those few days than there was in the classrooms. But with the end of the Thanksgiving weekend, the adult supervisors sought to restore order and squelch the holiday mood. Everyone, even the "heroes," was expected to return to routine. So the girls went back to studying their lessons and tending their chores.[4]

But life was far from ordinary, for the teammates were now the darlings of fans across Montana, and their superintendent intended to capitalize on their fame. He set about arranging tours for the spring and laying the groundwork for taking the team to yet another world's fair, the 1905 Lewis and Clark Exposition in Portland.[5]

However, the "world champions" would never again play as a unit. Flora Lucero, suffering the lingering effects of the tuberculosis that had hospitalized her in St. Louis, did not return from a Christmas visit home. In April Genie Butch went home to the Little Porcupine. The decision to leave Fort Shaw was a hard one, but she was nineteen years old, she had finished her schooling, and her father needed her help on the ranch.[6]

The team realigned itself. And as Josie had captained the 1902–1903 squad and as Belle had led them through their championship season, so now they chose Emma to serve as captain of the team that played only three match games that spring of 1905—all of them against Helena High, all of them overwhelming victories for the Indians.[7]

Superintendent Campbell did not let the lack of interscholastic competition hamper his scheduling of exhibitions for the Fort Shaw athletes and performers. There was an extended tour of Montana in the spring and new venues to visit en route to the Portland fair in August. Whether given in Great Falls, Helena, Boulder, or Anaconda, in Shelby, Browning, Kalispell, or Columbia Falls, the program the girls presented was a set piece. The mandolin club opened the pregame entertainment, followed by recitations by little Gertie LaRance, who had replaced Louis Youpee in this traveling troupe. The older girls then performed "The Famine" scene, and after a brief intermission, returned to the floor in their bloomers and middies to mount a four-against-four exhibition of basketball.[8]

~

The *Morning Oregonian* of August 21, 1905, headlined the arrival of the "famous basket-ball team" at the Lewis and Clark Exposition in Portland. This was the team, the reporter reminded his readers, "that won the cup at the St. Louis Fair . . . and is believed to be the best basket-ball team of any public institution in the country." This was not quite the same team that had "won the cup," however. It had undergone yet one more transition. Gen Healy had moved up to the first five, taking Katie's position at guard when Katie, overwhelmed by homesickness after two years away from the family, asked to be allowed to go home for the summer. Not that anyone on these fairgrounds would know— or care about—the altered lineup, for there would be no exhibitions in Portland.[9]

Perhaps because the girls were only visitors at this fair, perhaps because they had seen—and been an integral part of—the biggest and the best of the world's fairs the year before, for whatever reason Portland did not hold the excitement that St. Louis had. They were nevertheless at their most gracious in the interviews they did during the week. Belle alluded to the "beauty" of the fairgrounds; Emma said that they all had "found much to interest them in the western fair." And Minnie patiently responded each time she was asked: Yes, it was true that she was a member of the same tribe as Sacagawea, the young Shoshone woman who had accompanied the Corps of Discovery to the Pacific. But, as far as she knew, there was no familial connection.[10]

If a mood of anticlimax hung over the trip west, the energy was restored when, on Sunday, August 27, the entourage departed Portland, bound for Salem, some fifty miles to the south and the home of Chemawa Indian School. Long planned, this "challenge of the champions" testing the Fort Shaw Indians against the Chemawa Indians was finally to take place on the home court of the alleged champions of the Pacific Coast.[11]

On Monday evening, August 28, at the auditorium in Salem, the Fort Shaw girls gave their standard pregame "musical and literary" performance. Then the teams from Fort Shaw and Chemawa took the floor. But the game turned out to be little different from all the other long-anticipated games involving the Fort Shaw team. Minnie Burton, Emma Sansaver, Belle Johnson, Nettie Wirth, and Gen Healy simply overwhelmed the West Coast champions. At halftime the score was 26 to 6. At the final buzzer, the scoreboard read Fort Shaw 38, Chemawa 13.[12]

As jubilant as the girls were, a touch of melancholy pervaded the postgame celebration. The quest had come to an end. There were no new worlds to conquer. At least not on a basketball court, at least not in those middies with the "F" and the "S" on the collars.

~

The travelers were back on campus about the same time as Katie Snell returned from her summer break. There was much to share with her—the play-by-play of the game against Chemawa, the overwhelming vastness of the Pacific Ocean, the attention they had drawn on the fairgrounds, the fun they had had in Portland with the boys of the Chemawa band. . . . The chatter went on. It was as if the girls were trying to spill out all the stories—and by doing so, store up all the memories—for they were about to lose three more members of that St. Louis sorority.

Belle Johnson, Minnie Burton, and Rose LaRose were all nearing their twentieth birthdays. Their adult lives beckoned. Before September was over, Belle would be going north to her uncle's ranch near the Canadian border, and Minnie and Rose would be on their way home to Idaho. Although Minnie had a position as assistant matron at the Lemhi Agency School waiting for her, Rose had nothing so promising to go home to. A year earlier, her mother had left her father and, taking her two youngest children with her, had moved to the Uintah-Ouray Reservation near Fort Duchesne, Utah. Rose had not been home since the family upheaval. It was time to check on her father and remaining siblings and to begin her own life.[13]

~

Through the 1905–1906 school year, Emma Sansaver, Nettie Wirth, Katie Snell, Gen Healy, and Sarah Mitchell were the only members of the fabled Fort Shaw team remaining on campus. Nettie and Sarah were part of a six-member Fort Shaw squad that played only one game that year—against Great Falls High School. Playing for the first time by "girls' rules," Fort Shaw lost by a score of 26 to 18. The championship era was clearly over.[14]

The *Great Falls Tribune* published the team's obituary in November of 1906. "The girls who made Fort Shaw famous have scattered," the reporter said. "They composed probably the fastest and best trained team in the country." While proclaiming that the Fort Shaw team "belonged" to the fans of Great Falls, he confessed that when the rallying cry, "shoot, Minnie, shoot," had echoed through Luther Hall "at all their contests in this city," many in the stands would not have been able "to discern Minnie from any of the rest of the players."[15]

~

By the time that "obituary" appeared in print, the teammates had, for the most part, moved into their adult lives. There were five weddings in the span of six weeks from late November 1907 to early January 1908: Belle Johnson, Kate Snell, Sarah Mitchell, Genie Butch, and Emma Sansaver all pledged their vows. While their teammates were getting married that winter, Gen Healy and Nettie Wirth remained in school, though Fort Shaw was clearly a different place for them without the game and their teammates.[16]

At the close of the 1907–1908 school year, Fred Campbell resigned the Fort Shaw superintendency to take up duties as special Indian agent at large. With his departure, Gen Healy, now twenty, went home to Fort Belknap. A year later, Josie Langley Liephart, who had first brought basketball to Fort Shaw, resigned her staff position and moved with her husband, Harvey, to Great Falls.

Of all the heralded teammates, only Nettie Wirth remained on campus. At twenty-two she took a staff position as assistant seamstress under the new superintendent, John Brown. Her tenure—and Brown's—was a brief one. In 1910, in the face of declining enrollment and a shift in federal policy, Fort Shaw Government Indian Boarding School closed its doors. Nettie, who had entered those doors as a six-year-old on opening day, December 27, 1892, was on hand to assist in readying the institution for its closing day, May 5, 1910.[17]

Over the course of the twentieth century, the institution itself, along with the basketball team that had given the school a moment of international fame, was largely forgotten by history.

But not by those close to the story. As the centennial of the girls' triumph in St. Louis approached, residents of the Sun River Valley and descendants of the players came together to create a lasting memorial to the team. On Saturday, May 1, 2004, after three years of planning and fund-raising, vision became reality, and some four hundred people gathered on the site where Fort Shaw School had once stood. Not since the school's closing had so many Indians been in the valley. They came from towns across Montana, Idaho, and Wyoming, and from as far away as Washington, Nevada, Texas, and Rhode Island. They came to celebrate their heritage, to honor their grandmothers, and to dedicate

The memorial to the team, on the grounds of old Fort Shaw School,
May 2004.

the monument: a steel arch rising sixteen feet and spanning a circular
pad on which stands a granite obelisk topped by a bronze basketball.
The obelisk carries a photograph of the team and the names of the ten
teammates. The arch bears the legend "1904 World Champions."[18]

The girls from Fort Shaw Indian School will not be forgotten again.

Epilogue

AT THE CLOSE OF AN ARTICLE DESCRIBING HIS IMPRESSIONS OF the St. Louis World's Fair, a Montana journalist expressed his regret that "in six months practically all the wonderful beauty of the exposition will be a thing of the past." "Some time, maybe before the millennium," he continued, "there may be a national movement to create a permanent place for holding international expositions in this country, with permanent buildings erected for that purpose."[1]

Well intentioned as his remarks may have been, the journalist failed to take into account that world's fairs, especially the 1904 world's fair, are, by their very nature, marvels of a single time and place in history, assemblies of exhibits created to show the world as it was, as it is, as it might be—from the perspective of the organizers and exhibitors—at that very moment, in that very place. There is, in fact, no permanence possible.

There could never be another world's fair like the one in St. Louis.

Nor could there ever be another team like the one from Fort Shaw Indian School. The lives of those ten young women were shaped by the confluence of cultures set in motion by the Louisiana Purchase that opened the American West to exploration and exploitation. The girls came together and they came of age at an isolated moment in time and at an isolated outpost in Montana. And from that outpost they were swept inexorably toward an international event that exposed them to the world and exposed the world to them. Had they come together or come of age any earlier or any later, there would have been no journey, no quest for excellence in a game foreign to their cultures but not foreign to the spirit of the games of their foremothers.

They came of age during a brief window of time in which officials in Washington and administrators at Fort Shaw believed in the abilities of Indian youth and in the importance of providing them with academic, artistic, and athletic opportunities equal to those available to their white counterparts. They came of age at a time when a fledgling game was being embraced by women and girls whose gender had thus far excluded them from participation in team sports. And, finally, they came of age during the era of international fairs that culminated in the largest and grandest of them all—the Louisiana Purchase Exposition, which focused attention not only on the forward march of "civilization" but also on the indigenous peoples who were "acquired" along with the rest of the vast western wilderness.

Yet there was too much flux in the early years of the twentieth century, too much fluidity in government Indian policy and in the evolving game of basketball, to have sustained the conditions under which this team flourished. Even as the girls were center court and center stage in St. Louis, the Indian School Service was setting in motion sweeping changes that emphasized domestic and manual training to the exclusion of the very academic, artistic, and athletic programs that had been at the heart of a Fort Shaw education. Even as the girls were showing the world how well young women could play this game called basketball, the American Physical Education Association was adopting "girls' rules" that would so drastically change the game that the trademark skills of the Fort Shaw team would be subverted. And no future world's fair would ever again showcase anything like the Model Indian School, Indian Hill, or the Anthropology Days games. The stage that gave the young women from Fort Shaw their moment in history was that ephemeral.

Still, they seized that moment, and in doing so challenged the prevailing attitudes toward the athletic abilities of women and toward the abilities of Indian peoples. They did not set out to shatter preconceptions. They simply set out to play a new game and found they could play that game well. Then, when the game opened up new opportunities, they acquired the skills needed to seize those opportunities. They were placed in a landscape—Fort Shaw, St. Louis—not of their own choosing, but one they shaped to their liking. And in so doing they went on to achieve a level of success achieved by few other teenagers, white or Native, of their era.

That success, of course must be measured against its cost. The school—and the government—that fostered their achievements also sought to deprive them of their customs, cultures, and language and assimilate them into a world based on the customs, cultures, and language of the dominant white society. The losses incurred by the girls themselves, by their families, and their tribes as a result of the educational policies under which Fort Shaw and other such schools operated must never be underestimated.

Therein lies the irony of their situation. Had they *not* been in an off-reservation boarding school environment, without the responsibilities and distractions of family and tribal life, they would likely never have become stellar athletes, musicians, performers. Nor would they have forged ties across tribal lines, emerging as a tight-knit unit with a shared goal out of which developed that seemingly intuitive sense of teamwork.

Had there been no Fort Shaw, there would have been no world champions.

There is even more irony to be found in the fact that the gleaming silver trophy they brought home from St. Louis was theirs not by virtue of their defeat of the St. Louis All-Stars, but on the basis of their playing a single intrasquad game in front of the thousands who flocked to Francis Field to observe the fair's "primitives" engage in that bizarre and racist spectacle known as the Anthropology Days games. Only by virtue of participating in this "Olympic event" could the girls from Fort Shaw Indian School have been named the official "Basket Ball" champions of the St. Louis World's Fair and have been awarded a gleaming silver trophy similar to those received by all other winning athletes in the Olympic Games of 1904.

Had there been no Anthropology Days, there would have been no trophy.

In the eyes of those who see their victories on the court as the girls' greatest achievement, that trophy is of primary importance. But to those who know the story best, the trophy is more than a symbol of athletic excellence; it is the symbol of the emergence of a group of accomplished young women who knew who they were and where they had come from. "They were more than a skilled basketball team," Gen Healy's descendant, Turtle Woman, insists. "They were a rare gathering of young female warriors who, facing the same . . . [barriers] that caused many Indian people to become discouraged and defeated, chose a path that made them victors."[2]

The Years Thereafter

W. J. (Billy) Adams, a major force in bringing girls' basketball to Montana, and Fort Shaw's "athletic director" for one crucial year (1903–1904), was arrested in Butte, Montana, on September 27, 1905. He was accused of kidnapping nineteen-year-old Mamie McDonald, a member of one of his Butte basketball teams. A detective hired by the girl's father traced them to a Spokane hotel, an alert was issued, and she was taken into custody in Great Falls and returned to her parents. The charges against Adams were dropped a month later when McDonald refused to testify against him. Adams was twenty-six years old at the time, married, and the father of three very young children. As of 1920 he and family were still living in Butte, where he was employed as a bookkeeper at an ice company. The authors have not been able to uncover details of Billy Adams's life thereafter nor to find any evidence of the reaction of Fred Campbell or others to the scandal.

Sources: Anaconda Standard, September 29, 1905; *Butte Miner,* September 29, 1905; *Great Falls Daily Leader,* September 28 and 29 and October 20, 1905; 1900, 1910, and 1920 U.S. Manuscript Censuses, Silver Bow County, Montana.

Minnie Burton became a seamstress in the Indian School Service, working at the Lemhi Reservation School and later transferring to Wind River Agency School in Wyoming. On May 4, 1907, somewhere along Birch Creek near Leadore, Idaho, she gave birth to a daughter while on a forced march with her Lemhi people from their reservation in the Salmon River Valley to their new home at the Fort Hall Reservation. There she established her own household with the infant

Phoebe, whose father's identity remains a mystery to this day. Three years later Minnie married Stanton Gibson, with whom she had two children, Donner, who died as a toddler, and Virgie. After divorcing Gibson, Minnie married Robert Tindore in 1915, and a year later she gave birth to another daughter, Fay. In 1918, shortly after the birth of her fifth child, a son named Friday, Minnie Burton Tindore died. She was thirty-three years old. According to family members, her father and stepmother, William and Maggie Burton, raised her children, with William choosing to send the two middle children to boarding school and keeping Phoebe and Friday at home to be schooled in the Shoshone way and in the Shoshone language. Phoebe Burton seems to have inherited her mother's athleticism. Her speed was legendary, and stories are told of her racing against horses. Yet she never knew of her mother's achievements on the basketball court, because Minnie never told any of her children of her experiences at Fort Shaw. As a result, her descendants knew nothing about those years in her life until the authors went to the reservation in 2001 to share photographs and documents with them. Minnie's eighty-four-year-old son Friday, who spoke only Shoshone, cried as her great-granddaughter showed him photographs of the mother he had never seen and told him of her days as the star of a famous basketball team. Friday Tindore, Minnie's only surviving child, died three years later, in May 2004.

Sources: Fort Hall census records; Madsen, *The Lemhi,* 186; interviews and correspondence with Drusilla Gould, Minnie Burton's great-granddaughter.

Genie Butch went home to the Fort Peck Reservation in the spring of 1905. For the next two-and-a-half years, she helped her father run the ranch on Little Porcupine Creek. On January 6, 1908, at age twenty-one, she married Charles Hall, an Assiniboine classmate from Fort Shaw. Their son, Charles, Jr. (Curly), was born that year. Before the baby was eighteen months old, Genie gave birth to another little boy, Ralph. Her marriage to Hall was not a happy one, and there were rumors of abuse. On November 24, 1909, only four years after leaving Fort Shaw, Genie Butch Hall died under questionable circumstances. She was said to have

Genie Butch as a graduate, 1905.

taken a lethal dose of "salts," but few believed her death to be a suicide. Her obituary in the *Glasgow (Mont.) Democrat* noted that she had been "a member of the famous Fort Shaw basket ball team which won the worlds championship in 1904." Genie was buried next to her biological mother, and her infant son was laid to rest beside her six-and-a-half months later. Curly was raised by his Grandmother Butch.

Sources: Marriage certificate, Valley County, Montana; Urs, "Joe Butch," 149; obituary in the *Glasgow (Mont.) Democrat*, November 25, 1909; correspondence with Mary Helland, April 9, 2002; May 3, 2002; May 30, 2004.

F. C. (Fred) Campbell had a long and impressive career in the Indian Service. After leaving Fort Shaw in September 1908, he assumed various posts, among them special allotting agent at the Fort Peck Agency; superintendent of the Cheyenne River Agency in South Dakota; district superintendent, Montana, North Dakota, and Wyoming; and superintendent of the Flathead Indian Agency and later of the Blackfeet Indian Agency. By the time of his retirement at age sixty-eight in June 1932, he had spent forty-two years in the Indian Service and was widely regarded as one of its most able administrators. While at Fort Shaw, he had invested in a sheep ranch in Meagher County in central Montana, and he and the family spent much time there in the intervening years. While F. C. moved up in the Indian Service, his wife, **Ella Mead Campbell,** managed the sheep ranch from 1910 until failing health prompted her husband to take her to a sanitarium in San Antonio, Texas. She died there January 1918 at the age of fifty-one. Her body was taken home to Olathe, Kansas, for burial. Seven months later, the Campbells' younger son, twenty-five-year-old Fred, died in a training accident at flight school in Fort Worth, Texas. He was buried next to his mother in Olathe. In 1920 Campbell married **Sadie Malley**, former Fort Shaw teacher and his assistant basketball coach. Upon his retirement the couple moved to Meagher County, where F. C. took up the active management of the sheep ranch and entered politics, serving as a state senator in the late 1930s. In 1941, he and Sadie left the ranch and moved to Browning. He died in October 1942 in Portland, Oregon, while visiting his only surviving son. He was seventy-eight years old. His body was returned to Browning, where the funeral was held in the high school gymnasium, there being no other site in town large enough to hold the mourners. His wife, Sadie Malley Campbell, survived him by seventeen years.

Sources: "Campbell Mountain"; *Great Falls Daily Leader,* January 12, 1918; *Great Falls Daily Tribune,* August 11, 1918; "Personal Statement of F. C. Campbell"; Fred DesRosier correspondence of March 16, 2001; Wilcox, "Eulogy"; Stuwe, *Valley Ventures,* 44.

Lillie B. Crawford, who trained the girls in "pantomime and recitation" and then became their chaperone in St. Louis, remained at Fort Shaw through the 1907–1908 school year as teacher and assistant matron. She left the Sun River Valley at the same time the Campbells left, and all attempts to trace her life thereafter have yielded nothing.

Source: Fort Shaw Roster of Employees.

Delia Gebeau, a substitute on the 1902–1903 team, left school the next year to return to her father's home on the Flathead Indian Reservation. In 1905, at age eighteen, she married Isaac Ladderoute, who had also attended Fort Shaw. The couple lived out their lives in St. Ignatius, close enough to her many nieces and nephews to enjoy watching them play basketball. Said to have loved to talk sports "up until the last days of her life," Delia Gebeau Ladderoute died in January 1958 at age seventy-one. Her obituary in the local paper proudly, if mistakenly, noted that she was "a member of the world's basketball championship team in 1904 . . . that went to St. Louis."

Sources: Char-Koosta News (Pablo, Mont.), November 1957; *Ronan (Mont.) Pioneer*, January 23, 1958.

Genevieve Healy, who remained at Fort Shaw through June 1908, was one of the last two members of the championship team to leave the school. Sometime after 1910, she eloped with Charles Adams, a freighter who had been working out of Harlem, Montana, near the Fort Belknap Reservation. At the time of their marriage, Charlie was thirty-five years old; Gen was twenty-two. It was a tumultuous union, though an enduring one. They had seven children, and Gen also raised at least two grandchildren as her own. A tireless worker, she was known throughout the region as a skilled seamstress and a marvelous cook. She sang while she worked, and when she wasn't singing, she was whistling. She entertained her children and grandchildren with tunes on her "tater bug" and with stories of St. Louis, which she told over and over "so that the monologue almost became a part of her." The trickster of the Fort Shaw team, Gen maintained that reputation throughout her life. Her descendants are full of stories of Aunt Gen's adventures and misadventures. She was a "tough ol' darling," one friend recalled; to her family she was a "fierce and loyal friend, mother, grandmother, aunt, sister, wife, ally—and generous to a fault." Her basketball skills were passed on to granddaughters, great-nieces, and great-granddaughters, who played for their high school teams. The last surviving teammate, Genevieve Healy Adams died in April 1981 at age ninety-three and was buried next to Charlie at the Fort Belknap cemetery.

Sources: 1910 Choteau (Montana) County census; *Thunderstorms and Tumbleweeds,* 280; interviews with Donita Nordlund, Rita Nordlund, Thelma James, Cecilia James, and Jessie James Hawley; White, "She Was Born to Be a Basketball Star"; E. E. MacGilvra to Virginia Bird Mac-Donald, September 3, 1964; correspondence with Jessie James-Hawley, July 10, 2001.

Belle Johnson left Fort Shaw in September 1905 and lived for a while with her uncle and aunt on their ranch on the Milk River north of Browning, near the Canadian border. On November 29, 1907, in Kalispell, Montana, she married a former classmate, Marion Arnoux, a "redheaded Frenchman" with Indian blood. She was twenty-one years old, he was twenty-four. The couple and their three children, James, Thelma, and Carl, lived on a ranch north of Browning. As her children were growing up, Belle was employed as a nurse's aide at the Cut Bank Indian Boarding School outside Browning and at the Indian Agency hospitals in Blackfoot and in Browning. She also served as a translator for Indian patients and government physicians and, according to her niece, was "a godsend for the reservation." Even with three children of her own, Belle took in seven abandoned youngsters. After Arnoux's death, Belle married a Kansas native, Edward Swingley, and their son Meade was her last child. Belle was widowed again in 1940 and subsequently married Fort Shaw classmate William Conway. Belle Johnson Arnoux Swingley Conway died in St. John's Hospital in Helena, in January 1953. She was sixty-six years old. Her body was taken home to Browning for internment in the Catholic cemetery.

Sources: DeMarce, *Blackfeet Heritage,* 21, 22, 168; interviews with Valerie Goss, Myra Knopfle, and Lillian Smith; correspondence and conversations with Nora Connolly Lukin and Mary Lukin; Glenn Jeffrey family history; obituary, *Helena Independent Record,* January 29, 1953; *Fort Benton River Press,* February 4, 1953.

Josephine Langley worked at Fort Shaw as cook and housekeeper alongside her husband, Harvey Leiphart, the school's baker, until August 1909, a year before the school closed, when they moved to Great

Falls. The next year they relocated to the Blackfeet Reservation where at various times they operated a café/pool hall and a bakery. In 1930 Harvey and Josie Liephart, both fifty-one years old, moved to Spokane to be closer to their friend from Fort Shaw days, Louis Goings, and Harvey found work there as a baker. The Liepharts remained in Spokane for several years but eventually returned to Browning. In 1937, both rejoined the Indian Service, with Harvey becoming a baker at the Cut Bank Indian Boarding School outside Browning, and Josie serving as the school's matron. Childless themselves, they developed close ties with many of the children at the Cut Bank school as well as other children on the reservation. Throughout her life, Josie was plagued by bouts of trachoma, and at times—as had been the case at Carlisle—her vision was severely diminished. Josephine Langley Liephart died in September 1951 at the hospital in Browning and was laid to rest in the Browning cemetery. She was seventy-nine years old. Upon his wife's death, Harvey Liephart moved to Santa Clara, California, where he died twelve years later.

Sources: Conversations with Ramona DesRosier, Patricia Deboo, and Nora Connolly Lukin; Blackfeet Agency censuses; 1910 U.S. census for Great Falls, Montana; 1930 U.S. census for Spokane, Washington; California Death Index; *Browning (Mont.) Chief,* September 17 and 14, 1951.

Rose LaRose left Fort Shaw in September 1905 upon the team's return from Portland and, though only nineteen years of age, established a home of her own in a house next door to that of her recently divorced father on the Fort Hall Reservation. In 1913 she married John Cutler, a Shoshone-Bannock six years younger than she. Four years later, at age thirty-one, Rose gave birth to their only child, a son named Howard. Rose LaRose Cutler disappeared from public and family records in 1919. She was thirty-three years old and may have died in childbirth. In recent years family members have taken up the search for the rest of her story.

Sources: Correspondence with Rex LaRose, February 19, 2002; Kutch family tree; Fort Hall census 1906, 1913, 1917; interview with Ardith Peyope, Shoshone-Bannock Library.

Flora Lucero left school shortly after her return from St. Louis late in 1904. Some family members say that she later attended Haskell Indian School in Kansas or Genoa in Nebraska. However, lingering effects of the tuberculosis that hospitalized her in St. Louis eventually sent her back to the family home in Choteau. In December 1909, when she was twenty-one years old, she married James Dawson, a twenty-three-year-old Arikara from North Dakota who was working on a geological survey in Glacier Park. The Dawsons took up a farm near Minot, where Flora gave birth to two boys, Lawrence Eugene and James, Jr., and a little girl she lost at birth. Flora was remembered as a short, stout, stoical woman, who was skilled with a needle. Small as she was, she brimmed with self-confidence, and those around her knew that there were only two ways to do things: her way and the wrong way. She suffered from diabetes, which eventually led to the amputation of one of her legs. Flora Lucero Dawson was widowed in 1956 and died two years later in New Town, North Dakota, at age seventy.

Sources: Phone interviews with Grace Lavendis, Shirley Rust, and James Dawson; Dawson family tree; marriage records, 1893–1919, Choteau County, Montana; *Minot (N.D.) Daily News*, December 10, 1958.

Samuel M. McCowan recovered from the malaria that sent him to Hot Springs, Arkansas, in November 1904 and returned to St. Louis before the end of the year to close the books on the Model Indian School. By 1906 he was the highest-paid superintendent in the Indian School Service with an annual salary of three thousand dollars and enjoyed an enviable reputation—until claims of fraudulent accounting began to surface. In March of 1908, while a special agent of the BIA was investigating the situation at Chilocco, McCowan resigned the superintendency on the grounds of "rapidly developing diabetes." In February 1909, a federal grand jury indicted him on nine counts of embezzlement. He fought the charges for eleven years, but eventually pleaded guilty and paid the fines assessed. He died in Texarkansas in 1925 at the age of sixty-two. **Emma McCowan**'s life after St. Louis has not yet been traced.

Sources: Bradfield, "History of Chilocco," 71–75; Chilocco Superintendent's Files, OHS.

Sadie Malley Campbell, teacher and assistant coach of the Fort Shaw team, lived on in Browning after the death of her husband, F. C. Campbell, in 1942. She spent some years in the home of her stepdaughter, Freda Campbell DesRosier, and the last four years of her life close to family in Illinois. She died in Chicago in September 1959 at age eighty-four. Her body was returned to Montana, and she was interred beside F. C. Campbell in a Great Falls mausoleum.

Source: Undated obituary, Great Falls paper.

Sarah Mitchell left Fort Shaw School at the end of the 1906–1907 school year but returned to the Sun River Valley early that winter to prepare for her wedding to Phillip Courchene on December 31, 1907. Courchene, an Assiniboine who had grown up in the valley and had been a student at Fort Shaw, was by then the school disciplinarian. He

Sarah Mitchell and Phillip Courchene at the time of their wedding.

was twenty-one years old, Sarah was nineteen. After their wedding in the Great Falls cathedral, the young couple made their home at Fort Shaw, where Sarah became an assistant matron and cook. With the birth of their first child in September 1909, the Courchenes resigned their positions at Fort Shaw and moved to Wolf Point on the Fort Peck Reservation. There they ranched, raised eight children (having lost three others in infancy), and were leaders of their community. They hosted the weekly gatherings for Mass before there was a Catholic church in Wolf Point, and Sarah was president of the local Home Demonstration club. She also served as an interpreter for Indians on election day at the polls and helped Indians interpret their leases with white farmers. She was a skilled guitarist and seamstress. In February 1933, when her oldest child was twenty-one, her youngest barely two, Sarah Mitchell Courchene died of complications from "inflammatory rheumatism." She was forty-four years old. Phillip Courchene raised the children, never remarrying. He died in 1963 at age seventy-eight.

Sources: Fort Shaw employee rolls; correspondence with Sarah's daughter, Dorothy Courchene Smith; granddaughters, Therese Sain, Gena Aslanian, and Becky Yarbrough; and grandson Greg Courchene; Sarah's obituary, *Wolf Point (Mont.) Herald*, February 1933.

Emma Sansaver left school at the end of the 1906–1907 school year to take a position as housekeeper for a Canadian immigrant who was ranching on the American side of the border north of Havre. Six months later, in January 1908, Emma and the twenty-one-year-old bachelor rancher, Ernest Simpson, were married. Over the course of the next fourteen years their union produced eight children. In addition to child rearing and housekeeping, Emma helped with the ranch chores—and held to her memories. A treasured family photo, taken sometime during her early ranching years, shows her sitting confidently astride a chestnut mare. Her face framed by a cowboy hat, she is wearing dark bloomers and a middy blouse whose collar bears the "F" and the "S" of Fort Shaw. A disastrous fire in 1919 destroyed the family's log home. Although the Simpsons lost most of their possessions, no one was injured, and Emma's cherished piano and her box of memorabilia

Emma Sansaver as a graduate, 1908.

Emma Sansaver Simpson as a young wife on the ranch in Simpson, Montana. Note that she is wearing the Fort Shaw basketball middy.

from school and the world's fair were saved. In the face of mounting debt, the Simpsons gave up the homestead, and the family moved to Niehart in the mountains south of Great Falls. There they again took up ranching. But hard times gripped them, and in 1922 Ernest gave up ranching altogether and moved the family into Great Falls, where he took a job with the Great Northern Railway. In February 1925, three months after the birth of her ninth child, Emma underwent an emergency appendectomy in a Great Falls hospital. Three days later, Emma Rose Sansaver Simpson died of septicemia. She was thirty-nine years old. Her infant daughter died soon thereafter. Her two older girls, ten and five, were sent to live for several years with their aunt, their father's sister, in San Francisco, while Ernest raised his six sons to adulthood. Although her early death meant that her grandchildren and great-grandchildren never met "the Little One" or heard her stories, a number of them have enjoyed their own share of applause from basketball fans across the state of Montana.

Sources: correspondence and interviews with Emma's daughters, Betty Bisnett and Ella Barrow, and with her granddaughter, Barbara Winters; marriage certificate, Lewis and Clark County, Montana, January 7, 1908; death certificate, Cascade County, Montana, #9473.

Katie Snell left school in the spring of 1907, at the age of twenty-one, and was married six months later, on December 1, to Albert Wiegand, the thirty-seven-year-old son of a prominent Sun River Valley family. Shortly after the wedding the couple moved to the Fort Belknap Reservation, where they lived on Katie's allotment near what became known as the Wiegand Reservoir. There, their first child, a son, was born in September 1908. Over the next dozen years, there were six more babies, four of whom survived childhood. Katie was known as a quiet, peaceful woman, but a ceaseless worker, tending a large garden each year. Albert Wiegand died in 1921, and two years later, Katie married Irwin Burtch, a non-Indian from Kansas with whom she had four more children. Though Katie had sent her older children to Fort Belknap's agency boarding school, when that school closed, she left the family's ranch and the reservation behind each fall to set up housekeeping in Dodson, where her youngest pursued their schooling. It was during those long winter evenings that she began to share stories of Fort Shaw and St. Louis, stories of Coach Campbell, of Gen Healy and Genie Butch, Josie Langley, and Emma Sansaver. In time, several of her grandchildren and great-grandchildren who heard those stories became high school stars in Katie's tradition, with some receiving college athletic scholarships. When Katie lost her second husband in 1958, she lived out the last eighteen years of her life in the home of her married daughter, Rosie Burtch Stuart. There she would walk the banks of the Wiegand Reservoir with her arms raised in prayer, chanting Assiniboine—and English—supplications, and singing hymns from her days at Fort Shaw. Catherine (Katie) Snell Wiegand Burtch died of heart failure in a Havre hospital in October 1976, two days shy of her ninetieth birthday.

Sources: Interviews with daughter Rosie Burtch Stuart and grandson Douglas Stuart; granddaughter Thelma James, and correspondence with niece Pearl Wiegand Morton; marriage certificate, Choteau County, Montana, #1080; marriage certificate, Phillips County, Montana, #744; death certificate, Hill County, Montana, #114.

William Winslow, the founding superintendent of Fort Shaw, moved his family to Lawrence, Kansas, when he left the school in 1898. There he went into private practice but soon returned to the Indian School Service, becoming superintendent of the boarding school at Genoa, Nebraska. He was reunited with the Fort Shaw girls when he attended the Indian educators' conference both at St. Louis in 1904 and at Portland in 1905. A few years later the Winslow family moved to Fort Collins, Colorado, where Dr. Winslow again set up private practice. It would seem that he lived out his life in Fort Collins, although no death record has yet been found.

Sources: Correspondence and interviews with genealogist Gidget Fleming; U.S. censuses of 1900, 1910, 1920, and 1930.

Lizzie Wirth was twenty-five years old when, in May 1905, she married James Finley Smith, a thirty-five-year-old Texan who had come north to join his brother in the stock raising business The couple raised seven children on their ranch near Poplar on the Fort Peck Reservation. Smith worked with the Indian Field Service as an advisor to Indians on ranching and farming while Lizzie became an activist for Indian causes, making frequent trips to Washington, D.C., to lobby Congress for bills affecting Indian lands and people. Upon the invitation of Charles Curtis, Herbert Hoover's vice president, a man with Kaw and Osage Indian blood, she participated in the 1928 inaugural parade, riding a spirited horse. At the ceremonies she was pictured with Alice Roosevelt Longworth, whom she had most likely met during one of the visits the president's daughter made to the fair. At home the Smiths always set an "Indian table," ready to welcome anyone who stopped by at mealtime. Lizzie stayed busy with her beadwork, making beaded dresses, knife cases, necklaces, and moccasins. She loved being asked to perform the Indian club routine she had first learned at Fort Shaw and was proud that she could still work the clubs well into old age. Jim Smith died in 1944, and Lizzie married William Manning five years later. When Manning died in 1956, she lived with a daughter for several years until advancing senility prompted her move to a rest home in Poplar. Elizabeth (Lizzie) Wirth Smith Manning died in the Poplar Community Hospital in 1969. She was eighty-eight years old. Four sons and her daughter Elsie survived her.

Sources: Interviews with Terry Bender; Thomas, "Early Life," 111–12, 116, 121–27, 155–56.

Nettie Wirth joined the employee rolls as an assistant seamstress at Fort Shaw when her student days were over. In 1910, when the school closed, she returned to Fort Peck where she lived with her father and stepmother. In 1912, at age twenty-seven, she married John Mail. The couple had three sons, and in 1920, with jobs and money scarce on the reservation, the family set out for Seattle. There John worked as a mechanic, eventually owning his own shop—which was twice destroyed by fire. Losing all heart, he sank into alcoholism, and life became unpredictable and precarious for Nettie and her boys. She spent most of her life thereafter keeping house for others, though during the Great Depression, she consistently won cash prizes in walking competitions

Susan Wirth (Woman That Kills Wood) and daughters. Standing, left to right: Christine Wirth West, Louise Wirth Cain, Nettie Wirth Mail; seated on the arm of her mother's chair, Lizzie Wirth Smith; seated in front, Susan Wirth and Tina Archdale Davis.

in the Seattle area. Even through the worst of times her heart and her door were always open, and she frequently took in nieces, nephews, and grandchildren. She was remembered by all as a kind and gentle woman whose kitchen was always filled with wonderful aromas. She was honored by a Nettie Wirth Mail Day at the Seattle World's Fair in the summer of 1962, when her participation with the 1904 championship team in St. Louis was recalled and celebrated. Not long thereafter, a broken hip slowed her pace, and in September 1965, a week short of her seventy-eighth birthday, she died from complications from pneumonia. Her body was taken back to Fort Peck for burial.

Sources: Thomas, "Early Life"; Bye, "Shoot, Minnie, Shoot!"; Fort Shaw employee rolls; marriage certificate #1172, Valley County, Montana; correspondence and interviews with Elsie Bennett, Nettie's niece; her grandchildren, Winona Weber and Michael Mail; Terry Bender and Donna Claseman, her great-nieces; and Winfield Cain, a great-nephew.

Louis Youpee, the young boy who toured with the team and accompanied the girls to St. Louis, disappeared from the Fort Shaw rolls in 1907. He was fifteen years old. It is unknown where he finished his education, but as a young man, he joined the Indian Service and later became an activist for Indian causes. Settling in Duluth, he served in the Minnesota state legislature and established the *American Indian Journal.* In 1938 he published a testimonial to Fred Campbell in the *Journal,* citing his old superintendent as a benefactor of all Indians, but especially of the Blackfeet—and especially of "one small Indian boy" whom he raised "against his own wishes and educated him."

Sources: Fort Shaw student rolls; "A Friend of the Indian," *AIJ,* May 1938; Youpee to Hiram Clark, BIA, May 13, 1938, Fred Campbell Papers, MC 67, Montana Historical Society.

Acknowledgments

MANY, MANY PEOPLE HAVE TAKEN THIS JOURNEY WITH US, and we hesitate even to begin the roll call of acknowledgments for fear that some will be inadvertently left out. It is our hope that anyone whose name is missing below will nevertheless still know the satisfaction of having helped bring this story to light.

The journey began in the archives of the Montana Historical Society in Helena in January 1997, with the discovery of a photo of eight Indian girls dressed in buckskins and standing in a semicircle. This was obviously a studio portrait, taken in the city of Great Falls sometime in the fall of 1903. The caption drew Linda's attention: "Girls basketball team, old Fort Shaw Indian School." A girls' basketball team, arrayed in traditional dress, in 1903? Basketball was barely a decade old at that time, and in all her years in Montana, Linda had never heard of "old Fort Shaw Indian School."

Consultation with the society's resident historian, Dave Walter, brought confirmation that indeed there had been such a school and such a team. Dave shared the slim file of clippings he had on the players, and he told Linda of a Barbara Winters in Great Falls, who had very recently been in touch with him about the photograph. Linda contacted Barbara, who turned out to be a granddaughter of player Emma Sansaver, and the rest was, literally, history.

Barbara Winters became our first and our most faithful companion on this journey, accompanying us every step of the way—with phone calls and letters, with an open door on our many research trips, and with materials, contacts, and encouragement. But there are countless others to be acknowledged as fellow travelers: We begin with Kenneth

Robison, historian at the Overholser Historical Research Center in Fort Benton, Montana. An inveterate researcher and avid sports fan, Ken soon became as obsessed with this story as we were and devoted countless hours to scouring vintage Great Falls newspapers in search of accounts of basketball games and other Fort Shaw events. Dorothea Susag, whose students at Simms High School in the Sun River Valley had written about the team a year earlier as part of the school's Montana Heritage Project, invited Linda into her classroom as a poet/writer under a Montana Arts Council grant. During that residency, three of Susag's students—Tana Fleming, Sarah Green, and Ashle Wheeler—accepted the challenge of finding and interviewing descendants of three members of the Fort Shaw girls' basketball team. We are grateful for the work of these early collaborators.

Then there are the many, many others. We had the indispensable assistance of archivists and librarians and specialists who helped us uncover the records on Fort Shaw and its people in federal repositories, state and local historical societies, and libraries and museums across the country. These include Richard Fusick, archivist at the National Archives in Washington, D.C.; Eileen Bolger, director of archival operations, and Eric Bittner, archivist, at the National Archives in Denver; Barbara Bair, historian, at the Library of Congress; Rayna Green, director of the American Indian Program, and Ellen Roney Hughes and Jane Rogers, sports history, at the Smithsonian Institution's National Museum of American History; Bruce Bernstein, assistant director for cultural resources, and Sarah Demb, assistant archivist, at the Smithsonian's National Museum of the American Indian; Jake Homiak, director, Joanna Scherer, anthropologist, and Ruth Selig of the Department of Anthropology, along with Robert Leopold, director, Paula Fleming, photo archivist, and Jeannie Sklar, reference archivist, of the National Anthropological Archives at the Smithsonian's National Museum of Natural History; Duane Sneddeker, director of library and archives, and Ellen Thomasson, photoarchivist, at the Missouri Historical Society, St. Louis; Brian Shovers, librarian, Ellie Arguimbau, archivist, Lory Morrow, photoarchivist, and Jody Foley, state archivist, at the Montana Historical Society in Helena; Jodie Allison-Bunnell, archivist at the K. Ross Toole Archives, Mansfield Library, University of Montana, Missoula;

Kim Allen Scott, Special Collections librarian, Montana State University, Bozeman; Ellen Crain, archivist, at the Butte-Silver Bow Public Archives in Butte, Montana; Judy Ellinghausen, archivist at the Cascade County Historical Society in Great Falls, Montana; Mark Thiel, archivist, at Marquette University's Department of Special Collections and University Archives, Milwaukee, Wisconsin; Lorraine McConaghy and Mikala Woodward of the Rainier Valley Historical Society in Seattle, Washington; Karen Kearns, Laura Czyzewski, and Gary Domitz, Special Collections, Idaho State University in Pocatello; Ardith Peyope, library director, and Rosemary Devinney, museum curator, Fort Hall Reservation, Idaho; Gene Felsman, librarian at Salish Kootenai College in Pablo, Montana; Jackie Parsons, director of the Museum of the Plains Indian in Browning, Montana; Joyce Spoonhunter at the Blackfeet Tribal Office in Browning; Lyle MacDonald at the Blackfeet Boarding Dormitory in Browning; the staff and volunteers at the Genoa Indian School Museum in Genoa, Nebraska, and the Haskell Indian Nations University Archives, Lawrence, Kansas; the library and computer science staff at Fort Peck Community College, Poplar, Montana; David Carmichael, Kautz Family YMCA Archives, University of Minnesota, Minneapolis; Dean Rogers, Special Collections, Vassar College, Poughkeepsie, New York; Lynn Lucas, librarian, Adriance Memorial Library, Poughkeepsie; and Sherrill Redmon, director, and Amy Hague, curator of manuscripts, at the Sophia Smith Collection, Smith College Libraries, Northampton, Massachusetts. Although we put in thousands of miles of travel ourselves, we couldn't always be in the right place at the right time, and for follow-up research in the Denver archives, we gratefully acknowledge our daughter-in-law, Terese Higbie Smith, and for research on the girls at the 1905 World's Fair in Portland, we thank Gina McDermott, who not coincidentally is the great-granddaughter of the team's 1905 captain, Emma Sansaver.

The archivists and librarians—and our surrogate researchers—provided us with the records, facts and figures that formed the skeleton of the story. But the flesh and blood came through interviews and correspondence with the descendants and friends of the principal figures in the story. To all those listed below we owe a huge debt of gratitude for filling in so many missing pieces of the puzzle and, most of all, for helping us come to know just who these girls were. Drusilla Gould, great-granddaughter of **Minnie Burton**, Shoshone language scholar and anthropologist at Idaho State University, shared her family genealogy and her family stories. We learned **Genie Butch**'s story with the help of Mary Arnoux Helland of the Valley County Historical Society in Glasgow, Montana; Harold Dean Blount, genealogist, Frazer, Montana; Donald Clark, Butch's great-nephew, and Frank Archdale, both also of Frazer. While Donita Nordlund of Malta, Montana, was our primary guide in coming to know her grandmother **Genevieve Healy**, we were gifted as well with information from Rita Nordlund of Malta, Healy's great-granddaughter, Jessie James-Hawley of Harlem, Montana, a great-great niece; Cecilia Adams James of Dodson, Montana, a great-niece; and Harry Geer, Healy's son-in-law, of Great Falls. We learned much about **Belle Johnson**'s personality and later life from her three granddaughters, Valerie Goss, Lillian Smith, and Myra Knopfle, all of Browning, Montana. Belle's niece and great-niece, Nora Lukin and Mary Lukin of Browning, were equally generous with their stories and photographs, and much of our information came from Nora Lukin's memoir as well as from a reminiscence by Charles Connelly, Johnson's nephew, also of Browning. Glenn Jeffrey of Browning, a cousin by marriage, shared an extensive family genealogy with us. What we know of **Rose LaRose** came from her great-nephew, Rex LaRose, of Fort Duchesne, Utah, and from Sparrowhawk, LaRose family genealogist. We pieced the background to **Flora Lucero**'s story from multiple interviews with her nieces and nephews of Great Falls: Shirley Rust, Millie and Sam Lucero, Rosemary Cline, and Lorraine Walker. Jim Dawson of New Town, North Dakota, shared memories of his grandmother Flora with Barbara Winters and with us. Most helpful of all was Flora's niece Grace Lavendis of Las Vegas, Nevada. **Sarah Mitchell**'s daughter, Dorothy Courchene Smith of Amarillo, Texas, was a wonderful correspondent whose letters gave us a picture of her mother as an adult. And Sarah's grandson, Gregory Courchene of Browning, Montana, and her granddaughters, Gena Aslanian of Scottsdale, Arizona; Therese Sain of Phoenix; and Becky Yarbrough of Amarillo were enthusiastic in sharing their memories and materials with us. **Emma Sansaver** came alive for us through letters from and interviews with her daughter, Betty Bisnett of Augusta, Montana, and her granddaughter, the aforementioned Barbara Winters. Another of Emma's daughters, Ella Barrow of Billings, Montana, and Puyallup, Washington, also shared memories and photos. Beverly Braig, granddaughter, of Kalispell, Montana, shared documents and photographs and showed us the dress Emma wore in reciting "The Famine" scene. Emma's daughter-in-law, Olive Simpson, also of Kalispell, shared family stories. From the other line of Sansavers came the help and encouragement of Bill Sansaver, who in the last years of his life designed and spearheaded the construction of the team monument at Fort Shaw, and who, along with Mark Sansaver, Mary Ann Verwolf, and Donna Wimmer, all of Wolf Point, Montana, provided documents, photos, and genealogical information. Our many interviews and notes exchanged with Rosie Stuart of Harlem, Montana, have brought us close to her mother, **Katie Snell**. Douglas Stuart of Harlem, Montana, Charlotte Kelley of Clancy, Montana, and Sandy Wilson of Havre, Montana—Katie's grandson, daughter-in-law, and granddaughter, respectively—shared memories and photographs. Granddaughter Thelma James of Dodson, Montana, has been of invaluable assistance in helping us navigate the genealogy of the Snell family and the geography of the Snell-Wiegand landscape. Granddaughter Julia Cebulski of Zortman, Montana, and grandson Bruce Warren of Whitewater, Montana, contributed rich memories. And Pearl Wiegand Morton of Great Falls, a niece of Katie's, had answers to our questions. For background on **Nettie Wirth**, we have to start by acknowledging Bill Thomas and Terry Bender, whose ties to Nettie are through Nettie's sister **Lizzie Wirth**. Bill Thomas of Herndon, Virginia, Lizzie's grandson-in-law, not only researched the Wirth family tree, he has also written a comprehensive history of the life and times of his father-in-law, Tom Smith, from which we gleaned specifics on Nettie's heritage and on family dynamics within the Wirth household. Bill and his wife, Debbie, also opened their home to us during one of our research trips to the National Archives in D.C. Terry Bender of Helena, Montana, Lizzie's granddaughter, had safeguarded Nettie's schoolgirl scrapbook all these years and generously shared that material—and more—with us. Elsie Bennett, Lizzie's daughter, of Ashland, Wisconsin, had many memories of her aunt. Nettie's own offspring came forth with more rich information. We owe special thanks to her granddaughter, Winona Mail Weber of Aberdeen, Washington, and her grandson, Mike Mail of Taholah, Washington. We are grateful as well for interviews with Mildred McClury Mail Bumgardner, Nettie's daughter-in-law of Hoquiam, Washington, and a number of Mildred's children and grandchildren. Arline Skinner, great-niece of Seattle; Donna Claseman, great-niece of Federal Way, Washington; Winfield Cain, great-nephew of Taholah, Washington, and Malcolm Bailey, great-nephew of Billings, Montana, were also generous in sharing memories of Nettie with us.

Beside the descendants of the ten young women who played on the championship team, relatives and friends of other prominent figures in this story deserve our thanks: Fred DesRosier of Browning, Montana, grandson of **Fred C. Campbell**, Fort Shaw superintendent and coach/mentor of the girls, shared his grandfather's papers as well as his own personal memories of Campbell, who deserves a book all his own. Patricia Deboo of Valier, Montana, great-niece of **Josephine Langley**, gave us glimpses into Langley's adult life, as did Ramona DesRosier, Carol Murray, and Marion Selway, all of Browning. Insight into specific personalities on the team and details of their life on the road came from an interview Barbara Winters conducted with **Gertrude LaRance Parker** of Lame Deer, Montana, who served as the "mascot" of the team. Linda's later interview, and Barbara Winters's correspondence, with Beth Parker Riojas, Parker's daughter, fleshed out our knowledge of the little mascot herself. Virginia MacDonald of Polson, Montana, daughter of **Frank Bird**, an Irish lad who briefly coached the 1905 version of the championship team, proudly provided papers and photographs, and Helen Ellis of Helena, Montana, shared corroborating documents and photos. Curtis Madison of Corinth, New York, grandson of the Rev. **C. H. Madison**, shared some family papers and insights into his grandfather's missionary zeal. Peggy Fasbender, Erma Stinson, Ruth Merja, and other residents and former residents of the Sun River Valley shared memories and memorabilia concerning the valley and its citizens. Margaret Abbott, daughter-in-law of Frank Abbott, a Fort

Shaw student, shared her thesis on her father-in-law's experiences at the school.

Then there were those who helped us fill in the depth and the breadth of the full story and/or encouraged us in the work: the late Dave Walter of the Montana Historical Society in Helena; Emma Toman of the Sun River Valley (Montana) Historical Society; Irene Mahoney, OSU, historian of the Ursuline order of sisters; Gidget Fleming, genealogist extraordinaire; Cindy Kittredge, former director of the Cascade County Historical Society, Great Falls, Montana; Kathryn Shanley, director of Native American Studies, University of Montana, Missoula, and Jeanne Eder, associate professor, University of Alaska, Anchorage, both of whom are themselves descendants of Fort Shaw students; Jeffrey Safford, professor emeritus, Montana State University, Bozeman; Nancy Parezo, anthropologist, and Tsianina Lomawaima, American Indian Studies, University of Arizona, Tucson; Ann Cummins, creative writing, Northern Arizona University; and the late Pat Calliotte, associate editor, *News from Indian Country.*

We were partially sustained in our research and writing efforts by grants from several agencies. Funding from the Montana Committee for the Humanities helped support a spring 2000 speaking tour that included presentations at five of the state's seven reservations, an opportunity that connected us with a number of descendants and tribal kin of the Fort Shaw players. We received a 2002 Independent Research and Creative Work Award from the Charles Redd Center for Western Studies at Brigham Young University in Provo, Utah, and we were able to spend three weeks working at the Library of Congress, the National Archives, and the various museums of the Smithsonian Institution in Washington, D.C., all on the strength of Short-Term Visitors Awards from the Smithsonian. The receipt of individual eight-month National Endowment for the Humanities Fellowships for Independent Scholars in 2003 supported our writing during a crucial period of shaping the narrative. And the ongoing support of the Authors Guild is gratefully acknowledged.

Preparing presentations—especially for organizations and groups representing diverse constituencies—offered the challenge of approaching familiar material from fresh perspectives, afforded the opportunity for instant feedback and constructive criticism, and provided the energy boost that comes from having an audience remind us of why we set out on this seemingly endless journey in the first place. We are thankful to all of those who played a role in giving us a platform for sharing this story and to all of those who attended our sessions and encouraged our work.

The frustrations of having taken so many years to bring this book into print have been partly offset by having had the privilege of publishing a number of articles and essays in journals and books whose focus and readership reflect the interdisciplinary nature of this story. Editor Clark Whitehorn, now of the University of New Mexico Press, then of Montana Historical Society in Helena, paved the way by accepting "World Champions: The 1904 Girls' Basketball Team from Fort Shaw Indian Boarding School" for publication in *Montana The Magazine of Western History* (Winter 2001), and C. Richard King, sociology/comparative ethnic studies, Washington State University, reprinted that essay in *Native American Athletes in Sport and Society: A Reader* (University of Nebraska Press, 2005). Dee Garceau-Hagen, western/women's/Native American history, Rhodes College, Memphis, Tennessee, published "Unlikely Champion: Emma Rose Sansaver, 1884–1925" in *Portraits of Women in the American West* (Routledge, 2005). Mark Dyreson, sport historian, Pennsylvania State University, accepted "'Leav[ing] the White[s] Far Behind Them': The Girls from Fort Shaw Indian School, Basketball Champions of the 1904 Worlds Fair" for publication in the *International Journal of the History of Sport* (June 2007), and Susan Brownell, anthropologist, University of Missouri at St. Louis, included an expanded version of the article in *The 1904 Anthropology Days and Olympic Games: Sport, Race, and American Imperialism* (University of Nebraska Press, 2008). We are grateful for the guidance and support of these scholar-editors whose sharing of expertise and knowledge in their respective fields greatly enriched not only the articles but also the book itself.

Editors. Where would we be without them? As we scramble to clarify phrasing, verify spellings, and locate dates or names we know must be somewhere in all these copious files, we are especially grateful to Alice Stanton of the University of Oklahoma Press—not only for her copyediting expertise but also for her infinite patience. And, as everything is falling into place, we express our thanks to Charles Rankin, our editor at the Press, who believed in this story from the beginning and who, by the hardest, got us to tell it right.

Finally, we thank those personal friends and professional colleagues who have stood by us year after year without losing faith in this project—or in our ability to *finally* see it through. And we thank our families, who know us well enough to have understood why we could not move into the twenty-first century until we were able to take the girls from Fort Shaw Indian School along with us.

Notes

Preface

1. *St. Louis Republic,* June 15, 1904. The reporter actually referred to *eleven* "aboriginal maidens," since he included chaperone Lizzie Wirth.

2. Between February 1998 and July 2007, the authors conducted a series of interviews and/or engaged in correspondence with more than sixty-five descendants of team members, tribal kin, and Fort Shaw staff. For a more expansive discussion of the assistance provided by all these collaborators, see the "Acknowledgments" section of this book.

3. Extract from Jason Boyd, "The Fort," *Stories in Place,* 15.

A Confluence of Cultures

1. Pea-boa, born circa 1832, is variously listed in Lemhi census records as Pee-a-bob, Peeaboa, Pee-a-booie, and Pe-a-wa-boo-ee. She eventually became known as Sadie Burton. Lemhi Tribal Census Records, MC11, box 5, folder 2, Special Collections, Idaho State University (hereafter ISU). Pea-boa's Indian and white names are also found in Drusilla Gould's family history. The Bannock of the Lemhi Reservation were Northern Paiutes who had traveled with the Shoshones for generations. "Shoshoni and Northern Paiute Indians in Idaho," www.trailtribes.org.

Double-ball equipment varied from region to region, even band to band. The double ball used by the Northern Paiutes is described as a "ball, of buckskin, nearly cylindrical, and expanding at the ends, length, 11 ½ inches." A specimen is housed in the Museum of Science and Art, University of Pennsylvania, along with a playing stick described as "a forked, peeled sapling, 40 inches in length." Culin, "Games," 662–63. For a comprehensive treatise on this game as played by many different Native peoples, see Culin, "Games," 647–55.

2. Pea-wa-um (also Pee-a-waum and Pee-waum) was known among whites as Bob Burton. Gould family history; Lemhi Tribal Census Records, MC11, box 5, folder 2, ISU. According to Culin's treatise, double ball was the only *team* sport played exclusively by women of the Plains tribes. Culin, "Games," 647.

Minnie Burton's father, William, was born in 1860. The only surviving son of Bob and Sadie Burton, William married Jemima Osborne, daughter of Saw-voogan, a Northern Paiute woman, and Henry Osborne, an English immigrant. Their second daughter, Minnie, granddaughter of Pea-boa, was born in 1885 and became the most celebrated player on the Fort Shaw team. Lemhi censuses of 1885, 1889, 1890, and 1893, MC11, box 5, folder 2, ISU; Gould family history.

3. For a detailed description of the habits and habitats of the traditionally migratory peoples who would, by 1875, be confined to the 100-square-mile Lemhi Reservation, see Madsen, *Lemhi*. In essence, the Laramie Treaty of 1851 was negotiated in an attempt to bring an end to hostilities "between warring Indians and between the Indians and the advancing Americans." Malone, Roeder, and Lang, *Montana*, 116. For additional details on the provisions of the treaty, see Barker, *Preliminary Inventory*, 1, and Capps, *The Old West: Indians*, 163–64.

4. Barker, *Preliminary Inventory*, 1. Officially designated in 1851, these tribal reservations continued to shrink in size over the decades as gold strikes and homesteaders' demands voided the original terms of the U.S.-Indian treaties of 1851, 1855, and 1868. In 1855 the Salish, Kootenais, and Pend d'Oreilles were assigned to the Flathead Reservation, north of present-day Missoula, Montana. The Cheyennes, who had also contested the Shoshones during hunting expeditions in present-day southwestern Montana, were first moved to Indian Territory (present-day Oklahoma), although a band that became known as the Northern Cheyennes battled their way back to more familiar grounds, finally winning the rights to their own reservation in 1884. "Montana Indian Reservations."

5. Information on Got Wolf Tail, Walking Blue Mane, and their daughter comes from Thomas, "Early Life," 6. Can-kte-win-yan was born but a mile or so northeast of Fort Benton, Montana.

6. Thomas "Early Life," 10, 12–13. For more on women's work among the Assiniboines, see Long, *Land of the Nakota*.

7. Thomas, "Early Life," 15–16. On the frontier, marriages consummated "without benefit of clergy" were common. Described variously as *a la façon du pays* and "in the Indian way," they are today designated as "common law."

8. Long, *Land of the Nakota*, 19–20. Both men and women alike, however, still preferred moccasins to the leather shoes worn by whites.

9. According to family legend, Henry Archdale did not likely die but simply deserted his wife and children, being something of a "tepee hopper." Archdale interview, May 19, 2002. In addition to a son named for his father (born 1863) and a baby girl named Christina (born 1868), Susan Archdale had lost one daughter, Annie, in infancy. Thomas, "Early Life," 16–17, 19. Born in Wuerttemberg, Germany, Jacob Wirth had fled his native land to avoid obligatory service in Bismarck's war against Austria—only to end up enlisting in the U.S. army in December of 1865, just months after the Civil War. A member of the 13th Infantry, he went to Fort Buford to assist in construction of the post but ended up serving out his time as a cook and baker there. Thomas, "Early Life," 23–27. Further details on the marriage and children of Susan and Jacob Wirth can be found in Thomas, "Early Life."

10. Katie Snell's grandmother was Knocks, or Knocker, wife of Tattoo Arm, or Tattoo Face, both of whom were members of the Prairie Assiniboine band of the Nakotas. Katie's mother, Fanny Black Digger, married a German immigrant, James Snell. Family tree in possession of Thelma Warren James, granddaughter of Catherine (Katie) Snell Wiegand Burtch; Catherine Snell Wiegand's 1921 Fort Belknap enrollment application, #690, family records of Rosie Burtch Stuart, daughter of Catherine Snell Wiegand Burtch.

The name of Genie Butch's Assiniboine maternal grandmother has not yet been determined. Her birth mother was A-nin-ta-tca'n-gu Wa-ka'n, or Alone on a Sacred Path, and her father was Joe Butch. G. W. Wood to Commissioner of Indian Affairs (hereafter CIA), March 17, 1886, Record Group (RG) 75, Letters Received (LR) 1886, box 298, #8958, 75/11E3/4/13/6, National Archives, Washington, D.C. (NAW).

Likewise, the name of Sarah Mitchell's maternal grandmother remains unknown, although it is known that she was a Métis of Chippewa and French-Canadian stock. Sarah and her siblings were self-identified as Assiniboines, but their mother, Isabelle St. Germaine, came from a long line of Canadian-born Métis women, and their father was the son of David Dawson Mitchell, fur trader. Louise Courchene to David Charles Courchene, April 17, 1983, letter shared with authors by Gena Aslanian, Sarah Mitchell Courchene's granddaughter.

11. The Louisiana Purchase effectively doubled the size of the United States. In 1776 the nation comprised some 889,000 square miles. In 1803, with the conclusion of the treaty, the country added another 827,000 square miles. *New York Times 2005 World Almanac*, 613.

Built under the supervision of fur trader Alexander Culbertson, Fort Benton was named for Thomas Hart Benton, U.S. senator from Missouri and a major proponent of exploration and settlement of the trans-Mississippi West. Cheney, *Names*, 92–93. For more on the history of Fort Benton, see Overholser, *Fort Benton*.

12. The first steamboat arrived at Fort Benton 1860. By 1867 some forty boats were docking each year in the months the Missouri was open. Overholser, *Fort Benton*, 92.

Belle Johnson's maternal grandmother, a Piegan named Kills Inside, was born twenty years before the Blackfeet Reserve was created, but by the time Belle's mother, Nearly Died, came of age, her family, like many other Blackfeet families, was living in a camp not far from Fort Benton. Later known as Jenny, Nearly Died married Charles Johnson, a native of New York. U.S. Manuscript Census, 1880; Connelly, "My Mother's Life," 1; Lukin, "My Early Years," 2.

Genevieve Healy's grandmother, name unknown, was a full-blood Gros Ventre, as was Gen's mother, Honkow, or White Eagle, who married a white rancher. "Col. William H. H. Healy," 1574; Healy, "Reminiscence."

13. For more on Native peoples and their relationship to the 49th parallel, see LaDow, *Medicine Line*.

14. Dusenberry, "Waiting for a Day," 3, 37–38; Tanner, *Canadians*, 133.

For more on Métis community, see Peterson and Brown, *New Peoples,* and Stonechild, McLeod, and Nestor, *Survival of a People.*

15. Until 1947, the Bureau of Indian Affairs was called the Office of Indian Affairs. Because common usage, not to mention official records in archives, favors the designation Bureau of Indian Affairs, no matter the era, we have chosen to use "Bureau" throughout.

16. While Emma Rose Sansaver herself was born in Montana Territory, her mother, Marie Rose LaFromboise, was born near Prince Albert, Saskatchewan, and her father, Edward Sansaver (Sansauver, Sansavere), near Fort Pitt, Alberta. Because the birthplace of many Métis children was difficult to ascertain, the government's original policy was to deny such children—and their elders—educational opportunities as well as rations. Sansaver family record, provided by Barbara Winters, granddaughter of Emma Sansaver Simpson; Sansaver genealogical papers provided by Donna Sansaver Wimmer, great-niece of Emma Sansaver Simpson.

17. Emma Sansaver was born on August 15, 1886. Winters family record. The game of basketball was invented by James Naismith in December of 1891. Anderson, *Story of Basketball,* 9. By the early 1880s, as more and more settlers began demanding land, the government began dividing the Blackfeet Reserve into three separate and deliberately noncontiguous reservations. Barker, *Preliminary Inventory,* 1. Although originally called Camp Reynolds, within months of its establishment in 1867 the fort in the Sun River Valley was officially named Fort Shaw after Robert Shaw, the young colonel who led the nation's first black regiment, the 54th Massachusetts, in a courageous but disastrous attack on Fort Wagner, South Carolina. Cheney, *Names,* 104; Clark, "Fort Shaw," 147.

End of an Era

1. Founded in spring of 1867 and located some twenty miles west of present-day Great Falls, Montana, Sun River was one of the oldest towns in Montana and a way station for miners and settlers traveling from Fort Benton to the state's earliest goldfields. Cheney, *Names,* 259–60. Preparing a military post for closure was among the assignments carried out by the 25th Regiment, a black unit led by white officers. Clark, "Fort Shaw," 148.

2. Completed in 1862, John Mullan's six-hundred-mile road served the gold-rush towns of Bannack and Virginia City and extended all the way to Walla Walla, a key trading post in Washington Territory. Davis, *American Frontier,* 38. Known early on as Last Chance Gulch, Helena became the capital of Montana Territory in 1875. Malone, Roeder, and Lang, *Montana,* 213–14.

3. Col. Eugene Baker had set out to surprise the camp of Mountain Chief, a Piegan leader implicated in the deaths of some two dozen settlers. The camp he all but annihilated, however, during his infamous predawn raid of January 23, 1870, was occupied by a band of smallpox-ridden Piegans led by Heavy Runner. According to Baker's official report, 173 Indians died in that raid. Taking into account the deaths of those driven out of the camp and left to freeze or

starve to death, historians set the number of casualties at 217. Although the attack earned Colonel Baker "special commendation," the *Chicago Times* rightly described the incident as "the most disgraceful butchery in the annals of our dealings with the Indians." See Gibson and Hayne, "Notes," and Gibson and Hayne, "Postscript," for an overview of what became known as the Baker Massacre. For a slightly different view, see Miller and Cohen, *Military and Trading Posts*, 76–77.

4. For descriptions of the Fort Shaw complex, see Miller and Cohen, *Military and Trading Posts*, 76–77; Baldwin, "History of Fort Shaw," 2. For a reproduction of the "Plan of Fort Shaw," see *Pictorial History*, 149.

5. Miller and Cohen, *Military and Trading* Posts, 77; Baldwin, "History of Fort Shaw," 4–5; "John Gibbon," http://www.batteryb.com/gibbon/html. The sobriquet "the Queen of Montana's Military Forts," comes from the *Great Falls Tribune*, July 11, 1999.

6. Miller and Cohen, *Military and Trading Posts*, 77–79; Barsness and Dickinson, "Fort Shaw"; Clark, "Fort Shaw," 147–48.

7. Indian encampments near military forts—and trading posts—were the norm, and a significant number of the mixed-blood students who attended Fort Shaw School were the offspring of the soldiers and scouts and traders who frequented those camps. Bias among the valley's early settlers against American Indians is borne out by one woman's memory of her mother pulling down the shades and hiding her children under the bed whenever she saw an Indian approaching. Rockwell, "Memories," 273.

8. For the most part, white citizens in the valley accepted the presence of the buffalo soldiers, although some agreed with an outspoken resident who maintained that the presence of "a colored regiment . . .ha[d] kept many persons from settling [in the valley]." *Rising Sun*, October 9, 1889.

9. Although the arrival of the 25th in 1888 had, in effect, signaled the demise of the fort, the post was not closed until December of 1891. Clark, "Fort Shaw," 148. After more than a decade as territorial capital, Helena fought a successful ten-year battle to retain its position as capital following statehood in 1889. Cheney, *Names*, 134. The crusade to turn Fort Shaw into an agricultural college had been led by Granville Stuart, one of Montana's earliest pioneers. *Rising Sun*, July 1, 1891. The land grant college, now Montana State University, was established in Bozeman in 1893. Rydell, Safford, and Mullen, *In the People's Interest*, 9.

Birth of a Game

1. This account of the beginnings of basketball is drawn from the inventor's own recollections. Naismith, *Basketball*, 29–60. Founded in 1885 as the YMCA Department of the School for Christian Workers, the Springfield YMCA Training School is today's Springfield College.

2. That first game was played on December 21, 1891. It was not until 1897 that the Amateur Athletic Union (AAU) reduced the number of players to five. Robbins, *Basketball*, 3–5.

3. Naismith, *Basketball*, ix, xv. The centrality of the concept of "muscular Christianity" is evident from the YMCA insignia, proposed by Luther Gulick in 1889—a triangle depicting spirit, mind, and body as equally important elements in the organization's mission. "YMCA Worldwide History," www.heritageymca.org/ymca_worldwide.htm.

4. For more on the uses of basketball as a means to an end for organizations, ethnic groups, and nations, see Guttmann's *Games and Empires*.

5. Naismith, "Basket Ball," 144–47.

6. Ibid., 146. Some of the earliest adaptations included the installation of backboards (1893); twenty-minute halves, with a five-minute rest period between halves (1893); an official basketball to replace the soccer ball (1894); the free-throw line placed at fifteen feet from the basket (1895); a continuous dribble (1898); replacement of the basket by an iron rim and closed net (1900); and opening of the net in 1906. Robbins, *Basketball*, 3–5. For a comprehensive treatment of the worldwide popularity of basketball, see Wolff's *Big Game, Small World*.

Phoenix Rising, 1892

1. Greer, "Brief History," 38; Records of Bureau of Indian Affairs (hereafter BIA), Field Office Reports, Records of Non-Reservation Schools, Records of Fort Shaw Indian School, Record of Employees, 1891–1910, vol. 1, entry 1361, RG 75, National Archives, Denver (NAD). Hereafter Fort Shaw Record of Employees. Special Indian Agent J. A. Leonard had sent reports to the secretary of the Interior on March 15 and 22, and April 13, 1892. Greer, "Brief History," 3. Although he arrived in April, William Winslow was not officially appointed superintendent of the new facility until June 22, 1892. Baldwin, "History," 7. A native of North Carolina, Winslow had entered the Indian School Service as a physician soon after receiving his degree in medicine and had risen steadily through the ranks. He was thirty-seven years old and newly married when he accepted the appointment to Fort Shaw. Greer, "Brief History," 4; Gidget Fleming, census summaries, to authors, January 8 and 22, 2006. The authors' profile of Winslow is based on contemporary reports, including a September 21, 1892, article in the *Rising Sun*.

2. In 1892 Winslow would most likely have come into Montana via the Northern Pacific and into Great Falls from Helena on the Montana Central. Founded in 1884 by Paris Gibson, a New England–born visionary, Great Falls came into its own around 1887 with connections from both the St. Paul, Minneapolis, and Manitoba Railroad (soon to be the Great Northern) from the north and the Northern Pacific from the south. Cheney, *Names*, 126; *Great Falls Daily Leader*, December 10, 1902. Paris Gibson was also co-owner of the Park Hotel (constructed 1885–1886), one of the city's earliest and finest lodging establishments. Furdell and Furdell, *Great Falls*, 70.

In addition to Chilocco, other off-reservation schools operating in 1892 included the storied Carlisle in Pennsylvania, Haskell in Kansas, Chemawa in Oregon, Genoa in Nebraska, Albuquerque and Santa Fe in New Mexico, Grand

Junction and Fort Lewis in Colorado, Carson in Nevada, Fort Mohave and Phoenix in Arizona, and Pierre in South Dakota. Adams, *Education*, 57. Archuleta, Child, and Lomawaima's *Away from Home* is a comprehensive pictorial and textual overview of off-reservation boarding schools. Several studies of specific off-reservation schools have been published over the last few decades, most notably, Lomawaima, *They Called It Prairie Light*; Child, *Boarding School Seasons*; Trennert, *Phoenix Indian School*; and Scott, *Rapid City Indian School.*

3. Travel time estimates for a horse-drawn vehicle over that distance, in that era, during a Montana April were provided by two present-day wagon masters well versed in the rehabilitation and use of conveyances of the late nineteenth century. Barbara Winters interview with Bud Bisnett, March 13, 2003; Jan Dunbar interview with Rawhide Johnson, February 10, 2004.

4. *Rising Sun*, October 14, 1891.

5. Ibid., February 10 and March 25, 1892.

6. In addition to Agent Leonard's reports, Dr. Winslow also had access to the quartermaster's list of buildings and "property pertaining thereto" that the army had turned over to the Department of the Interior. Records of BIA, Field Office Reports, Records of Non-Reservation Schools, Records of Fort Shaw Indian School, Statement of Receipts and Disbursements, vol. 1, entry 1362, RG 75, NAD. Hereafter Fort Shaw Receipts and Disbursements.

7. Baldwin, "History," 7–8.

8. Report of Secretary of the Interior, *Indian Affairs*, 48, 472; Greer, "Brief History," 3, 38–39. Winslow had been instructed to choose 10,000 acres for the school, but once on site he requested permission to set aside 13,000 acres. In the end, his request was reduced to 4,999.5 acres. Greer, "Brief History," 3–5; Winslow to T. C. Power, January 11, 1893, MC55, T. C. Power Papers, Montana Historical Society (hereafter MHS), Helena. Although the river ran just north of the complex, gravity flow demanded that the water be drawn down to the fort via a ditch that originated nine miles to the west.

9. The BIA, on Special Agent Leonard's recommendation, had specified an expenditure of $50,000 for the initial rehabilitation of the buildings at Fort Shaw and a budget of $25,000 a year thereafter to maintain the institution. Report of the secretary of the Interior, *Indian Affairs*, 472; *Rising Sun*, September 21, 1892; Baldwin, "History," 8; Greer, "Brief History," 3–4.

10. Fort Shaw Record of Employees.

11. The items listed here are a sampling of the numerous texts, library books, and other school supplies ordered in fall of 1892. Fort Shaw Receipts and Disbursements, 15.

12. Ibid., 2–7, 8–10, 13, 17, 19.

13. Report of Secretary of the Interior, *Indian Affairs*, 472; Greer, "Brief History," 4. Children at off-reservation schools such as Fort Shaw were exposed to the "white man's religion" through mandatory attendance at chapel services and observance of Christian holidays. For a fuller treatment of the role of religious training at Indian schools, see Adams, *Education for Extinction*, 23, 164, 167–70. Pratt's oft-quoted mantra is found in Adams, 52.

14. Adams's *Education for Extinction* opens with a comprehensive overview of the federal government's theories and policies on Indian education.

15. Catholic mission schools were among the first schools established to serve Indian children. While agency schools did not have so rigorous a religious training program as mission schools, Christian principles were stressed, including celibacy outside marriage and abstinence from gambling and drinking. For more on education at mission and agency schools, see Reyhner and Eder, *American Indian Education*, and Coleman, *American Indian Children*. For more on such mission schools as St. Peter's in the Sun River Valley and St. Paul's on the Fort Belknap Reservation, see McBride, *Bird Tail*; Mahoney, *Lady Blackrobes*; Schoenbert, "Historic St. Peter's." A good treatment of a Protestant mission school is found in Pease, *Worthy Work*.

16. For their schooling prior to transfer to Fort Shaw, see the background given on each of the girls in subsequent chapters.

Routine and Ritual, 1892

1. No mention has been found of a "Mrs. Winslow" among the many reports of Fort Shaw activities in the local press, nor does her name appear on the Fort Shaw rolls. Only subsequent genealogical research by Gidget Fleming attests to the history of the Josephine and William Winslow family. Fort Shaw Record of Employees.

2. The official opening of Fort Shaw Indian School is listed as December 27, 1892. Winslow to T. C. Power, January 11, 1893, T. C. Power Papers, MC55, MHS; Greer, "Brief History," 39.

3. Thomas, "Early Life," 72; Bye, "History," 14. C. R. A. Scobey served as the Indian agent at Fort Peck from 1889 to 1893 and again from 1898 to 1904. "Roster of Superintendents, Fort Peck Indian Agency." www.montana.edu/ nwnfpcc/tribes/suprost. Fort Peck records in the Denver branch of National Archives do not go back far enough to include information on the fire that destroyed the reservation's school in fall 1892. Though mention of the fire has been included in various stories handed down from generation to generation and the sudden transportation of the Fort Peck children to Fort Shaw shortly thereafter can be documented, the authors have not yet been able to determine the exact date of the fire. Displaced by the fire, J. L. and Henrietta Baker accepted interim appointments to Fort Shaw. They both transferred to Fort Hall, Idaho, in June 1893. Fort Shaw Record of Employees.

4. The authors' speculations here are based on articles in the *Rising Sun* prior to and after the opening of the school. *Rising Sun*, August 23, September 21, and December 28, 1892. Also *Havre (Mont.) Advertiser* of July 25, 1893.

5. *Rising Sun*, December 28, 1892. Though the paper's editor cited "about fifty" children, according to enrollment records, thirty-five Assiniboines were aboard the wagons arriving at Fort Shaw that evening. Records of BIA, Field Office Reports, Records of Non-Reservation Schools, Records of Fort Shaw Indian School, Register of Pupils, 1892–1908, vol. 1, entry 1358, RG 75, NAD. Hereafter Fort Shaw Register of Pupils.

6. Though school records give Nettie's age at enrollment as seven, family records show her date of birth as September 18, 1886, making her barely six at the time she arrived at Fort Shaw. Wirth Family Genealogy.

7. Thomas, "Early Life," 15–17, 23–38; Wirth Family Genealogy.

8. Susan Wirth's sorrow over the departure of four of her daughters in the span of just a few months is easily understood, given the fact that of the eleven children born to her, three by her first husband, Henry Archdale, and eight by Jacob, she had buried five of them by that time and now her two oldest daughters, Christina (Tina) Archdale and Christine Wirth, were in California and Pennsylvania, respectively. In effect, there were no children remaining at home with the departure of the three girls for Fort Shaw. Her grief is documented by written and oral family history, and her anger toward Jacob for his compliance with the agent's orders would manifest itself in a dramatic way within a year. Thomas, "Early Life," 72, 74; 38, 91.

9. The journey from the railhead at Poplar to Great Falls on the Great Northern (formerly the St. Paul, Minneapolis and Manitoba) would take approximately eight-and-one-half hours. "History of the Great Northern Railway," 18. There would still be a transfer in Great Falls to a narrow-gauge railway owned and operated by the Alberta Railway and Coal Company (AR&C) and connecting Great Falls to Lethbridge, Alberta, Canada. Students bound for Fort Shaw went only as far as the railhead at Sunnyside (western edge of present-day Vaughn), where they were met by farm wagons that took them along the Sun River and down to the Indian School. Donald Malcolm West, "The Virtual Crowsnest Highway," www.crowsnest-highway.ca/index.htm. Cheney, *Names,* 259, 279. See also *Sun River Valley Pictorial History,* 52–54. Interview with Emma Toman of Sun River, February 5, 2005.

10. This scene is constructed on the basis of information found in Fort Shaw Record of Employees, 1892–1893, and Fort Shaw Receipts and Disbursements. It also takes into account the protocol established by the BIA for introducing students to off-reservation boarding schools. See Adams, *Education for Extinction,* 100–135, and Archuleta, Child, and Lomawaima, *Away from Home,* 26, 28, 29.

11. For more on life by the white man's clock, see Adams, *Education for Extinction,* 119–20. The authors have chosen to have reveille and taps open and close each day, with the sound of the bell acting as the call to the dining hall. *Great Falls Daily Tribune,* May 20, 1900. Dining hall described by Lydia Lefferts (Wilson), in interview by Friesen, "Golden Rule Days." A typical breakfast menu would include oatmeal, milk, fried potatoes, bread, syrup, and coffee. Reyhner and Eder, *American Indian Education,*153.

12. Winslow's philosophy of education is extracted from an article in the *Helena (Mont.) Weekly Herald,* May 28, 1896. The precision drills performed on the parade ground at Fort Shaw were modeled after those originated by Colonel Richard Pratt at Carlisle. For more on the militaristic nature of off-reservation boarding schools, see Adams, *Education for Extinction,* 117–18, and Archuleta, Child, and Lomawaima, *Away from Home,* 27.

13. Contents of the Fort Shaw classroom have been derived from the lists of materials ordered by Winslow in preparation for opening of the school. Fort Shaw Receipts and Disbursements.

14. For more expansive descriptions of the nature of and philosophy behind manual-arts training for boys and girls, see Adams, *Education for Extinction*, 149–54, and Archuleta, Child, and Lomawaima, *Away from Home*, 30–37.

15. Fort Shaw Record of Employees. For an overview on industrial education for girls, see Trennert's "Educating Indian Girls."

16. Schedules varied somewhat from school to school, and as yet no record of the rising hour at Fort Shaw school has been located. The authors have extrapolated from the schedule kept at the Model Indian School in St. Louis and from descriptions in Archuleta, Child, and Lomawaima, *Away from Home.*

Recruitment, Runaways, and Reinforcements, 1893

1. There were approximately 450 school-aged children on the Blackfeet Reservation in 1893, though only half of those were attending classes at the time of Dr. Winslow's visit. Both mission schools were run by Jesuit priests and Ursuline sisters. Parsons, *Educational Movement*, 19–20; Mahoney, *Lady Blackrobes*, 121, 123; McBride, *Bird Tail*, 163.

2. Soon after the death of her husband, Charles, Jenny Johnson (Nearly Died, but also known as Jane) moved herself and her children from Johnson's ranch in Kibby, Montana, to her allotment acreage on Blacktail Creek, east of Heart Butte. The Johnson children enrolled at Willow Creek School in fall 1892 were Mary, Charles, William, Belle, and James. Although one of Belle Johnson's granddaughters noted that two-year-old Ida was left in the care of her grandmother, Ma-Chew-ne-Ka (Kills Inside), Ida's daughter, Nora Lukin does not recall her mother ever mentioning this. Lukin, "My Early Years," 2–3.

3. While some sources indicate that forty Piegan students would be arriving on January 10, 1893, school records indicate that eighteen arrived on January 3, with more children from the Blackfeet Reservation coming to Fort Shaw over the course of the first two months of the year and still others arriving as late as April. Fort Shaw Register of Pupils.

4. *Rising Sun*, January 11, 1893. The newspaper identified the boys only as Piegan, but their names ultimately appeared in Dr. Winslow's final report for that first semester at Fort Shaw: William Croff, eighteen, Charles Powell, sixteen, and Thomas Spotted Eagle. Though Spotted Eagle's age is not given, he was likely at least sixteen. Records of BIA, Field Office Reports, Records of Non-Reservation Schools, Records of Fort Shaw Indian School, Discharge Records including Runaways, entry 1358, RG 75, NAD. Hereafter Fort Shaw Discharge Records. For more on running away and other forms of student resistance, see Adams, *Education for Extinction*, 222–38.

5. *Rising Sun*, January 11, 1893.

6. Ibid. Corporal punishment was a reality of boarding school life, with the severity of the punishment sometimes exceeding the seriousness of the trespass. The authors have come across written complaints about corporal pun-

ishment at Fort Shaw during their work in the National Archives, although such letters are relatively few in number, perhaps because not many reservation agents were willing to assist parents in lodging formal complaints with the BIA. While stories of harsh punishment at many boarding schools have been handed down orally or written into memoirs, further exploration into written complaints filed with the BIA seems called for.

7. There is no mention of runaways in early January in school records, indicating that Dr. Winslow must have decided against blotting his record so soon after his school officially opened. However, when the boys ran away again on March 24, he expelled all three. It was an easy decision on Winslow's part, as they were all close to the age limit for compulsory education anyway. Fort Shaw Discharge Records.

8. Fort Shaw Register of Pupils. David Dawson Mitchell, grandfather to the Mitchell girls, was instrumental in bringing the Plains tribes together in 1851 to sign the Treaty of Fort Laramie. Dorothy Smith, daughter of Sarah Mitchell Courchene, to authors, May 12, 2000. Later, Mitchell built a reputation as a partner in the American Fur Company before President Zachary Taylor appointed him as superintendent of Indian affairs for "the whole region drained by the Missouri and its tributaries." Verdon, "David Dawson Mitchell," 8. Josephine Mitchell is listed as age seventeen on the Fort Shaw Record of Employees, but family records show that she was fifteen at the time of her appointment as Indian assistant. Louise Courchene to David Courchene, April 17, 1983, per Gena Aslanian to authors, March 7, 2005.

9. Joe Butch, like many men in the nineteenth-century American West, was somewhat of a chameleon, changing his name with almost every move. Born in England to an impoverished family named Creasley, he emigrated to Canada in his teens and apprenticed under a tanner named Chamberlain. In 1863 he crossed into the United States and enrolled in the Union Army as Joe Chamberlain. At war's end he was sent to Dakota Territory with the 13th U.S. Infantry. Not yet twenty, he joined a small group of deserters, ending up as a woodcutter near present-day Frazer, Montana. He also worked as a butcher for buffalo hunters, calling himself "Joe Butcher," and finally Joe Butch, to avoid being found and imprisoned for desertion. Urs, "Joe Butch,"147–50; Rayner, *Montana*, 180. His first wife, A-nin-ta-tca'n-gu Wa-ka'n, or Alone on a Sacred Trail, the mother of his three daughters, drowned while crossing the Missouri River. Interview with Mary Helland, May 30, 2004. Josepha and Rosa Butch were enrolled at Fort Shaw on February 4, 1893. Fort Shaw Register of Pupils.

10. Winslow was able to secure one additional teacher, Hallie E. Bell, who arrived on January 17, 1893. Fort Shaw Record of Employees. Adams, *Education for Extinction*, 293.

11. The three Carlisle graduates were Richard Sanderville (Sanderval), twenty-three; Frank Guardipee, nineteen; and Nimrod Davis, twenty. Parsons, *Educational Movement of the Blackfeet*, 19; Fort Shaw Record of Employees. Over the course of the 1893 spring semester Winslow named three other Fort Shaw students as Indian assistants: Nora Ivy, Assiniboine, sixteen; Joseph McKnight,

Piegan, eighteen; and Frank Choate, Piegan, eighteen. All Indian assistants received a salary of sixty dollars a year. Fort Shaw Record of Employees.

12. The Bird Tail was a huge promontory rising up from the floor of the valley. Resembling a widespread bird's tail, it was a sacred site to Indians and a landmark to trappers and travelers. McBride, *Bird Tail*, vii.

13. Census records for 1880 list Many Kills as "Many" or "Mary," wife of military scout Louis Langley/Langlois and the mother of Annie and Josephine, both listed as age five. Many Kills appears elsewhere as Many Hills (DeMarce, *Blackfeet Heritage,* 150) and on Josephine Langley's marriage certificate as Louise Eagle Plume (marriage certificate, Cascade County, December 1903, per Kenneth Robison to authors, February 24, 2006). Eighteen months older than Josie, Annie Langley was actually her aunt, the last-born of Josie's maternal grandmother, Always Singing. Census of the Blackfeet Reservation, 1907–1908. Many Kills and Langley adopted Annie, gave her his name, and the two girls were raised as sisters. Patricia Deboo, granddaughter of Annie Langley Tatsey, telephone interview with authors, November 2004. The exact date, even the exact year, of Josephine Langley's birth has been impossible to determine, given the discrepancies found in various sources. Although her obituary in the *Browning (Mont.) Chieftain,* September 7, 1951, gives her birth date as June 15, 1870, this does not match the data found in various government, school, and tribal records. Based on all available records, the authors have settled on 1875 as the most likely year of her birth.

14. Louis Langley was still with Many Kills in the 1880 U.S. census for Fort Shaw, but he disappears from the records thereafter. In Blackfeet tribal records compiled in 1907–1908, he is listed as the "deceased" father of Josephine Langley Liephart. However, descendants of Josie's stepsister, Annie Langley Tatsey, have no knowledge of the nature or date of his death. It seems more likely that Louis Langley simply slipped from the frontier scene as unobtrusively as he had appeared upon it. Louise Langley's (Many Kills) marriage to Charles Choquette, who was about six years younger than she, occurred sometime between 1880 and 1885. Louise and Charles appear as a couple in Blackfeet tribal census records from 1891 onward, when they moved to Many Kills' family's allotment along Birch Creek. Blackfeet, Blood, and Piegan Census 1891; "History of the Blackfoot Indian . . . , 1907–1908." Census research courtesy of genealogist Gidget Fleming. Josie Langley/Langlois was enrolled at St. Peter's in the company of three of her stepfather's sisters, Rose, Josephine, and Elizabeth Choquette. McBride, *Bird Tail,* 71.

15. According to Patricia Deboo, Josie's dreams of going to Carlisle began during her years at St. Peter's. Telephone interview with Deboo, November 2004. Rampant in Indian boarding schools across the country, trachoma was an "unremitting problem" at St. Peter's. Mahoney, *Lady Blackrobes,* 55–57. Josie's recurring bouts with trachoma are documented in Fort Shaw infirmary records. Records of BIA, Field Office Reports, Records of Non-Reservation Schools, Records of Fort Shaw Indian School, Sanitary Reports, 1894–1899, RG 75, vol. 1, entry 1360, NAD. Hereafter Fort Shaw Sanitary Reports. For

more on illness and death in Indian boarding schools, see Adams, *Education for Extinction*, 124–35.

16. At the time Langley began working at Fort Shaw School, most of the Indians employed in the Indian School Service held staff positions, but many eventually worked their way up to higher-ranking posts. In 1895, the BIA mandated that Indian students who had attained a "normal school" education were to be given preferential treatment, in that they were exempted from the civil service exam and could begin work as teachers "without further examination." Adams, *Education for Extinction*, 293–94.

17. Description of Josephine Langley's personality and of her empathy for and support of the students in her care is drawn from interviews with her great-niece, Patricia Deboo, and with tribal elders who remember her service as a matron at Cut Bank Boarding School in Browning, Montana. Patricia Deboo interview, November 2004; Nora Lukin interview, April 2005.

18. By the end of spring semester, enrollment stood at 152. Fort Shaw Register of Pupils; Report of the Commissioner of Indian Affairs, vol. 2, 1895–1896, 179; *Choteau Montanian*, July 25, 1893. To add to the confusion, an early July *Great Falls Daily Tribune* article claims that year-end enrollment stood at 176. Article reprinted in the *Havre (Mont.) Advertiser*, July 28, 1893.

19. *Rising Sun*, June 28, 1893; *Havre (Mont.) Advertiser*, July 25, 1893. Patriotic music and Christian hymns were expected components of any program given by a school committed to "civilizing" Indian youth. For more on the content of Indian school programs held on national and religious holidays, see Adams, *Education for Extinction*, 191–206.

20. *Havre (Mont.) Advertiser*, July 25, 1893, as reprinted from the *Great Falls (Mont.) Daily Tribune*.

Foreshadowings, 1893

1. The Lemhi Reservation was the smallest Indian reservation in the United States. Created in 1875 and located between present-day Tendoy and Lemhi, Idaho, it consisted of one hundred square miles along the Lemhi River and had a population of fewer than five hundred Indians—Shoshones, Sheepeaters, and Bannocks. In 1907 the reservation would be closed and the people removed to Fort Hall Reservation some two hundred miles to the south.

Jemima Burton died in childbirth in 1893, exact date unknown. She appears in tribal censuses from 1885 through 1892 in the household of William Burton but is not listed in the 1893 census, though a two-month-old is then listed as a member of the household. Lemhi Tribal Census Records, MC11, box 5, folder 3, ISU. For a fuller description of the reservation, see Sandeen, *Inventory*, 3, 6–8: Madsen, *Lemhi*, 134–36, 168–69; Miller, "Resilient People."

2. Sandeen, *Inventory*, 3–4; Madsen, *Lemhi*, 135–36. George Monk was the agent on the Lemhi Reservation from 1891 to 1894. Although Chief Tendoy, son of Chief Cameahwait and nephew of Sacagawea, fought government officials, he was considered a friend by the white settlers of the Lemhi Valley. At his death in 1907, those settlers put up a monument in his memory. Sandeen,

Inventory, 1; Snook, Wilson, and Dinnell, "Lemhi Band," 49–52. Chief Tendoy's fears that the Shoshone language would be lost were not unfounded. In very recent years, however, William Burton's great-great-granddaughter, anthropologist Drusilla Gould, has codified the dialects spoken around the Fort Hall Reservation. See Gould and Loether, *Introduction to Shoshoni.*

3. Although it has proved impossible to establish the nature of Burton's education, it is known that he was fluent in English as well as Shoshone and Bannock and that he was an important aide to both the Indian agents and Chief Tendoy. A photograph of William Burton in a three-piece suit, standing with three tribal elders who are wearing traditional dress, hangs in the Lemhi County Historical Museum in Salmon, Idaho. Burton's status as tribal interpreter is found, among other entries, in Records of the Lemhi Reservation, Lemhi Agency Employee Rolls, MC11, box 1, folder 1, ISU.

4. Sandeen, *Inventory,* 7; C. F. Larabee to Edward Yearian, May 27, 1898, Records of the Lemhi Reservation, MC11, box 15, folder 2, ISU. In the late 1880s—and by extension, the authors assume, into the 1890s—there were approximately eighty school-aged children on the reservation. Sandeen, *Lemhi,* 6. At one point in the 1892 school year, it was reported that the agency school had a total of "two or three badly torn primers and first readers and geographys." Madsen, *Lemhi,* 136.

5. Willard Burton was born in 1888. The baby, Bob Burton, survived his mother by a matter of months. The authors have arbitrarily set the death dates for Jemima and Bob Burton in April and June, though only the year of their deaths is known for sure. Lemhi Tribal Census Records, 1889, 1890, 1891, 1893. The position of "grandmother's grandchild" conferred favors upon a child, primarily the favor of being always in the presence of the grandparent. See Snell, *Grandmother's Grandchild,* which tells of her relationship with the famous Crow medicine woman Pretty Shield.

6. For a detailed—and highly readable—account of the Columbian Exposition, see Erik Larson's *Devil in the White City.* For a comprehensive analysis of the motivations behind, and the impacts of, that fair and other nineteenth-century expositions, see Robert Rydell's *All the World's a Fair.*

7. Carlisle's *Indian Helper,* August 4, 1893. For the full story behind the eventual fate of the BIA's educational exhibit at the Chicago World's Fair, see Trennert, "Selling Indian Education."

Future Prospects, 1893–1894

1. Adams, *Education for Extinction,* 57–58. By the mid-1880s, some superintendents were rethinking the mandate to keep students on campus all summer, citing the need for boys and girls to remain familiar with life on the reservations to which some of them would inevitably return. McKinney, "History," 116.

2. Woman That Kills Wood gave Christina (Tina) Archdale as a three-year-old to an immigrant family traveling to California. Tina returned to the reservation to be officially enrolled and claim her allotment. Thomas, "Early Life," 15–16, 37–38, 71–72.

3. Friesen, "Golden Rule Days." Interview with Patricia Deboo. The Square Butte the girls climbed is in the Sun River Valley, near Fort Shaw, and is not to be confused with the Square Butte for which a town east of Great Falls was named.

4. The six reservations in Montana as of 1893 were Fort Belknap (Gros Ventres and Assiniboines) and Fort Peck (Assiniboines and Lakota Sioux) in the central and eastern parts of the state, respectively; the Crow and the Northern Cheyenne in the southeast, the Blackfeet in the northwest, and the Flathead (Salish, Kootenais, and Pend'Oreilles) across the Continental Divide from Fort Shaw. A seventh reservation, Rocky Boy's, in the very center of the state, was carved out in 1916 for the Chippewa-Cree Indians. The Lakota Sioux and Northern Cheyennes joined in June 1876 to defeat the command under Colonel George A. Custer. Known in American history books as the Battle of the Little Bighorn, it was known to Indians as the Battle of the Greasy Grass.

5. Fort Belknap's agency school opened sometime between 1888 and 1893. St. Paul's opened on September 18, 1888. Mahoney, *Lady Blackfeet,* 82.

6. James Snell served as a scout under both General George Crook and General Nelson Miles in their expeditions against the Sioux and the Nez Percé. For more on Snell's background and family life, see "James Snell" in *Thunderstorms and Tumbleweeds;* Snell's autobiographical entry in Noyes, *In the Land of the Chinook,* 112–15; and Alma Snell's *Grandmother's Grandchild,* 149–50. The daughter of Knocks (or Knocker) and Tattoo Arm, Fannie (Tahompe) Black Digger was born in 1865, near old Fort Browning, just south of present-day Dodson, Montana. One branch of Fanny Black Digger Snell's descendants has identified her father as Tattoed Face. Thelma Warren James' family tree; Katie Snell Weigand's 1921 Fort Belknap enrollment application #690; Jennie Snell Sherlock's Fort Belknap enrollment application #746; Snell family tree in possession of Douglas Stuart, Kate Snell's grandson; Assiniboine Census of 1897, Fort Belknap Agency.

7. Healy's biography appears in "Col. William H. H. Healy," *Progressive Men of Montana,* 1574. Although Healy scouted for General Nelson Miles and later General Oliver Howard, the authors have found no evidence of his having served in the army or earned military rank. Father Frederick Eberschweiler founded St. Paul's Mission and was responsible for bringing the Ursulines there to open a school. McBride, *Bird Tail,* 75–76; Mahoney, *Lady Blackrobes,* 79–80. Ursuline papers cited by McBride and Mahoney indicate that Eberschweiler petitioned the government for land for his mission, while Colonel Healy's "Reminiscence" mentions his donation of land to the Jesuits for the establishment of St. Paul's.

8. Telephone interview with Thelma Warren James, November 30, 2004.

9. By 1883 or 1884, at the time Fannie Black Digger married James Snell, *a la façon du pays,* she had a baby girl, Jennie. James Snell raised the child as his own. Jennie Snell Sherlock's Fort Belknap enrollment application, #746. At the time of his marriage to Fannie, James Snell had two other children, Lewis, who

lived with his Assiniboine mother on the Fort Peck Reservation, and Mary, whose mother, Her Cane—a niece of Sitting Bull—had died during childbirth. The names and birth dates of the offspring of Fanny Black Digger and James Snell come from James Snell's letter of March 14, 1910, to his daughter Mary Snell Sansaver. Letter in possession of Mary Ann Verwolf, granddaughter of Mary Snell Sansaver.

10. The four older Snell children, Jennie, Richard, Katie, and Mabel, were, indeed, enrolled at the agency school at Fort Belknap in the fall of 1893. Tribal records of Richard Snell, Jennie Snell Sherlock, and Catherine Snell Wiegand in possession of Thelma Warren James.

11. Colonel Healy married Honkow in 1881; she died early in 1893, soon after the birth of the infant Maude. Healy ran cattle and raised horses on his 160 acres and also served as postmaster of Lodge Pole (today called Lodgepole, though the creek is still spelled as Lodge Pole). "Col. William H. H. Healy," 1574. Ponley's role is documented by descendants of Genevieve Healy Adams, though his exact identity and origins remain unclear. Donita Nordlund interview, March 19, 2000. The only Ponley the authors have found appears in the 1900 Fort Belknap Agency Census, where he is listed as a thirty-two-year-old French-born rancher, head of a household, with a wife, also born in France, and seven children—five girls and two boys—all born in Montana. If this is the same Ponley that Genevieve Healy Adams spoke of as the caretaker for the Healy children—and later for the colonel himself—he would have been approximately twenty-five years old at the time of Winslow's visit.

12. The exact birth dates of the Healy children have been hard to establish. By extrapolation of birth dates given variously in the 1900 U.S. Manuscript Census for Lodge Pole, Montana; Fort Shaw Register of Pupils; and interviews with Genevieve Healy Adams's descendants, Donita Nordlund and Cecilia James, John Healy was nine years old in the summer of 1893, Harry was seven, Nettie, six, Genevieve, five, and William not yet two. The baby Maude was only a few months old. Characterization of the rowdy Healy household is drawn from anecdotal recollections of Healy descendants.

13. In fall 1893 four of the six Healy children, including five-year-old Genevieve, were enrolled at St. Paul's Mission School, near present-day Hayes, Montana. A year later, in fall 1894, Healy petitioned the BIA to allow his children— John, Harry, Nettie, and Genevieve—to transfer to the agency school at Fort Belknap on the grounds that it was a much better, healthier place for them to be. Healy to D. M. Browning, September 9, 1894, LR 1894, box 1124, #36194, 75/11E3/5/18/2, NAW.

14. Dr. Winslow's prediction turned out to be correct, for in October of 1895, eleven-year-old John Healy became one of the first Gros Ventre students to enroll at Fort Shaw School. Fort Shaw Register of Pupils.

15. Programs in Indian boarding schools went beyond academic and vocational training, as federal policymakers stressed the necessity of "attracting In-

dian students to 'civilized' artistry and music." Like its sister schools, Fort Shaw prided itself on its students' exposure to, and mastery of, music, both instrumental and vocal. For a comprehensive overview of music in Indian schools, see Troutman's *"Indian Blues."* For more on pageants, music, and dance, see Green and Troutman, "By the Waters of the Minnehaha," 60–83. Information on Eugene Parker comes from Fort Shaw Record of Employees; *Rising Sun*, December 19, 1894; Greer, "Brief History," 50–51. Sarah Patterson, a native of New York, served as assistant matron during the 1893–1894 school year but was promoted to a faculty position as music teacher the following year. Fort Shaw Record of Employees; *Rising Sun*, December 20, 1893.

16. *Rising Sun*, June 13, 1894.

17. *Rising Sun*, August 1, 1894. Barely two years after the opening of Fort Shaw, William Hailmann ranked the school as "the third best . . . in the service," behind Carlisle, the flagship of all Indian schools, and Haskell in Kansas. Winslow to T. C. Power, January 3, 1895, MC55, MHS. Pratt to George Monk, June 11, 1895, MC11, box 15, no folder number, ISU.

18. George Monk to Richard Pratt, August 30, 1894, MC11, box 15, no folder number, ISU.

19. Josephine Langley departed for the East in early January 1895. Fort Shaw Record of Employees. Her attendance at Carlisle is confirmed in Carlisle's newspaper, *Indian Helper*, as posted on Wotanging Ikche, http://native-net.org/aisesnet/discussion/1998/0149.html.

20. According to Thomas ("Early Life," 76–77), the Wirth girls were told of their mother's fight with their father by Susan (Woman That Kills Wood) herself. Had Lizzie gone to Carlisle at this time, she would have been joining her older sister, Christine, who had gone east to school in the fall of 1892.

"Basketball for Women," 1894

1. Berenson's "Basket Ball for Women" appeared in the September 1894 edition of *Physical Education*.

2. The only team sports for women in the late nineteenth century were doubles matches in tennis and a very constrained form of baseball. Spears, "Senda Berenson Abbott," 23–24. For more on the early years of women's basketball and, in particular, Berenson's role in introducing the sport to women and spearheading the move toward what would become known as "girls' rules," see Hult and Trekell, *A Century of Women's Basketball*; Grundy and Shackelford, *Shattering the Glass*, 12–33; and Lannin's *History of Basketball for Girls and Women*, 9–33. See also Anderson, *Story of Basketball*.

3. Accounts of exactly when Berenson introduced the game to her students vary. The authors have accepted Berenson's own statement in *Line Basket Ball*, 6. Helen Wheelock's well-researched website on women's basketball includes a reliable and comprehensive timeline of milestones in the sport. www.WomensBasketballOnline.com.

4. Berenson's written recollection of that first game is quoted by Hill, "Senda Berenson," 662. The date of that first game is given as March 22, 1893, in sever-

al sources, including notes compiled by graduate student Aynes Stillman during her 1971 perusal of the Senda Berenson papers, Sophia Smith Collection, Smith College Libraries.

5. Hill, "Senda Berenson," 662; Stillman notes.

6. *Northampton (Mass.) Daily Herald,* March 23, 1893, as quoted in Hill, "Senda Berenson," 662. That game was played according to Naismith's rules with nine players to a side.

7. Berenson, "Basket Ball for Women," 106, 109.

8. For the evolution of the rules, see Davenport, "Tides of Change," 83–108, and Wheelock, "Women's Basketball Online," http://www.WomensBasketball Online.com.

Elusive Dreams, 1895–1896

1. Interview with Belle Johnson Conway's granddaughter, Valerie Goss, March 2000; Lukin, "My Early Years," 2.

2. The photograph described is from a scrapbook preserved by Valerie Goss and other descendants of Charles and Jenny (Nearly Died) Johnson. Goss interview, March 2000.

3. Connelly, "My Mother's Life," 1, 2, 4; Lukin, "My Early Years," 2–3; Lukin interview, April 29, 2004; 1890 U.S. Manuscript Census, Fort Benton; Belle Johnson Conway obituary, *Helena Independent Record,* January 29, 1963. Birth dates for the Johnson children are extrapolated from Fort Shaw records and the Blackfeet, Blood, and Piegan Census of June 30, 1893.

4. Lukin, "My Early Years," 2–3; Connelly, "My Mother's Life," 1–4; Blackfeet, Blood, and Piegan Census of June 30, 1893; Fort Shaw Register of Pupils.

5. Reports of harsh treatment at the hands of Fort Shaw faculty and staff were periodically carried home to the Blackfeet Reservation by students, particularly runaways. According to Hart Schultz (Lone Wolf), Piegan son of writer/artist James Willard Schultz and himself a runaway from Fort Shaw, "Many boys ran away from the school because the treatment was so bad." Lone Wolf describes punishment that resulted in a broken collarbone for one of his classmates. Dyck, "Lone Wolf Returns," 24.

6. Description of the trip is based on information found in Thomas, "Early Life," 92–93, regarding Lizzie Wirth's ride to Carlisle in 1900.

7. The description of the campus and living quarters is based on Thomas, "Early Life," 93, and on Jenkins, *Real All Americans,* 99, 101–102.

8. Upon transfer from Fort Shaw, Josie would have been placed in the ninth grade, with her teaching training certificate attainable in two years. Despite initial reservations about introducing a brutal sport like football to Indian boys, Colonel Pratt had become aware of the recognition, both regionally and nationally, that a strong football team generated for the school. See Bloom, *To Show,* 12–18, and Jenkins, *Real All Americans,* 103.

9. Basketball was most likely brought to Carlisle by YMCA instructors, since that school was one of the earliest Indian schools to have a YMCA chapter on campus. Chauncey Yellow Robe, who came to Fort Shaw as disciplinarian

nine months after Josie's return to the school, was listed as secretary of the YMCA chapter at Carlisle in 1892. *Yearbook, 1892,* 166; Fort Shaw Record of Employees.

10. Until 1906, the referee was obliged to pull a chain releasing the ball from the net after each successful "basket." The center jump after every basket was finally eliminated in 1937, which in itself opened up the game and allowed higher scores. Until then, typical scores were low. The "Championship of America" tournament, played in Brooklyn in the spring of 1896, was won by a team representing the East District YMCA by a score of 4 to 0. Robbins, *Basketball,* 3–5; *Spalding's Catalogue, 1903–1904,* 28; Anderson, *Story of Basketball,* 9, 12.

11. There is little doubt that Josephine Langley brought basketball to Fort Shaw, and to Montana. The first YMCA chapters for American Indians on Montana's reservations were not established until 1897 and were possibly established due to the influence of F. C. Campbell, who took the Fort Shaw girls' basketball team to the 1904 World's Fair but who first served as the superintendent of the Fort Peck agency school from 1895 to 1898. However, there are no records of the YMCA chapters on the Fort Peck Reservation playing basketball before Josie organized the sport at Fort Shaw. *Yearbook, 1897,* 159. In February 1896, a month after Josie's return to her post at Fort Shaw, an item appearing in a Great Falls, Montana, paper noted local interest in forming a women's team, but there is no further mention of the game in the media until the Fort Shaw team began to gain public attention some seven years later. *Great Falls Daily Leader,* February 6, 1896.

12. Fort Shaw Record of Employees. Goings arrived on campus on April 30, 1895.

13. *Rising Sun,* June 26, 1895. Fort Shaw players included catcher Alvin Parker, fourteen, Cheyenne from Tongue River; first baseman Frank Conway, fourteen, Piegan; pitcher and coach Louis Goings, eighteen, Shoshone; third baseman Joseph Katon, fifteen, Piegan; shortstop Peter Adams, fourteen, Assiniboine, from Fort Peck; second baseman Charles Adams, twelve, Assiniboine from Fort Peck; right fielder Frank Choate, eighteen, Piegan; left fielder Paul Calf Looking, sixteen, Piegan; and center fielder Peter Marceau, eighteen, Piegan. *Rising Sun,* June 16, 1895; Fort Shaw Register of Pupils.

14. Fort Shaw Register of Pupils.

15. James Snell to Mary Snell Sansaver, March 14, 1910, letter in possession of Thelma Warren James.

16. Any information sent home by students spread quickly via the "moccasin telegraph." For evidence of the import of such letters, see Child, *Boarding School Seasons,* xxii–xvi.

17. James Snell to Mary Snell Sansaver, March 14, 1910, letter in possession of Thelma Warren James.

18. Jacob Wirth married Lydia Kennedy on January 13, 1895. Thomas, "Early Life," 78.

19. Fred C. Campbell, Kansas-born, began his career in the Indian School

Service in 1890 in Genoa, Nebraska. In 1895 he was named the superintendent of the Fort Peck Agency School. Smith, "Campbell Mountain," 164; F. C. Campbell papers in possession of Fred DesRosier, Campbell's grandson.

20. Interview with Patricia Deboo. Josie's eye infections did not end after her graduation from St. Peter's; infirmary records from Fort Shaw refer to bouts of chronic trachoma. Fort Shaw Sanitary Reports. Josie had returned to Fort Shaw by January 1896. Fort Shaw Record of Employees.

21. A required program for off-reservation boarding schools, "physical culture" still remained the stepchild at many institutions. With most Indian School Service teachers having received little or no training in the field themselves, physical culture classes were often handed to whichever teacher was willing to accept the extra assignment. Fort Shaw records make no mention of a physical culture position. While Josie Langley's official title for spring semester remained "Indian assistant" and her salary, at sixty dollars annually, was consistent with that position, her expanded responsibilities can be assumed from the pattern of promotions common after student employees returned from Carlisle.

22. Baldwin, "History," 5. Description of the outdoor "court" is derived from a photograph held by Terry Bender, granddaughter of Lizzie Wirth Smith.

23. Dribbling, which was not mentioned at all in Naismith's thirteen original rules, quickly became a prominent feature of the game. According to Naismith, the maneuver was developed by players who tried rolling the ball when they found themselves in a tight spot but soon discovered that bouncing it allowed for better—and longer—control of the sphere. By 1894, the soccer ball had given way to an official basketball. Naismith, *Basketball,* 65, 90.

A Wise Investment, 1896–1897

1. The fact that the girls' basketball shoes were made in the school's cobbler shop was communicated to the authors by Joseph Abbott, son of Frank Abbott, a Fort Shaw student from 1896 to 1899, in an interview conducted in March 2000. Fort Shaw Register of Pupils. See Margaret Abbott's "Writing the Journey" for Frank Abbott's memories of the dark side of student life at Fort Shaw.

2. Fort Shaw Register of Pupils.

3. Author interview with Donita Nordlund, granddaughter of Genevieve Healy Adams, March 19, 2000.

4. Emma Sansaver's father died in 1890, when she was six years old. *Chinook (Mont.) Opinion,* June 19, 1890. Genevieve Healy's mother died in 1893, when Gen was five years old. "Col. William H. H. Healy," 1574.

5. Descriptions of the girls' personalities are based on information given the authors in personal interviews with their descendants and classmates. Donita Nordlund, March 19, 2000; Cecilia James, great-niece of Genevieve Healy Adams, May 2000; Barbara Winters, granddaughter of Emma Sansaver Simpson, multiple times; Winters interview of Gertrude LaRance Parker, November 1990.

6. The description of Katie Snell's personality is based on information gleaned

in personal interviews with her daughter, Rosie Stuart, March 2000, and with her grandson, Douglas Stuart, May 2002. Fort Shaw Register of Pupils.

7. Fort Shaw Register of Pupils.

8. Ibid.

9. Ibid.; Fort Shaw Record of Employees; Lukin, "My Early Years," 3, 4; interview with Nora Lukin, Belle Johnson's niece, April 29, 2004. As at other Indian boarding schools, runaways were a chronic problem at Fort Shaw, especially among Piegan students whose homes were not as distant from campus as were the homes of students from other reservations. More often than not, the runaways were quickly apprehended and returned to campus—or became discouraged by the difficulties of finding their way home and returned voluntarily. But as will be seen later in this account, there were some tragic endings to winter attempts to escape the school.

10. Author interviews with Valerie Goss, granddaughter of Belle Johnson Conway, March 2000, March 2002, and May 2004.

11. Author interviews with Donita Nordlund, May 2002, and Cecilia James, May 2000.

12. *Great Falls Daily Tribune,* November 21, 1896.

13. Fred Campbell's years behind the plate were evidenced by his characteristic "gnarled and knotted baseball fingers." In the days when Campbell played, catchers wore gloves but not padded mitts. Harrington, "Semicentennial Visit," 166. Campbell played for the University of Kansas, but he also played semi-pro baseball as a means of paying his way through college and later just for the love of the game. Campbell Papers in possession of Fred DesRosier, Campbell's grandson.

14. When the girls took the field for that special exhibition, one team was clad in red uniforms, the other in white. The authors suspect that the irony of a Red team opposing a White team was unintended on the part of the girls. *Choteau Montanian,* July 2, 1897; Fort Shaw Record of Employees.

15. Rosa Lucero's lineage has been traced through DeMarce, *Blackfeet Heritage,* 159, and her Piegan tribal record, #5002, and those of her brother Richard, #5001 and #7442; Fort Shaw Register of Pupils; *Great Falls Daily Leader,* June 12, 1897; interviews with Millie Lucero, niece of Flora Lucero Dawson, May 20, 2001, and Grace Lavendis, niece of Flora Lucero Dawson, May 21, 2001. Although family records identify Philip Lucero as a native of Spain (Grace Lavendis fax to authors, September 22, 2001), the 1880 U.S. Manuscript Census for Teton County, Montana, lists Lucero as having been born in Mexico.

16. The events are listed in the program published in the June 12, 1897, *Great Falls Daily Leader,* which announced the June 30 closing exercises. The *Choteau Montanian* of July 2 reported that three hundred visitors attended the event.

17. The "White" team was victorious over the "Red" team. The lineups were not printed. *Choteau Montanian,* July 2, 1897.

18. *Great Falls Daily Leader,* June 12, 1897.

19. *Choteau Montanian,* July 2, 1897.

Widening the Circle, 1897

1. *Great Falls Daily Leader,* June 12, 1897. No other mention of basketball being played at a Montana school appears in newspapers until a year later when
the November 1898 issue of the *Exponent,* the weekly newspaper published by
Montana Agricultural College in Bozeman, cites the formation of an intramural basketball program on that campus.

2. In 1889, two years after finishing his degree at Kansas, Campbell married
Ella Mead, daughter of early pioneers of Olathe, Kansas. In 1890, the year their
first son, Mead, was born, Campbell entered the Indian School Service, beginning a forty-five-year career with the Bureau of Indian Affairs. The couple
was stationed at an off-reservation boarding school at Genoa, Nebraska, when
Ella gave birth to their second son, Fred. Then, in February 1898, the couple
welcomed a little girl, Mary Freda. DesRosier family records in possession of
Fred DesRosier.

3. Memories of her descendants indicate that Flora Lucero Dawson never
thought of herself as a scholar but that she excelled at needlework. Author
interviews with Shirley Rust, May 1, 2005; Millie Lucero, May 20, 2001; and
Grace Dawson Lavendis, May 21, 2001.

4. Rose Jocko's adoptive father traded her to Philip Lucero for a wagon.
Nothing Lucero offered Rose could assuage her bitterness at being forced to
wed a man twice her age. Sam and Millie Lucero, author interview, May 20,
2001; Grace Dawson Lavendis, author interview, May 21, 2001. During the
legendary winter of 1886–87, average livestock losses in the Choteau area approached 40 percent. Malone, Roeder, and Lang, *Montana,* 166. Ironically, William Hodgkiss, Lucero's one-time partner and the man to whom he sold his
surviving stock, eventually recouped all losses and even appears in *Progressive
Men,* 417. Author interview, Grace Lavendis, May 21, 2001.

5. According to family records, Flora Lucero, the oldest of Rose and Philip
Lucero's four children, was born on January 16, 1889, yet the Fort Shaw Register of Pupils lists her as being eleven in the fall of 1897, which would mean she
was born in 1886. Her marriage certificate indicates that she was twenty-one
on December 18, 1909. On the basis of further Fort Shaw data, the authors
have chosen to standardize on the 1888 date of birth. Family records indicate
that Lawrence Lucero was born on June 9, either 1890 or 1891, but more likely
1891, since school records show that Emma was born in 1890. Lena Lucero
was born on June 24, 1896. All of Rose Lucero's children were born in or near
Choteau. Family tree in possession of James Dawson, Flora's grandson; author interviews with Shirley Rust, May 1, 2005; Millie Lucero, May 20, 2001;
and Grace Dawson Lavendis, May 21, 2001. Surprisingly, there is no record
of Emma Lucero in family papers, and descendants had no knowledge of her
prior to the authors' research. Emma appears in Fort Shaw Register of Pupils
as a sibling of Flora's, two years younger.

6. That decision by Rose and Philip Lucero to raise the children in the "white
world" marks the longstanding reluctance of some family members to discuss

their American Indian heritage. Author interview with Shirley Rust, May 18, 2001.

7. Grace Lavendis fax to authors, September 22, 2001.

8. Betty Simpson Bisnett, Emma Sansaver Simpson's daughter, recalled her mother's talent as a pianist and her reports of having learned to play at St. Paul's. Emma Sansaver's love of the piano was so great that her husband, Ernie Simpson, gave her an upright grand as a gift on the birth of their first daughter, Betty. That same piano stands today in the home of Emma's great-granddaughter. Betty Bisnett interview, March 2000; multiple interviews with Barbara Winters, Emma Sansaver Simpson's granddaughter.

9. During Winslow's years as superintendent at Fort Shaw, no enrollee was listed as Métis, or as Chippew or Cree. Children whose fathers bore surnames like DeRoche, Henault, Jeneau, Lamont, and Pepion were designated by their mother's affiliation on the rolls. In this way Winslow conformed to the letter, if not always the spirit, of the BIA's edict against supporting and/or educating offspring of Indians who might well have been born north of the border.

10. Though direct descendants have standardized the spelling of "Sansaver," Emma's surname alternately appears in surviving records as St. Sauveur, St. Sevier, Sansavior, Sansauver, and Sansauvere. Barbara Winters' Family Group Record; Donna Wimmer's Sansaver Genealogical Papers. For more on the relationship of American Indians to the 49th parallel, see LaDow, *Medicine Line.* For more on the Métis, see Peterson and Brown, *New Peoples.*

11. Barbara Winters's Family Group Record; letter from Lillian DuBois Baker, Emma Sansaver's niece, to Betty Simpson Bisnett, Emma's daughter, January 11, 1974, in possession of Barbara Winters.

12. Mary, the Sansavers' first child, was born in July 1877 near Fort Benton; Isadore was born in March 1882 near Malta, Montana. Emma's date of birth is given variously as 1884 and 1886. School records are consistent in listing 1884, but according to a notation made by her husband after her death, Emma was born on August 15, 1886, and the authors have accepted that date. Emma and Flora were both born in the camp south of Havre. Fort Shaw Register of Pupils; Barbara Winters' Family Group Record; Betty Bisnett interview, March 2000; Winters interviews. For more on life in a Métis camp, see Dusenberry, "Waiting for a Day."

13. Notice of the death of "Edwin St. Sevier" appeared in the June 19, 1890, edition of the *Chinook (Mont) Opinion.* Baker to Bisnett, January 11, 1974; Campbell to CIA, October 24, 1901, LR 1901, box 1999, #61154, 75/11E3/6/13/3, NAW.

14. For more on St. Paul's Mission School, see Mahoney, *Lady Blackrobes.* The description of Emma Sansaver's life at St. Paul's is taken from an interview with Betty Bisnett, April 5, 2000, and multiple interviews with Barbara Winters. Mary Sansaver married Frank Dubois, a Métis contractor, and moved to Havre in 1895. Barbara Winters' Family Group Record; *Grit, Guts, and Gusto,* 270.

15. Fort Shaw Register of Pupils. Emma and Flora Sansaver arrived at Fort Shaw on September 29, 1897.

16. Madsen, *Lemhi*, 156–57.

17. Lannin, *History*, 20; *New York Times*, March 24, 1996; *San Francisco Chronicle*, April 5, 1896. Mabel Craft was the *Chronicle* reporter. Although this game is remembered as the first intercollegiate game between women, both colleges had been competing against area girls' schools for some time. The first recorded contest between teams on the West Coast was a November 18, 1892, game between Berkeley and Miss Head's School, with the prep-school girls winning 6 to 5.

Transitions, 1897–1899

1. Fort Shaw Register of Pupils. Known as the "Turkey Trail," the narrow-gauge railway that ran from the little whistle-stop station at Sunnyside (later Vaughn) into Great Falls was part of the Albert Railway and Coal Company line linking Lethbridge to Great Falls. Almost from the opening of the line, sparsely furnished, aging passenger cars had been interspersed between the coal cars. The ride was hardly luxurious, yet those who bumped and swayed their way along the precarious route found traveling ten miles by rail a welcome alternative to enduring the inteminably long—and not always reliable—wagon journey they would otherwise have faced. Pictorial History, 53; conversation with Emma Toman of the Sun River Valley Historical Society, February 5, 2005. A timetable for the route from Great Falls to Vaughn appears in the *Dupuyer (Mont.) Acantha*, September 20, 1900. See also www.crowsnest-highway.ca/index.htm.

2. Fort Shaw Register of Pupils. Although the Lucero girls were of Chippewa-Cree blood, they were listed on the Fort Shaw rolls as Piegans.

3. In a phone interview (May 21, 2001), Flora Lucero Dawson's niece Grace Lavendis described Flora's skills with the needle.

4. Measurements taken in St. Louis in 1904 show Emma Sansaver, at age eighteen, to be 4 feet 11 ¼ inches tall and 109 ¼ pounds. Document in possession of Emma's granddaughter Beverly Braig.

5. Campbell to CIA, October 24, 1901, LR 1901, box 1999, #611154, 75/11E3/6/13/3, NAW; *Havre (Mont.) Plaindealer*, June 13, 1903; *Fort Benton (Mont.) River Press*, June 17, 1903.

6. Fort Shaw Register of Pupils lists Mary Sansaver Dubois as the legal guardian of her younger siblings. The status of their mother, "living or dead," is left blank on the register.

7. Josephine and William's three children were born during their tenure at Fort Shaw: Irene in 1893, William, Jr., in 1895, and Hugh in 1897. Gidget Fleming, "William Winslow Biographical Data," compiled 2006. Though the authors believe he returned to practicing medicine in Lawrence, Kansas, after leaving Fort Shaw, by 1903 Winslow was back in the Indian School Service as superintendent of Genoa (Nebraska) Indian Boarding School. Samuel Mc-Cowan to Winslow, September 4, 1903, Chilocco Superintendent's Files, Oklahoma Historical Society (hereafter OHS).

8. *Great Falls Daily Tribune,* November 21, 1896; *Indian Helper (Carlisle),* August 6, 1897.

9. Campbell to A. C. Toner, August 11, 1898, LR 1898, box 1569, #37048, 75/11E3/5/26/3, NAW; Commissioner W. A. Jones to Winslow, August 11, 1898, LR 1898, box 1569, #37100, 75/11E3/5/26/3, NAW. In the late 1890s Great Falls, a planned city unlike most frontier towns, was a metropolis with a population of about 14,000. In Montana its only rival was the city of Butte, which was a little more than twice as large but hardly as elegant. U.S. Manuscript Census, Cascade and Silver Bow Counties, 1900; Murphy, *Mining Cultures,* 9.

10. According to Barbara Winters, Marie Sansaver's disappearance and death remained shrouded in mystery, with most of Emma Sansaver Simpson's children choosing not to delve into the matter. Interview with Barbara Winters; *Havre (Mont.) Plaindealer,* June 13, 1893; *Fort Benton (Mont.) River Press,* June 17, 1903.

11. Fort Shaw Register of Pupils; Campbell to CIA, October 24, 1901, LR 1901, box 1999, #611154, 75/11E3/6/13/3, NAW.

12. The Campbells arrived at Fort Shaw on September 9, 1898, the official date of Dr. Winslow's resignation. Fort Shaw Record of Employees; Campbell's "Report of School at Fort Shaw, Montana," August 28, 1899, in Reports of Independent Schools in Montana and Nebraska, 404. The authors' depiction of Campbell's personality is drawn from descriptions shared by his grandson, Fred DesRosier, as well as from many contemporary newspaper accounts.

13. Campbell began his career with the Indian School Service at Genoa, Nebraska, in 1890, and within two years, at age twenty-seven, he was named superintendent of the Omaha Agency School, the youngest man in the system to have attained that rank. Three years later, in mid-fall 1895, he was assigned to Fort Peck, Montana. F. C. Campbell, "Personal Statement," January 22, 1922. F. C. Campbell Papers in possession of Fred DesRosier.

14. Campbell, "Report of School at Fort Shaw, Montana," August 28, 1899, 404. Some three hundred students were enrolled at Fort Shaw at the time of Agent R. C. Bauer's inspection that fall. Bauer to CIA, Field Report, December 3, 1898, LR 1898, RG 75, no numbers available, NAW. In September 1898, a German-born physician, A. A. Wittke, replaced William Winslow as school physician. Fort Shaw Record of Employees.

15. Fort Shaw Sanitary Reports.

16. *Exponent,* November 1898 and November 1899.

17. *Kaimin,* June 1899. In actuality, lack of leadership and lack of a gymnasium would keep the university's women's basketball team from interscholastic competition for several years to come. *Kaimin,* November 1901. Adams's success in establishing girls' basketball in Butte would soon be apparent.

18. Fort Shaw Sanitary Reports. How many Fort Shaw children subsequently died at home during that epidemic of 1898–99 cannot be known. The seven students who were buried at the old military cemetery during that school year were Anna Koon, Assiniboine (age not in Fort Shaw or cemetery records); Jesse Lemon, Piegan, eleven; John Newrobe, Piegan, fifteen; Mary Purta [Putra],

Assiniboine, eight; Lulu Stepping, Assiniboine, twelve; Robert Stone, Piegan, eight; Charles Whitebear, [tribe uncertain, possibly Piegan], fifteen. "Fort Shaw Military Cemetery," compiled by Sun River Valley Historical Society members Burnette Batista, Herb Sharp, and Dick Thoroughman and entered on computer by Willard Cook. Tribes of students taken from Fort Shaw Register of Pupils. According to this cemetery survey, twenty-nine children from Fort Shaw Indian School were buried there between 1892 and 1910, the year of the school's closing.

19. Fort Shaw Sanitary Reports. Josie Langley "resigned on account of a temporary sickness" with the understanding that she "would be pleased to have the position again" upon her recovery. Campbell to CIA, April 19, 1899, LR 1899, box 1650, #19478, 75/113E/7/27/3, NAW.

20. Sadie Malley came to Fort Shaw from her native Jerseyville, Illinois. Fort Shaw Record of Employees; Campbell "To Whom It May Concern" Department of the Interior, United States Indian Service, June 22, 1906, LR 1906, box 1728, #57849, 75/11E3/5/29/3, NAW.

21. Frail from birth, Berenson was largely educated at home, but in her late teens she entered the New England Conservatory, intending to pursue a career as a pianist. When the course proved too stressful, she realized the extent to which she had been debilitated by years of inactivity. In 1890, at twenty-one, she enrolled at the newly established Boston Normal School of Gymnastics. Her improvement was so dramatic that, rather than return to music, she accepted a post as gymnastics instructor at Smith College, where she ran a rigorous program in Swedish gymnastics—and introduced her students to the game of basketball. Spears, "Senda Berenson Abbott," 20–22.

22. Berenson, "Basket Ball," 106.

23. Lannin, *History of Basketball*, 25.

24. Other aspects of Berenson's rules mandated two fifteen-minute halves and two points for a "field goal," one point for a successful foul shot. Fouls were called when a player held the ball for more than three seconds, when a player dribbled the ball more than three times, and when a player "snatched" the ball from an opponent. Berenson strongly advised six players to a team, although her rules allowed up to nine. Berenson, *Basket Ball for Women*, 39–41, 66–85; Davenport, "Tides of Change," 84–86.

More to Be Learned, 1899–1900

1. Agent Edward Yearian was still bemoaning Chief Tendoy's interference in his attempts to enroll students in the white man's school, writing, "not a single Indian on this reservation . . . will oppose him." Yearian to CIA, August 23, 1899, as quoted in Miller, "Resilient People," 11.

2. Pratt to Yearian, April 29, 1899, MC11, box 15, folder 3, ISU; Yearian to Pratt, September 4, 1899, MC11, box 7, folder 1, ISU; Pratt to Yearian, September 14, 1899, MC11, box 15, folder 3, ISU. Willard Burton went on to the Phoenix Indian Boarding School, where he was discovered to be almost blind.

Fitted with glasses, he did well in his work there. C. W. Goodman to August Duclos, September 23, 1905, MC11, box 16, folder 4, ISU.

3. Pratt to Yearian, September 14, 1899, MC11, box 15, folder 3, ISU.

4. Lemhi Tribal Census, 1898. Maggie Tingo Burton's Indian name was Dengutsi'i. Stories of the respect Minnie Burton and her siblings had for their stepmother and reports of Blind Maggie's beading expertise have been handed down through the generations. Interview with Drusilla Gould, July 24–25, 2000. Admiration for Maggie's work went beyond the family circle, as evidenced by the pair of beaded moccasins on display at the Lemhi County Historical Museum in Salmon, Idaho.

5. Fort Shaw Record of Employees. Crawford's role as recruiter to the Idaho reservations is documented in a letter from Campbell to August Duclos, May 21, 1906, MC11, box 61, folder 5, ISU. Curiously, Lillie Crawford's arrival date at Fort Shaw is variously listed as July, August, and October 1898. While published records of school employees at Fort Shaw from 1898 to 1908 consistently list Crawford as assistant matron, her name is conspicuously absent from handwritten faculty rosters between 1899 and 1904.

6. Merceline Rose LaRose was born "about 1886." Kutch genealogy drafted for authors by genealogist Gidget Fleming. Fort Shaw enrollment records show Rose LaRose to be fifteen years old in 1901. The other children born to Nettie and Fred LaRose include Leonard, born in 1889; Milton, 1891; Carnes, 1894; Ethel, circa 1895; Irene, 1898; and Raymond, 1899. Kutch genealogy; tribal family records in the Shoshone-Bannock Library at Fort Hall, Idaho.

7. *Great Falls Daily Tribune*, October 22 and 25, 1899.

8. Louis Goings's baseball team continued to acquit itself well in games against local clubs, and the nascent football squad was learning the fundamentals of the game under Perry Sargent, who came to Fort Shaw from the agency school at Fort Peck in the fall of 1899 as principal teacher. Fort Shaw Record of Employees; *Great Falls Daily Tribune*, October 13, 1901. Eventually, Chauncey Yellow Robe, Fort Shaw disciplinarian and Carlisle graduate, would take over the coaching duties for the football team. *Great Falls Daily Leader*, February 1, 1923.

9. For more on the development of basketball in the state of Illinois, see Johnson, "Not Altogether Ladylike," www.iha.org/initiatives/hstoricbasketball_girls_early.htm. The athletic schedule of the St. Louis High girls' basketball team is found in school yearbooks from the turn of the century and kept at the school district's central office in St. Louis.

10. While it is possible Sadie Malley was able to obtain a copy of Senda Berenson's rules as set forth in a June 1899 Springfield, Massachusetts, meeting of physical educators, it is more likely she would have read about the rules in articles found in various journals and newspapers of the day.

11. Campbell was correct in his assessment of the brand of basketball being played by the newly organized club in Great Falls. The members were young women, both single and married, who had "almost forgotten tennis and other

evening pleasures" as engrossed as they were in this new sport. *Great Falls Daily Leader*, July 26 and September 2, 1900.

12. Minnie Scoldbear—or Scold Bear or Scolding Bear—stood 5' 2" and weighed 130 pounds when she transferred to Fort Shaw on April 26, 1900. Her father, Scoldbear, was a farmer. Fort Shaw Register of Pupils. She would twice be listed in the lineup of the Fort Shaw team—in its first-ever game at Butte in November 1902 and in a game against the college at Missoula in January 1903. *Butte Daily Inter Mountain* November 26, 1902; *Missoulian*, January 29, 1903. According to Crow elder Joseph Medicine Crow, the people of the Crow Reservation have long assumed Minnie Scoldbear to be the Minnie whose play inspired the legendary "shoot, Minnie, shoot." Author interview with Medicine Crow, June 26, 2007.

13. Nine-year-old Emma Lucero's death was reported in the *Choteau Montanian*, August 18, 22, and 25, 1899. Rosa's infant was taken to the Sisters' Orphanage in Helena. Rosa married in 1903 and went on to make a good life for herself and her children. Fort Shaw Discharge Records; Richard Lucero's entry in *Blackfeet Heritage*, 159. Lawrence Lucero entered Fort Shaw on October 11, 1898. Fort Shaw Register of Pupils.

14. Jenny Johnson had married John Kicking Woman sometime before her death of unknown cause in spring or summer 1900. Nora Lukin, "My Early Years," 3; Mary Lukin to authors, January 8, 2006. Though the census records are inconsistent, she was likely in her late thirties or early forties. The Blackfeet census of 1893 gives her age as thirty-eight, the Blackfeet census of 1900 lists her as thirty-two. Mary was twenty, Charlie nineteen, William sixteen, Belle fourteen, James thirteen, and Ida ten at the time of their mother's death.

15. Campbell, "Report of School at Fort Shaw, Montana," August 24, 1900, 490–91.

Gateway to a World's Fair, 1900

1. Williams, *State of Missouri*, 257.

2. Leighton, "Year," 38.

3. Francis established a successful grain brokerage business before becoming mayor of St. Louis, 1885–89; governor of Missouri, 1889–93; and secretary of the Interior, 1896–97. He would later serve as U.S. ambassador to Russia, 1916–17. Jensen, "St. Louis Celebrates," 6–7; Rydell, *All the World's a Fair*, 157; Leighton, "Year," 38.

4. The Louisiana Purchase treaty, concluded by agents of Thomas Jefferson with Napoleon Bonaparte, added more than 827,000 square miles to the United States. The states eventually created out of that area included Arkansas, Colorado, Iowa, Kansas, Louisiana, Minnesota, Missouri, Montana, Nebraska, North Dakota, Oklahoma, South Dakota, and Wyoming.

5. Parezo and Fowler, *Anthropology*, 15. The "C" in F. C. Campbell stood for "Choteau," the name given him by his father to honor his friendship with Fred Chouteau, an early Indian trader in the Shawnee, Kansas, area and member of the legendary Chouteau family. Campbell to Clyde Campbell, April 22,

1932, F. C. Campbell Papers in possession of Fred DesRosier. Flora Lucero's hometown, Choteau, Montana, northwest of Fort Shaw, was also named for the Chouteau family, founders of the city of St. Louis and influential traders throughout the West. Cheney, *Names*, 51.

6. Jensen, "St. Louis Celebrates," 6–7.

7. Fox and Sneddeker, *From the Palaces*, ix; Leighton, "Year," 39.

8. Jensen, "St. Louis Celebrates," 7.

9. Fox and Sneddeker, *From the Palaces*, 8.

School Spirit, 1900–1901

1. Campbell to CIA, July 16, 1900, LR 1900, box 1809, #35072, 75/11E3/6/7/6, NAW; Campbell to CIA, November 20, 1900, LR 1900, box 1848, #58527, 75/11E3/6/8/5, NAW.

2. Lizzie Wirth departed for Carlisle in November 1900. Thomas, "Early Life," 93. Author interview with Grace Lavendis, May 20, 2001.

3. Lawrence Lucero's trip to Dupuyer is based on descendants' accounts of his being sent there to bring his father home, only to witness Philip Lucero's death. Author interviews with Millie Lucero, May 20, 2001, and Grace Lavendis, May 21, 2001.

4. Though newspaper accounts do not specify the tavern in which Lucero spent his final night, authors have cited F. H. Dean as the owner of the saloon on the basis that Dean held a gambling license in addition to a liquor license. Business Licenses, Teton County, Montana.

5. *Dupuyer (Mont.) Acantha*, September 27, 1900; *Choteau Montanian*, September 28, 1900.

6. *Choteau Montanian*, September 28, 1900.

7. Fort Shaw Register of Pupils. Isadore Sansaver had become a night watchman and Indian assistant shortly after his arrival on campus. Eugene Parker was the school farmer and band director. Fort Shaw Record of Employees.

8. *Great Falls Daily Tribune*, November 9 and 11, 1900.

9. *Great Falls Daily Tribune*, November 30, 1900. The Fort Shaw team that met Great Falls on Thanksgiving Day included Louis Matt, Thomas Bud, and David Ripley, Piegans; John Koon and James West, Sioux; William Bigby, Gros Ventre; Alex Sansaver, Chippewa; Roy Faulkner, Shoshone. The one non-Indian on the team was the captain, twenty-three-year-old Leo Grove, the school's new manual-training teacher. *Great Falls Daily Tribune*, November 29, 1900; Fort Shaw Record of Employees.

10. *Anaconda Standard*, December 9, 1900. At the turn of the century, Butte was the largest city between Spokane and Minneapolis and north of Salt Lake City, with a population of approximately 30,000. U.S Manuscript Census, Silver Bow County, 1900; Murphy, *Mining Cultures*, 9. Minstrel shows were a popular form of entertainment in which whites in "black face" performed skits in "Negro" dialect, with no recognition of—or apologies for—the inherent racism. In a case of high irony, Fort Shaw's own "entertainments" also frequently included recitations presented by Indian students in black face, for instance, a

soliloquy titled "Alphabetic Sermon" as given by John Minesinger, a Flathead student and staff member, mimicking a "colored preacher." *Great Falls Daily Tribune,* May 30, 1904.

Carlisle's football team, coached by the legendary Glenn "Pop" Warner, had risen to prominence by the turn of the century. See Jenkins, *Real All-Americans,* for the full story of the Carlisle program, including its impact on the game as well as the players.

11. Two hundred fifty pounds of turkey and six gallons of cranberries were ordered for the Christmas 1900 dinner. The other menu items came from the school's fields and kitchens. Campbell to CIA, November 19, 1900, LR 1900, box 1857, #58525, 75/11E3/6/8/5, NAW; Friesen, "Golden Rule Days."

12. By the time football became an interscholastic sport at Fort Shaw, safety had become a major issue, and players were required to wear helmets, an India rubber nose-guard, a broad rubber collar around the neck, leather wristlets, a padded frame across the abdomen, shin guards, and spiked leather shoes. *Great Falls Daily Leader,* October 19, 1901. At the turn of the twentieth century, Butterick's pattern was the choice of most schools that made their own basketball uniforms. The pattern is found in the sports equipment archives of the American History Museum, Smithsonian Institution. Authors' visit, September 2002.

New Connections and Old, 1901

1. Yearian to CIA, April 2, 1901, MC11, box 9, folder 1, ISU.

2. Rose LaRose and her brother, Leonard, entered Fort Shaw on April 3, 1901. Leonard appears as nineteen on the record, but he was actually twelve at the time of his enrollment. Fort Shaw Register of Pupils; tribal family records in the Shoshone-Bannock Library, Fort Hall, Idaho; Kutch Genealogy.

3. The Shoshone and Bannock peoples were originally distinct nations, and their primary difference was language. But because the two tribes often intermarried, most Shoshone and Bannock were bilingual by 1900. Zimmerman, "Fort Hall Story," 10. The LaRose and Kutch families know very little about Rose's father, Fred, though the name LaRose would suggest that he was Métis. Author interview with Rex LaRose, January 26, 2002.

4. Richard Snell ran away on March 14, 1901 (after reentering school on March 1), and would run away again on November 15, 1901. William Healy ran away on April 22, 1901. James Johnson ran away twice in the 1901–1902 school year, once in the early fall, once during spring term. He was dismissed after the second offense. Fort Shaw Discharge Records. Though many, if not all, white fathers of Indian children expressed support of those children remaining in school, in reality once a boy was old enough to take on farming and ranching responsibilities, his running away was often accepted by parents. Whatever their own reasons for deciding not to force their runaway sons to return to school might have been, James Snell and Colonel Healy were by no means alone in that decision.

5. *Great Falls Daily Tribune,* May 26, 1901. Paris Gibson was the "father of Great Falls," having founded the settlement in the early 1880s. He subsequently

served as the city's mayor before taking his seat in the U.S. Senate in March 1901. Malone, Roeder, and Lang, *Montana*, 179, 220.

6. *Great Falls Daily Tribune*, May 26, 1901.

7. Campbell, "Report of School at Fort Shaw, Montana," August 27, 1901, 543. Campbell made sure that year that both statesmen received copies of his annual report to the commissioner of Indian affairs.

8. Susan Wirth was described as a "stout, distinguished woman." Thomas, "Early Life," 75–76.

9. A series of letters between the Fort Peck agent, C. R. Scobey, and Washington between April 1900 and March 1901 documents the inspector's accounts of Wirth's problems as a baker. Scobey to CIA, April 28, 1900, LR 1900, box 1780, #21536, 75/11E3/6/7/3, NAW; February 28, 1901, LR 1901, box 1895, #12581, 75/11E3/6/7/3, NAW.

10. Jacob Wirth's letter is enclosed in Scobey's February 28, 1901, letter to the CIA.

11. Lukin, "My Early Years," 3; Connelly, "My Mother's Life," 2.

12. Author interviews with Barbara Winters. Frank Dubois, husband of Mary Sansaver Dubois, was of Métis descent. The couple had ten children, seven sons and three daughters. Mary Sansaver Dubois obituary, *Havre (Mont.) Daily News*, February 19, 1935.

13. Born at the agency hospital on November 24, 1900, Alice Snell died there on January 3, 1901. A baby boy, James, was born to Fanny Black Digger Snell on September 9, 1901, within weeks of Katie's return to Fort Shaw. James Snell to Mary Snell Sansaver, March 14, 1910.

14. According to Erma Stinson, a native of Sun River, the local team was formed by Superintendent Campbell and was not connected directly with the Sun River School. Author interviews with Erma Stinson, May 2001; Emma Toman, Sun River Valley (Mont.) Historical Society, January 3, 2006; Judy Ellinghausen, Cascade County (Mont.) Historical Society, January 11, 2006. Edna Blossom Jenkins was the daughter of Howard Blossom, co-owner of the Hastie and Blossom Saloon. *Pictorial History*, 105; author interview with Emma Toman, April 19, 2001. The Sun River team that was eventually formed had Edna Blossom, captain, at center, Norma Robertson and Ida Rhein at forward, Eva Strong and Julia Price at guard, and Mazie Sherman as a substitute. *Great Falls Daily Tribune*, May 21, 1903.

Staking Out the Fair, St. Louis 1901

1. Jensen, "St. Louis Celebrates," 8.

2. Fox and Sneddeker, *From the Palaces*, 9.

3. Ibid., 5–7

4. Ibid., 6–7

5. Jensen, "St. Louis Celebrates," 8.

6. Parezo and Fowler, *Anthropology*, 19, 26; Rydell, *All the Word's a Fair*, 159–60.

7. Parezo and Fowler, *Anthropology*, 26–27; Rydell, *All the World's a Fair*, 160–62. McGee's initials are used here without periods and closed up, in the

way he himself treated the name. McGee was a complex man. Though he was frequently referred to as "Dr. McGee," he had no such academic degree. Though he had headed the Bureau of American Ethnology, he had left that post under a cloud of financial irregularity. Rydell, *All the World's a Fair*, 160. William Holmes, whose reputation actually exceeded McGee's in anthropology and museology, was the LPEC anthropology committee's initial contact, but McGee was eventually appointed the director of the fair's anthropology department. Parezo and Fowler, *Anthropology*, 24, 26.

8. Parezo and Fowler, *Anthropology*, 27.

The Team Takes Shape, 1901–1902

1. Urs, "Joe Butch," 149; Genie Butch's name appears variously on tribal and school records as "Genie" and "Jennie." Her Valley County (Montana) marriage license of January 6, 1908, lists her as "Gennie." Because she is most often identified as "Genie," the authors have chosen to standardize on that form.

2. Joe Butch was fifty-one at the time he married thirty-six-year-old Susan. 1897 Fort Peck Assiniboine Census; 1900 Valley County (Montana) Census; Mary Helland to authors, May 30, 2004; *Wolf Point (Mont.) Herald*, March 27, 1931.

3. Fred Campbell's love of fine horses was legendary. During his years at Fort Shaw he kept a trotting team of "as lusty a pair of sorrel bronchos as ever faced a Montana blizzard." "Old Timers," 252. Fred DesRosier, Campbell's grandson, recalls the fine horses Campbell kept on his sheep ranch in Meagher County. Interview with Fred DesRosier, April 29, 2002.

4. A-nin-ta-tca'n-gu Wa-ka'n (Alone on a Sacred Trail), Joe Butch's first wife, had drowned in the Missouri River in November 1892. Mary Helland interview with Bob Westland, May 30, 2004. Her name is taken from G. W. Wood to CIA, March 17, 1886, LR 1886, box 298, #8958, 75/11E3/4/13/6, NAW. Genie Butch's horsemanship was widely acknowledged. During her years at Fort Shaw, she rode in races at the Cascade County Fair. *Great Falls Daily Tribune*, September 21, 23, and 25, 1905.

5. Genie Butch entered Fort Shaw as a fifteen-year-old on September 10, 1901. She was placed in the fourth grade. She was 5' 3" and 113 pounds. Fort Shaw Register of Pupils.

6. *Great Falls Daily Leader*, October 11, 1901.

7. Ibid.; *Anaconda Standard*, September 9, 1900.

8. The Fort Shaw/Great Falls team defeated the university in Missoula by a score of 5 to 0; defeated Helena High at Black Eagle Park in Great Falls by a score of 10 to 0; played to a scoreless tie in a rematch in Helena; and were defeated in Butte by a score of 7 to 0. *Great Falls Daily Leader,* October 21, 22, and 29, November 1, 2, 27, 29, and 30, 1901; *Anaconda Standard*, October 27 and November 3, 1901. Just as shoemaking instructor Louis Goings had pitched for the Fort Shaw baseball team, at least two adult men played for the Great Falls/Fort Shaw football team: Leo Grove, the manual training teacher at the

Indian school, and F. W. Preston, professor at Great Falls Commercial College. *Anaconda Standard*, November 29, 1901.

9. *Great Falls Daily Leader*, November 29, 1901; *Anaconda Standard*, November 29, 1901. This was the first girls' basketball game to be played before the public in Butte, although an earlier game against the girls from the university at Missoula had been scheduled for November 16 in Butte, with a rematch scheduled in Missoula. These games may or may not have actually materialized, and if the university team did come to Butte on November 16, that game was apparently another example of a behind-closed-doors contest. *Kaimin*, November 1901. From 1901 to 1908 St. Patrick's High School was housed with St. Patrick's Elementary School and had no "athletic department" as such. The girls from St. Patrick's were first called the "Parochials" and by 1903 were the "Independents." Authors' interview with Patrick Kearney of Butte, August 31, 2006.

10. *Anaconda Standard*, November 29 and December 8, 1901. Though many, perhaps most, of the proposed games failed to materialize, enough were played to call the 1901–1902 series of matches "a season." W. J. Adams seemed to have primary control over all the girls' and women's basketball teams in Butte, and Butte High was declared unofficial state champions that first season of intercity play. *Anaconda Standard*, December 8, 12, 13, and 29, 1901, and January 16 and February 28, 1902. The authors have assumed that the basketball team from Dillon represented the state normal teachers' college located there.

11. Yearian to W. J. McConnell, July 9, 1900, MC11 box 8, file 1, ISU; and Caldwell to CIA, August 5, 1900, MC11, box 8, file 1, ISU.

12. The Lemhi students who were enrolled at Fort Shaw on April 23, 1902, included Leland Bear, sixteen; Billy Warjack, twelve; Bessie Gunn, thirteen; Gladys Tyler, twelve; Julia Woodozano, twelve; Alice Pandoah, fifteen; and Minnie Burton, seventeen. Yearian to CIA, April 20, 1902, MC11, box 10, file 1, ISU; Fort Shaw Register of Pupils.

13. The women's basketball program at the university at Missoula was "severely retarded" in its progress due to delays in the completion of the gymnasium, which was not finished until early in 1903. Too impatient to wait any longer, the women's team played their first home game in Missoula's Union Hall on Friday, December 12, 1902, defeating Helena 12 to 7. Zach Dundas, "Hundred-Year-Old Hoops, http://www.umt.edu/comm/s99/sports.html.

"Basket Ball Is the Thing," Fall 1902

1. *Great Falls Daily Tribune*, September 16, 1902.

2. Gray, "Miss Estelle Reel," 384. Estelle Reel served as superintendent of Indian education from 1898 to 1910, a tenure almost exactly spanning Fred Campbell's years at Fort Shaw. For a comprehensive overview of Reel's career and policies, see Lomawaima, "Estelle Reel."

3. *Great Falls Daily Tribune*, September 16, 1902.

4. Gray, "Miss Estelle Reel," 385. The *Uniform Course of Study* was, in large part, based on the assumption that relatively few Indian children were capable

of mastering academic courses and even those who did would find little practical application for what they learned in the classroom. Reel advocated adding traditional arts and crafts to the domestic sciences to give Indian girls a means of earning a living. For the evolution of pedagogy in relation to Indian children, see Lomawaima and McCarty, *To Remain an Indian.*

5. *Great Falls Daily Leader*, November 17, 1902. Scheduling interscholastic games in the early years of the twentieth century seems to have been a haphazard operation at best. Campbell had begun negotiations with Butte and Helena High principals sometime that summer, but it was not until mid-November that the Great Falls newspapers spoke of the schools having finally "completed arrangements" for the Thanksgiving weekend games. And Campbell was not able to finalize the plans for the anticipated game with Helena until less than a week before the proposed game. *Great Falls Daily Tribune*, November 17, 1902.

6. *Anaconda Standard*, November 23, 1902.

7. After a number of boys from Butte High—as well as a significant number of male spectators who "do not attend the high school or never did"—engaged in a postgame row with fans of Butte Business College, the board of education declared that nothing like that would ever again be associated with the name of Butte High. The girls' basketball program was to be abolished—but not before the Butte High girls played the Fort Shaw Indians. *Anaconda Standard*, March 8, 9, and 23, 1902; November 23, 1902. Description of Josie Langley's weight comes from the *Great Falls Daily Tribune*, January 30, 1903.

8. The relative sizes of the girls have been established through news accounts of early games and descendants' memories of the heights of their mothers and grandmothers. *Great Falls Daily Tribune*, January 30, 1903; "Indian Girls Win Out" and "Fort Shaw Wins Again," undated news clippings in Nettie Wirth Mail's scrapbook in possession of Terry Bender, Mail's great-niece; *Bozeman (Mont.) Avant Courier*, April 3, 1903. Ironically, the exact measurements of the girls on the team could have been established had they not been en route to St. Louis that day in June of 1904 when all student heights and weights were recorded. Fort Shaw Register of Pupils.

9. Testimony to Nettie Wirth's long arms and strong legs is the inheritance of a great-granddaughter, a volleyball player with a thirty-inch standing leap. Interview with Winona and Nicole Weber, granddaughter and great-granddaughter of Nettie Wirth Mail, September 2004.

10. Delia Gebeau arrived at Fort Shaw on September 10, 1902, two days after her fifteenth birthday. Fort Shaw Register of Pupils. The year she turned six, she had followed three older sisters to St. Ignatius. Delia Gebeau Ladderoute obituary, *Ronan Pioneer*, January 23, 1958. Delia's father, Henry Gebeau, was a soldier posted to Fort Spokane who had settled among the Colville band in the mid-nineteenth century, adopted their customs, and married one of their number, Cecile Shaw. When the Colville band was ordered to join the Southern Spokanes on a new reservation on the Spokane River, the Gebeaus loaded up their goods and eight children and made the wagon journey to Montana,

moving onto the Flathead Reservation as soon as the Spokanes were allowed to claim allotments there. Born on the reservation on September 8, 1887, Delia was the last of the ten Gebeau children and far younger than her oldest brothers and sisters. Her mother died when she was still an infant, and at the time she entered Fort Shaw she and her father were making their home with her brother, Oscar. Two of Oscar's children, Mary and Joe, were also attending Fort Shaw. Flathead Records, Salish Kootenai College, Pablo, Montana; Frenchtown Historical Society, *Frenchtown Valley Footprints*, 24.

The Flathead Reservation was established in 1855 for the combined Salish, Kootenai, and Pend d'Oreilles tribes; other related tribes were later allowed to move onto the reserve. Interview with Gene Felsman, librarian and tribal archivist at Salish Kootenai College, Pablo, Montana, March 2000.

11. Born in 1876, Fred C. Preston, a native of Platteville, Wisconsin, established Great Falls Commercial College in 1900 in partnership with Samuel H. Bauman. Young and single (though not exactly high-school age), Preston played on the Fort Shaw/Great Falls football team in 1901. Information compiled by Kenneth G. Robison from census records, Great Falls city directories, and newspaper accounts of athletic events in Cascade County and around the state. Preston was to remain a major figure on the local sports scene, serving as umpire or referee for many athletic events. Undated clippings about games in Helena and Bozeman in Nettie Wirth Mail's scrapbook; *Anaconda Daily Standard*, March 14, 1903; *Great Falls Daily Tribune*, June 25, 1903. Preston's unsuccessful attempts to get a football team organized for the 1902–1903 season are noted in the *Great Falls Daily Leader*, October 2 and November 8, 1902; *Great Falls Daily Tribune*, October 4 and 5, 1902. As of early October, some of the Great Falls girls were "planning to organize a basketball team, but no great progress in the movement has yet been made." *Great Falls Daily Tribune*, October 4, 1902.

12. *Great Falls Daily Leader*, November 17, 1902.

13. During a visit to the Smithsonian's Museum of American History in the summer of 2002, the authors were shown the Butterick pattern utilized by most girls' basketball teams at the turn of the nineteenth century. Blue serge bloomers and a middy blouse of the kind worn by the Fort Shaw girls were also seen in the Smithsonian's archival storage.

14. Jennie Parker, wife of Eugene Parker, Fort Shaw farmer and band director, was the school seamstress in 1902–1903. Fort Shaw Record of Employees. Gen Healy Adams described the uniforms in "Three Survivors in This Area of Famous Indian Girls' Team," undated *Phillips County News* clipping in Donita Nordlund's family scrapbook. Joe Abbott, son of one of the boys in Louis Goings's cobbler shop, told the authors in a spring 2000 interview that at one point the basketball shoes were made on the campus.

Because no newspaper accounts—other than the game-day *Butte Inter Mountain*—list Fort Shaw's lineup beyond the girls on the starting five, the authors have assumed that Minnie Scoldbear and Mattie Hayes, both of whom were mentioned in the *Inter Mountain* article and both of whom were pictured

in Helena's *Daily Montanian* of November 29, 1902, were the substitutes chosen for the November games. Neither saw action, since only injury would allow
substitutes to come into the game.

15. *Anaconda Standard,* November 23, 1902. The paper noted that the
Assiniboine, Cheyenne, and Crow tribes were represented on the Fort Shaw
team. In actuality the Assiniboine, Crow, Lemhi Shoshone, Chippewa-Cree,
and Piegan tribes were represented. Two of the girls were "full-blood" Indians,
Minnie Burton and Minnie Scoldbear. In contrast to Butte's emphasis on the
clash between the races, the November 17, 1902, *Great Falls Daily Tribune* article placed no emphasis on race.

16. *Butte Inter Mountain,* November 23, 1902.

Testing Their Mettle, Thanksgiving 1902

1. The authors' assignment of drivers for the wagons is based on their
knowledge of staff members listed on the Fort Shaw faculty roster. Harvey
Liephart (also spelled Leiphart) was a twenty-four-year-old native of Indiana
when he requested a transfer to Montana from the Indian school at Chilocco
the previous spring. The National Archives carry many of Liephart's requests
for transfer within the Indian Service. See letters of May 19, 1900, August 27,
1900, August 31, 1901, September 30, 1901, October 1, 1901, August 2, 1902,
and October 6, 1902. LR 1900, box 1823, #42102, 75/11E3/6/8/2; LR 1901, box
1788, #24920, 75/11E3/6/7/4; box 2000, #61276, 75/11E3/6/13/3; box 2092,
#27559, 75/11E3/6/6/1; LR 1902, box 2138, #54367, 75/11E3/6/17/3; box 2169,
#60444, 75/11E3/6/17/4. At Fort Shaw Liephart quickly became enamored of
Josie Langley, with whom he worked as the school baker when she was assistant cook. Fort Shaw Record of Employees. The couple would be married at
the school in December 1903.

Though the *Anaconda Standard* of November 23, 1902, indicated a "party of
20" was expected to travel from Fort Shaw to Butte on Wednesday, November
26, 1902, the authors have concluded that the number was closer to thirty,
given the membership of the mandolin club, the gymnastics drill team, the
chaperones, and the players, as well as John Minesinger and Louis Youpee.

2. John Minesinger was sixteen and living on the Flathead Reservation when
he enrolled at Fort Shaw in March 1899. By 1902 he is listed as a twenty-year-
old and, like most Indian assistants, he had held many positions, including laborer, gardener, and laundry assistant, which post he held in November 1902.
Fort Shaw Register of Pupils and Record of Employees.

Since there is no "Lone Calf" listed on the Fort Shaw Register of Pupils, the
authors have concluded that for the purposes of showmanship, Louis Youpee either used the English translation of his Indian name—which would
not have appeared on the rolls—or, more likely, chose a name for his mascot
role. Youpee, a Chippewa child from Cascade, Montana, was eight in October
1900 when he followed two older brothers to Fort Shaw. Fort Shaw Register of
Pupils. His repertoire in entertainments from 1902 through 1904 included at

least three comic pieces, "Nothin 't' All," "The Clever Parson," and "Our Girl Elizabeth Ann." *Great Falls Daily Leader*, February 5 and 6, 1904.

3. Still called the "Turkey Trail," the narrow gauge linking Sunnyside and Great Falls, had, by 1902, become the Great Falls and Canada line. The Montana Central connected Great Falls to Helena and Butte. Taylor and Taylor, *Butte Short Line*, 9. The broad news coverage of the games is known from *Butte Inter Mountain*, November 27, 1902.

4. At the turn of the twentieth century, Butte, Montana, "the richest hill on earth," was one of the largest cities west of the Mississippi. Open pit firing of ore and smelter stacks contributed to the air pollution that gave the town the sobriquet "the Smoky City." Novelist Dashiell Hammett described Butte as "an ugly city . . . set in an ugly notch between two ugly mountains." Hammett, *Red Harvest*, as quoted in Malone's *Battle for Butte*, 62. But among Butte's redeeming features were the mansions built by its mining magnates and the unique Columbia Gardens, a park of gorgeous gardens and amusement rides. See Kearney, *Butte's Pride*.

5. *(Helena) Montana Daily Record*, November 27, 1902. The description of Lone Calf's outfits come from reports in the *Great Falls Daily Leader* of February 6, 1904.

6. *Anaconda Standard,* November 28, 1902. The Fort Shaw lineup was the one Campbell and Preston had chosen. The Butte lineup included Vera Ledwidge, Jessie Hickox, Ona Proebstel, Floyd [*sic*] Patterson, Madge Bray, Margaret Driscoll, and Laura Mills, according to *Butte Inter Mountain* of November 27. However, on the day after the game the *Anaconda Standard* listed Mabel Brady, rather than Madge Bray, and Miss Lee rather than Laura Mills.

7. *Anaconda Standard*, November 23, 1902.

8. *Anaconda Standard*, November 28, 1902. *Montana Daily Record*, November 27, 1902; *Butte Inter Mountain*, November 28, 1902. Jessie Hickox is called "Bessie" by the *Daily Record*.

9. *Butte Inter Mountain*, November 28, 1902. While the Butte paper's account is more colorful and likely based on firsthand observation of the collision, the Helena paper noted only that "Miss Ledwidge fainted and was unable to play for a few minutes." *Montana Daily Record,* November 28, 1902. Curiously, while the Butte and Helena papers gave generous pre- and postgame coverage to the Thanksgiving game, the only account of the contest appearing in a Great Falls newspaper was a single sentence in the *Leader* of November 28, 1902: "The Fort Shaw basket ball team played in Butte last evening, [winning] by a score of 15 to 0 [*sic*]."

10. *Butte Inter Mountain*, November 28, 1902; *Anaconda Standard*, November 28, 1902. The *Inter Mountain* of November 28, 1902, published a cartoon with the heading, "Why Our Girls Lost." The cartoon depicts two of the Indian girls holding up a figure representing Louis Youpee, "the Little Red Warrior," with a tomahawk in hand and feathers atop his head.

11. *Anaconda Standard*, November 28, 1902; *Montana Daily Record,* Novem-

ber 28, 1902. The Pythian Hall was also known as the "Pythian Castle." *Anaconda Standard,* November 23, 1902. The authors have assumed here, from the *Standard's* wording, that the boys from Butte High sought out the Fort Shaw girls as dance partners. They have assumed that the racial mixing occurred as well at the dance the next night in Helena. Though such racial mixing in a social setting would have been unusual at that time in Montana, it is confirmed in a report from the *Bozeman Chronicle* of April 1, 1903, which describes a postgame dance where "the dusky bells [*sic*] had no cause to complain of a lack of partners among the college boys." Racial barriers became porous, at least where these particular girls were concerned.

12. *Montana Daily Record,* November 29, 1902. Though minstrel shows were in fashion, these two little performers were not in blackface but were members of Helena's black community, which was relatively significant in size at the turn of the twentieth century. For more on Helena's black community, see Lang, "Nearly Forgotten Blacks."

13. *Montana Daily Record,* November 29, 1902. The Fort Shaw lineup was the same as in the Butte game of the previous evening. Helena's players were Lucy Stevens at center, Winnie Cooney and Elsie Abrahamson at forward, and Maude Sagle [Nagle] and Polly Eckle[s] at guard.

14. Ibid.

15. Ibid. The game caught the attention of the press statewide. The next morning's edition of the *Missoulian* touted the Helena–Fort Shaw game as "the athletic event of the season." *Missoulian,* November 29, 1902.

16. *Montana Daily Record,* November 29, 1902.

17. Ibid.

18. *Anaconda Standard,* December 4 and 12, 1902; January 2, 1903; *Montana Daily Record,* December 7, 1902. The league remained unofficial, having not yet been sanctioned by the regional athletic board in Seattle.

19. The Butte school board's decision to ban girls' high school basketball was in line with similar decisions being made in other parts of the country. The original Butte Parochials had played several games in 1901, defeating more than one girls' team and trouncing a local boys' team 17 to 0. *Anaconda Standard,* January 22, 1902. This reincarnation of the team put together by Adams seems to have been a combination of girls from St. Patrick's High School and recent graduates from several parochial elementary schools in the city. Kearney interview, August 31, 2006.

20. *Great Falls Weekly Tribune,* January 22, 1903.

Samuel McCowan's Indian Exhibit, December 1902

1. Parezo and Fowler, *Anthropology,* 33.

2. Trennert, "Selling Indian Education," 212; Bradfield, "History of Chilocco," 61–62.

3. Chilocco Indian School (1882–1980) was located in north-central Oklahoma, very near the Kansas state line. The forty-year-old McCowan was a farm boy, a native of Peoria County, Illinois, who had worked his way through high school and college on farms and in coal mines. He then taught in district

schools in Peoria County and worked on a local newspaper before entering the Indian School Service in 1889. Bradfield, "History of Chilocco," 61–62.

4. The appropriation had been approved by Congress on June 28, 1902. LPEC "Final Report," 344. With the acquisition of the 614 acres to the north and west of the original Forest Park tract of 657 acres, the grounds of the 1904 World's Fair exceeded that of any other in size, before or since. Fox and Sneddeker, *From the Palaces*, 24–27; LPEC "Final Report," 344; McCowan to CIA, April 7, 1903, LR 1903, box 2274, #23155, 75/11E3/6/19/4, NAW. The vast amount of site work and organizational problems stalled progress on construction so drastically that, in the spring of 1902, even Francis had to concede that the fair could not possibly open on April 30, 1903. Parezo and Fowler, *Anthropology*, 31. He would cover this embarrassment by scheduling a "Dedication Day" of the fairgrounds on April 30, 1903.

5. C. H. Spencer to secretary of the Interior, February 12, 1903, LR 1903, box 2240, #11457, 75/11E3/6/18/6, NAW; Trennert, "Selling Indian Education," 214.

6. Parezo and Fowler, *Anthropology*, 61; Trennert, "Selling Indian Education," 215. WJ McGee was not officially appointed the director of the anthropology department until July 1903. Parezo and Fowler, *Anthropology*, 33. McCowan eventually developed a way to manage Indian Hill with little interference from McGee. Parezo, paper given at International Congress on the 1904 St. Louis Olympic Games and Anthropology Days, St. Louis, Missouri, September 10–11, 2005.

"Like Lambent Flames . . . across the Polished Floor," Winter 1903

1. *Anaconda Standard*, January 2, 1903. Weather report from *Great Falls Tribune*, January 4, 1903.

2. *Anaconda Standard*, January 2, 1903.

3. Ibid.

4. Ibid.

5. Ibid.

6. *Great Falls Daily Leader*, January 8 and 9, 1903. The game-day edition of the *Leader* would note that Campbell had guaranteed expenses for visiting teams—amounting to "between $200 and $300"—meaning "a considerable audience" was needed in order to come out even. At an admissions cost of fifty cents per person, breaking even meant enticing four hundred to six hundred spectators into Luther Hall. *Great Falls Daily Leader*, January 15, 1903.

7. The only mention in either Great Falls paper of Fort Shaw's New Year's Day game in Butte against the Parochials appeared in a succinct entry in the *Leader* on January 8: "The girls have met before and are evenly matched, the Indians winning out in a game played in Butte on the evening of the 1st by a margin of two points." However, thereafter the *Leader* printed a series of pregame articles of varying length and emphasis. See *Great Falls Daily Leader*, January 8, 9, 14, and 15, 1903. The *Tribune* seems to have adopted a wait-and-see attitude concerning the worth of this new craze, publishing its sole article on game-day morning. *Great Falls Daily Tribune*, January 15, 1903.

8. *Great Falls Daily Leader*, January 9, 1903. In fact, the *Tribune* of January 16, 1903, reported that the "Butte maids dressed in natty, short dresses of gray, trimmed with red."

9. *Great Falls Daily Tribune*, January 15 , 1903; *Great Falls Daily Leader*, January 16, 1903. Luther (or Luther's) Hall, later the Eagles Lodge, stood at First Avenue South and Fourth Street. *Great Falls Tribune*, June 8, 2000.

10. *Great Falls Daily Leader*, January 10, 1903. The Butte Parochials started Mabel Baker and Frances Dillon at forward, Stella O'Donnell at center, and Mary Rodgers and Annie Cosgrove at guard, with "Miss Sherman" and "Miss Kipp" as substitutes.

11. *Great Falls Daily Leader*, January 16, 1903. Regulations gave the referee the power to make decisions of this kind, even over the coaches' protests.

12. Ibid.

13. Ibid.

14. Ibid.

15. Ibid.

16. Ibid.

17. *Great Falls Daily Tribune*, January 17, 1903; *Great Falls Daily Leader*, January 16, 1903.

18. *Great Falls Daily Leader*, January 16, 1903.

19. *Great Falls Daily Tribune*, January 17 and 30, 1903.

20. *Great Falls Daily Tribune*, January 17, 1903; *Great Falls Daily Leader*, January 16, 1903.

21. *Great Falls Daily Tribune*, January 17, 1903.

22. *Missoulian*, January 29, 1903. The two teams did, indeed, stay at the Park Hotel, perhaps with a substantial discount for the Fort Shaw girls, who, on the basis of a single "home" game—and a loss at that—were already said to "represent this city in the games they play." *Great Falls Daily Leader*, January 30, 1903.

23. See, for instance, *Great Falls Daily Tribune*, January 23, 1903.

24. Simplistic as was Campbell's assessment of the improved relations between Indians and whites, there could be no doubt there had been a shift in the thinking of white Montanans who had come into direct contact with Fort Shaw students.

Before moving into Great Falls, Rocky Boy's band of Chippewas had been living around present-day Babb in the northwestern corner of the Blackfeet Reservation. Not until 1916 were the landless Chippewa-Crees given their own reservation when Rocky Boy's Reservation, by far the smallest of the state's Indian agencies, was carved from the large Fort Assinniboine Military Reserve south of Havre. Malone, Roeder, and Lang, *Montana*, 20–21. The characterization of the Crees is taken from the *Great Falls Daily Leader*, August 8, 1902.

25. *Great Falls Daily Tribune*, January 23, 1903.

26. *Great Falls Daily Tribune*, January 30, 1903; *Missoulian*, January 28, 1903.

27. *Great Falls Daily Tribune*, January 30, 1903. Though the article was more

accurate than anything that had appeared before in the press about the Indian girls, it misrepresented Emma Sansaver as Assiniboine rather than Chippewa and said that Minnie Burton had come from Fort Lapwai rather than the Lemhi Reservation. It placed Belle Johnson at the mission school on the Blackfeet Reservation rather than the agency school and spoke of her father as if he were still alive, despite his death a dozen years earlier. Joe Butch, Genie's father, is identified as a Scotsman rather than an Englishman. It is interesting to note that several fathers were mentioned by name, while mothers were identified only by their tribal affiliations. In citing the exemplary family life of the teammates, the article did *not* mention the scandalous divorce of Nettie Wirth's parents, or the mysterious disappearance of Emma Sansaver's mother, or the desertion of Josie Langley's father. While subsequent editions of both Great Falls papers would at times fall back on pejorative terms in describing the Indian girls, they were more often found in out-of-town papers.

The lineup given for the university women had Lucia Merrilees, the captain of the squad, at center; Maud Bryan at left guard and Elouise Bigbee at right; Dorothy "Joe" Polley at left forward and Mabel Jones at right. The substitutes were Ruth Ward and Carolyne Wells. Though the *Tribune* listed only two substitutes, the *Leader* of that same day listed four: Ward, Wells, Miriam Hathaway, and Agnes McBride.

28. *Great Falls Daily Tribune*, January 30 and 31, 1903; *Great Falls Daily Leader*, January 31, 1903. The start of the game was delayed because of time lost in dealing with such a huge crowd.

29. Despite the earlier criticism of Coach Billy Adams having served as the only official in Butte Parochial's win over Fort Shaw at Luther Hall, there seems to have been no question as to the appropriateness of having Fred Preston, an advisor to Coach Campbell, serve as one of the two officials chosen for Fort Shaw's game against the university team. The second official, Professor Tenney of Montana Wesleyan University in Helena, could be assumed to have kept things balanced. Ten fouls were called against the Indians, six against the university team. *Great Falls Daily Leader*, January 31, 1903.

In contrast to the play-by-play report of the game published by both the *Tribune* and the *Leader*, the *Missoulian* offered a single paragraph on the game: "The squaws were too much for their opponents and they virtually swept them off their feet." *Missoulian*, January 31, 1903.

30. The *Leader* described the hospitality of Great Falls and Fort Shaw at the close of the lengthy article of January 31, 1903, and again—in slightly different tone and wording—on the society page of that same issue.

31. *Great Falls Daily Leader*, February 4, 1903. Rev. George Edwards recalled attending such Saturday night "entertainments" at the Fort Shaw Indian School during his periodic weekend visits there. Edwards, "Reminiscence." As noted by Adams in *Education for Extinction* (173–81), Saturday evening socials, typically featuring checkers, beanbag tosses, and other quiet indoor games, were a sometime aspect of Indian school life. They were intended to "ritualize" male-female relationships "according to civilized standards." Dances were also held

on special occasions, with attention given to dance-floor etiquette. Boys bowed to girls in asking for a dance, then escorted their partners back to their chairs and thanked them for the honor. Gertie LaRance, mascot for the 1905 Fort Shaw girls' team, recalled learning to dance the minuet at Fort Shaw. Winters interview with Gertrude LaRance Parker, November 1990.

32. Josie's entanglement with the gentleman spectator was reported in the *Great Falls Daily Leader,* February 4, 1903. The authors have simply chosen to relay it through Belle Johnson.

33. *Great Falls Daily Tribune,* February 5, 1903. The story of the little girls' improvised game appeared in the *Tribune* in a press release from Fort Shaw. Neither the faculty roster nor the Department of the Interior's *Official Register* of government employees, vol. 1, 994, lists anyone named Stark as serving in any position at the school at that time.

34. Fort Shaw Register of Pupils; Fort Shaw Discharge Records. The three Piegans were sixteen-year-old Thomas Bird and eighteen-year-olds Parick Bullshoe and Michael Dayrider. Campbell's glowing year-end report for 1902–1903 makes no mention of the sizeable number of runaways, including Lawrence Lucero and James Johnson, during that school year. Campbell, "Report of School at Fort Shaw, Montana," August 29, 1903, 422–23.

"Like a Wall of Fire through a Cane Break," Winter 1903

1. W. J. Peters—once the school's tailor and now its disciplinarian—organized a boys' basketball team in the fall of 1902. Their first public appearance took place in a game against Helena High in the capital city on January 23, 1903, when they won in an upset, 13 to 11. Fort Shaw Record of Employees; *Great Falls Daily Tribune,* January 24, 1903. The editors at the *Tribune* were so accustomed to reporting on the girls' team from Fort Shaw that the headline announcing the boys' victory read, "The Indian Maids Win." The *Tribune* of January 31, 1903, mistakenly reported that the Helena boys' team would "accompany the girls' team" to Great Falls and play two ten-minute halves against the Fort Shaw boys after the February 6 girls' matchup.

2. *Great Falls Daily Tribune,* January 30 and February 5, 1903; *Great Falls Daily Leader,* January 30 and February 6, 1903. William Merrill was a thirty-five-year-old native of Michigan. Fort Shaw Record of Employees.

3. *Great Falls Daily Tribune,* February 5, 1903; special to the *Great Falls Daily Leader* from Helena, February 6, 1903. Kate Merville—her name is spelled Merrill in the special release from Helena—had actually played at least once previously for Helena High, but at forward, rather than center. Winnie Cooney and Elsie Abrahamson, Maude Nagle and Polly Eckles rounded out the starting five for the visitors, while Coach Campbell would be going with his usual lineup. Once again Genie Butch and Delia Gebeau were the Fort Shaw substitutes. Helena listed three substitutes—Agnes Hildebrecht, Mary Sheriff, and Lucy Stephens [Stevens]. *Great Falls Daily Leader,* February 6 and 7, 1903.

4. *Great Falls Daily Leader,* February 5, 1903. *Corianton* was based on the Book of Mormon and was written by a young Utah playwright, Orestes Bean.

5. The girls' game-day routine is described by Campbell in the *Great Falls Tribune* of April 28, 1903. The young carpenters had possibly seen games against the Sun River Valley team, but never a game on this level.

6. The Helena team was stranded somewhere "above the Nelson place at Riverdale." The Nelsons sent wagons to ferry the passengers across the river, and "a special train was made up" and dispatched to bring the travelers into Great Falls. Unnamed newspaper, undated clipping in Nettie Wirth Mail scrapbook. While the *Leader* of February 6 cites an attendance of eight hundred, the account in the *Tribune* of February 7 put the number attending at seven hundred.

7. The lineup for the Reds included team captain Eddie Gobert and John Ledeau, guards; George Rock and William Pierce, forwards, and Max Moon, center. Taking the floor for the Blacks were team captain Baptiste Couture and John Matt, guards; Charles Parker and Leland Bear, forwards; and Clay Rowland, center.

8. *Great Falls Daily Leader,* February 9, 1903.

9. *Great Falls Daily Leader,* February 7, 1903. As befitted an event sponsored by a women's club, the paper's society page carried a detailed account of the day.

10. *Great Falls Daily Tribune,* February 8, 1903; *Great Falls Daily Leader,* February 9, 1903. According to the *Tribune* reporter, there was "a noticeable difference in the height of members of the two teams," with some of the Helena girls "being head and shoulders over the Indians." The rallying cry "Shoot, Minnie, shoot!" first heard this night, has, for a century, been associated with the "world champions" of Fort Shaw.

11. *Great Falls Daily Leader,* February 9, 1903. During this first year of the unofficial girls' basketball league, rules were flexible, to say the least. The season seems to have been extended to fit the wishes of various coaches or to generate income. There was no firm notion of how to determine which team had earned the title of "champions." Indeed, Adams's invitation implied there should be two games, one at Fort Shaw and one at Butte. Campbell's reply specified only one game—at Luther Hall.

12. *Great Falls Daily Leader,* February 10, 16, 17, and 18, 1903.

13. Ibid., February 18, 1903. Though basketball was well established as a sport for men and boys in the East—and had been since its invention by a man, for men, in 1891—it was not until 1905 that it caught on among Montanans as a proper activity for boys. Late that year the *Anaconda Standard* ran a lengthy article extolling it as "not merely a girl's sport" and quoting "an authority" as saying, "[It] is not a game of 'beef against beef,' but essentially a game of brain, physical endurance and athletic activity. It is not a one-man game, but one in which five are engaged, displaying science, skill and tact[ics]." *Anaconda Standard,* December 6, 1905.

14. *Great Falls Daily Leader,* February 27, 1903.

15. Ibid., March 10, 1903. In 1921 Montana Agricultural College became Montana State College, and in 1965, when the name of the school in Missoula

was changed to the University of Montana, the school in Bozeman became Montana State University. See Rydell, Safford, and Mullen, *In the People's Interest*, 93–96.

16. *Great Falls Daily Leader*, March 12, 1903.

17. Ibid., March 14, 1903; *Bozeman Chronicle*, March 18, 1903; (Montana Agricultural College) *Exponent*, April 1903; "Fort Shaw Wins Again," unnamed newspaper, undated clipping in Nettie Wirth Mail scrapbook. Bozeman's team included captain Amy McPherson, Nellie Pease, Agnes Morris, Helen Jeffers, Belle Francisco, Carrie Penwell, Edith Houston, and Edna Kiser. Professors C. W. Tenney of Wesleyan University in Helena and F. C. Preston of Great Falls Commercial College were referees.

18. *Bozeman Chronicle*, March 18, 1903. The April edition of the college *Exponent* was generous in praising the "hospitable treatment" the team received as guests of Fort Shaw.

19. *Great Falls Daily Leader*, March 14 and 24, 1903.

20. The old school cheer "Bum-a-ling! Bum-a-ling!" was dusted off again and used as a rallying cry during the championship game played in St. Louis in 1904. *Great Falls Daily Tribune*, September 9, 1904.

21. *Anaconda Standard*, March 28, 1903. Fort Shaw's substitutes, who saw no action in this game, were Genie Butch and Delia Gebeau. Four starters for the Butte Parochials, Stella O'Donnell, Gertrude Kipp, Frances "Frankie" Dillon, team captain, and Mary Rodgers, were joined by May O'Connor, with Minnie McDonald serving as substitute. The Parochials may have been handicapped because of the absence of starter Annie Cosgrove, who was out because of illness. *Anaconda Standard*, March 27 and 28, 1903. Most likely "Minnie" McDonald is the "Mamie" McDonald who is listed in the *Anaconda Standard* of January 24, 1903, and appears in subsequent papers by that name.

22. "Indians Win," unnamed newpaper, undated clipping in Nettie Wirth Mail scrapbook. The *Great Falls Daily Leader*, March 30, 1903, gives the Boulder score as 34 to 6, while the *Leader* of April 28, 1903, cites it as 65 to 6, which is likely a misprint given the forty minutes of play and the constraints of center jumps after every basket. Only the Buffalo Germans, a men's YMCA team in the East, was recording such scores at that time. Boulder is some thirty miles northeast of Butte, on the route to Helena.

23. *Bozeman Chronicle*, April 1, 1903; (Bozeman) *Avant Courier*, April 3, 1903. The *Chronicle* listed the Fort Shaw girls by their tribal affiliations (not always correctly) as well as their names and positions. The starters for the college were Nellie Pease, center, Amy McPherson and Carrie Penwell, forwards, and Agnes Morris and Edna Kiser at guard. *Exponent*, April 1903.

24. *Bozeman Chronicle*, April 1, 1903; *Exponent*, April 1903; *Great Falls Daily Leader*, March 31 and April 2, 1903.

25. *Bozeman Chronicle*, April 1, 1903.

26. *Great Falls Daily Leader*, March 31, 1903.

27. *Great Falls Daily Tribune*, April 28, 1903.

28. *Missoulian*, April 2, 1903; *Kaimin*, April 1903.

29. *Kaimin*, April 1903; *Missoulian*, April 2, 1903. At a time when prejudice against American Indians ran deep in the state, indeed throughout the West, it is notable that the Fort Shaw Indians would go to Utah, not as representatives of their school, but as representatives of Montana. In a letter to the manager of the University of Utah team, Campbell explained that Fort Shaw played "20-minute halves and [by] men's rules." *Great Falls Daily Tribune*, April 26, 1903.

McCowan in St. Louis, April 1903

1. Fox and Sneddeker, *From the Palaces*, 18–23. Staff, a mixture of plaster of Paris and fiber, was made in shops on the northern edge of the fairgrounds. Lightweight and easily molded and cut, it was lifted and nailed into place on wooden frameworks. Construction of this sort—state-of-the-art for expositions of the era—resulted in buildings designed to look solid and permanent, though, with the exception of the Palace of Fine Arts, every building on the grounds was scheduled to be dismantled immediately after the fair's closing in December 1904.

2. Commissioner Jones was adamant that McCowan's exhibit be as distanced as possible from the Pike, or midway, where the concessions were likely to conjure distasteful representations of Indians. McCowan to CIA, April 7, 1903, LR 1903, box 2274, #23155, 75/11E3/6/19/4, NAW. Though McCowan saw the site as "a half mile from the Midway," it was in fact a mile from the Pike. The Philippine Reservation was designed to introduce American fairgoers to the country's newest possession, the spoils of the recently concluded Spanish-American War. During the fair eleven hundred Filipino people lived on the reservation, which included clusters of native settlements and a replica of the "Walled City of Manila." Fox and Sneddeker, *From the Palaces*, 181. Rydell gives the population of the Philippine Reservation as twelve hundred. Rydell, *All the World's a Fair*, 167.

3. Fox and Sneddeker, *From the Palaces*, 27. When the LPEC contracted for the lease of the new Washington University campus on the western edge of Forest Park for the duration of the world's fair, they took over the school's administration building, Brookings Hall, as their own. Brookings stood just a few blocks to the north of the Indian exhibit site.

McGee was not officially made the head of the anthropology department until July 1903, although the LPEC directors had long since decided that anthropology would be a major focus of the fair and were constantly consulting with him. Parezo and Fowler, *Anthropology*, 33.

4. McCowan to CIA, April 7, 1903, LR 1903, box 2274, #23155, 75/11E3/6/19/4, NAW; *Indian School Journal*, June 1, 1904, and October 1904.

5. *World's Fair Bulletin*, 6:43; Trennert, "Selling Indian Education," 214; *Indian School Journal*, June 16, 1904; McCowan to CIA, telegram, June 25, 1903, LR 1903, box 2317, #3933, 75/11E3/6/25/3, NAW. Like every other building on the fairgrounds, the Model Indian School would be ivory in color and built of wood covered with staff. McCowan to CIA, August 6, 1903, box 2345, #49926, 75/11E3/6/21/6, NAW.

6. McCowan to CIA, March 20, 1903, LR 1903, box 2261, #18545, 75/11E3/ 6/19/2, NAW. Haskell in Kansas and Genoa in Nebraska, along with Chilocco, provided the majority of students for the Model Indian School. In the end, in order to get the representation of skills he wanted, McCowan brought in students and encampment Indians from schools and reservations outside the Louisiana Purchase Territory, specifically from the Southwest.

7. The quote from Inspector Chalcraft was published in the *Great Falls Daily Tribune* on April 25, 1903, but McCowan would likely have picked it up much earlier in a communiqué from the BIA. Sometime late in 1902, McCowan had approached Campbell about a position at Chilocco. Campbell to McCowan, January 16, 1903, Chilocco Superintendent's Files, OHS. In May 1903 McCowan first approached Campbell in regard to sending Fort Shaw students to St. Louis, as reported in the *Montana Daily Record*, February 29, 1904.

Montana's Champions, Spring 1903

1. *Great Falls Daily Tribune*, April 7, 1903.

2. Delia Gebeau is not listed with the Fort Shaw team after the last game with the university women in Missoula. She may even have gone home to the Flathead Reservation from Missoula, though there is no record of her withdrawal from school. Her father was elderly, she was the youngest child in the family, and having completed the eighth-grade level at Fort Shaw, she had effectively finished her education. She would marry a Fort Shaw classmate, Isaac Ladderoute, two years later. Fort Shaw Register of Pupils; 1901 Flathead census; Salish-Kootenai tribal records, Pablo, Montana.

3. *Great Falls Daily Tribune*, April 17, 1903. Members of the Sun River team were Edna Blossom, captain and center, Norma Robertson and Ida Rhein, forwards, Eva Strong and Julia Price, guards, and Mazie Sherman, substitute. *Great Falls Daily Tribune*, May 21, 1903.

4. *Great Falls Daily Tribune*, April 17, 1903.

5. Ibid.

6. Ibid.

7. *Great Falls Daily Tribune*, April 25 and May 8, 1903. The total points (242) the *Tribune* (May 8) credited to Fort Shaw include the 65 points reported by the *Leader* in the Boulder game of March 28, 1903. A more accurate total might be 211. The legend that has attached to the Fort Shaw team over the years includes at least two victories over boys' teams—one at home in Montana, one at the fair in St. Louis. The authors have found no verifiable evidence of either game, though it is more than likely the girls would have scrimmaged frequently against the Fort Shaw boys in the gym at home.

8. *Great Falls Daily Tribune*, April 28 and May 7 and 8, 1903. In all, sixty-six business and individuals contributed to the reception and banquet. "Weather permitting," the postgame event was to be held at the dance pavilion at Black Eagle Park. *Great Falls Daily Tribune*, April 28, 1903.

9. *Great Falls Daily Tribune*, May 8, 1903.

10. *Great Falls Daily Tribune,* May 8 and 9, 1903. For the Independents, May O'Connor was playing guard alongside Tina Merkle, a newcomer to the squad. Another newcomer, "Miss Payne," joined Frankie Dillon at forward. The given name of "Miss Merkle" appears in the *Tribune,* June 26, 1903.

11. *Great Falls Daily Tribune,* May 9, 1903.

12. Ibid. The score was reported as 33 to 6 in the *Anaconda Standard* of May 9, 1903.

13. *Great Falls Daily Tribune,* May 9, 1903; *Anaconda Standard,* May 9, 1903.

14. *Great Falls Daily Tribune,* May 10 and 8, 1903.

15. *Great Falls Daily Tribune,* May 10, 1903. The Chippewa women had bound their heads "in vari-colored shawls."

16. Ibid. At one point the *Tribune* confuses Nettie with Emma as the injured player, though is later consistent that in noting that it was Emma who, after the game, "was compelled to visit the dentist."

17. *Great Falls Daily Tribune,* May 10, 1903; *Anaconda Standard,* May 10, 1903.

Taking the Gospel Back Home, June 1903

1. In late April Campbell announced an exhibition tour that included towns "along the line of the Great Northern." *Fort Benton (Mont.) River Press,* April 29, 1903; *Great Falls Daily Tribune,* April 28, 1903.

2. *Great Falls Daily Tribune,* June 3 and 9, 1903. The tour was originally scheduled to open with a Friday, June 5, exhibition at Cascade, but there is no evidence this game took place. *Great Falls Daily Tribune,* June 1, 1903.

3. *Great Falls Daily Tribune,* June 9, 1903. Though the "Great Falls Grays" were touted in the newspapers as representing Great Falls High School, Montana sports historian Ken Robison suggests that, like the "Great Falls Blues," the Grays were more likely a "club" team of young women. Robison to authors, February 2, 2006.

4. *Fort Benton (Mont.) River Press,* June 9, 1903. This article mistakenly notes that Emma Sansaver was "formerly of Fort Benton," perhaps because there were those who remembered her parents living in the vicinity when her older sister Mary was a baby. Belle Johnson's family had lived south of Fort Benton in Kibby, a small town on the Shonkin, before moving onto her mother's allotment on the Blackfeet Reservation.

5. No pregame article from the *Havre Plaindealer* has as yet been found, so it cannot be known if Emma Sansaver's name appeared in print before the game.

6. *Havre Plaindealer,* June 27, 1903. A special June 10 dispatch from Havre to the *Tribune* in Great Falls meant the citizens of that city—and likely Emma's teachers and classmates at Fort Shaw—read the details of her mother's murder days before the *Plaindealer* published the rest of the story. *Great Falls Tribune,* June 11, 1903. For further details on the disappearance and murder of Marie Lafromboise Sansaver, see Peavy and Smith, "Unlikely Champion."

7. *Havre Plaindealer,* June 13, 1903. In Havre, as in all the towns included on this tour, Superintendent Campbell spoke briefly of "the benefits of Indian education and of the progress made with the Indians who have come under Uncle Sam's educational wing in this section of the state." Although the two teams were identified as the "Blues" and the "Browns" on this tour, at other times they were designated the "Blues" and the "Reds." In no reports were the actual lineups of the two squads given.

8. *Havre Plaindealer,* June 13, 1903; *Great Falls Daily Tribune,* June 11, 1903.

9. *Havre Plaindealer,* June 13, 1903. Despite Emma's skepticism, Havre authorities had continued to work on the case since Marie Sansaver was first reported missing. They had, in fact, searched the well behind the slaughterhouse twice, in 1901 when Sansaver's brother first made that claim and again this June of 1903. No body was ever found. Inconclusive evidence and conflicting testimony finally forced the district attorney to close the case. *Great Falls Daily Tribune,* June 11, 1903; *Havre Plaindealer,* June 20, 1903.

10. *Great Falls Daily Tribune,* June 14, 1903; *Chinook Opinion,* June 18, 1903.

11. James H. Snell was born on September 9, 1901. James Snell to Mary Snell Sansaver, March 14, 1910.

12. *Chinook Opinion,* June 18, 1903. Dated June 12, this report appeared six days later under the heading "Harlem Hearsay."

13. *Great Falls Daily Tribune,* June 17, 1903.

14. Ibid., June 19, 1903; *(Glasgow) North Montana Review,* June 20, 1903. The Glasgow paper reported a score of "about 30 to 40 in favor of the blues."

15. *Great Falls Daily Tribune,* June 19, 1903. In noting "the very large attendance of delighted old bucks and squaws," the *Tribune* reporter betrayed the prejudice still attending Indian families back on the reservations, even if attitudes toward Fort Shaw students seemed to have shifted.

16. Sarah Mitchell entered school on September 9, 1903. Fort Shaw Register of Pupils.

17. *Great Falls Daily Tribune,* June 17, 1903.

18. Ibid., June 19, 1903.

19. Ibid.

20. Josephine Langley's name does not appear in the lineup after this tour, while Genie Butch is listed at guard in all subsequent games. It is notable that in late May Genie had played for the Sun River team in a game against a newly organized Great Falls team. She was the star as Sun River handily defeated Great Falls. *Great Falls Daily Tribune,* May 22, 1903.

"In All Ways Most Deserving," Summer 1903

1. *Great Falls Daily Leader,* June 23, 1903.

2. Ibid.

3. *Fergus County (Mont.) Argus,* May 31, 1931; Baldwin, "History," 12. Elmer Elsworth was a Shoshone from the Fort Hall Reservation, who was nineteen years old when he enrolled at Fort Shaw in April 1901. The authors have been

unable to find a record of a Charles Feather at Fort Shaw. Nor were they able to find mention of this time capsule in the contemporary press.

4. Campbell received the letter in late May 1903, as reported in *Montana Daily Record*, February 29, 1904. McCowan to CIA, March 20, 1903, LR 1903, box 2261, #18545, 75/11E3/6/19/2, NAW.

5. *Great Falls Daily Tribune*, June 26, 1903.

6. For the game, canvas was laid down over a section of the park's harness racing track. *Great Falls Daily Tribune*, June 26, 1903.

7. Ibid., June 26, 1903. Other papers around the county and state were following with interest the ongoing battles between the Indians and the Independents, and Fort Benton's *River Press* of July 1, 1903, carried accounts of both games played at Black Eagle Park.

8. *Great Falls Daily Tribune*, June 26 and 27, 1903; *Great Falls Daily Leader*, June 27, 1903. All five of Butte's points came on free throws.

9. *Great Falls Daily Tribune*, June 27, 1903. No newspaper accounts or other documents have been found to suggest that a tour to either Washington State or Utah ever materialized.

10. Emma Sansaver's attachment to the Campbell family is attested to by the fact that she named her second daughter Ella, after the superintendent's wife. Author interview with Barbara Winters.

11. Campbell, "Report of School at Fort Shaw, Montana," August 29, 1903, 422.

12. Ibid. Campbell's report also remarked upon the "noticeable change" in attitude toward the "importance of the Indian question to the State," a change to which he attributed "the friendliness and interest of the press and friends of Indian education." The two Great Falls papers—the morning *Tribune* and the evening *Leader*—were cited as having been "especially kind in this respect."

Looking to the Future, Fall 1903

1. *Great Falls Daily Leader*, July 28, 1903. Sullivan had served as assistant director for sports events at the Paris Exposition in 1900 and as director of athletics for the Pan American Exposition held at Buffalo, New York, in 1901. Lucas, "Early Olympic Antagonists," 261-62.

2. *Great Falls Daily Leader*, July 28, 1903.

3. The funeral service was conducted by an Episcopal minister from Great Falls. Campbell to Yearian, September 3, 1903, MC11, box 15, folder 8, ISU. Campbell wrote Yearian that Pandoah had died on September 3, but the death record in the Fort Shaw Sanitary Reports gives September 1 as the date of death.

4. Campbell set out for Idaho around September 6. *Great Falls Daily Leader*, September 9, 1903. The authors have based their depiction of Minnie Burton's means of dealing with loss on the fact that she seems to have always kept her counsel. For instance, until the authors showed photographs of Minnie in her basketball uniform to her great-granddaughter, Drusilla Gould of Pocatello, Idaho, no one in the family had ever heard of Minnie's career at Fort Shaw. Author interview with Gould, June 2001.

5. Sarah Mitchell arrived at Fort Shaw on September 9, 1903, in the company of her twelve-year-old niece, Lucy, daughter of her older brother, Daniel. Fort Shaw Register of Pupils.

6. The 320 pupils on campus that fall ranged in age from five to twenty, and, according to J. E. Mountford, Fort Shaw spokesman, those children represented "every tribe in the northwest." *Great Falls Daily Leader*, October 29, 1903.

7. *Great Falls Daily Leader*, October 29, 1903. Adams was not listed on the Fort Shaw Record of Employees and the source of his salary remains a mystery. His wife, Winnie, and their two very young children, Arthur and Walter, presumably stayed on in Butte. U.S. Manuscript Census, 1910. It is even likely that Adams only periodically spent time in the Sun River Valley as part-time athletic director.

8. *Great Falls Daily Tribune*, October 27, 1903; *Great Falls Daily Leader*, October 20 and 29, 1903.

9. Belle may have been made the captain by Campbell, but it is more likely that she was chosen by the girls. In any event, she exhibited the same qualities that were so valuable in Josie—a caring personality and leadership skills, which were also to serve her family and her community well in later years.

10. *Great Falls Daily Leader*, October 29, 1903. From mid-October to mid-November, Campbell was in Chicago to sell Fort Shaw cattle; in Olathe, Kansas, on family business; and in St. Louis to interview McCowan. *Great Falls Daily Leader*, October 14, 1903; Campbell to McCowan, December 2, 1903, Chilocco Superintendent's Files, OHS.

11. The boys who played for Fort Shaw that fall included William Pierce, Leland Bear, Standing Rye, Fred Roundstan, Bernard Striker, Jack Frye, George Rock, August Decell, Clay Roland, Clayton Lester, George Conner, Ben Strike, Philip Cockran, and Elmer Ellsworth. *Great Falls Daily Leader*, November 21, 1903. It has been difficult to piece together the 1903 football season. Two losses were noted in the papers, one to Butte High, 5 to 0, on November 26, and another to Montana Agricultural College, date unknown. *Great Falls Daily Leader*, November 27, 1903; *Great Falls Daily Tribune*, November 23, 1903.

12. The authors have had to use their own insights in assigning positions to the individual girls on the second team. Gen Healey and Katie Snell, both from Fort Belknap Reservation, were mentioned by name—but not by position—in connection with the exhibition game played in June 1903 in Harlem. It is known for sure that Katie Snell took Emma's position at forward when Emma suffered a badly sprained ankle in St. Louis.

13. *Great Falls Daily Tribune*, November 23, 1903. Although construction of the Model Indian School was to have begun in October, the contract was not let until December 2, 1903. McCowan to CIA, August 6, 1903, LR 1903, box 2345, #49926, 75/11E3/6/21/6, NAW; Francis, *Universal Exposition*, 6:43.

14. LPEC, *Final Report*, 344–45.

15. The Model Indian School was to be a means of showing the progress the nation's Indian children had made under the government's educational system.

McCowan's vision of how best to accomplish this goal expanded with time, but "entertainments" such as those assigned to the Fort Shaw contingent had been a part of his plan from the first, though the exact nature of those "entertainments" and the youngsters best suited to provide them came only as he began to gather the student body. *Great Falls Daily Leader*, December 28, 1903.

16. *Indian School Journal*, June 1, 1904; Campbell to McCowan, December 2, 1903, Chilocco Superintendent's Files, OHS. Club swinging was developed in India and imported to the West by British soldiers in the late eighteenth century. "Indian clubs" were swung in a series of relatively intricate routines designed to make the body supple. Todd, "From Milo to Milo," 8–9. Early programs published in local newspapers note club-swinging and dumbbell exercises by the Fort Shaw girls (*Rising Sun*, June 13, 1894; July 10, 1895; and July 3, 1896), but an article in the *Great Falls Daily Leader* of February 6, 1904, noted that barbells were a "new departure in Fort Shaw athletics." Early barbells were described as a cross between a wand and dumbbells, in that they were four-to six-foot-long wooden poles with wooden balls on each end. While men used iron barbells loaded with heavy weights for strength training, the lightweight wooden barbells used by women were a means of developing graceful movement while toning muscles. Todd, "From Milo to Milo," 10–12.

17. Frederica (Fern) Evans was a twenty-three-year-old native of Nebraska when she first came to Fort Shaw in the spring of 1901. Fort Shaw Record of Employees.

18. Such recitations were being performed at that same time at Carlisle and Haskell and other Indian schools across the county. For Lillie Crawford's work in readying the girls for these performances, see, in particular, *Great Falls Daily Leader*, December 28, 1903. Campbell assured McCowan that "a very good elocutionist has this work ["The Famine"] in hand." Campbell to McCowan, December 2, 1903, Chilocco Superintendent's Files, OHS. Scenes from *Hiawatha* were among the most popular pieces performed at government Indian schools in the late nineteenth and early twentieth centuries. For more on various "entertainments" at Indian boarding schools, see Green and Troutman, "By the Waters of the Minnehaha," 67–83.

19. The authors have assigned instruments to the ten players on the basis of interviews with descendants. For instance, Gen Healy's love of her "tater bug" was described by her granddaughter, Donita Nordlund. Rose LaRose's parents were professional fiddlers, according to Fred LaRose, Rose's great nephew. Katie Snell's daughter and granddaughter, Rosie Stuart and Thelma Warren James, recalled her playing the guitar. Sarah Mitchell played guitar and violin as well as the mandolin and was a member of the Fort Shaw orchestra, according to her granddaughter Gena Aslanian. While Emma Sansaver's favorite instrument was the piano, she also played several stringed instruments, according to her granddaughter Barbara Winters. In a letter to McCowan, Campbell mentions only "guitars, mandolin and violin," but the authors have determined that the mandolin club also traveled with a cello. See Greer, "Brief History," 50.

20. *Great Falls Daily Leader*, December 14, 1903. Harvey Liephart entered the Indian School Service in 1899 as a baker, assigned first to Chilocco, then to Fort Shaw a year later in the same position. BIA records in the National Archives are filled with correspondence pertaining to Liephart's frequent requests for transfers—to Haskell, to Phoenix, to Riverside, to Fort Shaw. A note attached to one Liephart request for transfer sums up the situation: "He is a nice young fellow, but too vacillating to stay long at one thing." Liephart to C. W. Goodman, superintendent of Phoenix Indian School, October 17, 1902, LR 1902, box 2176, #63120, 75/11E3/6/17/5, NAW.

21. *Great Falls Daily Leader*, December 23, 1903.

"A Great Thing for Girls' Sport," Fall 1903

1. Kindersley, *Chronicle*, 25–27; *Des Moines (Iowa) Leader*, September 8, 1903, Louisiana Purchase Exposition (hereafter LPE) Scrapbook, n.p. Missouri Historical Society, St. Louis (hereafter MoHS).

2. *Colorado Springs Telegraph*, September 6, 1903; LPE Scrapbook, n.p., MoHS.

3. Ibid.

4. McCowan to Sullivan, January 12, 1904, LR 1904, Chilocco Superintendent's Files, OHS.

Getting Ready, Winter 1903–1904

1. *Great Falls Daily Leader*, December 26, 1903.

2. Ibid. Rhoda Parker, who had come to school with Josie as an Indian assistant in 1893, attended her friend as bridesmaid. Joseph Mountford, the school farmer, stood up for Harvey, and the Reverend J. H. Little "joined the two in wedlock." The couple would continue to live and work on the campus through the 1908–1909 school year. Fort Shaw Recrod of Employees.

3. *Great Falls Daily Leader*, December 26, 1903.

4. Ibid., December 23, 1903, and January 8, 1904. At seven hundred, Chemawa's enrollment was over twice that of Fort Shaw. See "Chemawa History," http://www.chemawa.bia.edu/history, and Larson, "History of Chemawa." Campbell did not mention to his team or to the press what he confided to Superintendent McCowan in St. Louis. The Fort Shaw girls "will no doubt loose [sic] some games but then they will profit by defeat" since losing would "give them a chance to overcome their weak points," making them all the stronger by the time they got to St. Louis. Campbell to McCowan, December 26, 1903, Chilocco Superintendent's Files, OHS.

5. In requesting a game with Spokane, Campbell felt a need to assure the high school principal there that his girls were comparable in age and size to non-Indian girls, noting, "The Indians are from 15 to 17 years of age and with two exceptions are all about 118 pounds in weight." *Great Falls Daily Leader*, December 30, 1903.

6. Ibid., December 28, 1903. In fact, 150 students were selected for St. Louis, and only five schools—Chilocco, Haskell, Genoa, Fort Shaw, and Sacaton—

sent delegations of any size. Fort Shaw entry records for Lewis Snell are not found, but in the 1907–1908 record of students he is listed as a 22-year-old Sioux from Fort Peck. He is variously listed as Lewis and Louis. The authors have chosen Lewis because his father used that spelling in a letter to Lewis's half sister Mary Snell Sansaver, March 14, 1910.

7. *Great Falls Daily Leader*, December 28, 1903.

8. When examined in a photograph from the Montana Historical Society archives, the dresses appear to be almost identical, though the beaded breast-plates differ in color and pattern. Some descendants have questioned the authenticity of these dresses in terms of tribal identity—and the authors have no way of knowing whether team members ended up with dresses representing their own lineage or with dresses borrowed from another tribe. The beaded belt that was a feature of Katie Snell's apparently authentic Assiniboine buck-skin dress is in possession of her granddaughter Thelma Warren James. Emma Sansaver's buckskin dress has been preserved by her granddaughter, Beverly Braig; her beaded buckskin gloves have been preserved by her granddaughter, Barbara Winters.

9. Campbell to Yearian, January 4, 1904, MC11, box 15, folder 9, ISU.

10. Yearian to Campbell, January 17, 1904, MC11, box 11, folder 1, ISU.

11. *(Helena) Montana Daily Record*, February 29, 1904. Eschewing rhyme altogether, Longfellow depended upon rhythm and repetition to give his lengthy narrative poem the "feel" of incessant drumbeats leading inevitably to tragedy. The Delsartian movements taught by Lillie Crawford—and hundreds of physical culture and dance instructors in Europe and America—were developed in Europe by Francois Delsarte around the middle of the nineteenth century. Delsarte made thousands of sketches of prescribed movements, and those sketches were widely circulated and taught. See Delsarte, *Delsarte System of Oratory.*

12. *Great Falls Daily Leader*, January 15, 1904. There could be several reasons behind the exclusion of Fort Shaw—prejudice against the Indian and/or the desire to "even the playing field" come to mind—but the most apparent reason, or excuse, was that membership was limited to accredited schools and Fort Shaw was not an accredited high school. At best, it provided education through the eighth-grade level. Friesen, "Golden Rule Days."

13. Ibid. If there was any consolation to be found in their exclusion, Fort Shaw might well have focused on the fact that the league mandated girls' rules for basketball. When the conference actually came into being in January 1905, its membership included high schools in Helena, Butte, Billings, and Boulder, as well as the colleges in Missoula, Bozeman, and Dillon. The young women from Billings would claim the first conference championship in March 1905. *Anaconda Standard*, January 20, 1905; *Montana Daily Record*, March 27, 1905.

14. *Great Falls Daily Leader*, February 5 and 6, 1904.

15. Ibid., February 4 and 5, 1904.

16. Ibid., February 5 and 6, 1904. James M. Keller, program notes, San Francisco Symphony's February 16–18, 2005, performance of Schubert's Opus 50,

Das Paradies Und Die Peri (Paradise and the Peri), poem from *Lalla Rookh* by Thomas Moore. A Peri is an elfin-like, ethereal offspring of a fallen angel and a mortal. Though the child is barred from entering the gates of heaven, an angel offers a ray of hope: The Peri may be admitted if she brings a gift "most dear to Heaven." The Peri brings a repentant criminal to the angel, who declares "a soul forgiven" to be the gift most dear—and admits the flawed Peri to heaven. The moral of the story, as taught to Indian children, was clear. Repentance, rejection of their former ways, and acceptance of Christian doctrine were prerequisites for entry into the white world as well as for passage into heaven.

17. The movements adopted for the pantomime performance of "Paradise and the Peri," as well as for "Song of the Mystic," which would soon replace "Paradise" in the Fort Shaw repertoire, mimicked the Isadora Duncan style of modern dance. Given Lillie Crawford's roots in Pennsylvania, it seems plausible that she would have seen Duncan in performance during Duncan's years in New York (1895–99).

18. Fort Shaw Record of Employees. Clara Holt was a twenty-nine-year-old native of Indiana.

19. *(Helena) Montana Daily Record,* February 2, 1904.

Showcase Season, February–April, 1904

1. *Great Falls Daily Tribune,* February 5, 1904.

2. *Great Falls Daily Leader,* February 6, 1904; Longfellow, *Hiawatha,* part 2, chapter 20, "The Famine," lines 24–28 .

3. *Great Falls Daily Leader,* February 6, 1904. Performances in blackface were popular in the early years of the twentieth century, and the irony of having an Indian in blackface render a recitation in "Negro" dialect probably escaped the audience. It is hard to know if it escaped Minesinger and his superintendent.

4. Ibid.; *Great Falls Daily Tribune,* February 6, 1904, as reprinted in the *Chilocco Farmer and Stockgrower,* March 15, 1904.

5. *Great Falls Daily Leader,* February 6, 1904; *Great Falls Daily Tribune,* Feburary 6, 1904, as reprinted in the *Chilocco Farmer and Stockgrower,* March 15, 1904.

6. *Great Falls Daily Leader,* February 8, 1904.

7. Ibid., February 16, 1904. Weather conditions on that Monday can be inferred from newspaper reports of the tragedy to come. *(Helena) Montana Daily Reporter,* March 3, 1904.

8. *Anaconda Standard,* March 1, 1904.

9. Ibid. Campbell would have received the news late in the day on Tuesday, March 1, though the tragedy itself was not reported in the papers until Thursday, March 3. *Anaconda Standard,* March 3, 1904.

10. The authors have based this assumption on the fact that the Helena performance did, indeed, proceed as planned. Had the young players and performers been aware of what had happened back at Fort Shaw, it is hard to imagine they would have been able to carry on.

11. *Anaconda Standard,* March 2, 1904. The two Fort Shaw squads, first called

the "Blues" and the "Browns," were later called the "Blues" and the "Reds" and the "Reds" and the "Blacks." In the beginning the Blue team was composed of the first stringers, but the authors believe that in time Coach Campbell began to mix the lineups.

12. *Anaconda Standard*, March 3, 1904; *Great Falls Daily Tribune*, March 2, 1904; *Great Falls Daily Leader*, March 3, 1904. Fort Shaw enrollment records for both George Snell and Fred Kuhnahan are missing. In fact, the only mention of Fred Kuhnahan in Fort Shaw records is found in the death records in Fort Shaw Sanitary Reports.

13. Dan Kuhnhan returned to campus on March 2, the day after his brother's body was found. The four other teenaged runaways, all from Fort Peck, were Paul Dakotah, Willie and Frank Donsick, and Morris Tricot. Apparently assuming the older boys had waited out the storm in the barn of some friendly farmer, Isadore Sansaver and Lewis Snell, Katie's and George's older half brother and cousin of Fred Kuhnahan, had given priority to searching for the younger boys. Ultimately it was Dan Mitchell, a resident of Poplar and Sarah Mitchell's older brother, who rounded up the teens and brought them back to Fort Shaw on March 5, a full week after their escape. *Anaconda Standard*, March 5 and 6, 1904.

14. Richard Snell, William and James Johnson, William and Nettie Healy, and Lawrence Lucero are all listed as runaways on the Fort Shaw Discharge Records during 1900–1902.

15. Barbara Winters letter to authors, October 25, 1999, which contains a quotation from an interview with a Sun River Valley resident who told of her grandmother's memory of hearing the sobs of the students passing through town that early morning.

16. Fred Kuhnahan's grave is found in the cemetery to the west of the old fort complex. Fort Shaw cemetery list compiled by Dick Thoroughman, Herb Sharp, Willard Cook, and Burnette Batista, 2005.

17. Campbell to McCowan, March 9, 1904, Chilocco Superintendent's Files, OHS.

18. Ibid.

19. *Great Falls Daily Leader*, March 17, 1904.

20. *Anaconda Standard*, March 1, 24, and 25, 1904.

21. The Fort Benton exhibition game, played on March 29 in Green's Opera House, was won by the Reds, 14 to 13. *Fort Benton (Mont.) River Press*, March 23 and April 6, 1904.

22. Lizzie Wirth had completed a five-year course of study in less than four years, including nurse's aide training. She was also a trained pianist and skilled in Indian-club exercises, being able to work with as many as five clubs at one time. Thomas, "Early Life," 99–102. Her Indian clubs are in the possession today of her granddaughter Terry Bender.

23. On April 9, Campbell evidently still anticipated leaving for St. Louis "in three weeks," but McCowan was at that point notifying Washington, and everyone involved, including the Fort Shaw contingent, that the Indian exhibit on

the fairgrounds would not open until June 1. *Great Falls Daily Leader*, April 9, 1904; McCowan to CIA, April 8, 1904, Chilocco Superintendent's Files, OHS.

"Open, Ye Gates! Swing Wide, Ye Portals!" April 30, 1904

1. Heathcott, "Out of the Wilds," 18.
2. Daily Official Program, LPE Collection, box 30, folder 6b, MoHS; Fox and Sneddeker, *From the Palaces*, 37.
3. Leighton, "The Year," 43; Fox and Sneddeker, *From the Palaces*, 37.
4. Heathcott, "Out of the Wilds," 18. On opening day, construction continued on many of the displays. For instance, the Palace of Varied Industries, where some of the opening-day festivities took place, had been roofed over but was otherwise unfinished. Leighton, "The Year," 43.
5. Fox and Sneddeker, *From the Palaces*, 42; Leighton, "The Year," 43.
6. McCowan to CIA, April 8, 1904, Chilocco Superintendent's Files, OHS. In the same communiqué, McCowan advised Washington that he did not have enough funds—a total of $65,000, including $17,000 for the construction of the building—to support the school's operations for the seven-month duration of the fair. Given that the students would not be arriving at the school until late May, for an official opening on June 1, and that the school would likely have to end operations once the cold months of autumn set in, McCowan projected that he could maintain the school for five months, June through October. McCowan, "Resume of Government's Indian Exhibit," *Indian School Journal*, October 1904; *Official Guide to the LPE*, 110–11.
7. Francis, *Universal Exposition*, 6:43.

"Everybody Is Going," May 1904

1. *Great Falls Daily Leader*, May 4, 1904; *Fort Benton (Mont.) River Press*, June 3, 1903; Governor's Papers, MC 35, box 315, folder 10, MHS; *Great Falls Daily Tribune*, May 29, 1904. Within two weeks of opening day, fifty delegates and dignitaries had set out for St. Louis from Billings, Montana, including several members of the committee in charge of designing, opening, and staffing the Montana Building. *Great Falls Daily Tribune*, May 14, 1904.
2. *Great Falls Daily Leader*, January 9, 1904.
3. The Sun River game and "entertainment" occurred on Friday, April 22. *Great Falls Daily Leader*, April 19, 1904. The material from which the new uniforms were made remains unknown, since none of the uniforms worn in St. Louis have been located. The typical basketball uniform of the day was made from worsted wool, yet from her analysis of extant photographs of the Fort Shaw team at St. Louis, Patricia Warner, a fashion historian whose expertise lies in athletic dress for women, has concluded that the new uniforms were made of heavy cotton sateen. Warner, "Dressed to Win"; Warner to authors, November 18, 2004.
4. Campbell to McCowan, March 17 and April 10, 1904; McCowan to Great Northern Railway, March 23, 1904; McCowan to Campbell, April 30, 1904; voucher 86; all in Chilocco Superintendent's Files, OHS. Contemporary Great

Falls papers were advertising the price of a round-trip ticket to St. Louis via Denver as $49.50. *Great Falls Daily Tribune*, June 9, 1904. The route requested by Campbell, with allowance for stopovers en route, may account for the difference between the cost to McCowan ($53.35) and the price being advertised in Great Falls.

5. Campbell to McCowan, March 9, 1904; McCowan to Campbell, March 23, 1904; both in Chilocco Superintendent's Files, OHS.

6. *Great Falls Daily Leader*, May 10, 19, and 31, 1904. The Fort Shaw cemetery also contained the graves of some fifty-eight soldiers and scouts who had served at the military post between 1868 and 1892. Fort Shaw military cemetery records compiled by Batista et al., 2005. See 397–98n18, above.

7. *Great Falls Daily Leader*, May 31, 1904; *Great Falls Daily Tribune*, May 31 and June 1, 1904. The new pantomime was based on "Song of the Mystic," a poem written in the mid-1880s by Father Abram Ryan (1839–86). The elegy speaks to the soul's search for God and opens with the lines "I walk down the Valley of Silence/ Down the dim, voiceless valley—alone!" By mid-1904 Louis Youpee would have been almost twelve years old.

"Something to Remember," June 1, 1904

1. McCowan to CIA, June 2, 1904, LR 1904, box 2534, #36905, 75/11E3/7/14/3, NAW; *Indian School Journal*, June 2, 1904; C. H. Spencer to the secretary of the Interior, February 12, 1903, LR 1903, box 2240, #11457, 75/11E3/6/18/6, NAW.

2. The 150 students who would eventually populate the Model Indian School came primarily from five institutions—Chilocco, Haskell, Genoa, Fort Shaw, and Sacaton. A few were offspring of the traditional Indians who lived in the encampments on Indian Hill, but other BIA boarding schools—Phoenix, Chemawa, Santa Fe—also sent individuals, selected mostly for their musical talents in order to bolster the Indian School Band or to perform in afternoon concerts. In all, the student body came to represent forty different tribes. *Indian School Journal*, June 6, 1904; *Indian School Journal*, October 1904, 30.

3. *Report of the Commissioner of Indian Affairs, 1904*, 55.

4. Ibid.; *Indian School Journal*, June 16 and July 8, 1904.

5. *Indian School Journal*, June 6, 1904; *Report of the Commissioner of Indian Affairs, 1904*, 55.

6. Parezo and Fowler, *Anthropology*, 157–58.

7. Ibid.; Fox and Sneddeker, *From the Palaces*, 230. The electric railway ran on a double track, partly on the surface, partly on an elevated structure. A passenger could make the seven-mile round trip between the seventeen terminals in about forty minutes. *Official Guide to the LPE*, 24.

8. Daily Official Program, May 18 and June 4, 1904, LPE Collection, box 30, folder 6b, MoHS.

9. *Report of the Commissioner of Indian Affairs, 1904*, 55; Francis, *Universal Exposition*, 1:526; C. W. Crouse to McCowan, May 31, 1904, Chilocco Superintendent's Files, OHS.

10. Emma McCowan, who had served alongside her husband at his various posts, was a major figure at the school on Indian Hill. Their son, Roy, was also in St. Louis as a member of the Model Indian School Band. Parezo and Fowler, *Anthropology*, 97, 372.

The Adventure Begins, June 1904

1. The rainy weather is noted in the *Great Falls Daily Leader*, June 1, 1904.

2. The hand-crafted items traveling to St. Louis with the basketball girls were the second of two such collections of student work. The first collection had gone off with the Montana state delegation a month earlier to be displayed in the Montana Building at the world's fair. *Great Falls Daily Leader*, January 9, 1904; Campbell to McCowan, May 31, 1904, Chilocco Superintendent's Files, OHS.

3. *Great Falls Daily Leader*, June 2, 1904.

4. Ibid., May 31, and June 2, 1904.

5. Ibid., June 2, 1904.

6. Ibid.

7. The authors have inferred the girls' attitudes from multiple conversations with their descendants. The Montana Central took the travelers as far as Helena, where they boarded a Northern Pacific spur line that took them to Bozeman, a point on the main NP route by which they would travel across Montana and North Dakota and into St. Paul.

8. *Great Falls Daily Leader*, June 2, 1904. The schedule in the June 2 *Leader* differs from one appearing in Helena's *Montana Daily Record* a week earlier, with Livingston listed in place of Big Timber and with the North Dakota games listed as Dickinson, June 8; Bismarck, June 9; Valley City, June 10; and "possibly later dates in Minnesota." *Montana Daily Record*, May 25, 1904. Adams's role as the "advance man" is cited in the *Morning Call and Fargo (N.D.) Daily Argus*, June 11, 1904.

9. *Great Falls Daily Tribune*, June 3, 1904; *Miles City (Mont.) Independent*, June 1, 1904.

10. *Miles City (Mont.) Independent*, June 9, 1904. According to Valley City archivists, there are no records of a June 9, 1904, game between Fort Shaw and the "North Dakota state champions." Liz Hoskisson, Valley City/Barnes County Public Library to authors, September 15, 2003; M. Wieland, Allen Memorial Library, Valley City State University to authors, September 8, 2004. An article in the *Fargo Forum* of June 19, 1904, indicated the girls were in that city to play "an All Star Girls team of Fargo," not a North Dakota All-Star team. The second game is cited in the *(Fargo) Morning Call and Daily Argus*, June 11, 1904.

11. Glendive's involvement in interscholastic play is a reminder that the game had spread to the far eastern corners of the state by fall 1903. *Great Falls Daily Tribune*, November 23, 1903.

12. *Mandan (N.D.) Pioneer*, June 3 and 10, 1904. The second game in Mandan, the "match game," pitted "four Indians against five white girls." The Indi-

ans won by a score of 25 to 2, in an abbreviated, fifteen-minute contest. *Great Falls Daily Leader*, June 16, 1904.

13. The racism met in Fargo is evidenced in Campbell's letter to the *Leader* describing the team's reception in that town of some nine thousand people. *Great Falls Daily Leader*, June 16, 1904.

14. *Morning Call and Fargo (N.D.) Daily Argus*, June 11, 1904.

15. *Great Falls Daily Leader*, June 16, 1904.

16. Ibid.

17. *Morning Call and Fargo (N.D.) Daily Argus*, June 11, 1904.

18. Ibid.

19. *Great Falls Daily Leader*, June 16, 1904.

20. *Morning Call and Fargo (N.D.) Daily Argus*, June 11, 1904.

"A Veritable Fairyland," St. Louis

1. Twenty-seven railroads from all across the country came into and out of Union Station at that time. "St. Louis Union Station," http://www.stlouisunionstation.com/info. Though the *Indian School Journal* of June 15 does not include Lillie Crawford among the Fort Shaw party that arrived at the Model Indian School, she had left Great Falls with the group (see *Great Falls Daily Leader*, June 2, 1904) and there are multiple subsequent citations as to her presence and work at the fair. That particular *Journal* entry has other errors, most notably including W. J. Adams in the party, even though he had returned to Montana from Fargo.

2. For more details on the window, the architecture, and the history of Union Station, see "St. Louis Union Station," http://www.stlouisunionstation.com/info/aboutus.cfm.

3. For the life and career of Sarah Mitchell's grandfather, see Verdon, "David Dawson Mitchell."

4. A part of the infrastructure that the city had upgraded for the fair, a "train" of ten streetcars, each capable of carrying a hundred passengers, ran between downtown and the fairgrounds every minute or two. St. Louis Public Library, World's Fair website, "World's Fair," http://www.exhibits.slpl.org.

5. The fairgrounds were described as a "veritable fairyland" in an article in the *Great Falls Daily Tribune* of May 29, 1904.

6. Entrance to the fair cost fifty cents, or ten dollars in early twenty-first-century terms. The press of crowds at the ticket booths soon led to the adoption of automated coin machines. *St. Louis Globe-Democrat*, June 28, 1904. The Jefferson Guard, largely composed of veterans of the Spanish-American War, served as the police force for the fair. They carried no firearms, only ceremonial swords. Bennitt, *History*, 737; *1904 World's Fair Society Bulletin*, April 2005.

7. The wheel, designed by George Ferris for the 1893 Columbian Exposition in Chicago and transported to St. Louis, was 265 feet in height. Its thirty-six cars could hold sixty people each. A ride, two revolutions, twenty minutes in duration, cost fifty cents. Fox and Sneddeker, *From the Palaces*, 231.

8. Within a week of the opening of the Model Indian School, fair officials

had added an extra station on the Intramural Railway to serve the visitors to Indian Hill. *Indian School Journal,* June 7, 1904; *Official Guide to the LPE, 1904,* 24.

9. *St. Louis Globe-Democrat,* June 16, 1904; *Indian School Journal,* June 15, 1904. The travelers from Montana, coincidentally, arrived on Montana Day at the fair. Daily Official Program, LPE Collection, box 30, folder 6b, MoHS.

10. *Indian School Journal,* September 17 and June 15, 1904.

11. Despite signs posted on the main floor saying there were no exhibits upstairs, visitors to the school frequently attempted to slip past the guards and climb the stairs to see the student quarters. Parezo and Fowler, *Anthropology,* 139.

12. The number of boys among the students outnumbered girls by the forty members of McCowan's specially assembled Indian School Band. McCowan to CIA, March 20, 1903, LR 1903, box 2261, #18545, 75/11E3/6/19/2, NAW. Dorm furnishings were Spartan, but the rooms were clean, bright, and well ventilated. Washstands with running water were provided in the rooms, but the flush toilets were downstairs in the basement. Because electricity served the school, as indeed it served every building on the grounds, the girls were able to enjoy the pleasures of electric lights, rather than gas lamps. McCowan to John Dunn, January 14, 1905, LR 1905, box 2716, #11530, 75/11E3/7/17/5, NAW; Parezo and Fowler, *Anthropology,* 139; *Great Falls Daily Tribune,* May 29, 1904.

13. *Indian School Journal,* June 15, 1904. The Scenic Railway was an early version of a roller coaster. The ride was just a few minutes long, and the fare was fifteen cents, though students at the Model Indian School were often given free passes to it and all other Pike attractions. "Scenic Railway," http://www.tlaupp.com/scenicrailway.html; *Great Falls Daily Leader,* July 23, 1904.

14. *Indian School Journal,* June 15 and 16, 1904.

"Eleven Aboriginal Maidens"

1. The daily schedule is taken from multiple issues of the *Indian School Journal.* The Model Indian School uniform was specified by McCowan in a letter to Campbell of March 23, 1904, Chilocco Superintendent's Files, OHS.

2. *St. Louis Republic,* June 15, 1904.

3. Ibid.

4. H. B. Peairs was the superintendent of Haskell Indian School in Kansas. Parezo and Fowler, *Anthropology,* 97.

5. For years Geronimo and his band warred against the encroachment of the whites, and he was among the last of the famous Indian warriors to be subdued. Though he was now a federal prisoner at Fort Sill, Oklahoma, he had taken up farming, converted to Christianity, and enjoyed special privileges such as government-sponsored appearances at major events. He died at the age of eighty in 1909, five years after his summer in St. Louis. Trennert, "Selling Indian Education," 215. On the basis of proceeds from their spring exhibitions and the games played en route to St. Louis, the girls were each assured of a credit of twenty-five dollars upon arrival at the Model Indian School. Campbell to McCowan, April 25, 1904, Chilocco Superintendent's Files, OHS.

6. *Indian School Journal*, June 15, 1904. The previous day's *Journal* had announced that the concert would be held in the open air on the east porch of the school building, though all other sources cite the chapel. It cannot be known with certainty where the program took place.

7. *St. Louis Globe-Democrat*, June 16, 1904.

8. Ibid.

9. At times the school had more than fifty thousand visitors a day. Parezo and Fowler, *Anthropology*, 161, 141–50. The fairgrounds were closed on Sundays, and after chapel services, students were taken on chaperoned outings or were given the day to spend as they wished. *Official Guide to the LPE*, 146; Parezo and Fowler, *Anthropology*, 157–58. The classroom curriculum at the school included "mental and written arithmetic, language, geography of the U.S. and particularly of the Louisiana Purchase, and history." McCowan to Campbell, March 23, 1904, Chilocco Superintendent's Files, OHS.

10. Daily Official Program, multiple issues; *Great Falls Daily Tribune*, June 24, 1904; *Indian School Journal*, June 20, 1904.

11. *Indian School Journal*, June 16 and 18, 1904. The only aunt of Belle's known to the authors is Maude Martin, the wife of Belle's uncle Charles Martin, and Maude was a white woman, an unlikely creator of the dress. Lukin, "My Early Years," 3.

12. Daily Official Program, June 23, 1904. Annie Lucero was born circa 1898 and would have been five or six years old at this time. Telephone conversation with Grace Lavendis, May 21, 2001. James and Tom LaRose would have been two and one, respectively. Family Register, Shoshone-Bannock Library. Jimmy Snell would have been three. James Snell to Mary Snell Sansaver, March 14, 1910.

13. *Indian School Journal*, June 1 and 14, 1904. There were actually more than fourteen encampments, as the Pueblo peoples were represented by Acoma, Laguna, and Santa Clara groups, all of whom had separate camps, as did the White Mountain, Chiricahua, and Jacarilla Apaches and the Lakota and Dakota Sioux.

14. *Indian School Journal*, July 2 and September 12, 1904.

15. Ibid., July 1, 1904. Ella Campbell and Freda had spent the spring in Olathe, Kansas, with her parents, while the boys were in boarding school. In the summer of 1904, Mead would have been fourteen, Freddy eleven, and Freda six.

16. *Indian School Journal*, July 1, 1904; *St. Louis Republic*, August 24, 1904.

17. *St. Louis Globe*-Democrat, June 26, 1904; *Indian School Journal*, June 27 and 28, 1904. Dr. Winslow, who had ostensibly gone into private practice in 1898 when he left Fort Shaw, had soon rejoined the Indian School Service and by the turn of the century was superintendent at Genoa. McCowan to Winslow, September 4, 1903, Chilocco Superintendent's Files, OHS.

18. *St. Louis Globe-Democrat*, July 2, 1904. According to McCowan, Fern Evans "remained here but a short time and not long enough for her to earn free transportation here and back." McCowan to Campbell, August 16, 1904, Chilocco Superintendent's Files, OHS. Ada Breuninger, a Cherokee from Ar-

kansas, was twenty-four years old that summer of 1904. Having attended Haskell, she was teaching at Chilocco when Estelle Reel observed her in the classroom and offered her a scholarship at a teacher-training institution in Philadelphia. Completing her work there, Breuninger returned to Chilocco, and then came to the Model Indian School. Miles, "My Genealogy."

19. *St. Louis Globe-Democrat,* June 28, 1904.

20. Reel arrived in Great Falls on a tour of Indian schools in the Northwest on August 12. *Great Falls Daily Leader,* August 12, 1904.

21. *Indian School Journal,* June 29, 1904. The menu for the banquet included roast turkey, cream potatoes and peas, hot biscuits, fruit salad, lemon sherbet, and cherry pie.

22. *Indian School Journal,* July 2, 1904.

23. Ibid.; Daily Hotel Reporter, July 12, 1904, LPE Scrapbook, no page; Fox and Sneddeker, *From the Palaces,* 230.

24. After leaving St. Louis, Ada Breuninger accepted a position at Fort Shaw, where she and Minesinger were married in November 1904. Miles, "My Genealogy"; Fort Shaw Record of Employees.

25. Voucher #86, filed by Campbell on September 26, 1904, Chilocco Superintendent's Files, OHS, confirms the family's transportation to Kansas City, where Ella and the children stopped over with her family, and Campbell's continuation on to Great Falls, where he arrived on July 9. Jesse McCallum, harness maker from Genoa, had remained a friend of Campbell's since the latter's service as a teacher at the school in the early 1890s. "Personal Statement of F. C. Campbell" in Fred DesRosier's possession. McCallum appears with the team in several photos throughout that summer.

The Observers and the Observed

1. The eight Pygmies were all males. *Indian School Journal,* July 2 and 7, 1904. The positioning of the encampments on Indian Hill was intended to convey the degree of civilization achieved by the residents, from the supposedly most highly civilized—the Kickapoo, Pima, and Navajo who were closest to the Model Indian School—to the Patagonians, Ainu, and Pygmies at the far end of the village. The rising temperatures were first noted in the *St. Louis Globe-Democrat* of July 8, 1904, and reported in the *Indian School Journal* of July 15 and 16, 1904.

2. Genevieve Healy Adams recalled that rarely, if ever, were their exhibitions cancelled because of weather conditions. "She Was Born to Be a Star," *Great Falls Tribune,* April 3, 1977. According to her daughter, Rosie Stuart, one of Katie Snell Burtch's most vivid memories of that St. Louis summer was the bad taste of the water and her introduction to soft drinks. Rosie spoke of "Coke," but the authors have assumed that Katie would have been drinking the soda that was popularized at the fair, Dr. Pepper. Truax, http://ftp.apci.net/~truax/1904wf.

3. *Indian School Journal,* July 6, 1904, confirmed by an article in the *Great Falls Daily Leader,* August 1, 1904.

4. From a letter to the editor of the *New York Tribune*, which was signed "Impressed" and reprinted in full in the *Indian School Journal*, August 22, 1904. Though it can't be known that the letter writer was actually referring to the Fourth of July dress parade, the authors have chosen to use his remarks to illustrate that day's ceremony.

5. Ibid. Geronimo was frequently an unofficial participant in the dress parades.

6. Parezo and Fowler, *Anthropology*, 113.

7. *World's Fair Bulletin*, 5:6.

8. The July 11 storm caused damage from hail, wind, and lightning. Truax, http://ftp.apci.net/~truax/1904wf. The roof of the school building had suffered leaks from the very beginning. McCowan to Widmann, Walsh, & Boisselier, April 26, 1904, Chilocco Superintendent's Files, OHS.

9. *Indian School Journal*, July 18 and 19, 1904. The remaining children were taken home in early August. *Indian School Journal*, October 1904, 46.

10. Dyreson, *Making the American Team*, 80–81; Francis, *Universal Exposition*, 539; Sullivan, "Report of the Department of Physical Culture," chap. 5, p. 2. The "Olympic World's Basket Ball Championship" competition was held on July 11–12 on the infield of Francis Field. The event was dominated by the Buffalo German YMCA team, conceded to be the greatest team of that era and later enshrined in the Basketball Hall of Fame in Springfield, Massachusetts. It won the championship game against the Missouri Athletic Club by a score of 97 to 8. Mallon, *1904 Olympic Games*, 212–18.

11. Sullivan, as quoted in the *Colorado Springs Telegraph*, September 6, 1903, LPE Scrapbook, n.p., MoHS.

12. *Great Falls Daily Leader*, July 13 and 23, 1904.

13. The mining and metallurgy exhibit was just west of the Montana Building, and according to a contemporary publication, "the noise and the activities of 'the Gulch' [made] the Montana people feel the surroundings to be homelike." Stevens, *Forest City*, 299.

14. The Philippine Reservation was the largest, most expensive—and best-attended—exhibit on the fairgrounds. It encompassed forty-seven acres, cost a million-and-a-half dollars to erect and maintain, and was home for five months to some twelve hundred natives. Parezo and Fowler, *Anthropology*, 164–66, 172–75.

15. *Indian School Journal*, July 12, 22, and 26, 1904; *Official Daily Guide*, 146.

16. *Mandan (N. D.) Pioneer*, July 10, 1904. Cummins' Wild West show was akin to Bufallo Bill's show, which had appeared at the Chicago World's Fair but which was touring Europe in 1904.

17. The Pomo woman was identified as Mrs. Benson. *Indian School Journal*, July 7 and 8, 1904. Reports of visitors' comments such as these come not only from the *Indian School Journal*—where they appeared almost daily as proof of the educational value of the "living exhibits" on Indian Hill—but also from memories the players, most notably Genevieve Healy Adams, shared with their

children and grandchildren. Author interview with Donita Nordlund, March 19, 2000.

18. *Indian School Journal*, July 20 and 21, 1904.

19. Ibid., July 20 and 25, 1904. See Philip Deloria's insightful commentary on this phenomenon of the public's perception of Native abilities in *Indians in Unexpected Places*.

20. "Fairy fluff" would become known as cotton candy. Dr. Marshall saw Sarah Mitchell on July 6 and 14. The Model Indian School covered all student medical expenses of the summer. McCowan voucher of November 21, 1904. Chilocco Superintendent's Files, OHS.

21. Ibid. Katie saw Dr. Marshall on July 25 and again on July 26.

22. Trachoma was rampant in Indian boarding schools. Mild occurrences usually cleared up without permanent damage. Youpee saw Dr. Shoemaker on July 22, 23, 25, 26, 27, and 28. The initial visit was charged to the school at five dollars, with subsequent visits costing three dollars. McCowan was given a 20 percent discount. McCowan to CIA, December 31, 1904, Chilocco Superintendent's Files, OHS.

23. *O'Fallon (Ill.) Progress*, July 22, 1904.

24. *Indian School Journal*, July 27, 1904

25. *O'Fallon (Ill.) Progress*, August 5, 1904; *Indian School Journal*, July 29, 1904; *Great Falls Daily Tribune* of August 10, 1904, quoting the *St. Louis Republic* of July 29, which gave the score as 13 to 3. The O'Fallon team included Mary Howtrow, Ellen Zinkgraf, Eleanor Delscher, Carrie Ahring, Leonore Stites, Anna Neville, and Lucille Bug. *O'Fallon (Ill.) Progress*, July 22, 1904. Gen Healy was the other substitute beside Katie for the games in St. Louis, though it is assumed that all the girls suited up. *Fargo Forum*, June 10, 1904.

26. *O'Fallon (Ill.) Progress*, August 5, 1904; *Great Falls Daily Tribune*, August 10, 1904; *Indian School Journal*, July 29, 1904; *St. Louis Post-Dispatch*, August 27, 1904.

27. *Indian School Journal*, July 29, 1904.

28. McCowan to CIA, December 31, 1904, Chilocco Superintendent's Files, OHS.

A Silver Trophy

1. The fireworks display took place on Tuesday, August 9, 1904. *Indian School Journal*, August 12, 1904. Francis Field, the Olympic Stadium, had been an added enticement in James Sullivan's campaign to bring the 1904 Olympics to St. Louis.

2. Daily Official Program, August 11, 2; *St. Louis Globe-Democrat*, August 13, 1904. For a full treatment of Anthropology Days and the 1904 Olympic Games, see Brownell, *1904 Anthropology Days*.

3. Ibid. Though others have cited August 12 and 13 as the dates for the Anthropology Days games, the contemporary media—including the official report of the Department of Anthropology—cite Thursday and Friday, August 11 and 12. McGee, "Report," 42–44, LPE Collection, box 30, folder 6b, MoHS.

4. Guttman, *The Games Must Go On,* 19; "Novel Athletic Contest," *World's Fair Bulletin,* 5:50; *St. Louis Globe-Democrat,* August 13, 1904; O'Brien, "Meet Me in St. Louis," 13. Dr. Martin Delaney of St. Louis University explained the basics of the contest to the participants before the start of each event, but unfortunately, he had no interpreters to help him convey his instructions. Parezo and Fowler, *Anthropology,* 350. From the Model Indian School, George Mentz from Genoa took first in the 100-yard dash, the 440, and the high jump; Leon Poitre, also from Genoa, finished first in the 120-yard hurdles; and Blake Whitebear (home school unknown) won the mile. Second place finishes were recorded by Mentz in the hurdles, Whitebear in the high jump, Simon Marques (home school unknown) in the 440, and Frank Moore (Haskell) in the baseball throw. *Indian School Journal,* August 13, 1904.

5. "Novel Athletic Contest," *World's Fair Bulletin,* 5:50.

6. *Indian School Journal,* August 13, 1904; Parezo and Fowler, *Anthropology,* 353–54. Sullivan wanted nothing to do with another such meet, so McGee proceeded on his own, and the second "anthropological meet" took place in mid-September. According to a reporter for the *Globe-Democrat,* the event was "a grand success from every point of view," serving "as a good example of what brown men are capable of doing with training." *St. Louis Globe-Democrat,* September 16, 1904.

7. *Indian School Journal,* August 13, 1904.

8. *Great Falls Daily Leader,* August 12, 1904. The celebrity of the Fort Shaw girls was echoed in the Great Falls press a few days later when Dr. C. I. Jones, a local dentist, returned home from his visit to St. Louis to report that the "basket ball team has won great renown for itself." *Great Falls Daily Tribune,* August 16, 1904. Parezo and Fowler, 356.

9. *Indian School Journal,* August 25, 1904. While the girls were given this trophy, other winners of the Anthropology Days contests were taken into the Physical Culture building immediately after their events and given a cash prize—three dollars for first place, two for second place, and a dollar for third place. "Novel Athletic Contest," *World's Fair Bulletin,* 4:50. The authors have compared the girls' trophy with the Olympic trophy won by the St. Louis Rowing Club, as described by Karl Heilman, April 25, 2006, and with photos of other trophies seen in Kindersley, *Chronicle of the Olympics,* 25–27.

10. *Indian School Journal,* August 25, 1904; *Great Falls Daily Leader,* September 6, 1904.

Champions of the World's Fair

1. Lucas, *Modern Olympic Games,* 54–55; *New York Times,* July 20, 1904. Of the forty-some sports that were a part of the "real" 1904 Olympics, only archery was open to women. Lucas, *Modern Olympic Games,* 53.

2. *St. Louis Post-Dispatch,* August 27, 1904. The All-Star lineup included Florence Messing and Paula Fisher, forwards, Lillian Randall, center, and Laura Strong and Birdie Hoffman, guards. *St. Louis Republic,* October 9, 1904; *Indian School Journal,* July 29, 1904.

3. *Great Falls Daily Tribune,* September 9, 1904.

4. *St. Louis Post-Dispatch,* September 4, 1904.

5. Ibid. Lillie Crawford had been a journalist in Pennsylvania before she joined the Indian School Service. Crawford to McCowan, July 28, 1904, Chilocco Superintendent's Files, OHS.

6. *Great Falls Daily Tribune,* September 9, 1904. Miss Crawford did not mention "Coach" McCallum, though he is in the team photo at Kulage Park.

7. *Indian School Journal,* September 12, 1904.

8. *St. Louis Republic,* September 12, 1904. Nine girls appear in the photo; Flora Lucero is missing, and the authors assume that it was at about this time that she began to suffer the symptoms of tuberculosis. See note 14 below.

9. McCowan invoice, per Genevieve Healy, to Wm. Barr Dry Goods, September 14, 1904, OHS.

10. *Indian School Journal,* September 17, 1904.

11. Ibid.; McGee, chief of anthropology, to Frederick Skiff, director of exhibits, August 18, 1904, in McGee, "Report," 410.

12. Daily Official Program, May 25.

13. Dr. Frank G. Bruner's report of Emma Sansaver, September 30, 1904, held by the family. Bruner was a professor of psychology at Columbia University. Emma's is the only record available to the authors. Other measurements noted on the chart are hard to decipher without a standard reference. For instance, Emma's lung capacity was 135 cubic inches, the strength of her right forearm is given as 23 kilos (51 pounds), her left arm 17 kilos (39 pounds). Her eye acuity was 135, the distance between her eyes was 1 ½ inches. Known to have been measured as well were sensitivity to temperature, delicacy of touch and taste, and reaction times to disparate sensory impressions. Scientists believed the results obtained from the laboratories would be "a real contribution to science." The claim was later made that the findings showed that "racial differences exist." Rydell, *All the World's a Fair,* 164.

14. S. H. Cadwallader, Missouri Baptist Sanitarium, to McCowan, November 12, 1904, Chilocco Superintendent's Files, OHS. The charges for the week's confinement amounted to $12.50, not counting the physician's fees. Cadwallader's letter to McCowan does not give the dates for Flora's confinement. Given the date of the correspondence, a best guess is mid-September.

15. *Great Falls Daily Tribune,* October 14, 1904.

16. Ibid.

17. Ibid.

18. *Great Falls Daily Tribune,* October 14, 1904; *St. Louis Republic,* October 9, 1904. The *Republic* gave the score as 17 to 5.

19. "Basketball Champions," undated *Great Falls Daily Tribune* article in Nettie Wirth Mail scrapbook; McCowan to Miss Lillian Randall, October 14, 1904, Chilocco Superintendent's Files, OHS; *Great Falls Daily Tribune,* October 11, 1904.

20. "Basketball Champions," undated *Great Falls Daily Tribune* article in Nettie Wirth Mail scrapbook.

21. *History of Poughkeepsie,* 251; *Great Falls Daily Tribune,* October 31, 1904; *Great Falls Daily Leader,* November 4, 1904; A. F. Caldwell to CIA, Monday, October 24, 1904, LR 1904, box 2646, #78711, 75/11E3/7/16/3, NAW.

22. McCowan to Madison, October 24, 1904, LR 1904, not otherwise attributed, NAW.

23. McCowan to CIA, October 27, 1904, LR 1904, box 2646, #78711, 75/11E3/7/16/3, NAW.

24. McCowan to Madison, October 24, 1904.

25. Brewer to McCowan, October 26 and November 14, 1904, LR 1904, not otherwise attributed, NAW. The list of girls in favor of going to Poughkeepsie is assumed from the revised travel vouchers, of November 10 and 21, 1904, in Chilocco Superintendent's Files, OHS.

26. *St. Louis Republic,* October 19, 1904. Keller was twenty-four years old and had just completed a degree at Radcliffe when she visited the fair.

27. Ibid.

28. Keller to McCowan, October 24, 1904, Chilocco Superintendent's Files, OHS.

29. McCowan to CIA, October 15, 1904, LR 1904, box 2629, #72479, 75/11E3/7/16/1, NAW; Emma Sansaver Simpson's memory book, in the possession of her granddaughter, Barbara Winters. Upon Geronimo's departure, McCowan wrote the commandant of the Apache prisoners at Fort Sill that Geronimo had "behaved admirably throughout his stay with us. He . . . endeared himself to whites and Indians alike. With one or two exceptions when he was not feeling well, he was gentle, kind, and courteous." McCowan to Capt. Sayer, October 3, 1904, Chilocco Superintendent's Files, OHS.

30. Emma Sansaver's memory book.

31. Campbell's thoughts are inferred from an item released to the *Anaconda Standard* of December 18, 1904, by W. J. Adams; vouchers of November 10 and 21, 1904, in Chilocco Superintendent's Files, OHS. The *Great Falls Leader* of November 4, 1904, reported that "seven of the Fort Shaw girls—Nettie Wirth, Emma Sansaver, Sarah Mitchell, Katie Snell, Belle Johnson, Minnie Burton, and Rose LaRose—had started for Poughkeepsie, New York, with Lillie B. Crawford." The *Indian School Journal* of December 15, 1904, also reported that the Fort Shaw team had traveled to Poughkeepsie and were demonstrating their musical talents as well as their basketball skills to people on the East Coast. However, the travel vouchers ($2.50 for each girl's "incidentals" on the train trip home) in McCowan's files clearly support the fact that ten girls started for Fort Shaw in mid-November. In February 1905 the commissioner of Indian affairs, Francis Leupp, wrote Campbell that he thought the Poughkeepsie plan most unwise. That was the last heard of it. Leupp to Campbell, February 20, 1905, LR 1905, box 2721, #12962, 75/11E3/2/11/9, NAW.

32. Parezo and Fowler, *Anthropology,* 372; Francis, *Universal Exposition,* 533.

33. Vouchers for lodging and meals at Hotel Warner, Cascade, Montana,

filed November 18, 1904, Chilocco Superintendent's Files, OHS. According to the *Montana Daily Record* of November 15, 1904, Belle Johnson, Flora Lucero, Genie Butch, and Gen Healy arrived in Helena on November 13 and were "staying over in Cascade" to await their teammates. Lizzie traveled with them. Cascade is fifteen miles south of Great Falls.

34. Reedy, "The End of the Fair," *Mirror*, December 1, 1904.

35. C. I. Jones, quoted in the *Great Falls Daily Tribune*, August 16, 1904.

"Forget Me Not," 1904–1910

1. Nettie Wirth, Rose LaRose, Emma Sansaver, Minnie Burton, Sarah Mitchell, and Katie Snell were reported by the *Great Falls Leader* of November 21, 1904, to have arrived in Cascade on November 18. The scene at the depot is reconstructed according to F. C. Campbell's typical way of celebrating Fort Shaw accomplishments.

2. The names of the siblings and special friends have been drawn from the Fort Shaw enrollment and attendance records of 1904–1905. Mary Johnson had married Eddie Gobert, a fellow Fort Shaw student, on January 2, 1901. Lukin, "My Early Years," 5. Ada Breuninger and John Minesinger were married at Fort Shaw on November 15, 1904. Ada was hired at that same time as clerk and singing instructor for the school. Fort Shaw Record of Employees.

3. Ruby-flash-glass vases and engraved spoons were favored souvenirs of fairgoers. Emma Sansaver's own cup and spoon from St. Louis are among her family's treasures today.

4. In a 1977 interview in the *Great Falls Tribune*, Gen Healy Adams told the reporter that despite their world's fair adventures there was no special treatment accorded the girls once they were back at Fort Shaw: "[We] went back to work tending the school's pigs and cattle and digging weeds in the vegetable patch," she said. *Great Falls Tribune*, April 3, 1977.

5. *Great Falls Daily Leader*, December 16, 1904.

6. Flora Lucero does not appear on the school rolls again after her return from St. Louis. There is no record of Genie Butch's withdrawal from school. It is known only that Genie did not accompany the team on the swing around the state in May 1905 and was not listed among the travelers to Portland in August. From a report that appeared in the *Great Falls Daily Tribune* of September 25, 1905, it appears that she was at that point still home at Frazer, and she never again appears in the school records.

7. Emma sits front and center, holding the ball inscribed "1905" in the portrait of the team taken that year. Photo courtesy of Betty Bisnett, daughter of Emma Sansaver Simpson. Katie's position on the team is taken from news reports found in the *Montana Daily Record*, May 8, 1905, and the *Great Falls Daily Leader*, May 16, 1905. Two of the games against Helena High were held in the capital city, one in Great Falls. *Montana Daily Record*, April 25 and May 1, 1905; *Great Falls Daily Tribune*, June 17, 1905.

8. The Fort Shaw program is described in articles in the *Great Falls Daily Leader*, January 28, 1905; reprint in *Indian School Journal*, March 1905; *Great*

Falls Daily Tribune, June 17, 1904; *Kalispell (Mont.) Bee,* August 15, 1905; *(Portland) Evening Telegram,* August 23, 1905; *Morning Oregonian,* August 24, 1905. Gertrude LaRance was the Chippewa daughter of Jackson LaRance, a rancher from Choteau, and his unnamed wife. She was five years old when she entered Fort Shaw in September 1900, and she was at the school when it closed in 1910. Fort Shaw Register of Pupils. While Louis Youpee's recitations were in the comic tradition, Gertie's were in the tragic, not to say melodramatic, mode. Though Youpee was still at Fort Shaw in 1905, he was thirteen years old and his change of voice had lessened his entertainment value. In those venues where the Fort Shaw team had not appeared before, Campbell explained that the four-man teams were not standard basketball.

9. *Morning Oregonian,* August 21, 1905. It is not known exactly what would have drawn Katie Snell home that summer, but Fort Shaw records show that she withdrew from school in August 1905. She was back at Fort Shaw, however, for the beginning of the 1905–1906 school year.

10. *Morning Oregonian,* August 21 and 24, 1905; *(Spokane) Spokesman-Review,* September 3, 1905.

11. *Chemawa American,* September 8, 1905. The Fort Shaw contingent "spent a couple of days at Chemawa" in the course of their visit to Portland. The third off-reservation boarding school established by the Indian School Service, some fifteen years before Fort Shaw opened, Chemawa continues to operate today. www.chemawa.bia.edu/history.htm. The claim of a West Coast championship is reported only in a manuscript history of Chemawa, written at the turn of the twentieth century by Charles Larson: "The Chemawa girls' basket ball team of 1903 holds the championship of the entire Pacific coast and as yet remains undefeated, although they have played the principal teams from San Francisco to Seattle." Larson, "History of Chemawa."

12. *Chemawa American,* September 8, 1905. The Chemawa lineup included Woods and Clark at forward, McKay at center, and Munny and Lashpell at guards. *(Salem) Oregon Journal,* August 29, 1905.

13. Belle Johnson disappears from the Fort Shaw records in fall 1905. The leave-taking of the other two is documented in newsprint and archival files: *Great Falls Daily Leader,* September 21, 1905; Campbell to August Duclos, September 13, 1905, MC11, box 16, folder 4, ISU; Family Register, Shoshone-Bannock Library, Fort Hall, Idaho. On his trip into Great Falls on September 21 to start Minnie and Rose on their way home, Campbell had hoped to meet Genie Butch coming in from Fort Peck. Genie was to be one of the featured riders in the horse races at the upcoming county fair, but the plan was scuttled when Joe Butch declined to give Genie permission to race. *Great Falls Daily Tribune,* September 21 and 25, 1905.

14. *Great Falls Daily Tribune,* March 24, 1906. This was the inaugural season for the Great Falls girls' basketball team, which had joined the Montana State Interscholastic Athletic Association. The game was therefore played by the girls' rules enforced by the league. The Fort Shaw team was composed of forwards Nettie Wirth and Lucy Mitchell, Sarah's niece; centers Rose Putra and

Mazie Longee; and guards Sarah Mitchell and Nora Porcupine. The substitutes were Nellie Black Dog and Sophia Lambert. The Great Falls team started Elizabeth Embleton and Edna Johnson at forward, Ethel Reid and Anna Olsen at centers, and Frances Dailey and Geraldine Lawrenson at guards.

15. *Great Falls Daily Tribune,* November 5, 1906. The *Tribune's* obituary was somewhat premature. In March of 1907, Emma Sansaver, Katie Snell, and Gen Healy formed the heart of a team that Superintendent Campbell took to Bozeman to play the women of the agricultural college. The game was again played under "girls' rules"; the Indians won 8 to 6. Rosa Putra, Mazie Longee, and Eliza Delorme at "running center," "jumping center," and guard, respectively, filled out the starting squad. That was the last public notice given to Fort Shaw basketball. *Great Falls Daily Tribune,* April 3, 1907; *Exponent,* April 1907. The photo of this 1907 team shows Katie Snell in the captain's position, holding the ball. Emma Sansaver sits to Katie's right, and Gen Healy stands behind Katie's left shoulder. Photo in the possession of Thelma Warren James, Snell's granddaughter.

16. Belle Johnson was married on November 29 (Glenn Jeffrey's Arnoux family history); Katie Snell on December 1 (marriage certificate #1080, Choteau County, Montana); Sarah Mitchell on December 31 (Dorothy Courchene Smith to authors, June 8, 2000); Genie Butch on January 6 (marriage certificate [no number], Valley County, Montana); and Emma Sansaver (marriage certificate [no number], Lewis and Clark County, Montana). Three of the five girls—Belle, Sarah, and Genie—married Fort Shaw classmates. Katie and Emma married non-Indians.

17. *Great Falls Daily Tribune,* October 25, 1908 and April 18, 1910; Greer, "Brief History," 58; Campbell, "Personal Statement"; Fort Shaw Discharge Records; Fort Shaw Record of Employees.

18. Barbara Winters, granddaughter of player Emma Sansaver and chair of the Sun River Valley Historical Society's monument committee, and Bill Sansaver, kinsman of three of the teammates, spearheaded the fundraising, design, construction, and dedication of the monument.

Epilogue

1. H. B. Curtis, *Great Falls Daily Tribune,* May 29, 1904.

2. Jessie James-Hawley (Turtle Woman), letter to authors, March 26, 2001.

Bibliography

Official Records and Government Reports

Annual Report of the Department of the Interior, Commissioner of Indian Affairs, 1894, 1905.

Assiniboine Census of 1897, Fort Belknap Agency.

Blackfeet, Blood, and Piegan Censuses of 1891, 1893, 1895.

Department of Indian Affairs, 56th Congressional Documents, 1900.

Flathead Records. Salish Kootenai College, Pablo, Montana.

"History of the Blackfoot Indian or Blackfeet-Piegan Tribe of Northwest Montana, East of the Rockies, Called the Blackfoot Reservation, Browning, Montana, Taken about 1907–1908." Blackfeet Agency Office, Browning, Mont.

Lemhi Tribal Census Records, Special Collections, Idaho State University, Pocatello.

Louisiana Purchase Exposition Commission. "Final Report of the Louisiana Purchase Exposition." Louisiana Purchase Exposition Files, Missouri Historical Society, St. Louis.

McGee, WJ. "Report of the Department of Anthropology to Frederick Skiff, Director, Universal Exposition of 1904, Division of Exhibits, May 1905." Louisiana Purchase Exposition Files, file series III, subseries XI, Missouri Historical Society, St. Louis.

Records of the Bureau of Indian Affairs, Letters Received, Letters Sent. Record Group 75, National Archives, Washington, D.C.

Records of Fort Shaw Indian School, including Descriptive Record of Students as Admitted 1892–1901, Entry 1358, vol 1; Record of Employees, 1891–1910, Entry 1361, vol. 1; Statements of Receipts and Disbursements, 1892, Entry 1362, vol. 2; Sanitary Reports, 1894–1899, Entry 1360, vol. 1; Discharges, in Records of the Bureau of Indian Affairs, Field Office Reports, Records of Non-Reservation Schools, Record Group 75, National Archives, Denver.

Records of the Lemhi Reservation, MC 11, Special Collections, Idaho State University, Pocatello.

Records of the Shoshone Bannock Peoples. Shoshone-Bannock Library, Fort Hall, Idaho.

Report of the Commissioner of Indian Affairs, Register of Pupils, Descriptive Record of Students as Admitted [Fort Shaw Indian School], vol. 2, 1895–1896, National Archives Denver.

Report of Secretary of Interior. *Indian Affairs*, vol. 2, 1893. Washington, D.C.: Government Printing Office, 1895–1896.

Reports of Agencies in Montana, including George Steele, Report of Blackfeet Agency, August 26, 1891, 265–66; A. O. Simms, Report of Belknap Agency, August 1891, 280–81, National Archives, Washington, D.C.

Reports of Independent Schools in Montana and Nebraska, including Annual Report of Fort Shaw School, August 16, 1898, August 28, 1899, June 17, 1901, National Archives, Washington, D.C.

Reports of Inspection of Field Jurisdiction of Office of Indian Affairs, 1893–1900. Record Group 75, National Archives, Washington, D.C.

Scobey, C. R. A. Report of the Fort Peck Agency, August 3, 1901, 282. In Report of the Secretary of the Interior, *Indian Affairs*, vol. 1, 1901.

Sullivan, James E. "Report of the Department of Physical Culture to Frederick Skiff, Director, Universal Exposition of 1904," May 1905. Louisiana Purchase Exposition Files, file series III, subseries XIV, Missouri Historical Society, St. Louis.

Tulley, John. Report of Tongue River Agency, August 18, 1891, 286–87. In Report of the Secretary of the Interior, *Indian Affairs*, vol. 2, 1891.

U.S. Manuscript Census, 1880, 1900, 1910.

U.S. Official Register: Employees of the Federal Government, vol. 1, 1901.

Wyman, W. P., Report of Crow Agency, October 22, 1891, 270. In Report of the Secretary of the Interior, *Indian Affairs*, vol. 2, 1891.

Books and Articles

Adams, David Wallace. *Education for Extinction: American Indians and the Boarding School Experience, 1875–1928*. Lawrence: University Press of Kansas, 1995.

Anderson, David. *The Story of Basketball*. New York: William Morrow, 1988.

Archuleta, Margaret, Brenda Child, and K. Tsianina Lomawaima. *Away from Home: American Indian Boarding School Experiences, 1879–2000*. Phoenix, Ariz.: Heard Museum, 2000.

Barker, Joel, comp. *Preliminary Inventory of Records of the Blackfeet Agency*. Washington, D.C.: Government Printing Office/Bureau of Indian Affairs, n.d.

Barsness, John, and William Dickinson. "Fort Shaw on the Sun." In *Montana Centennial, 1864–1964 Sun River Valley*. Self-published. Found in Montana Historical Society Library, Helena.

"Basketball Dynasty." *Montana Magazine*, March/April 1988, 63.

Bender, Albert. "Women's Stickball Makes Historic Comeback." In *News from Indian Country*, late November 2000, 18B.

Bennitt, Mark, ed. *History of the Louisiana Purchase Exposition, Illustrated*. St. Louis: Universal Exposition Publishing Co., 1905. Reprint, New York: Arno Press, 1976.

Berenson, Senda. "Basket Ball for Women." In *Physical Education* 3, no. 7 (September 1894), 106–109.

———, ed. *Basket Ball for Women.* New York: American Sports Publishing Co., 1903. Originally published as *Line Basket Ball or Basket Ball for Women,* 1899.

———. "Significance of Basket Ball for Women." In *Basket Ball for Women, by Senda Berenson, 31–43.* New York: American Sports Publishing Co., 1903.

Bloom, John. *"To Show What an Indian Can Do": Sports at Native American Boarding Schools.* Minneapolis: University of Minnesota Press, 2000.

Boyd, Jason. "The Fort." In *Stories in Place: Our Sun River Valley Heritage,* vol. 1. Simms, Mont." Simms High School, 1998.

Breitbart, Eric. *A World on Display: Photographs from the St. Louis World's Fair of 1904.* Albuquerque: University of New Mexico Press, 1997.

Brown, Estelle Aubrey. *Stubborn Fool: A Narrative.* Caldwell, Idaho: Caxton, 1952.

Brownell, Susan, ed. *The 1904 Anthropology Days and Olympic Games: Sport, Race, and American Imperialism.* Lincoln: University of Nebraska Press, 2008.

Bye, John O. "'Shoot, Minnie, Shoot!' Lusty Cry of Unbeaten Indian Girls," *Montana Post* 3 (8), August 1965, 1–2.

Capps, Benjamin. *The Old West: The Great Chiefs.* New York: Time-Life Books, 1973.

———. *The Old West: Indians.* New York: Time-Life Books, 1973.

Cheney, Robert Carkeek. *Names on the Face of Montana.* Missoula: Mountain Press, 2003.

Child, Brenda. *Boarding School Seasons: American Indian Families, 1900–1940.* Lincoln: University of Nebraska Press, 1995.

Clark, Banbridge. "Fort Shaw." In *Pictorial History of the Sun River Valley,* 147–52. Shelby, Mont.: Promoter Publishing, 1989.

Clevenger, Martha, ed. *"Indescribably Grand": Diaries and Letters from the 1904 World's Fair.* St. Louis: Missouri Historical Society, 1996.

Coleman, Michael. *American Indian Children at School, 1850–1930.* Jackson: University Press of Mississippi, 1993.

"Col. William H. H. Healy." In *Progressive Men of the State of Montana,* 1574. Chicago: A. W. Bowen, 1901.

Coubertin, Pierre de. *Olympic Memories.* Lausanne: International Olympic Committee, 1979.

Culin, Stewart. "Games of the North American Indians." In *Twenty-fourth Annual Report of the Bureau of American Ethnology* 647–64. Washington, D.C.: Government Printing Office, 1907. Reprint, Mineola, N.Y.: Dover Press, 1975.

Cummings, Louise. "St. Peter's Mission." In *A Pictorial History of the Sun River Valley,* 26–33. Shelby, Mont.: Promoter Publishing, 1989.

Davenport, Joanna. "The Tides of Change in Women's Basketball Rules." In *A Century of Women's Basketball: From Frailty to Final Four,* edited by Joan

Hult and Marianna Trekell, 83–108. Reston, Va.: National Association of Girls and Women in Sport, 1991.

Davis, William. *The American Frontier: Pioneers, Settlers, and Cowboys.* Norman: University of Oklahoma Press, 1992.

Deloria, Philip. *Indians in Unexpected Places.* Lawrence: University Press of Kansas, 2005.

Delsarte, Francois. *Delsarte System of Oratory.* Paris: n.p., 1893.

DeMarce, Roxanne, ed. *Blackfeet Heritage, 1907–1908, Blackfeet Indian Reservation, Browning, Montana.* Browning, Mont.: Blackfeet Heritage Program, 1980.

Dusenberry, Verne. "Waiting for a Day That Never Comes." *Montana The Magazine of Western History* 8, no. 2 (Spring 1958): 26–39.

Dyck, Paul. "Lone Wolf Returns," *Montana The Magazine of Western History* 22, no. 1 (Winter 1972): 18–41.

Dyreson, Mark. *Making the American Team: Sport, Culture and the Olympic Experience.* Champaign: University of Illinois Press, 1998.

Ewers, John. *The Blackfeet: Raiders of the Northwestern Plains.* Norman: University of Oklahoma Press, 1958.

"Fort Shaw at State Fair." *Anaconda (Mont.) Standard.* October 12, 1903.

Fox, Timothy, and Duane Sneddecker. *From the Palaces to the Pike: Visions of the 1904 World's Fair.* St. Louis: Missouri Historical Society, 1997.

Francis, David. *Universal Exposition of 1904.* 6 vols. St. Louis: Louisiana Exposition Co., 1913.

Frenchtown Historical Society. *Frenchtown Valley Footprints.* Missoula, Mont.: Mountain Press, 1976.

Friesen, Phyllis. "Golden Rule Days Recalled." *Great Falls (Mont.) Tribune.* December 15, 1968.

Furdell, William, and Elizabeth Furdell. *Great Falls: A Pictorial History.* Richmond, Va.: Donning, 1983.

Garceau-Hagen, Dee, ed. *Portraits of Women in the American West.* New York: Routledge, 2005.

Gilluly, Sam. "1904 Women's Basketball Team Were World Champions." *Choteau (Mont.) Acantha,* December 30, 1976.

Gould, Drusilla, and Christopher Loether. *An Introduction to the Shoshoni Language.* Salt Lake City: University of Utah Press, 2003.

Graetz, Rick. "Plains Warriors Settled in Scenic but Harsh Area." *Great Falls (Mont.) Tribune,* January 25, 2001.

Gray, Lillian. "Miss Estelle Reel and Her Work." *Chilocco Farmer and Stock Grower* 4, no. 3 (June 1903): 383–85.

Green, Rayna, and John Troutman. "By the Waters of the Minnehaha: Music and Dance, Pageants and Princesses." In *Away from Home: American Indian Boarding School Experiences, 1879–2000,* by Margaret Archuleta, Brenda Child, and K. Tsianina Lomawaima, 60–83. Phoenix: Heard Museum, 2000.

Grit, Guts, and Gusto: A History of Hill County. Havre, Mont.: Hill County Centennial Commision, 1976.

Grundy, Pamela, and Susan Shackelford. *Shattering the Glass.* Chapel Hill: University of North Carolina Press, 2007.

Gulick, Luther, ed. *Spalding's Athletic Library: Official Basketball Guide.* New York: American Sports Publishing Co., 1896, 1908, 1912.

Guttmann, Allen. *Games and Empires: Modern Sports and Cultural Imperialism.* New York: Columbia University Press, 1995.

———. *The Games Must Go On: Avery Brundage and the Olympic Movement.* New York: Columbia University Press, 1984.

———. *The Olympics: A History of the Modern Games.* 2nd ed. Urbana: University of Illinois Press, 2002.

Haig-Brown, Celia. *Resistance and Renewal: Surviving the Indian Residential School.* Vancouver: Tillacum Press, 1988.

Harrington, Grant Woodbury. "A Semicentennial Visit." *The Delta,* March 1943, 166.

Heathcott, Joseph. "Out of the Wilds: Visions of an Urban Order." *Gateway Heritage* 24, no. 4 (Spring 2004): 10–19.

Hill, Edith. "Senda Berenson." *Research Quarterly* 12, no. 3 (October 1941): 658–65.

"History of the Great Northern Railway." Reprint of article in *Shipper and Carrier,* February 1925. In C. B. Griffin Papers, Museum of the Rockies, Bozeman, Montana.

Hitchcock, Edward, Sr. "Basket Ball for Women." *Physical Education* 3, no. 6 (August 1894): 100.

Hollander, Zander, ed. *The Modern Encyclopedia of Basketball.* New York: Fourwinds Press, 1969.

Hult, Joan, and Marianna Trekell, eds. *A Century of Women's Basketball: From Frailty to Final Four.* Reston, Va.: National Association of Girls and Women in Sports, 1991.

"The Indian Belles of Fort Shaw, Montana's Only World Champions." *Montana Sports Magazine,* n.d.

"James H. Snell." In *In the Land of the Chinook: The Story of Blaine County,* by A. J. Noyes, 112–15. N.p., n.d.

"James Snell." In *Thunderstorms and Tumbleweeds, 1887–1987,* by East Blaine County Centennial Book Committee. Visalia, Calif.: Jostens, 1988.

Jenkins, Edna Blossom. "Reminiscence." *Montana Centennial, 1864–1964.* Sun River: Sun River (Mont.) Valley Historical Society, 1963.

Jenkins, Sally. *The Real All Americans: The Team That Changed a Game, a People, a Nation.* New York: Doubleday, 2007.

Jensen, Billie Snell. "St. Louis Celebrates." *Gateway Heritage,* October 1954, 5–26.

Kappler, Charles, comp. *Indian Affairs: Laws and Treaties.* Vol. 3, *Laws.* Washington, D.C.: Government Printing Office, 1913.

Kearney, Pat. *Butte's Big Game: Butte Central vs. Butte High.* Butte, Mont.: n.p., 1989.

————. *Butte's Pride: The Columbia Gardens.* Butte, Mont.: n.p., 1994.

Kelly, Laverne Fitzgerald. "Journey to Ft. Shaw in 1908." *Great Falls Tribune,* April 5, 1959.

Kindersley, Dorling. *Chronicle of the Olympics.* New York: DK Publishers, 1996.

Kinley, Henry. "An Indian School Diary," In *A Pictorial History of the Sun River Valley,* p. 268. Shelby, Mont.: Promoter Publishing, 1989.

LaDow, Beth. *The Medicine Line.* New York: Routledge, 2001.

Lang, William. "The Nearly Forgotten Blacks on the Last Chance Gulch, 1900–1912." In *Pacific Northwest Quarterly* 70, no. 2 (April 1979): 50–57.

Lannin, Joanne. *A History of Basketball for Girls and Women: From Bloomers to Big Leagues.* New York: Lerner Sports, 2000.

Larson, Erik. *The Devil in the White City: Murder, Magic, and Madness at the Fair That Changed America.* New York: Vintage Books, 2004.

Leighton, George. "The Year St. Louis Enchanted the World." *Harper's,* August 1960, 38–47.

Lomawaima, K. Tsianina. "Estelle Reel, Superintendent of Indian Schools, 1898–1901: Politics, Curriculum, and Land." In *Journal of American Indian Education* 35, no. 3 (Spring 1996): 5–31.

————. *They Called It Prairie Light: The Story of Chilocco Indian School.* Lincoln: University of Nebraska Press, 1994.

Lomawaima, K. Tsianina, and Teresa McCarty. *To Remain an Indian: Lessons in Democracy from a Century of Native American Education.* New York: Teachers College Press, 2006.

Long, James. *Land of the Nakota: The Story of the Assiniboine Indians.* Helena, Mont.: State Publishing Co., 1942.

Lucas, John. "Early Olympic Antagonists: Pierre de Coubertin and James E. Sullivan." In *Stadion* 3, no. 2 (1977): 258–72.

————. *Modern Olympic Games* New York: Barnes and Co., 1980.

Lutz, Dennis. *Montana Post Offices and Postmasters.* Rochester, Minn.: Johnson Printing, 1986.

Madsen, Brigham. *The Lemhi: Sacajawea's People.* Caldwell, Idaho: Caxton, 1979.

Mahoney, Irene, OSU. *Lady Blackrobes: Missionaries in the Heart of Indian Country.* Golden, Colo.: Fulcrum, 2006.

Mallon, Bill. *The 1904 Olympic Games. Results for All Competitors in All Events, with Commentary.* Jefferson, N.C.: McFarland, 1999.

Malone, Michael. *The Battle for Butte: Mining and Politics on the Northern Frontier, 1864–1906.* Seattle: University of Washington Press, 1981.

Malone, Michael, Richard Roeder, and William Lang. *Montana: A History of Two Centuries.* Rev. ed. Seattle: University of Washington Press, 1991.

McBride, Genevieve, OSU. *The Bird Tail.* New York: Vantage, 1974.

McKinney, Lillie G. "History of the Albuquerque Indian School." In *New Mexico Historical Review* 20 (April 1945): 116.

Miles, Walker. "My Genealogy." In *Native Families,* 9 vols, vol 9, 115–21. Bound volumes in Salish Kootenai Library, Pablo, Mont.

Miller, Don, and Stan Cohen. *Military and Trading Posts of Montana.* Missoula, Mont.: Pictorial Histories Publishing Co., 1978.

Minkin, Bert. *Legacies of the St. Louis World's Fair.* St. Louis: 1904 World's Fair Society, 1998.

"Montana Indian Reservations." Helena: Travel Montana, 1994.

Murphy, Mary. *Mining Cultures: Men, Women, and Leisure in Butte, 1914–1941.* Urbana: University of Illinois Press, 1997.

Naismith, James. "Basket Ball." *[YMCA] Triangle,* January 1892, 144–47.

———. *Basketball: Its Origins and Development.* Lincoln: University of Nebraska Press, 1996.

Noyes, A. J. *In the Land of the Chinook: The Story of Blaine County.* N.p, n.d..

O'Brien, Frank. "Meet Me in St. Louis." In *Washington University Magazine* 44, no. 3 (Spring 1974), 7–13

Official Guide to the Louisiana Purchase Exposition. St. Louis: Official Guide Co., 1904.

"Old Timers." In Fred C. Campbell Papers, MC 67, Montana Historical Society, Helena.

Overholser, Joel. *Fort Benton: World's Innermost Port.* Helena, Mont.: Falcon Press, 1987.

Oxendine, Joseph. *American Indian Sports Heritage.* Lincoln: University of Nebraska Press, 1988.

Parezo, Nancy, and Don Fowler. *Anthropology Goes to the Fair.* Lincoln: University of Nebraska Press, 2007.

Parsons, Jackie. *The Educational Movement of the Blackfeet Indians, 1840–1979.* Browning, Mont.: Blackfeet Heritage Program, 1980.

Paul, Joan. "Clara Gregory Baer: Catalyst for Women's Basketball." In *A Century of Women's Basketball: From Frailty to Final Four,* edited by Joan Hult and Marianna Trekel, 37–52. Reston, Va.: National Association of Girls and Women in Sport, 1991.

Pease, Margery. *A Worthy Work in a Needy Time: The Montana Industrial School for Indians (Bond's Mission) 1886–1897.* 2nd ed. Billings, Mont.: n.p., 2007.

Peavy, Linda, and Ursula Smith. "'Leav[ing]] the White[s] Far Behind Them': The Girls from Fort Shaw (Montana) Indian School, Basketball Champions of the 1904 Worlds Fair." *International Journal of the History of Sport* 24, no. 6 (June 2007): 819–40. Reprinted in *The 1904 Anthropology Days and Olympic Games: Sport, Race, and American Imperialism,* edited by Susan Brownell. Lincoln: University of Nebraska Press, 2008.

———. "Unlikely Champion: Emma Rose Sansaver, 1884–1925." In *Portraits of Women in the American* West, edited by Dee Garceau-Hagen, 179–206. New York: Routledge, 2005.

———. "World Champions: The 1904 Girls' Basketball Team from Fort Shaw Indian Boarding School. *Montana The Magazine of Western History* 51, no. 4 (Winter 2001): 2–25. Reprinted in *Native American Athletes in Sport and*

Society: A Reader, edited by C. Richard King, 40–78. Lincoln: University of Nebraska Press, 2005.

Peterson, Jacqueline, and Jennifer Brown, eds. The New Peoples: Being and Becoming Métis in North America. Winnipeg: University of Manitoba Press, 1985.

A Pictorial History of the Sun River Valley. Shelby, Mont.: Promoter Publishing, 1989.

Platt, Edmund. The Eagle's History of Poughkeepsie, for the Earliest Settlements, 1683 to 1905. Poughkeepsie, N.Y.: Platt and Platt, 1905.

Rayner, Robert. Montana: The Land and the People, vol. 3. Chicago: Lewis Publishing, 1930.

Reedy, William. "The End of the Fair." The Mirror, December 1, 1904.

Reyhner, Jon, and Jeanne Eder. American Indian Education: A History. Norman: University of Oklahoma Press, 2004.

Riney, Scott. The Rapid City Indian School, 1898–1933. Norman: University of Oklahoma Press, 1999.

Robbins, Celia, ed. Basketball Was Born Here. Springfield, Mass.: Springfield College, 2002.

Rockwell, Mary Woodrow. "Memories and History of Sun River Valley and Fort Shaw." In A Pictorial History of the Sun River Valley, by the Sun River Valley Historical Society, 266–77. Shelby, Mont.: Promoter Publishing, 1989.

Roeder, Richard. "A Settlement on the Plains: Paris Gibson and the Building of Great Falls." In Montana The Magazine of Western History 42, no. 4 (Autumn 1992), 4–19.

Roosevelt County, Montana, Bicentennial Committee. Roosevelt County's Treasured Years. Great Falls, Mont.: Blue Print Co., 1976.

Rydell, Robert. All the World's a Fair. Chicago: University of Chicago Press, 1984.

———. World of Fairs: The Century-of-Progress Expositions. Chicago: University of Chicago Press, 1993.

Rydell, Robert, Jeffrey Safford, and Pierce Mullen. In the People's Interest: A Centennial History of Montana State University. Bozeman: Montana State University Foundation, 1992.

Sandeen, Eric. An Inventory of Papers of the Lemhi Indian Agency. Pocatello: Idaho State University Press, 1982.

Schoenbert, Wilfred, S. J. "Historic St. Peter's Mission." Montana The Magazine of Western History 11, no, 1 (Winter 1961), 68–85.

"Shoot, Minnie, Shoot!" Montana Sports Magazine, Spring 1968.

Smith, Gary. "Shadow of a Nation." Sports Illustrated, February 18, 1991, 60–73.

Smith, LaRue. "Campbell Mountain in Glacier National Park: The Story of a Sigma Nu and His Huge Namesake." The Delta, March 1943, 164–66.

Snell, Alma. Grandmother's Grandchild. Lincoln: University of Nebraska Press, 2000.

Snook, Fred, Jed Wilson, and Teri Wilson Dinnell. "The Lemhi Band of the

Shoshone Indians" In *Centennial History of Lemhi County*, vol. 1, 51–58. Pocatello, Idaho: Lemhi County History Committee, 1992.

Spalding Official Basketball Guide, 1901–1902. New York: Spalding, 1901.

Spears, Betty. "Senda Berenson Abbott: New Woman, New Sport." In *A Century of Women's Basketball: From Frailty to Final Four*, edited by Joan Hult and Marianna Trekell, 19–36. Reston, Va.: National Association for Girls and Women in Sports, 1991.

Stevens, Walter. *The Forest City.* St. Louis, Mo.: Thompson Publishing, 1904.

Stonechild, Blair, Neal MacLeod, and Rob Nestor. *Survival of a People.* Regina, Sask.: Indian Studies Research Centre, First Nations University of Canada, 2003.

Stories in Place: Our Sun River Valley Heritage, vol. 1. Simms, Mont.: Simms High School, 1998.

Stuwe, Jane Willits. *Valley Ventures.* Havre, Mont.: Hi-Line Herald, n.d.

Tanner, Ogden. *The Canadians.* New York: Time-Life Books, 1973.

Taylor, Bill, and Jan Taylor. *The Butte Short Line: The Construction Era, 1888–1929.* Missoula, Mont.: Pictorial Histories, 2003.

"Three Survivors in This Area of Famous Indian Girls' Team." Malta (Mont.) newspaper, n.d.

Thunderstorms and Tumbleweeds, 1887–1987. Visalia, Calif.: Jostens, 1988.

Todd, Jan. "From Milo to Milo: A History of Barbells, Dumbells, and Indian Clubs." In *Iron Game History* 3, no. 6 (April 1995), 4–16.

"To See Fort Shaw Indians." *Anaconda (Mont.) Standard*, March 1, 1904.

Trennert, Robert. "Educating Indian Girls at Nonreservation Boarding Schools, 1878–1920." *Western Historical Quarterly* 13 (July 1982), 271–90.

———. *The Phoenix Indian School: Forced Assimilation in Arizona, 1891–1935.* Norman: University of Oklahoma Press, 1988.

———. "Selling Indian Education at World's Fairs and Expositions, 1893–1904." *American Indian Quarterly* 11 (1987), 203–22.

Troutman, John. *"Indian Blues": American Indians and the Politics of Music, 1890–1935.* Norman: University of Oklahoma Press, forthcoming.

U.S. Department of Interior. *Indian Affairs*, vol. II, *1895–96.* Washington, D.C.: Government Printing Office, 1896.

Urs, Byrnece. "Joe Butch." In *Footprints in the Valley: A History of Valley County, Montana*, vol. 2, 147–50. Glasgow, Mont.: Friends of the Pioneer Museum, 1991.

Verdon, Paul. "David Dawson Mitchell: Virginian on the Wild Missouri." *Montana The Magazine of Western History* 27, no. 2 (April 1977), 2–15.

Wandell, H. B. *Story of a Great City in a Nutshell* 5th ed. N.p., 1901.

White, Stuart. "She Was Born to Be a Basketball Star." *Great Falls (Mont.) Tribune*, April 3, 1977.

"William Hodgkiss." Progressive Men of Montana, 3:417. Chicago: A. W. Bowen, n.d.

Williams, Walter, ed. *The State of Missouri: An Autobiography.* Columbia, Mo.: Stephens Press, 1904.

Winslow, W. H. "Fort Shaw," *Montana Illustrated*, n.d., 32–34

Wolff, Alexander. *Big Game, Small World: A Basketball Adventure*. New York: Warner Books, 2002.

World Almanac and Book of Facts, 2005. New York: World Almanac Books, 2005.

World's Fair Bulletin, vols. 4, 5, and 6. St. Louis: Universal Exposition of 1904, 1904.

"World's Fair Indian Exhibit." *Chilocco Farmer and Stock Grower* 4, no. 2 (December 1903), 114; 4, no. 6 (April 1904), 282.

Yearbook, 1892, 1897, Young Men's Christian Associations of North America. Kautz Family YMCA Archives, University of Minnesota Library, Twin Cities.

Youpee [Youpe], Louis. "A Friend of the Indian." *American Indian Journal*, May 1938, 6.

Zimmerman, William, Jr. "The Fort Hall Story: An Interpretation." In *Historical Society Journal*, Indian Rights Association, 1959, 5–12.

Unpublished Documents

Abbott, Margaret, "Writing the Journey." Master's thesis, University of Montana, 1997.

Baldwin, Dorothy. "History of Fort Shaw." Montana Historical Society file, 1932.

Bradfield, Larry. "A History of Chilocco Indian School." Master's thesis, University of Oklahoma, 1963.

Buysee, JoAnn Marie. "An Historical Analysis of Women's Athletics at Montana State University from 1893 to 1971." Master's thesis, 1979.

Bye, John. "The History of Fort Shaw." Sun River Valley Historical Society files, Sun River, Montana.

Campbell, F. C. "Personal Statement of F. C. Campbell." In possession of Campbell's grandson, Fred DesRosier.

Connelly, Charles. "My Mother's Life with the Martins."

Courchene, David Charles. Courchene Family Genealogy.

Cunniff, Jeff. "Fort Shaw Indian School," Montana Historical Society vertical file.

Dawson, James. Dawson Family Tree.

Edwards, Rev. George. "Reminiscence." Montana Historical Society files.

Family Group Record (Sansaver). In possession of Barbara Winters.

"Fort Shaw Military Cemetery." Typewritten list in possession of the Sun River Valley (Mont.) Historical Society.

Greer, John. "A Brief History of Indian Education at the Fort Shaw Industrial School." Master's thesis, Montana State University, Missoula, 1958.

Gould, Drusilla. Family History, 2000.

Healy, William H. H. "Reminiscence of William H. Healy, 1869–1916." SC 814, Montana Historical Society, Helena.

Kutch Family Genealogy.

Larson, Charles. "The History of Chemawa." In possession of SuAnn Reddick, historian, Chemawa Indian School, Salem, Oregon.

Lukin, Nora Connolly. "My Early Years, a Memoir."

Miller, Julianne, "A Resilient People." Idaho State University, December 1993.

Nordlund, Donita. "Grandmother." In possession of the authors.

Parezo, Nancy. "The Special Olympics: Testing Racial Strength and Endurance at the 1904 Louisiana Purchase Exposition." Paper delivered at the International Symposium on Athletics at the 1904 World's Fair, St. Louis, Missouri, September 2004.

Sansaver Family Genealogy. In possession of Donna Wimmer.

Snell Family Tree. In possession of Douglas Stuart.

Snell Family Tree. In possession of Thelma Warren James.

Thomas, Bill. "Early Life and Times of the Montana Smith Family," 1995.

Warner, Patricia. "Dressed to Win: The Fort Shaw Indian School Champions of the World." Paper delivered at the Costume Society of America, Region III, October 9, 2004.

White, Edna, "Women's Activities as I Knew Them at MSC from 1904–1908." Montana State University Archives, Bozeman, Montana.

Wilcox, Rev. Allen. "Eulogy for Fred C. Campbell." Fred DesRosier Papers in posession of Fred DesRosier.

"William Healy Reminiscence, 1869–1916." SC 814, Montana Historical Society, Helena.

Wirth Family Genealogy. In possession of Bill Thomas.

Newspapers

Anaconda (Mont.) Standard
Billings (Mont.) Gazette
Bozeman (Mont.) Avant Courier
Bozeman (Mont.) Chronicle
Browning (Mont.) Chieftain/Chief
Butte (Mont.) Inter Mountain
Butte (Mont.) Miner
Char-Koosta News (Pablo, Mont.)
Charleston (S.C.) Evening Post
Chemawa (Indian School) American
Chilocco Farmer and Stock Grower, later *Indian School Journal*
Chinook (Mont.) Opinion
Choteau (Mont.) Acantha
Choteau (Mont.) Montanian
Colorado Springs (Colo.) Telegraph
Des Moines (Iowa) Leader
Dupuyer (Mont.) Acantha
The Exponent (Montana State College, Bozeman)
Fargo (N.D.) Forum
Fergus County (Mont.) Argus

Fort Benton (Mont.) River Press
Glasgow (Mont.) Democrat
(Glasgow) North Montana Review
Great Falls (Mont.) Daily Leader
Great Falls (Mont.) [Daily] Tribune
Great Falls (Mont.) Weekly Tribune
Havre (Mont.) Advertiser
Havre (Mont.) Daily News
Havre (Mont.) Plaindealer
Helena (Mont.) Daily Record
Helena (Mont.) Weekly Herald
Indian Helper (Carlisle)
Indian School Journal
Kaimin (Montana State University, Missoula)
Kalispell (Mont.) Bee
Mandan (N.D.) Pioneer
Miles City (Mont.) Independent
Minot (N.D.) Daily News
Missoula (Mont.) Missoulian
Montana Record Herald (Helena)
Morning Call and Fargo (N.D.) Daily Argus
Morning Oregonian
New York Times
1904 World's Fair Society Bulletin
Northampton (Mass.) Daily Herald
O'Fallon (Ill.) Progress
Pocatello (Idaho) Tribune
Portland (Ore.) Journal
Portland (Ore.) Evening Telegram
Prairie (Mont.) Advocate
Rising Sun [Sun River (Mont.) Sun]
Ronan (Mont.) Pioneer
St. Louis Globe-Democrat
St. Louis Post-Dispatch
St. Louis Republic
(Salem) Oregon Journal
Spokane (Wash.) Evening Chronicle
Spokane (Wash.) Spokesman-Review
Sun River (Mont.) Sun [Rising Sun]
Wolf Point (Mont.) Herald
World's Fair Bulletin

Websites

"Archeology Program." http://www.nps.gov/archeology/PUBS/lee/Lee_CH3.htm.

"Barbarous Dialects Should Be Blotted Out . . ." Excerpts from the 1897 Report of the Commissioner of Indian Affairs. http://ourworld.compuserve.com/homepages/JWCRAWFORD/atkins.htm.

Chemawa History. http://www.chemawa.bia.edu/history/htm.

Everett, Marshall. *The Book of the Fair*, chapter 19, "The Study of Mankind." http://www.bboondocksnet.com/expos/wfe_1904_book19.html.

Dundas, Zack. "Hundred-Year-Old Hoops." http://www.umt.edu/comm/s99/sports.html.

Gibson, Stan, and Jack Hayne. "Notes on an Obscure Massacre." http://www.imdiversity.com/article_detail.asp?Article_ID=1536.

————. "Postscript to the 1870 Marias Massacre." http://www.dickshovel.com/parts3.html.

"History of Great Falls, Montana." http://www.100megsfree3.com/mick-mc/1800.html.

"History of Shawnee, Kansas." www.cityofshawnee.org/cityclerk/history/hist.

"John Gibbon." http://www.batteryb.com/gibbon/html.

Johnson, Scott. "Not Altogether Ladylike: The Premature Demise of Girls' Interscholastic Basketball in Illinois." www.iha.org/initiatives/hstoricbasketball_girls_early.htm.

Krause, Jan. "Saint Ignatius Mission, St. Ignatius, Montana." www.lakeshorecountry/journal.com.

McIlhaney, Marueen, "1916 Basketball." www.dickinson.edu/departments/hist/publication/eyeongame/1916bball.

"Roster of Superintendents, Fort Peck Indian Agency." www.montana.edu/nwnfpcc/tribes/suprost.

Sahr, Robert. Consumer Price Index (CPI) Conversion Factors. http://www.orst.edu/dept/pol_sci/fac/sahr/sahrhome.html.

"St. Louis Union Station." http://www.stlouisunionstation.com/info.

"Scenic Railway." http://www.laupp.com/scenicrailway.html.

"Shoshoni and Northern Paiute Indians in Idaho." www.trailtribes.org.

Sparrowhawk. Kutch genealogy. www.geocities.com.

Truax, Mike. "Mike's 1904 St. Louis World's Fair Web Pages." http://ftp.apci.net/~truax/1904wf.

Wheelock, Helen. "Women's Basketball Online." http://www.WomensBasketballOnline.com.

"World's Fair," St. Louis Public Library. http://www.exhibits.slpl.org.

"Wotanging Ikche." http://native-net.org/aisesnet/discussion/1998/0149.html.

"YMCA Worldwide History." Heritage YMCA Group. www.heritageymca.org/ymca_worldwide.htm.

Correspondence

Aslanian, Gena, granddaughter of Sarah Mitchell Courchene. To authors, numerous documents, March 2003–November 2007.

Bender, Terry, granddaughter of Lizzie Wirth Smith. To authors, numerous documents, June 2000–November 2007.

Bennett, Elsie, daughter of Lizzie Wirth Smith. To authors, May 16, 2000; June 1, 2000; September 9, 2001.

Bisnett, Betty, daughter of Emma Sansaver Simpson. To authors, numerous documents, June 1999–February 2002.

Campbell, Fred C., to Clyde Campbell, April 23, 1932. Campbell Papers in possession of Fred DesRosier, Browning, Montana.

Chalcraft, Edwin, to S. M. McCowan, March 29, 1905. Letters to Superintendent, Oklahoma Historical Society files.

Claseman, Donna, great-niece of Nettie Wirth Mail. To authors, numerous documents, September 7, 2004; August 16, 2006.

Courchene, Gregory, grandson of Sarah Mitchell Courchene. To authors, Feburary 10, 2004; February 1, 2005.

Courchene, Louise, to David Courchene, April 17, 1983. Letter in possession of Gena Aslanian.

DesRosier, Fred, grandson of F. C. Campbell. To authors, numerous documents.

Fleming Gidget, genealogist. To authors, numerous documents.

Helland, Mary Arnoux, president, Valley County (Montana) Historical Society. To authors, numerous documents.

James, Thelma Warren, granddaughter of Katie Snell Wiegand Burtch. To authors, September 2007.

James-Hawley, Jessie, great-niece of Genevieve Healy Adams. To authors, March 26, 2001; July 10, 2001.

LaRose, Rex, great-nephew of Rose LaRose Cutler. To authors, February 19, 2002.

Lavendis, Grace, niece of Flora Lucero Dawson. To authors, September 22, 2001.

Lukin, Mary, great-niece of Belle Johnson Arnoux Swingley Conway. To authors, numerous documents, September 2000–November 2007.

MacDonald, Virginia Bird, daughter of Frank Bird. To authors, January 5 and 23, 2002.

Mail, Michael, grandson of Nettie Wirth Mail. To Linda Peavy, August 20, 2006.

Morton, Pearl, niece of Katie Snell Wiegand Burtch. To authors, September 5, 2003.

Parks, Janet, Branch of Tribal Enrollment, Department of the Interior, to Shirley Lucero Rust, February 18, 1977.

Reddick, SuAnne, historian, Chemawa Indian School. To authors, September 22, 2000; March 14, March 18, March 19, May 16, 2006.

Riojas, Beth Parker, daughter of Gertrude LaRance Parker. To Barbara Winters, September 26, 1998; February 7, 2001.

Robison, Kenneth, historian, Overholser Historical Research Center, Fort Benton, Montana. Numerous e-mail messages, August 2004–February 2008.

Sain, Therese, granddaughter of Sarah Mitchell Courchene. To authors, numerous documents, March 2003–October 2007.

Skinner, Arline, great-niece of Nettie Wirth Mail. To authors, August 2004.
Smith, Dorothy, daughter of Sarah Mitchell Courchene. To authors, May 12, June 14, and July 11, 2000.
Snell, James, to Mary Snell Sansaver, March 14, 1910. In possession of Mary Ann Verwolf.
Stuart, Douglas, grandson of Katie Snell Wiegand Burtch. To authors, April 28, May 6, December 12, and December 14, 2002.
Stuart, Rosie, daughter of Katie Snell Wiegand Burtch. To authors, numerous documents, March 22, 2000–August 21, 2007.
Thomas, Bill, grandson-in-law of Lizzie Wirth Smith. To authors, numerous documents, February 2000–July 2007.
Toman, Emma, archivist, Sun River Valley Historical Society. To authors, numerous documents, February 7, 1999–December 31, 2007.
Verwolf, Mary Ann, granddaughter of Mary Snell Sansaver. To authors, May 26 and August 10, 2000.
Weber, Winona Mail, granddaughter of Nettie Wirth Mail. To authors, numerous documents, February 2004–May 2007.
Winters, Barbara, granddaughter of Emma Sansaver Simpson. To authors, numerous documents, January 1997–February 2008.
Yarbrough, Becky, granddaughter of Sarah Mitchell Courchene. To authors, numerous documents, July 2004–August 2005.

Interviews

Abbott, Joseph, son of Fort Shaw student. Interview by authors, Poplar, Montana, March 2000.
Abbott, Margaret, daughter-in-law of Fort Shaw student. Telephone interview by authors, October 19, 1998.
Archdale, Frank, descendant of Henry Archdale. Interview by authors, Wolf Point, Montana, May 19, 2002.
Bailey, Malcolm, great-nephew of Nettie Wirth Mail. Interviews by authors, Billings, Montana, March 2000; Fort Shaw, Montana, May 2004.
Barrow, Ella, daughter of Emma Sansaver Simpson. Interview by authors, Billings, Montana, April 2000.
Bender, Terry, granddaughter of Lizzie Wirth Smith. Numerous interviews by authors, Brockton and Helena, Montana, multiple dates.
Bisnett, Betty, daughter of Emma Sansaver Simpson. Interview by authors, Augusta, Montana, April 5, 2000; Great Falls, Montana, March 5, 2000.
Bisnett, Bud, son-in-law of Emma Sansaver Simpson. Interview by authors, Augusta, Montana, April 15, 2000; Great Falls, Montana, March 5, 2000; interview by Barbara Winters, March 13, 2003.
Braig, Beverly, granddaughter-in-law of Emma Sansaver Simpson. Interviews by authors, Kalispell, Montana, March 2000; Great Falls, Montana, May 1, 2004.
Cain, Winfield, great-nephew of Nettie Wirth Mail. Interview by Linda Peavy, Hoquiam, Washington, July 2004.

Clark, Donald, great-nephew of Genie Butch Hall. Telephone interview by authors, April 25, 2001.

Cline, Rosemary, niece of Flora Lucero Dawson. Interview by Linda Peavy, Great Falls, Montana, May 20, 2001.

Courchene, Gregory, grandson of Sarah Mitchell Courchene. Interview by authors, Browning, Montana, March 2000.

Dawson, James, grandson of Flora Lucero Dawson. Interview by Barbara Winters, New Town, North Dakota, September 14, 2001.

Deboo, Partricia, great-niece of Josephine Langley Liephart. Telephone interviews by authors, May 2000; October 2003; November 2004; December 7, 2004.

DesRosier, Fred, grandson of Fred C. Campbell. Interviews by authors, Browning, Montana, February 1999; April 29, 2000; April 29, 2002; April 29, 2004.

Ellinghausen, Judy, archivist, Cascade County (Mont.) History Museum. January 11, 2006.

Felsman, Gene, Tribal archivist, Salish Kootenai College. Interview by authors, Pablo, Montana, March 2000.

Geer, Harry, son-in-law of Genevieve Healy Adams. Telephone interview by authors, January 19, 2005.

Goss, Valerie, granddaughter of Belle Johnson Arnoux Swingley Conway. Interviews by authors, Browning, Montana, and Great Falls, Montana, March 2000, March 2002, and May 2004.

Gould, Drusilla, great-granddaughter of Minnie Burton Tindore. Interviews by authors, Pocatello, Idaho, July 2000; June 2001.

Helland, Mary Arnoux, president, Valley County (Montana) Historical Society. Interviews by authors, Glasgow, Montana, May 30 and June 14, 2004.

James, Cecilia, great-niece of Genevieve Healy Adams. Interview by authors, Dodson, Montana, May 2000.

James, Thelma Warren, granddaughter of Katie Snell Wiegand Burtch. Interviews by authors, Dodson, Montana, May 2000; May 2001; Sun River, May 2004; November 30, 2004.

James-Hawley, Jessie, great-niece of Genevieve Healy Adams. Interview by authors, Harlem, Montana, May 2002.

Johnson, Rawhide, board member, Buffalo Bill Historical Center, Cody, Wyoming. Interview by Janice Dunbar, West Yellowstone, Montana, February 10, 2004.

Kearney, Patrick, sport historian, Butte, Montana. Telephone interview by authors, August 31, 2006.

Kelley, Charlotte, daughter-in-law of Katie Snell Wiegand Burtch. Interview by authors, Havre, Montana, May 2002.

Knopfle, Myra, grandaughter of Belle Johnson Arnoux Swingley Conway. Interview by authors, Great Falls, Montana, May 2004.

LaRose, Rex, great-nephew of Rose LaRose Cutler. Telephone interviews by Linda Peavy, January 26, 2002; February 19, 2002.

Lavendis, Grace Dawson, niece of Flora Lucero Dawson. Numerous telephone interviews by Linda Peavy, May 21 to October 30, 2001.

Lucero, Millie, niece of Flora Lucero Dawson. Telephone interview by Linda Peavy, May 20, 2001.

Lucero, Sam, nephew of Flora Lucero Dawson. Telephone interview by Linda Peavy, May 20, 2001.

Lukin, Mary, great-niece of Belle Johnson Arnoux Swingley Conway. Numerous interviews by authors, Bozeman, Montana, multiple dates.

Lukin, Nora Connolly, niece of Belle Johnson Arnoux Swingley Conway. Interviews by authors, Browning, Montana, April 29, 2004; April 2005.

MacDonald, Virginia Bird, daughter of Frank Bird. Interview by authors, Pablo, Montana, May 2000.

Madison, Curtis, grandson of C. H. Madison. Interview by authors, Corinth, New York, July 2002.

Mail, Francine, grandaughter-in-law of Nettie Wirth Mail. Telephone interview by authors, February 2002; interview by authors, Hoquiam and Taholah, Washington, July 2004.

Mail, Michael, grandson of Nettie Wirth Mail. Telephone interviews by authors, February 2002; April 2004; interview by Linda Peavy, Hoquiam and Taholah, Washington, July 2004.

Mail, Mildred McClury Bumgardner, daughter-in-law of Nettie Wirth Mail. Interview by Linda Peavy, Hoquiam, Washington, July 2004.

Medicine Crow, Joseph, historian and Crow tribal elder. Interview by Linda Peavy, Fort Smith, Montana, June 26, 2007.

Murray, Carole, Blackfeet Community College. Interview by authors, Browning, Montana, March 2000.

Nordlund, Donita, granddaughter of Genevieve Healy Adams. Interviews by authors, Malta, Montana, March 19, 2000; June 2001; October 2001, May 2002.

Nordlund, Rita, great-granddaughter of Genevieve Healy Adams. Interview by authors, Malta, Montana, March 19, 2000.

Parker, Gertrude LaRance, mascot of 1905 Fort Shaw team. Interview by Barbara Winters, Lame Deer, Montana, November 1990.

Riojas, Beth Parker, daughter of Gertrude LaRance Parker. Interview by Barbara Winters, September 8, 1999; telephone interviews by Linda Peavy, September 8, 1999; February 7, 2000.

Robison, Kenneth, historian, Overholser Historical Research Center. Interview by authors, Great Falls, Montana, September 2006.

Rust, Shirley, niece of Flora Lucero Dawson. Telephone interviews by Linda Peavy, May 18, 2001; May 1, 2005.

Sansaver, Bill, grandson of Mary Snell Sansaver. Interviews by authors, Wolf Point, Montana, May 2000; May 2001; telephone interview March 20, 2000.

Sansaver, Mark, great-grandson of Mary Snell Sansaver. Interviews by authors, Wolf Point, Montana, May 2000, May 2001.

Simpson, Olive, daughter-in-law of Emma Sansaver Simpson. Interview by authors, Great Falls, Montana, May 1, 2004.

Smith, Dorothy, daughter of Sarah Mitchell Courchene. Telephone interview by Ursula Smith, March 2000.

Smith, Lillian, granddaughter of Belle Johnson Arnoux Swingley Conway. Interview by authors, Great Falls, Montana, May 2004.

Spoonhunter, Joyce, Blackfeet Tribal Office. Interview by authors, Browning, Montana, April 29, 2002.

Stinson, Erma, Sun River Valley Historical Society. Telephone interview by authors, May 2001.

Stuart, Douglas, grandson of Katie Snell Wiegand Burtch. Interviews by authors, Middletown Springs, May 2002; May 2004.

Stuart, Rosie, daughter of Katie Snell Wiegand Burtch. Interviews by authors, Harlem, Montana, March 2000; March 2002; Middletown Springs, May 2002.

Thomas, Bill and Debbie, descendants of Lizzie Wirth Smith and Nettie Wirth Mail. Interview by authors, Herndon, Virginia, May 2000.

Toman, Emma, archivist, Sun River Valley Historical Society. Interviews by authors, Sun River, Montana, March 13, 2000; April 19, 2001; February 5, 2005; January 3, 2006.

Verwolf, Mary Ann, great-granddaughter of Mary Snell Sansaver. Interviews by authors, Wolf Point, Montana, May 2000; May 2001.

Walker, Lorraine, niece of Flora Lucero Dawson. Interview by Barbara Winters, Great Falls, Montana, February 3, 2000.

Warren, Bruce, grandson of Katie Snell Wiegand Burtch. Interview by authors, Malta, Montana, May 2004.

Weber, Winona Mail, granddaughter of Nettie Wirth Mail. Interviews by authors, Hoquiam, Washington, September 2004; Middletown Springs, Vermont, September 2006.

Westland, Bob, local history buff, Valley County, Montana. Interview by Mary Arnoux Helland, Glasgow, Montana, May 30, 2004.

Wimmer, Donna, great-granddaughter of Mary Snell Sansaver. Interview by authors, Wolf Point, Montana, May 2001.

Wilson, Sandy, granddaughter of Katie Snell Wiegand Burtch. Interview by authors, Havre, Montana, May 2002.

Winters, Barbara, granddaughter of Emma Sansaver Simpson. Numerous interviews by authors, Great Falls, Montana, and Middletown Springs, Vermont, 1997–2004.

Index

References to illustrations are in italic type.

Illustration Credits

Gena Aslanian: **263 (top left), 355.**

Authors' Collection: **342** (photograph by Linda Peavy).

Ella Barrow: **265** (restoration by Clearwater Photo, Great Falls, Montana).

Terry Bender: **116–117** (restoration by Clearwater Photo), **121 (top), 121 (bottom), 256 (top), 256 (bottom left)** (restoration by Clearwater Photo), **256 (bottom right), 263 (top right), 361.**

Butte (Mont.) Inter Mountain, November 28, 1902: **120** (cartoon).

Cascade County Historical Society, Great Falls, Montana: **262 (bottom left)** (Fred DesRosier Collection).

Stewart Culin's "Games of North American Indians." In *Twenty-fourth Annual Report of the Bureau of American Ethnology*. Government Printing Office: Washington, D.C., 1907: **111 (top)** (fig. 879), **111 (bottom)** (figs. 856, 857).

Fred DesRosier: **118.**

Kathy Fehlig and *Montana the Magazine of Western History*: **24.**

Gladys Jackson: **349.**

Thelma James: **263 (bottom right).**

Nora Lukin: **114 (top), 114–115 (bottom).**

Missouri Historical Society, St. Louis: **259** (photograph by Jessie Tarbox Beals), **260–261, 264** (photograph by Frank Behymer), **286** (by Parker Engraving Company), **289** (from *Official Catalogue of Exhibitors, Universal Exposition*), **291** (from *World's Fair Bulletin*).

Montana Historical Society, Helena: **112–13 (top), 112–13 (bottom)** (courtesy Fred DesRosier), **119, 257** (photograph by G. M. Eddies), **262 (top right)** (photograph by Andrew P. Williams).

Oklahoma Historical Society: **261 (bottom right).**

Shoshone-Bannock Library, Fort Hall, Idaho: **262 (top left).**

Barbara Winters: **iii, 258, 266** (photographs by Barbara Winters), **267** (photograph by Barbara Winters); **268, 357 (top), 357 (bottom).**